11 $\frac{80}{EN}$

E

Theory and Explanation in International Politics

Theory and Explanation in International Politics

Charles Reynolds
DEPARTMENT OF POLITICS, UNIVERSITY OF DURHAM

Martin Robertson

First published in 1973 by Martin Robertson and Co. Ltd., 17 Quick Street, London, N1 8HL.

ISBN   0   85520   025   1

Printed in Britain at The Pitman Press, Bath.

Contents

To Colette

Preface

THIS book is an attempt to do what is probably impossible: to write about international politics and, at the same time, to write about writing about international politics. There is a long tradition that theory and practice are distinctive and separable entities. But while this schizophrenia is perhaps unavoidable, my intention is to present a self-consciously critical analysis of various approaches towards an explanation of international politics with a fairly detailed exposition of major empirical aspects, in the belief that the best teaching book is one which does not make the complex simple but renders it intelligible without making it the less complex. Hence the structure of the book is based on an enquiry into what constitutes an explanation in this field. The problem here is that, unlike other social sciences or the traditional fields of philosophy, law and history, the study of politics is peculiarly eclectic. It embraces most of the approaches associated with these fields while its subject-matter is exceedingly diverse. The student of international politics needs to know where he is and where he is going, and this means, in my view, putting his study in the context of other disciplines and areas. A book which confined itself solely to the materials of international politics would be very thin indeed and the best books in the field extend outside it.

Consequently, the first part of this study consists of an examination of the various modes of explanation found in the social sciences in general. The rest of the book is an examination of the application of these modes combined with an attempt at providing sufficient empirical analysis to make these intelligible to the student without begging too many theoretical questions. Thus four chapters, on the origins of the Cold War, on nuclear strategy and defence policy, on economic explanations of international politics and on international organisation, examine theoretical and methodological problems involved in attempts at explaining these phenomena and also contain interpretations asserted to be adequate, together with a final critical discussion of the grounds for this assertion.

It must be admitted, however, that this attempt has produced a chimera: in this case a beast with a rationalist head, a positivist body and an idealist tail, which has the disconcerting tendency of disappearing when it thinks, as if the effort of synthesis was too much for it. It is neither a systematic theoretical enquiry, a historical work, nor an epistemological tract, but contains something of all of these. My excuse for this, apart from the innate eclecticism of my subject, is that I am not convinced that any one of these preoccupations would provide a satisfactory answer for those concerned with explaining international politics. The worlds of philosophy, history and the social sciences tend to be over-exclusive. Moreover, although my own predilections will be apparent to those who read this book, I am not primarily concerned with formulating an answer to the problem of explanation but rather with the questions arising from it. The chimera is a beast whose chase is more enjoyable than its capture.

It is true that this approach will be considered frivolous by those who consider the study of international politics as a means of relieving mankind from the burden of some at least of its problems, but it possesses a number of advantages, notably that of providing a more human form of truth which fits the world of practice more closely than proffered alternatives. This book is thus an exercise in criticism and a contribution to education rather than to knowledge. It is intended for those who wish not simply to learn more about international politics but wish to know something of the nature of the exercise of explaining empirical phenomena in whatever field. In some places, where interpretation and criticism rather than exposition seem to me to be called for, I have taken short-cuts, while in others, especially where the theoretical literature is very abstract and difficult, I have explained more fully. But the best way of making use of this book is to read concurrently those references given in the notes and, of course, to follow up the books given in the select bibliography at the end.

A teacher is of necessity something of a critic of other peoples' work, and criticism, so it is said, is a less exacting exercise than creation. Although I have tried to be constructive, I am conscious that in this book I have not only drawn on a wide variety of creative works as sources for my own inspiration and education, but that I have ventured to exercise critical judgement in cases where my knowledge is incomplete and perhaps inadequate. If I have been unfair in my judgement, then this is unintentional; if I have been ignorant, then this is entirely my own fault.

Apart from these debts, I owe a great deal to the intellectual stimulus of my colleagues Henry Tudor and David Manning and to the encouragement and helpful criticisms of Jack Spence. My thanks are due also to Mrs E. Manning and Mrs C. Bates, who coped so adequately in typing up an ever-increasing pile of manuscript.

C.R.

CHAPTER 1

The Study of International Politics

THERE are problems and modes of explanation common to all enquiries and some which are specific to particular enquiries. The questions whether the study of international politics is based upon an eclectic collection of data, which owes its coherence to the idiosyncrasies of the scholar, or whether it has a corpus of material and explanatory methods peculiar to itself, and with its own theoretical justification, will be examined in the first part of this study.

It has often been claimed that a particular academic field is interdisciplinary, or that its study calls for an awareness of approaches and scholarship which emanate from outside it, or simply that it stands at the frontiers or the crossroads of knowledge. While no unique claims are made here for the study of international politics, it is certainly true that its literature and its problems extend into, and are derived from, a wide variety of sources and academic fields. We shall be considering in ensuing chapters a range of arguments and theories culled from the natural sciences, sociology, social anthropology, jurisprudence, economics, political thought, cybernetics, literature, moral philosophy and various ideologies (notably Marxism-Leninism), all related to attempts to explain the phenomena of international politics.

The main focus, initially at least, is the examination of explanations of international politics. Clearly, such a focus cannot simply be confined to this field, for even if a superriding and valid explanation existed for this class of phenomena, it is unlikely that it would be solely applicable to international politics, or that the criteria for its evaluation are purely internal. In other words, any type of explanation offered in the general field of human activities and experience poses problems relating to the nature of knowledge and truth, which extend beyond the specific phenomena to which it is applied. Such problems are innately philosophical. Consequently, much of the analysis and argument contained in the first part of this study will be concerned with theoretical questions which apply not only to international politics but to the whole of the social sciences. The notion of explanation is central to this enquiry. Before discussing it, however, some preliminary definition of the area of phenomena covered by the term 'international politics' would seem appropriate. For the moment, it will be

1

assumed that its study is part of the general examination of human behaviour, characteristic of historical study and the social sciences.

The content of this field may be described as consisting of phenomena which are non-national although made up of national elements. By this is meant the organised aspects of inter-state relations comprising international organisations, international technical agencies of 'mixed' composition, and those institutions which possess an international bureaucracy. Such organisations include not only the complex group of associated agencies known as the United Nations, but also include a number of technical, economic, social and political institutions, with regional or general membership, which have relevance for international politics. Not all of these are exclusively political in the sense that they are standing diplomatic conferences, or are extensions of national diplomacy. They constitute both an area of international political activity with its own peculiarities of organisation and procedures, as well as being a reflection of, and an influence on, national policies.

The second broad category of international political phenomena which forms the subject of our study is that of relations between states proper. Neither of these two areas are exclusive and their common element is that of political activity which takes place beyond the boundaries of the state. Even this rough delineation requires some qualification, since a distinction between foreign and domestic politics appears arbitrary, especially when questions of motivation and policy are considered. Moreover, there are a number of purely national bodies outside the policy-making process which nevertheless exercise, directly or indirectly, an influence upon it. There are, for example, various lobbies and pressure groups in the major countries, as well as organisations such as C.N.D., Oxfam, anti-*apartheid* groups and pacifist or anti-war bodies which seek to direct their government's policy on specific issues. International politics is thus not solely concerned with observed interactions between states, but with an explanation which relates these to motivation, policy and decision-making within the nation-state itself. All this is simply a convenient means of isolating a phenomenon in order to begin an explanation of it. The choice of approach and the selection of data are related to various assumptions which have theoretical implications and pose certain questions which will form the subject of the first part of this study.

Some writers[1] introduce a confusing element into the study by making a distinction between international 'relations' and international 'politics'. These terms are often used interchangeably. When such a distinction is made, it is usually based upon the assumption that some relations between states are non-political, as for example in the case of cultural exchanges or economic transactions. This depends very much on what is meant by 'politics'. A view which asserted the presence of conflict as the factor defining a situation as political would make relevant to the student of politics all questions which involved conflict regardless of their apparent substance. An Aristotelian view of politics[2] would be more confined and so would any enquiry which used consensus or authority as a central concept for a definition of political activity. If the former position were adopted, then a study of legal, economic, social, cultural, technological and ideological aspects of international intercourse would be relevant to international politics, provided that the element of conflict was present.

A distinction which is exclusive in this way may conceal a value or ethical premise; if, for example, consensus and the avoidance of war are conceived of as preferable to conflict and violence, then a concept of normative order will prescribe the phenomena to be examined. Similarly, a Marxist's interest in class struggle and in the process of capitalist evolution will result in an emphasis on inter-state conflict, and on divisions between capitalist countries, in his interpretation of international politics. The point here is not that the criterion for selection can be established beyond cavil, but that it should be made explicit. It should not pose as an objective standard without theoretical validation, nor should it constitute a concealed referent based upon a value judgement.

Of course, aspects of international relations, such as trade or investment, may be said to be economic and afford a subject for different questions and a different mode of analysis and explanation. But even here it is no longer possible, if indeed it ever was, to make a clear distinction between what is the province of the economist and what is the exclusive concern of the political scientist, sociologist or historian. The real distinction lies not in the phenomena but, as will be seen later, in the nature of the explanation. For example, the government of an underdeveloped country will relate to its development programme not only theories of economic development and the achievement of specific economic goals, but also sources of foreign capital, both in the form of export earnings and investment. It will be concerned with increasing the flow of capital or with altering the terms of trade in its favour. Such a concern is placed in relation to other governments. Thus an improvement in the terms of trade for the primary producing countries depends not only on the attitudes and behaviour of the countries which provide markets, and which produce capital goods, but also on competition between them. It has been said, with some justification, that the developed western countries are concerned with applying pre-Keynesian economics to international trade with underdeveloped countries, while applying welfare economics to their own societies. In the area of economic relationships there is a competition between the developed and the underdeveloped countries, based on conflicting interests, and which is essentially political. Similarly, the growth and organisation of economic co-operation between the developed countries reflects a form of political, as well as of economic, activity which requires explanation. It is thus difficult, and sometimes highly artificial, to separate categories of phenomena, without first establishing a specific mode of explanation as the basis of such a separation. All enquiries are selective and, in the absence of a universalist theory of human behaviour, all aspects of international phenomena considered to be germane to a particular enquiry should be included in it. There is on this argument no finite or exclusive discipline of international politics in terms of facts or of phenomena.

There is, however, contained in this study, an assumption that international political activity is both distinctive and capable of definition. Much here hinges on empirical analysis which will be considered later, and these remarks will therefore be prefatory. It has been argued by some writers that international politics are not really politics at all. Crick, for example,[3] following the arguments of Aristotle,[4] has provided a definition of politics which, *inter alia,* would exclude inter-state relations. He argues[5] that politics is a means of obtaining public order, and that it consists of the conciliation of multiple and actual or potentially conflicting interests. The important part of this conception of politics is the notion that it is an activity of conciliation. The study of politics in this view is the study of consensus-making within the boundaries of some definable political unit which alone possesses autonomy. Only the process of government itself can give rise to the phenomenon of politics. Politics is confined to the state, because only the state has a centralised and recognisable authority and identity. Without such coherence there is no body politic and consequently no politics.

In international relations there is no centralised legitimate authority and no social or political coherence. If, then, there is no international body politic, but only sets of changing relationships between national body politics, then on this argument there can be no genuine international political activity. The only genuine political context is the state itself, and international politics consists of the extension of national political activity, and not something which exists in its own right. One of the assumptions of this argument[6] is that there is no condition of normative order in international politics, and that conciliation and consensus are absent from the international area. As will be seen, empirically, this is a dubious assumption. But there are objections to this argument as applied to the state itself. Only democratic or pluralist states can be true body politics, since the main characteristic of the latter is asserted as being the conciliation of different interests by according them a share of power, in proportion to the welfare and the conditions of survival for the community as a whole. Non-democratic states are not, therefore, body politics since they do not possess this characteristic, although the evidence on which this presumption is made is rather scant. In other words, according to this view, there can be no genuine political activity in centralised communist or one-party states, since the central element in politics, that of conciliation, is absent, although these states possess governments. If this view is accepted, then this would reduce the study of politics to some five or six countries out of over a hundred extant sovereign states.

The difficulty with such a narrow definition of politics is that its very narrowness reduces the force of the associated explanation. In seeking to refine definition in this way the baby is thrown out with the bathwater, for whatever the label, there are events and phenomena which still require examination and explanation, after the body politic has been examined in its pristine state. While it does not matter much what the label is, it does matter if the assumptions contained in the definition of area prejudice the argument. If, for example, we assume the existence of normative order or its absence, then it should not be surprising that the conclusions, and the selection of the evidence on which the conclusions are based, should so perfectly reflect and reify the assumptions. The western pluralist society is perhaps a genuine phenomenon, and it deserves explanation in its own right, but it should hardly be taken as an archetype for all political phenomena. An element of prescriptive analysis and the intrusion of a concealed value judgement enters the explanation. Democratic pluralist societies, like world peace, may be conceived of as desirable things, but they should not be taken as the norms for a general explanation of political behaviour.

We may regard the conception of politics, as a conciliating activity conducted between opposed interests, within the framework of state and government, as being a special case. It can perhaps be argued that within the state itself only the government can legitimise the use of violence, and that this constitutes a characteristic of the state, in that violence is both monopolised and used in a way which is not found outside it. But again, the past affords many examples of violent conflict within the state, both in the form of the assertion of individual or collective interests against the government, or as a competition for control over the state itself, in the form of insurrection, revolution or civil war. Such competitions may perhaps be regarded as more characteristic of certain periods of history than of others. They may, however, be considered as endemic to political activity. If the element of concealed or explicit force is ignored in political analysis and enquiry concentrates on non-violent means of conflict resolution as the only legitimate kind of politics, then this leaves the question of the relevance of violence in political activity unanswered. This is as much a bias as the emphasis placed on violent conflict itself in an explanation of international relations.

In any case, it is possible to argue that consensus-making itself presupposes conflict and, from this, that conflict resolution may be achieved through violence as well as through conciliation. A definition of politics which asserts the latter as its central principle is really only emphasising one aspect of conflict, and that only in a number of selected instances. In the field of international politics most of the aspects of conflict found in the state, such as negotiation, agreement, conciliation and the accommodation of opposed interests, occur in addition to wars and other forms of violence. The central criterion for a definition of political activity, or a political situation, in this study is the existence of conflict itself. The resolution of conflict, whether through violent or non-violent means, constitutes political activity. It is true that, historically speaking, there is no permanence in the relationships which emerge out of the incessant competition between states, but it would be a very strong statement to assert the permanence of the nation-state, or of one particular kind of polity, as political phenomena. It is a truism that change is endemic in human behaviour and organisation, but one worth making in this context. Clearly, the nation-state is a more easily identifiable phenomenon than international political relationships, but it is well to be aware that it is only a comparatively recent one in human history. One may conclude by saying that what might be termed the organising concept for the study of international politics, as well as for national politics, is the notion of conflict in human relationships.

Since the last major war there has grown up a considerable amount of publication and scholarship in the field of political science, much of it concerned with theoretical problems connected with the study of the state, and with socio-political groupings within the state. The study of international politics itself, that is, with relations *between* states, has been relatively neglected, and before the war, with some notable exceptions, most research took place in the traditional schools of history and international law. This academic framework reinforced the general view that inter-state relations were the products of the states themselves, and of a particular kind of politics, known as *Realpolitik*.[7] Such a view was perhaps influenced by two world wars and the policies which brought them about. International politics was conceived of as power politics in which the central problem for the state was the achievement of local or global hegemony. The failure of collective security, and of idealistic notions of alternatives to the free exercise of national sovereignty, tended to strengthen this attitude. More recently, however, the influence of ideas developed in the social sciences has produced a number of studies which take a reduced view of the free will of the sovereign nation-state, and which stress the interactive nature of political relationships.

These studies[8] accept that the sources of international political behaviour are to be found in the states making up international society at any given time, but assert that the area of inter-state action is beyond the control of any individual state, as is the nature of the interaction between the state and its environment. The world, on this argument, is inherently unstable. Consequently the nation-state is constantly forced to adjust to the operations of variables and to situations beyond its control. Such adjustments themselves produce, or reinforce, international instability and thus create, in turn, the necessity for further adjustments. The result is not only the omnipresence of organised violence between states, and of a continually developing and innovative weapons technology, but also the centralisation of the state, and its political and economic organisation, as conditions for survival. Nation-states thus contribute to international politics but they are also influenced as states by their participation in international politics. This interaction between states and their international, or external, environment is one of the most important foci in our study. It is not explicable solely in terms of the nation-state and its foreign policy. Although we are concerned with questions of foreign policy-making, with particular decisions taken by politicians, and with the relationship between domestic politics and foreign policy, in our study of international politics, these do not provide the main area of our interest, since by themselves they do not explain international political phenomena; yet they themselves are partly explicable at least by reference to external phenomena.

For example, the phenomenon of war can be studied as a thing in itself, that is, as a recurring phenomenon which requires explanation. It is, of course, possible to examine as a separate problem the effects of a war on a particular polity or national society, or to isolate a specific national policy in terms of its contribution to a war. But any explanation of war itself is a total one. By this is meant that the criteria of relevance would include a number of apparently disparate phenomena. In explaining the origins of the Second World War, for example, it would be necessary to examine all the attitudes of the belligerents, as well as those of the non-participants, as a first step. But for a full explanation, motivation and the domestic political situation in each of these countries would have to be taken into account, and gradually the explanation would move away from isolable facts or events into a consideration of international relationships, with the outbreak of war as its only tangible focus. An explanation of international political behaviour thus cannot rest on one element which is found in actual behaviour, i.e. the struggle between states with violence as the *ultima ratio,* although this affords one 'explanation' for war. Nor can it rest on the ideological or value elements in an individual politician's conception of the world and in the decisions which appear to stem from them. Both these categories of elements are found in behaviour, but an explanation is concerned with relationships which themselves influence the things related.

The difficulty is that the nation-state, superficially at least, appears to possess concrete institutions, and to have a corporate identity capable of description, and which acts as a focus for analysis. It is not, therefore, merely that international history has tended to be nationalist history, but that the apparently tangible attracts more attention than the diffuse and complex area of inter-state relations. In international politics there is no identifiable political unit or society which can be examined or explained in

political or sociological terms derived from the study of national societies;
although, as we shall see later in this study, there have been attempts to
apply sociological method to the examination of what has been termed
'international society'.[9] A great deal depends upon the assumptions made
about the phenomena selected for examination and, in the case just cited,
the conception of society has been lifted from one context and applied to
another without theoretical justification.[10] This is possible because the
boundaries of the social unit are usually left undefined and thus an analogy
is translated into a political reality. In practice, although there are exceptions, the social unit tends either to be subsumed within, or to coincide
with, the political unit. Such an assumption may perhaps be possible
without prejudicing a specific sociological enquiry, but it has very different
consequences when applied beyond the nation-state. What are the boundaries of an international society, and what assumptions may be made
about parameters in international politics, are questions which are left
unanswered in this type of analysis.

It has been argued so far in this introduction that international politics
are not explicable solely as an extension of the politics of the nation-states
which make up the world at any one time. Indeed, it has aptly been
described by some commentators as 'politics in the absence of central
authority'. But is this the sum total of our focus, that is, are we concerned
with the politics of interaction between sovereign states, each equipped
with differential capacities for action, with conflicting demands on each
other, and with differing views of the world? If this is so, how can the
study of *ad hoc* relationships be organised? As we shall see later in this
study, these questions have been answered more by the examination of
particular problems than by any teleological vision. The nature of political
power, of the national interest, of decision-making and negotiation, of the
relationship between strategy, diplomacy and war, and of the adjustment
of the state to radical technological developments involving their external
relations, have all been examined as specific problems by scholars, without
arriving at any holistic view of the subject. There is an important exception
to this assertion, and that is the application of structural-functional theory
and systems analysis to international politics. This will be examined in
the first part of this study.

The empirical focus in this work consists of the first two decades after
the Second World War and of the relations between the United States,
the Soviet Union, France and the United Kingdom. From what has been
said previously there are assumptions which underly this selection of
phenomena. The choice of period is arbitrary and involves no value judgement or theoretical premise. The error is not committed, for example, of
believing that contemporary history is more significant because it coincides
with the lifetime of the author, nor that such a choice posits an interest
in solving major human problems, or influencing the attitudes and policies

of politicians, or the public in general. The attitude here is the reverse of that taken by one theoretician in this field, who said:

> science for science's sake and theory for theories' sake students of international relations may deplore the fact, but it is the widespread belief that better understanding of the international system will lead to better policies of the actors in that system that accounts for whatever influence and prestige international relations scholars now enjoy.[11]

This may well be true in certain countries, where scholars are recruited into the political system as advisers, but analysis which is prescriptive in its orientation, and which is concerned with problem-solving, either with the intention of fulfilling value or ethically based objectives, or the promotion of a national foreign policy, tends to be biased. It is of course entirely possible that utility may emerge out of academic pursuits, but this can be considered a fortuitous by-product and depends upon factors which lie outside the area of academic enquiry. But it is difficult to avoid the feeling that the search for a predictive science of human behaviour is motivated by some very dubious assumptions about the prescriptive value of such a science. It has been aptly said, by the commentator just quoted, among others, that the concern for international peace as a value has been to the study of international politics what the disease of cancer has been to medical research; although it might also be said that the heaviest investment of public money into an academic field, outside science and technology, has been in the area of defence studies and strategy, where there is clearly a direct link between research and a government's foreign and defence policies.

Nor is the period of time chosen because it is considered to be historically significant as being a time of profound revolutionary changes, or involving major secular movements. One writer has urged that 'contemporary history begins when the problems which are actual in the world today first take visible shape'.[12] This can only be an impressionistic criterion and its application to historical argument will be discussed in the first part of this study. The question at this stage is, are we really concerned in our enquiry into the nature of international politics with the study of what has been called the human condition or with any overtly prescriptive end? Does this not properly belong to other modes of thought and enquiry? It may indeed be relevant to our study, as we shall see subsequently, but its relevance is conditional upon other questions and other empirical foci, as for example in any attempt to explain political behaviour in terms of motivation and values. The recent past has been chosen as a focus for the study of international politics largely on the grounds of interest, that is, on purely aesthetic and subjective grounds. An additional reason is that the recent past has one feature which is not found in the more distant past, namely the practitioners in international politics are for the most part still alive, and thus provide another dimension, and another source of evidence and data, which are absent for earlier periods of time. In this sense the issues and controversies surrounding international politics and foreign policy are still very much 'alive', and this constitutes an additional interest.

The second choice of focus, that of relations between the major powers, is less arbitrary. There is an explicit assumption about power in this selection. The main justification for emphasising these particular states is empirical, in that the concern of this enquiry is with the pattern of relationships which has developed in the post-war world. Consequently, an explanation will be grounded on the actions of those states which have provided the parameters for the behaviour of other states. The language of common sense singles out specific states as being important in politics, perhaps in the same way as particular politicians are regarded as being above their fellows. Obviously, no enquiry will get very far, or be more than superficial, if it is inspired solely by common sense, but it is useful in making tentative assumptions at its outset. But any assumption about power requires very careful examination, and all that is being said at this stage is that the emphasis in treatment will be on those states which were most prominent in recent international history. How far this is justified, and what power or prominence means, will constitute part of the enquiry. Before going on to the subject of treatment or the kinds of explanation found in this field, it might be advisable to consider some of the more practical problems involved in studying contemporary international politics. There are certain difficulties inherent in this study. These have been summed up by one distinguished commentator, who argued:

> it is said that recent events are particularly difficult to sort into focus, that the survival of prejudice hinders detachment and that the evidence to be mastered is at once vast in bulk and at the same time frustratingly incomplete. And it is said that 'official' enquiry into the past is liable to be qualified by the presence of interests other than that of the discovery of the truth.[13]

These comments are generally true, although whether they apply only to the study of the recent past is questionable.

There are, however, difficulties peculiar to this study, such as the problem of language. In this respect the study of national history presents no such technical difficulty unless a dead language is involved. Students of European history before the seventeenth century must equip themselves with a knowledge of Latin and of palaeography, as a necessary preliminary for their study. But the student of international politics is concerned with the world and its babel of tongues. Few scholars would claim to be proficient in Russian, Chinese, French, German and English, yet if they are students of international politics they are concerned with the politics of the countries in which these languages are used. French is no longer the language of diplomacy, although it has left its mark on its vocabulary. Linguistic difficulties may be surmounted through translation services, and the Anglo-

Saxon scholar is perhaps fortunate in the possession of a lingua franca. Nevertheless, the problem of language tends to reinforce a nationalist bias found in some monoglot scholars who explain the world almost exclusively in national terms.

This kind of bias exists in one major source of evidence for contemporary historians, namely the press. International events tend to be reported and interpreted in terms of partisan argument within the domestic political system. On major issues where policy objectives are either the subject of controversy, or transcend the national scene, there may be a freer discussion in the press, but even this tends to be cast in a prescriptive mould. Discussion concentrates on the question of which particular action should be taken by the government, without regard for the contextual relationships of foreign policy. These criticisms are, of course, relevant only for countries which possess a free press with no direct governmental control over reporting. It should be stressed, however, that few governments have abandoned censorship in all its forms, and the area of defence and foreign policy is peculiarly sensitive to government influence over the press in most countries.

Perhaps the worst failing in the national press, and in its reporting of international politics, is its habitual *suppressio veri* of facts and news deemed to be un-newsworthy. The selection of stories and a concern for the present and its fashions and attitudes are permanent features of contemporary journalism. Editorial policy dictates the selection of news, and even where there is no specific bias, the definition of what constitutes 'news' may be based on criteria other than a concern for full coverage or for the truth. Studies in depth are rarely undertaken by the mass media. Unfortunately, the press is important to the student of the recent past in two ways: firstly as a source of information, and secondly as an influence upon policy and public opinion on matters relating to foreign policy. One might not fully agree with George Kennan that '98 per cent. of the information needed as background for judgements on questions of foreign policy can be found in the *New York Times*',[14] but the press constitutes a significant source for our study.

What of other sources? The restrictions on public access to official documents imposed by governments vary, but generally those relating to the recent past are totally excluded from scrutiny. Whether this is a major handicap to the student of international politics is open to some doubt, since a great deal of potential evidence is lost from official archives. This is especially true of material relating to international negotiations, and complete records of discussions rarely exist. It is unusual for foreign policy to be discussed in the same way, and with the same extent of documentation, as domestic political questions. The major source of evidence for policy-making consists of the official pronouncement and the official and unofficial act. There are, of course, autobiographies and memoirs produced

by participants in international politics in which they explain their participation and their respective views of the world. These must necessarily be
partial, since for the most part they consist of *post facto* justification.
Nevertheless, *in toto,* they constitute a valuable source of material, especially
for the evaluation of motives and reasoning in the policy-making area. An
examination of memoir and autobiographical sources will be found in a
later chapter concerned with various explanations of the origins of the Cold
War.

The evaluation of political statement, as part of an explanation of policy
or behaviour, presents some difficulties in the area of international politics.
Unlike domestic politics in democratic countries where someone, or some
faction, has an interest at some time or other in exposing the truth, no one
stands to gain from frankness in the field of foreign policy. There are of
course exceptions to this generalisation, as for example in the crisis after
Munich where controversy over the British government's attitude towards
Hitler provoked a public controversy and factional argument. There are
occasions when international politics obtrude directly into domestic politics
and become the subject of public and partisan debate. The Suez crisis of
1956 is a more contemporary example. These are, however, relatively
infrequent, and the absence of sustained criticism or of debate of a government's conduct of foreign policy, except perhaps in the area of defence
expenditure, is more characteristic. This area tends to be more bipartisan
than any other area of public policy. The possibility of an international
situation becoming the subject of a political crisis, or of policy intentions
being made known to other states through public debate, tends to exacer-
bate the normal secretiveness of a government in respect of its policies.
Clearly, these remarks are valid only for countries which have a democratic
political system or where party politics is a characteristic of the political
process.

Diplomacy must be concealed not only in order to avoid unwelcome
debate in the national legislature or the press, but also to preserve an
advantage for national policies in the external environment. The most
famous exponent of 'open covenants, openly arrived at', Woodrow Wilson,
did not himself observe his own principle in practice, during the negotiation
of the peace treaties after the First World War. His neglect of his own
legislature led to the rejection of his policies. Frankness only occasionally
promotes a national position, as for example in publicly stating a position
in order to establish a framework for negotiation. General de Gaulle let
it be known that he favoured the Oder–Neisse as an international frontier
between Germany and Poland, although his allies had not so committed
themselves. The reasoning behind this apparent concession to the Eastern
European states was that in the event of a reopening of the frontier questions, and of the German peace treaty, the French government would not
be excluded, as she had been during the Potsdam negotiations, because her

nominal opponents would insist on such a favourable voice being heard at any conference. The major French allies reserved their position on this question until recently, when the Federal Republic of Germany concluded agreements with Poland and the U.S.S.R.

Thus a government is not only interested in putting forward a favourable case for its policy for internal consumption, but it is also engaged in a contest of deception with other countries. It may also be concerned with persuading uncommitted countries into supporting its policies. Public pronouncements on foreign policy have multiple audiences and are intended to further a number of different purposes. As increasingly foreign policy statements are concerned with reconciling these diverse positions, so it becomes more and more difficult to disentangle from them what national attitudes on an issue really are. We turn away from the conception of policy, and from the difficulties of interpreting political statement, to an examination of behaviour itself in order to find an explanation. An understanding both of the domestic political context, and of the external environment, is essential for any evaluation of national policy.

This problem of interpretation is not of course confined to the study of international politics, but is found in any historical study. The concern of the historian for sources and evidence reflects this. As Elton puts it, 'the study of the past is really the study of present traces of the past, and it is therefore partial and arbitrary to an extent which cannot be established'.[15] The study of past, as well as of recent, events is seriously limited by the nature and extent of surviving material. But the participants, unlike those involved in recent events, are dead, so that they cannot be asked what they really meant when they publicly defended their policies or negotiated the terms of a treaty. We have the additional problem of reconstructing their values and motivations, as well as trying to avoid intruding our own upon them as anachronisms. The advantage that a contemporary historian has in having the participants alive and available as a source of evidence may, however, be illusory, in that this presents the additional problem of a re-editing of the past by those involved in making history. Essentially the problem of interpretation is the same, and we might conclude from this that all historical interpretation, both ancient and modern, is impressionistic and subjective, but this is to anticipate later arguments.

It was said at the beginning of this introduction that the concern of this study was with the notion of explanation as an essential preliminary to the understanding of particular 'explanations' which are offered in the literature of the phenomena of international politics. Perhaps it is appropriate at this point to ask why the problem of explanation is considered so important. Even a cursory survey of the literature reveals a considerable variety of approaches as well as the existence of controversy between scholars over the most appropriate way of achieving an adequate explanation.[16] Disputes over what is called methodology and over the status and nature of extant explanations are often considered to be arid and excessively scholastic. Indeed, the kind of writing which may be termed 'theoretical' is often extremely difficult to read and frequently leaves the reader wondering whether the results were really worth the effort incurred. It is tempting to argue that a concern with methodology is irrelevant to the actual pursuit of an enquiry, and that the student of international politics, like the creative artist, should not theorise about his work. But to adopt this attitude is to abandon critical evaluation and ultimately to abandon the attempt at communication fundamental to academic understanding.

The intention in this analysis is not to write a philosophical treatise on explanation and knowledge, but to present in their proper context the difficulties which face any attempt to explain international politics. Thus in examining the arguments of scholar X and relating them to those of scholar Y, the intention is not to set up an inconclusive academic cock-shy or to illustrate the superiority of one approach by revealing the inadequacies of its ostensible opposition, but to try to establish a proper basis for criticism which extends outside parochial controversy. But in order to do this we must establish the nature of the various explanations proffered in our chosen field, and this necessarily involves us in philosophical problems. What is explanation? What, for example, do we mean when we give reasons for a political act or event? How do we distinguish between motives and causes? What is the distinction between an interpretation, an understanding and an explanation of political phenomena? Can we distinguish between explanation and meaning, and on what grounds? When we are confronted with two conflicting explanations of the same facts or event, what criteria do we use, firstly to distinguish between them, and secondly to evaluate them? What are the appropriate criteria for an evaluation of a historical interpretation, a scientific explanation, a causal hypothesis or a model? In what sense are these categories meaningful? All these questions are not simply internal to particular arguments involving questions of logic, or the status of premises and assumptions, but are central to the notion of explanation itself. Before we can communicate or formulate any critical judgement, we must arrive at some agreement as to the nature of the explanation which is the subject of our communication and our criticism. Clearly, the basis of academic disagreement (or agreement) on these questions and of this kind of preoccupation with theoretical and methodological analysis is of major importance, not only to the field of international politics in particular, but to all attempts at explaining human activities and experience. It involves both how and what we know.

If we take a closer look at the field of international politics, we can see that the kind of simplification produced by the polarising of controversies over approaches into the 'classical' or 'traditional' versus the 'scientific' or 'systematic' tends to have too narrow a basis to be meaningful.[17] This is not to say that particular approaches are not distinctive, but that in the criticism of one such approach the validity of the alternative implicitly recommended is often begged or taken for granted. This is to say yet again that the grounds for evaluation must be stated and accepted before there can be genuine agreement or disagreement between proponents of conflicting explanations. In a sense, much of contemporary theoretical and methodological discussion is concerned with establishing these grounds and, indeed, its catholicity is one indication of the importance of this problem.

In a general sense it is broadly true that there are two schools of thought on how to study and explain international politics. These are really different approaches to the problem of theory and methodology rather than interpretations proper. But this is more of a historiographical judgement than one which has theoretical substance. Proponents of, for example, the scientific approach are often unclear as to what 'science' is as an explanation, and the same is true of the so-called traditionalists and their notion of historical understanding. It will be shown later in this study that these apparently conflicting approaches have more in common than their advocates have perhaps realised. However, before undertaking a detailed analysis of the notion of explanation and of the nature of explanations offered in this field, an examination of the characteristics of these two approaches might be appropriate as an introduction. It should be emphasised that the question of their theoretical nature is left open at this stage.

The first school can be called loosely that of political science, and it advocates a systematic and scientific orientation in the study of international politics. Although there are numerous applications of this approach concerned with specific aspects of politics, such as decision-making, crisis behaviour, bargaining and communication between states, or with concepts such as power, the national interest or conflict, the most developed general theoretical approach is that of systems analysis.

The main postulate of this theory is the existence of a system in which all those engaged in action in international politics, the nation-states, governments, diplomats, politicians, interest groups, and national and international organisations, are elements in relationships the interactions of which contribute to the system as a whole. Such a formulation stresses factors which lie outside the demands of politicians and the capacities of their states to fulfil them. It reduces the importance of values and of psychological factors, since the participants in international politics are regarded as actors who take part in a performance which they have not written and which they only partly understand; although this last statement must be qualified, since if the premises of this view are accepted, the rational observer is given the means to comprehend this world and, from this, the power to influence it. In such an approach there is a strong prescriptive element which ignores the difficulty of reconciling participation in events with the detached understanding of their significance and causation. Its focus is that of an international system which is conceived of as being an identifiable set of relationships and which is subject to interactive forces which either maintain it or change it in some recognisable way.

A simplified example of such a system is that of the balance of power in which, whatever the ostensible desires of peoples or of governments, the participating nation-states behave according to the rules of the system. On this argument the persistent refusal of British governments over the inter-war period to maintain an alliance with France, and to support the provisions of the Versailles Treaty, is explained by the necessity for Britain to preserve the balance of power in Europe by preventing any accretion to French power arising out of the defeat of Germany. When German re-armament tipped the balance against France, then Britain shifted her influence in favour of the French, and opposed Germany. This rationalisation of British foreign policy over the inter-war period is presented not as a description, or even as a conceptual framework for an examination of policy and motivation, but as a scientific argument by some commentators. They argue that the determinant of international behaviour, given the factors predominant at the time, was the preservation of a theoretical balance between several equally powerful states. This situation determined the behaviour of the participating states, and the statesmen of the period had little choice in what they did; their justifications and statements of policy merely disguised or rationalised their actions. Any challenge to the *status quo* had to be met by countering alliances and countervailing power. This kind of theorising generally discounts the element of political free will or of idiosyncratic behaviour in international politics and foreign policy-making.

The deterministic element in such explanations, in which the emphasis is placed on the understanding of the mechanics of the system, or its optimal conditions for survival, stems from the attempt to study politics scientifically. A historical situation, such as for example the international situation immediately preceding the Second World War, is treated not as a unique sequence of events, but as an example of certain regularities in politics which constitute the subject of scientific explanation. The purpose of such enquiry is not simply to explain a particular situation but all such situations. As in science – and this is why this school is termed scientific – the method of enquiry depends on the application of a theory, or is intended to produce a theory. The distinction between a 'theoretical explanation' which is purely hypothetical, or which takes the form of a model, and a theory proper, is that the latter must do things.[18] It must both explain and predict and it must have an exact correspondence between its conclusions and empirical reality. The results of an experiment, in terms of human behaviour, must correspond to what is or can be observed, as is the case for explanations of material behaviour in science. In short, such a theory must be both testable or verifiable and explain specific aspects of human behaviour.

Although verification has not yet proved possible for scientific analyses of international politics, this school remains convinced that with greater knowledge and perseverance it will eventually be possible to postulate a general theory of political behaviour, much as a theory of dynamics or mechanics can be postulated for material behaviour. The main difficulty in such an approach is that of recognising and quantifying the variables which form part of a hypothesis of human behaviour. If only, for example, the determination of political leaders in a crisis, their propensity to act rationally, or the degree of desire for one choice among many in policy decisions, were measurable, then political behaviour could be explained scientifically, and the political scientist could not only explain what has happened in political history, and why, but he could then go on to predict what will happen. In the field of international politics this is very much an idea influenced by contemporary power relationships between states, and it is, in the main, the product of American scholars who have been pre-occupied with American foreign policy in relation to the conflict with communist countries over the post-war years and to radical changes in weapons, technology and strategy.

Scientific method has been used in order to achieve such a theory, and various techniques, as will be seen in the following chapter, have been borrowed from other disciplines in the social sciences as well as from science itself. However, no attempt at formulating a theory has yet proved successful and, as was pointed out earlier, the reason appears to lie in the difficulty of defining and measuring the variables for human behaviour, and in the problem of making valid and testable propositions about human cognition and volition. Untestable hypotheses exist in all forms of explana-tion, but in this case the problem lies in making the critical jump from hypothesis to theory. If this problem is not solved, that is, if no valid theory can be attained, then we have the difficult task of evaluating the link between the levels of hypothesis, conceptualisation or general propositions, and the interpretations of international politics which contain them. As will be seen later in this study, the scientific and the historical approaches have more in common, in this respect at least, than would superficially appear.

An example of the interpretation of an actual historical situation might serve to clarify some of the general problems involved in formulating a theory in the field of international politics. The first task of the political scientist concerned with explaining the origins of the Second World War as part of a general theoretical enquiry into international conflict would be the isolation of the relevant variables in conflict behaviour. The question of relevance is of course dependent on assumptions which are themselves open to question. From this stage he then proceeds to examine their relationships in terms of the outbreak of violence, with a view to establishing general propositions about the behaviour of states in such situations. Such proposi-tions form part of a hypothesis and lead to specific conclusions which are then related back to empirical reality for verification.

What does this *modus operandi* entail so far as our historical example is concerned? The central area with which such an examination is concerned is that of the attitudes and policies of the states in conflict. The demands of these states, together with their relative capacities to achieve them by force, must therefore be elucidated and explained. We might say that, in general, the participant states fell into three categories: the satisfied states, desirous of maintaining the extant international situation; their opponents, the unsatisfied states; and those not directly involved in the conflict, but whose attitudes were relevant to it, as for example the United States and the Soviet Union. This is, of course, a crude division, but nevertheless the conflict apparently arose because of competing national demands, and the basis of the competition rested on differing conceptions of the national interest and the means of fulfilling it. However – and this is the point – regardless of our initial assumptions, in order to formulate a theory which explains wars in general, and this war in particular, we must isolate the relevant and significant factors in such a way as to produce testable generalisations about the nature of war. If there is no means of testing our hypothesis, then although it may be coherent and appear reasonable, it is not scientific.

What are these factors? One such factor is that of the objectives or demands of the states in conflict. This can be taken as an external factor, that is, in terms of its outward manifestation as a set of explicit demands made of other states, or it can be examined in terms of motivation. Alternatively, motivation may be expressed in mechanical terms, as was the case in the example of the balance-of-power system given earlier. In this last case the demands of states are explained according to the rules of the system. Thus in examining the factor of national objectives as an element in a theoretical approach to the conflict, unless we take them as given, or as part of a systemic hypothesis, we are forced to examine their motivation. It is clearly simpler to adopt the former approach, that is, to assume that the substantive content of national policy objectives is not important, or that the conceptions of those making these demands are peripheral to the real situation; but, as will be seen, this has its dangers. It is difficult to generalise about each national decision- and policy-making context, since this involves not only problems of historical reconstruction, but also further hypotheses concerning decision-making itself. Theories about international politics tend to be isolated from theories of national political behaviour for this reason. Nevertheless, if a theory of international conflict is desired, then it must involve a consideration of national motivation, as well as of the actual interactions between states. The difficulty in this instance is that the notion of objectives implies both a constant and isolation from related factors. National demands are couched both in value and in conceptual terms, the most fundamental concept being that of national security and the most dominant value being that of nationalism.

The British position, for example, prior to the declaration of war on Germany, was expressed as being the maintenance of naval supremacy in the North Sea and the Channel, the neutralisation of the Channel coast and the prevention of any potential danger to these demands by the rise of one dominant power on the European continent. Related to these was the additional interest in preserving the British Empire from external attack. In this sense Britain was activated in her policies immediately before the war by security interests. Yet, paradoxically perhaps, Britain was concerned with promoting international order, thus: '. . . it will be found politically and strategically impossible for Great Britain to secure her own advantage or her special interests in the present anarchical condition of the world without concerning herself, first and foremost, with the task of converting this anarchy into order'.[19] In defending what was, in effect, the *status quo,* Britain clearly identified peace with her security. But for Germany, security was closely related to the recovery of her former military strength as well as with the unification of all German-speaking peoples within a German Reich. In pursuing these objectives, a conflict with her neighbours seems inevitable, and the war can be explained in terms of conflicting security interests. This does not explain the significance of another factor related to security, and that is the value element in policy- and decision-making. If Britain conceived of her security as being related to international co-operation and the avoidance of war, then this element was clearly relevant to any explanation of motivation. Similarly, the racialist element in German policy can be related both to the aggrandisement of Germany and also to the element of pragmatism and opportunism in German policy. Thus while Hitler demanded the Sudetenland from Czechoslovakia, forced the *Anschluss* on Austria and invaded Poland on the pretext of resolving the Danzig question, he made no demands on Switzerland, Italy, the Soviet Union or France for the restoration of 'German' territory incorporated in their states or within their area of influence.[20] The point here is that the influence of these factors on policies and decisions is extremely complex, and an explanation which abstracts from this context, and projects the abstractions as a variable in international politics, is an over-simplification.

The selection of variables such as capacity, objectives, communication and motivation really reflects *post facto* judgements and generalisations which are non-scientific and descriptive. Some variables, notably that of capacity, also tend to be tautological, in that the question of 'capacity for what?' is begged. It is possible to conceive of capacity hypothetically as an optimal condition for some specific action, but the problem of explaining international conflict is an empirical one and it cannot be answered by abstractions. The statement that a strong power is one which has capacity, and a weak one is one which lacks it, does not take us very far in explaining inter-state relationships. The concern of statesmen in the late 1930s was with the problem of interpreting each other's demands and in trying to relate these to their respective military capacities and interests, in a constantly changing political context. The selection of variables, quite apart from the problems associated with their definition, tends to freeze such political situations and to ignore their dynamic nature. As will be seen later in this examination, explanations which are based upon such variables tend to be models rather than hypotheses or theories.

Turning to the general hypothetical level of explanation, that is, the area of relationships between the conflicting states, it can be seen that it depends on concepts such as interest, power and security. Of the present century it could be said that the question of world dominance has been an open one in spite of two major wars. National security is usually defined in terms of power, and this in turn is defined, *inter alia,* as the national capacity to fight a successful war. But no war has been successful in the sense of finally providing security for a victor nation, and all victories in the past have been transient. What has been termed the security dilemma remains unresolved and the consequence has been that one state's security implies another state's insecurity.

From this general situation the political scientist has extracted a concept of security and turned it into a theory which explains the occurrence of wars. War, it is argued, is caused by the belief that national security depends on military superiority. Consequently, national defence policy seeks to arm to a level superior to that of any potential opponent, and national foreign policy seeks to reinforce this by alliance with other states. Clearly, the number of states with the organisation, technology and resources to do this will be limited. The rest of the world is composed of states which are either victims, neutrals or allies of these major powers. Thus the effect of this notion of security is to induce a competition between states and hence the phenomenon of an arms race makes its appearance. From the arms race itself, war is a comparatively short step, since the temptation will exist of stopping or winning the competition by a trial of strength. The paradox in this situation is that the pursuit of national security leads to the perpetuation of international violence, until the war which ends all wars is fought, and one state finally achieves the hegemony which alone guarantees its security.

This brief description is a good example of the interconnection between national policies, technology and organisation, and the international environment. The argument is reasonable and coherent, and it explains why disarmament talks between states are really discussions over security and not about peace. It provides a general explanation of the occurrence of violent conflict in the world and of the responsive, if anarchic, nature of international politics. But what it does not explain is why particular wars have occurred in the past. Nor does it explain adequately the role of technology as a variable, although it is clearly extremely important as a factor. Moreover, the role of individual politicians and of domestic political activity and of diplomacy are treated almost as irrelevances.

The objections to the selection of one process in international politics, an arms race, as a prime cause of war are, firstly, that specific causes of war are ignored in the analysis since they are regarded as being incidental or symptomatic to the basic conflict. Secondly, arms races may lead to stability, and not to violence, as the present nuclear balance seems to indicate, and as the balance-of-power theorists argue. Thirdly, the race is subject to factors not directly controlled by the participating states, for example social and political pressures within them, economic and technological changes and so on. Finally, it does not take into account other factors of importance in determining national policies in conflict situations, commitments to an appeasing position, for example, changing alliance relationships, or the prior existence of international commitments and the revaluation of policy in response to another state's actions.

If we apply these criticisms to our example, we could argue that Britain went to war in 1939 not to restore the balance of power and to remove a challenge to her security, but because of the triumph of a war party in domestic politics, moral indignation over the breach of the Munich agreement by Germany, and the obligations incurred to Poland as a consequence of the unconditional guarantee of Polish integrity, as well as a reaction to the actions and demands of other states such as France and the Soviet Union. It can be said of this situation that values can act as an influence on policy, and that questions of prestige are sometimes important as an influence on governments. On the German side it can also be said that Hitler made a major miscalculation as to British intentions and in believing that his pact with the Soviet Union would effectively deter Britain from implementing her guarantee to Poland.

It is clear from this brief treatment of this international situation that the major difficulty in applying scientific method to situations of this kind lies in separating factors and their relationships without distorting the explanation. We can perhaps agree that conceptions of national security may create international conditions, which then exert an influence on national policies, but we would probably disagree in particular cases as to the importance of this factor. On the general level the security explanation of war appears convincing, but when a specific war is the subject of explanation, then other factors and relationships assume importance, and the question of their significance remains a matter of interpretation and not of objective certainty. There are also considerable theoretical difficulties in achieving the kind of explanation found in science, apart from these general considerations, and these will be discussed in the following chapter.

What of the other general approach towards the study of international politics? For want of a better term the second approach may be called that of historical interpretation. It is concerned with the examination of phenomena without attempting to formulate a general theory and without making any attempt at either prescription or prediction. In this sense it is non-scientific. Yet it cannot, as we shall see, avoid a level of generalisation which implicitly, at least, is theoretical. The historian of international politics, like the political scientist, seeks to make order out of chaos and to render complex events and behaviour intelligible. In so doing he is involved in the application of concepts and assumptions, in creating a rational argument and in explaining why things happened as part of a larger explanation. But the interpretations which emerge from the historian's view of the past are not explicitly theoretical, in the sense that a general theory of human or political behaviour is either advanced or forms the basis for more limited interpretations.

There are certain difficulties in avoiding a deliberately systematic theoretical approach as well as advantages in doing so. Since the premises and assumptions are largely implicit, or left undefined, the dangers of value judgement and anachronistic argument are perhaps greater than in the scientific approach. In the latter a conscious attempt is made to state premises, and to construct a logical deductive argument as a testable hypothesis. Such an argument provides its own terms for verification and is therefore easier to evaluate. Another problem related to the implicit hypothetical content of historical explanation is that of its subject-matter. The historian is concerned with what he conceives of as actuality; in the case of international politics, with decisions and events which actually occurred in the past. Once something has happened, then the explanation proffered is related to the concrete event, and not to events which have not occurred, or which might be expected to occur. What might have happened is not the subject of history, although as a possibility it may be relevant to the participant. However, while the corpus of past, rather than present or future, occurrences constitutes the subject-matter of the historian, it cannot be said that it is in any way neutral, in the sense that it is concrete or self-evident. This is firstly because, as was pointed out earlier in this introduction, the historian is concerned with the surviving traces of the past in his present, and his historical knowledge is confined to these; and secondly, because if an explanation of the past is offered which is less than total, then some selection must take place, and this involves, as we have seen, the question of criteria related to specific assumptions. The activity of interpreting the past may or may not take the form of a distinctive explanation, distinctive that is as an explanation, but it does involve the construction of a coherent and communicable argument dependent on concepts, premises and assumptions. So far as contemporary history is concerned there is clearly a difficulty in that finite events are not so easily recognisable, and detachment therefore both of the historian's viewpoint and of the isolation of significant facts is more difficult. History has not done its editing. It should be pointed out that this is a practical and not a theoretical distinction between the study of the recent and the remote past. There are some lacunae in the contemporary historian's knowledge of the immediate past, but his main problem is one of profusion of material, not its scarcity.

This involves him in rather more emphasis on the criteria used for the selection of material, since he is not aided, or hindered, by historical accident. Historical anachronism is perhaps less of a problem. The element of value judgement is more intractable, especially since the contemporary historian is inevitably involved in evaluating questions which are still live controversies, and which are subject to continual reassessment or revaluation as the pattern of events unfolds. Our personal beliefs may well influence our behaviour as members of society, or equally well may not, since human beings permit themselves the convenience of inconsistency. It is obvious that someone with a strong conviction that the world is flat or that the dimensions of the Great Pyramid have some relevance to the prediction of the future will have a somewhat idiosyncratic interpretation of the past and the present. What is less obvious is the case where an implicit assumption, apparently unexceptionable, colours an interpretation of contemporary history. Where an underlying value system is explicitly related to historical interpretation, such as for example Marxism-Leninism or Christianity, then the bias is clear. But much of recent historical writing on international relations is coloured by such assumptions as, for example, that the Soviet Union is an expansionist or aggressive power,[21] or that the United States is primarily motivated in its foreign policy by the desire to promote and protect its economy.[22] Such assumptions are the more dangerous when they are unrelated to any theoretical argument which can be examined in its own right, and when they are taken as axiomatic by those who make them. The point here is not that a value-orientated argument is wrong, but that it should be made clear that it is such an argument, and not something else. We may be interested in the reduction of social and economic inequalities between people, or in promoting the fortunes of our own country, and thus selecting some aspects of the recent past and rejecting others in our interpretations of international politics. The basis of such a selection should, however, be made explicit.

If the scientific approach is rejected, and validity, or truth, is not regarded as certainty, or subject to an unequivocal test, then we are thrown back on interpretations which are subjective in the sense that they cannot be verified. If these interpretations are arrived at with half of the questions already answered, either through prejudice or through unexamined assumptions, then either we make out of history self-fulfilment, or vindication, or we are unable to communicate. It can of course be maintained that historical explanation is not so relativistic as all that, and that there are recognisable criteria for the evaluation of good and bad history. The question as to whether historical explanation is a distinctive form of explanation, with its own methodological rules, and its own criteria for validity, will be examined in Chapter 4 of this study. The point which is emphasised here is that whatever the grounds for asserting that a particular mode of enquiry has its own characteristics or its own truth, any explanation of human behaviour, political or otherwise, should make these grounds explicit, and this applies as much to the historical as it does to the scientific approach to the study of international politics. The first four chapters of this study seek to establish the nature of the various modes of enquiry offered as explanations of international politics, and to establish the conditions necessary for their evaluation. Succeeding chapters are concerned with the applications of these modes of enquiry in various empirical fields of international politics, both as a means of studying the nature of explanation in these areas, and of providing particular interpretations of the various phenomena found in them.

If there is a theme common to all aspects of this introductory study of international politics, applicable to both theoretical and empirical areas of enquiry, it is that the terms of an argument should always be stated as far as is possible within the limits of language and understanding. In particular, the terms on which the argument may be evaluated should always be part of any interpretation. It is the contention of the author that, in so far as this field of study is concerned, the apparent choice of different modes of explanation, which hinges on the notion that one is more likely to lead to the truth than another, has no justification. The choice, as will be argued later in this work, is essentially one of taste. For while some arguments are better than others, no one argument contains the whole truth, and thus invalidates all the rest.

REFERENCES

1. See, for example, Fred A. Sonderman, 'The Linkage between Foreign Policy and International Politics', in James N. Rosenau (ed.), *International Politics and Foreign Policy* (New York; Free Press of Glencoe, 1961) p. 9.
2. i.e. the notion of politics as being exclusively concerned with a polity.
3. Bernard Crick, *In Defence of Politics* (Harmondsworth: Penguin Books, 1964).
4. Aristotle, *The Politics* (Harmondsworth: Penguin Books, 1962) bk xi, pp. 55-100.
5. Crick, op. cit., p. 30.
6. Ibid., p. 29.
7. For a critical exposition of this view, see Hedley Bull, 'Society and Anarchy in International Relations', in Herbert Butterfield and Martin Wight (eds.), *Diplomatic Investigations* (London: Allen & Unwin, 1966) pp. 35ff.

8. For example, see George Liska, 'Toward an Equilibrium Theory of International Relations and Institutions', in Rosenau, op. cit., pp. 330ff., and Harold and Margaret Sprout, 'Environmental Factors in the Study of International Politics', ibid., pp. 106ff.

9. See Talcott Parsons, 'Polarisation of the World and International Order', in *Sociological Theory and Modern Society* (New York: Free Press, 1967) pp. 466-89.

10. See Talcott Parsons, 'Order and Community in the International Social System', in Rosenau, op. cit., pp. 120ff., and 'Certain Primary Sources and Patterns of Aggression in the Social Structure of the Western World', first published 1947 and reprinted in *Essays in Sociological Theory,* rev. ed. (New York: Free Press, 1954) pp. 298ff.

11. Unpublished paper by W. T. R. Fox, 'Growing Points in the Study of International Relations', for the Seventh World Congress of the International Political Studies Association held at Brussels, 18–23 Sept. 1967, p. 4.

12. Geoffrey Barraclough, *An Introduction to Contemporary History* (London: C. A. Watts, 1964) p. 12.

13. Michael Oakeshott, 'The Activity of Being an Historian', in *Rationalism in Politics and Other Essays* (London: Methuen, 1962) p. 161.

14. George F. Kennan, *Memoirs,* vol. i: *1925–1950* (New York: Bantam Books, 1969) p. 428.

15. G. R. Elton, *The Practice of History* (London: Collins, Fontana Library Series, 1969) p. 20; see also the section on 'Evidence and Criticism', pp. 96-108.

16. See in particular Klaus Knorr and James N. Rosenau (eds.), *Contending Approaches to International Politics* (Princeton Univ. Press, 1969).

17. See Knorr and Rosenau, 'Tradition and Science in the Study of International Politics', ibid., pp. 3ff.

18. See Anatol Rapoport, 'Various Meanings of Theory', in Rosenau, op. cit., pp. 44ff.

19. Royal Institute of International Affairs, *Political and Strategic Interests of the United Kingdom* (London: Oxford Univ. Press, 1939) p. ix.

20. There were sizeable ethnic German communities in various cantons of Switzerland, in the Alto Adige, the Baltic states and in Alsace–Lorraine.

21. For example, see John W. Spanier, *American Foreign Policy since World War II* (London: Pall Mall Press, 1962) pp. 19-33.

22. For example, see Gabriel Kolko, *The Roots of American Foreign Policy* (Boston: Beacon Press, 1969).

CHAPTER 2

Scientific Theory and International Politics

ANY piece of empirical investigation, whether it is consciously systematic or not, contains premisses and assumptions made about the subject investigated. In other words, all explanations of events, action or behaviour have theoretical implications even when these are not explicitly stated or considered. This is no less true of explanation in the fields of international politics and contemporary history. The main problem in evaluating such interpretations is in answering the question, what is theory? Or more precisely, which theory is relevant to which explanation? It is assumed here that no extant theory has a universal validity. An assessment of whether an explanation is valid or applicable depends upon agreement as to its nature as an explanation and on the relevance of its theoretical criteria to the subject explained. This is more than agreement on what constitutes a valid method of enquiry or an appropriate analytic technique, for it involves the nature of the enquiry itself.

It would be inappropriate, for example, to apply the criteria of literary or aesthetic criticism to an explanation whose purpose was different from that of literature or art. Intentions are not enough, for explanations are judged not only by the explicit statement of purpose made by the author, but also by their nature as explanations. It is insufficient to state that a particular method or theoretical form is being applied to a field of study. The purpose of a theory is to explain, and the main criterion which must be established before the question of validity can properly be answered is, what is being explained? Of course, it is possible to apply a number of different criteria to certain kinds of argument and to make evaluations on different levels. The main point is that such criteria and evaluations should be distinguished one from the other.

In the social sciences there is an unresolved problem of which kind of explanation is most relevant to the study of human behaviour. The debate over this question has taken the form of two broad, and apparently opposed, schools of thought. One has argued that the model of scientific explanation is the most appropriate for the social sciences, while the other, when it is not resisting this claim, has taken the view that 'subjective' historical interpretation constitutes the only viable approach. In part this last view is negative, in the sense that any systematic theoretical approach towards the study of human activities is rejected. It has also been argued, however, that there is a form of explanation termed historical and which possesses characteristics distinct from those of other explanations. Clearly, if such an explanation could be validated, then it would be as inappropriate to apply to it the criteria for a valid scientific theory, as it would be to judge it by literary or aesthetic standards.

There are perhaps two stages in making evaluations of particular interpretations in the social sciences. The first is in establishing the nature of the enquiry, and the second is in validating its application. It is of value, as will be argued later, to assess argument and interpretation on the basis of a clearly defined explanatory model, but such an assessment should not ignore the dangers of over-idealisation, nor should an inappropriate model be chosen. This chapter will be concerned with the model of scientific explanation, as applied to the social sciences in general, and to the field of international politics specifically. The question as to whether there is a distinctive historical explanation, with its own criteria and validity, will be examined in a later chapter. When social scientists claim to be theoretical and scientific in their approach to the study of human behaviour, what is the nature of their claim, and what is the nature of their explanation? In order to answer these questions it is first necessary to establish the nature of scientific explanation. What is sometimes called an exact science consists of a set of propositions derived from a logical argument and from which are established generalisations which 'explain' the existence and behaviour of phenomena. The assumptions and hypotheses themselves cannot be 'proven', but the validity of the conclusions derived from them is established by direct reference to experience. Such a theory is true if its conclusions correspond to every instance of the phenomenon it seeks to explain. It is refuted if this correspondence fails to appear in any one instance. A theoretical argument which is not tested or is not testable in this way remains a hypothesis.

In theories of this kind the assumptions may be empirically derived, that is, from the observation of phenomena, but the ultimate test of their validity lies in the relationship between hypothetical conclusions and behavioural reality. Such assumptions can be approximate or idealised and need not be rigorously defined. The problem of precise definition occurs in the course of the deductive argument, for example in the selection and measurement of variables. Where there is no agreement on their recognition, as in astrology or alchemy, there can be no measurement, or at least no communicable theory which explains the occurrence and behaviour of phenomena. It would be more apposite to regard these kinds of theories not as early and unsuccessful attempts at scientific explanation, but rather as arguments in their own right of a metaphysical or ideological nature, or as myths. The point is not that alchemists sought to achieve science through metaphysics, but that such an attempt if it were made would prove unsuccessful, since they are two radically different forms of explanation with their own evaluatory criteria.

A science is thus a rigorous deductive argument from which are induced generalisations which bear a sufficiently close correspondence to real behaviour as to enable predictive statement. Such a theory may provide only a partial explanation of all classes of behaviour, but it must provide specific and exact conclusions which are empirically verifiable. It need not be dependent upon a general theory with universal laws in order to have explanatory efficacy. It has validity and utility in that it permits accurate predictions and, from this, makes prescription possible. If future states in the behaviour of a group of phenomena are known, and if the processes and rules governing their relationship can be deduced, then behaviour can be controlled or induced. Of course, prediction does not necessarily mean more than a statement that, if the laws governing sequences of relationships are known, then future states in that relationship may be deduced from them. If this can be verified empirically, then the explanation advanced is a valid one. But it does not follow that such an explanation has the sole claim to validity, since an alternative may produce the same conclusions. Nor does the notion of validity constitute an absolute truth, for, as Popper has pointed out,[1] while hypotheses can be falsified, they cannot be absolutely verified. In this sense we can know whether a hypothesis is false but we cannot establish its truth. Yet whether we accept falsification or verification as a means of testing scientific argument, it is clear that it is the capacity for predictive statement which is subject to an empirical test, that distinguishes science from other kinds of explanation. It is not its logical structure, or the methods which it uses. An argument is not scientific because it uses methods commonly found in science, nor can it be presumed, as we shall see in the next chapter, that the use of such methods will produce a valid scientific explanation. The use of symbolic logic, mathematics, experiment and analysis is found in a variety of different explanations and theories.

There is another kind of theory which has been termed scientific, and that is probabilistic explanation.[2] The conclusions produced by this form of argument are valid according to a proportion of empirical instances. Unlike the kind of explanation in which one contrary instance invalidates the theory, probability theory admits exceptions but with reference to a specified statistical norm. Both explanations are similar in construction, argument and method, but in the former case validity consists of an absolute conformity between conclusions and empirical instances, while in the latter it consists of a specified conformity. Prediction is made possible in the one case, while the other can make only 'probability' statements. It has been argued that all generalisations about behaviour are probability statements in the sense that absolute prediction is not possible. Not only is the uniformity of nature a basic assumption which cannot be proven, but it is impossible to establish that the correspondence between theoretical conclusions and empirical instances is infinite. As Reichenbach puts it, 'observational facts can make a theory only probable but will never make it absolutely certain'.[3] All general propositions can be expressed as having a statistical conformity with observation, of a ratio between 1 and 100. If this argument is accepted, then scientific explanation is concerned with probabilities and not certainties, and its general propositions are not universal laws. Nevertheless, both kinds of explanation depend upon recognisable and quantifiable variables and on general propositions derived from a deductive argument. They differ according to their explanatory power in terms of a correspondence between theoretical conclusions and behavioural reality. But although absolute certainty is not possible in scientific explanation, hypotheses are testable in a meaningful sense and on these grounds it is possible to establish whether a theoretical explanation is a good or a bad one.

This brief examination of the nature of explanation in science glosses over a number of important philosophical problems. But although the model is a simplistic one and does not correspond exactly to extant theorising in science, nor resolve philosophic debate on the nature of science, it establishes a major distinction between scientific explanation and other kinds of explanation. There may be similarities in the process of enquiry and in the logical form of the arguments used, but the touchstone lies in the notion of validation contained in the explanation. As Braithwaite puts it, 'it is this hypothetico-deductive method applied to empirical material which is the essential feature of a science and if psychology or economics can produce empirically testable hypotheses *ipso facto* they are sciences'.[4] The question asked in this chapter is whether such an explanation has been produced in the fields of political science and international politics.

A further reason for accepting this model is that it is the one which is almost invariably used by social scientists in their attempts to provide a theoretical explanation of human behaviour. In Easton's words:

> In its ideal and most powerful form, a general theory achieves maximal value when it constitutes a deductive system of thought so that from a limited number of postulates, assumptions and axioms, a whole body of empirically valid generalisations might be deduced in descending order of specificity.[5]

How far has this idealisation of scientific explanation been fulfilled in the social sciences? Can the criteria for a valid theory in science be met in this field? Are social scientists concerned with a distinctive kind of explanation which may be termed scientific?

There are perhaps three ways of approaching an answer to these questions. The first is to examine specific statements of intent made by social scientists, that is, to take objectives and structure as the criteria. The second is to apply the criteria of the model described above, and the third is to establish another, more appropriate model. It may be true that theory in the social sciences is not scientific theory, but alternatively another form of explanation may be offered which has its own autonomy and which is not susceptible to the evaluatory criteria appropriate for science.

What attempts have been made in the social sciences to produce a theoretical explanation of human behaviour? According to Runciman[6] there is only 'one serious candidate' for theory in political science, and that is the functionalist approach. The central question asked by this theory is not how a phenomenon came about but what contribution it makes to maintaining other phenomena. In other words, what are its functions? The notion of function tends to have a number of different meanings. It can be taken, for example, to refer to the necessary preconditions for action or for a phenomenon, to the consequences of action, to purposive action or to characteristic activity in relation to an organism. In general it is the former concept which is used in this analysis. The major assumption in functional theory is that social phenomena are interdependent and that specific phenomena make a necessary contribution to the existence of other phenomena. An interaction takes place between them and a distinguishable aggregate is formed.

The idea of an organ or an entity comprising a number of functional relationships to which they contribute is central to functional theory. It is sometimes argued that what is called a 'communication flow',[7] or specific relationships, are 'functional', but this is really to assert that phenomena may be interactive. A full explanation of such specific interactions would involve an explanation of their context. If phenomena are simply coeval, then an explanation of them must be found elsewhere. They may be functional for other phenomena but not for each other. The theorist must concern himself with sequential or system relationships, unless he is advancing an alternative explanation based upon a principle of spontaneity or has a concept of system which is not dependent upon specific phenomena. Yet if relationships are examined in isolation, some of the coeval phenomena and relationships are being ignored. A functional explanation must establish criteria for relevance and significance which would include the context and validate the selection.

Functional theory thus asserts a property in a set of relationships over and above the sum of its respective parts. Such an entity is conceived as being self-maintaining in the sense that its needs are satisfied by particular phenomena. These phenomena are functional for the entity and operate according to the principle of regulation asserted in the theoretical explanation. If they do not, then the functional entity either changes or, in any case, disappears altogether. It is necessary in such a theory, as Hempel points out,[8] to establish the regulative principle in order to explain what is functionally necessary for the system. Otherwise it is difficult to argue that one particular phenomenon rather than another is functionally necessary. The establishment of such a principle would enable prediction and would form part of a theory corresponding to the scientific model considered above and with its explanatory power.

In order to assert a functional need or a functional prerequisite, it is necessary to define what it is which has this need. The problem of establishing a norm for survival also poses the question of what exactly is in jeopardy. In a general sense, all social phenomena may be related in that they have a time or spatial connection. Unless a referent exists in the form of some recognisable or definable entity comprising the set of conditions and resultant relationships, then the functional approach simply asserts a form of holism in which all coeval social phenomena are 'necessary' and functional. If, for example, 'society' is left undefined, then this implies a concept of total unity or conceals an implicit empirical referent. To argue that functions are, as Merton puts it,[9] 'those observed consequences which make for adaptation or adjustment of a given system; and dysfunctions, those observed consequences which lessen the adaptation or adjustment of the system', is to leave unanswered the question, what is the system? There is a tautological element in a concept of functional relationship which is not causal and which does not provide an empirically testable theory. This difficulty, as will be seen later, is only apparently avoided by the assertion of a conceptual entity such as 'society', 'system' or 'polity' to which functional relationships are directed and which have functional needs. This appears less tautological than the general assertion of all coeval phenomena as being necessarily related, but still leaves open the problem of validating the organising concept and establishing a theoretical basis for assessing functional necessity. An explanation of functions must also explain what it is which articulates needs which these functions satisfy. This is a difficult problem, for, as Sorokin[10] points out, if a causal functional unity is said to exist 'with interdependent components contributing to the maintenance of the unity, then while in biology empirical distinctions can be made between classes of such unities the boundaries are far from distinct for systems of human behaviour'. If such boundaries are not established, then the concept of functional unity is analogous and not theoretical.

In short, the basic questions in structural-functional theory are, which and why certain conditions are necessary for the existence of what? Such questions lead on to a theory of causation, for while a causal explanation may not necessarily be a functional one, a functional explanation is always causal. Why should this be so? In what way is a thing explained by its relationship with other things? Does such an explanation depend upon general propositions as in science, or does it assert only that certain phenomena are interdependent in some loose way? A scientific theory, as we have seen, establishes generalisations about phenomena which are validated by referring them to the events explained by the supporting hypothesis. It is the assertion of necessary relationships between things which brings into question the nature of the theory underlying this assertion. As Malinowski put it:

> The functional isolate that I have labelled institution differs from the culture complex or trait complex, when defined as 'composed of elements which stand in no necessary relationships to each other' in that it does postulate such a necessary relationship.[11]

The argument that X is necessary for the existence of Y is a causal one so far as Y is concerned. Otherwise, if it is only asserted that X and Y are related in some way, the level of this generalisation is non-theoretical. The assertion of a *necessary* relationship requires a supporting hypothesis, which would have the effect of saying that the conditions for the existence of Y would always result in Y (or according to a stated statistical probability), or that Y could be deduced from the conditions and the hypothesis. Such an argument is only applicable if a necessary relationship is asserted. If it is not, then all that is being said is that an optimal set of conditions are necessary, or that an indeterminate relationship exists, or that X is not necessary for the existence of Y but constitutes only one of a number of unspecified preconditions for Y. Whether it is a sufficient precondition depends on the theoretical argument advanced. A full causal explanation would provide such a statement. If X and Y are said to have a causal relationship, then such a theory is implied.

To refer back to the earlier definition of scientific explanation, we can see that such an explanation explains why things happen in such a way as to be able to say that, given the same conditions, factors, variables and relationships, the same phenomenon will recur. Such an explanation, *inter alia,* is causal or genetic, and permits, if not the absolute certainty of prediction, at least a statement of the probability of its occurrence. If the preceding argument is accepted, that is, that structural-functional explanations are causal in nature, then some statement of prediction or of probability should be possible if they are to be considered scientific. Such statements should be capable of empirical verification.

As will be seen later when systems analysis is examined, the problem of establishing causality is sometimes avoided by emphasising the structural part of the analysis and ignoring its dynamics or processes. An alternative way of evading causal laws is the assertion of necessary but not sufficient conditions for functional relationships. Such an argument leads on to what has been called capacity or survival theory, that is, to the assertion of optimal conditions for the existence of phenomena. Such arguments have been termed by Taylor[12] 'what-explanations', that is, they are really descriptions which are non-scientific. In other words, they make a phenomenon intelligible by defining it or fitting it into a context which confers meaning upon it, but they do not 'explain' in the sense of providing a causal generalisation. For example, a war may be 'explained' by a description of its characteristics and its diplomatic and political antecedents. Hence from this we know what the Second World War was, but unless the antecedents are treated as necessary and sufficient preconditions for the class of events of which it was an example, and thus provide us with a general proposition about wars, such an 'explanation' remains non-scientific. It may, of course, have its own explanatory autonomy, and this possibility will be considered later on in this study.

This argument indicates that it is very difficult to avoid the assertion of a general proposition when relevant or significant conditions for the occurrence of a particular phenomenon are asserted. As we shall see in a later chapter, the notions of unique properties, of innate qualities or of propensity pose theoretical problems. But the point here is that while it may be possible to say that non-events are explicable by the absence of particular factors, the explanation of actual events requires some causal proposition.

The question as to how far such a level of explanation has been achieved in the social sciences is beyond the scope of this work,[13] as is a full exposition of the major theoretical developments in this field. The intention rather is to indicate the general relationship between these developments and explanations specific to the field of international politics. It will be apparent from the foregoing discussion that a functional theory requires the assumption of an organising concept. Even where a system is conceived of as a set of interactions, this involves some notion, either of a state of equilibrium or stability to which change is related, that is, a normative principle, or of some conceptual entity comprising the sum of the relationships involved. Otherwise there is no theoretical justification for the selection of specific phenomena which are asserted to be in relationship. For reasons which will be more apparent when the empirical content of international politics is considered in later chapters, the choice of an organising concept as a referent and as an assumption is difficult. The notions of group, mass, individual, class, culture, or of state, nation, bodypolitic, institution or organisation, are not easily applied to this field. Nor, it must be admitted, can equivalent notions peculiar to international politics be substituted as empirical referents. Assumptions of 'actors' or of 'nation-states' do not permit the same identification; for example, the idea of 'Britain' is as cloudy as that of 'society' or of 'class' but less useful in organising an explanation.

An emphasis on the nation-state as the source of international political behaviour paralleled the earlier concentration in the social sciences upon the individual and his behaviour within the large and ill-defined entities of society and state. Structural-functional theory appeared to resolve some of the difficulties involved in this emphasis, which then shifted to the conception of interactions within a framework or system. The emphasis in the study of international politics similarly changed, and an explanation of individual and national behaviour was found in interactions between them rather than in a projection of national foreign policies and behaviour. The problem was the same as that in the social sciences generally; to isolate variables and referents as a preliminary for an explanation. Durkheim,[14] for example, found his referent in the concept of 'social facts' and in the demarcation of a 'social consciousness' as the proper focus for sociological explanation. Malinowski[15] found his focus in the concept of group and of 'social institutions'. The only such referent which appears to permit the application of functional theory to international politics is the apparently neutral one of system.

From this it would appear that theories which have some coherence as explanations in the social sciences fit but uneasily where a recognisable organising concept is absent. The concept of society imposes its own general limits upon explanations and may be appropriate when it is applied to identifiable groups, such as pre-literate peoples, or communities within a given political framework such as the nation-state, but is inadequate where such a focus does not exist. Some writers have sought to extend theories based upon such organising concepts, derived from generalisations about social behaviour within a society or a body politic, to explain international behaviour. For example, Parsons[16] extends his notion of social structure and system to international politics and refers to an 'international society'. Other writers have not attempted to widen the application of their theories and have either argued that the phenomena of international politics are subsumed within their own explanations, or that the field has no valid separate existence. The absence of any definable or recognisable entity in this field has inhibited a direct functional explanation and has severely limited those general analyses which are based upon conceptual entities. One might conclude by saying either that the field of international politics does not constitute a class of phenomena requiring specific explanation, or that extant functional theories are incomplete or lacking in some way since they do not explain satisfactorily phenomena existing beyond the boundaries of the nation-state or of society.

An examination of systems theory in the social sciences might help to clarify some of the theoretical problems involved in this type of explanation. The concept of system has been considered by some writers as avoiding any preconception as to the significance of single factors or of specific phenomena in an explanation of human behaviour. It is, in this view, empirically 'neutral', in that it does not presuppose any particular organising concept based upon empirical generalisation or interpretation. According to this argument it permits a multivariate analysis without either prescribing its content or prejudicing the enquiry. So far as the study of politics is concerned, the most developed systems theory is contained in the work of David Easton,[17] although this writer explicitly rejects the functionalist approach on the grounds that it is 'fundamentally devoid of theoretical content'.[18] Whether this is so or not, the outline of his intentions appears to be identical with those of functional theorists. Thus he talks of the recognition of 'units of analysis', of 'the fundamental processes or activities without which no society could continue',[19] and of 'those fundamental functions without which no system could endure'.[20] The distinction would appear to be semantic rather than substantive, since Easton argues that the focus of his enquiry is 'the kinds of activities that go on in a political system, what we might at other times and places have called the political functions, if this concept itself had not become virtually unusable because of the enormous variety of slippery meanings currently attached'.[21]

From his description of purpose it seems clear that he is seeking an explanation of the workings of a set of relationships which function in such a way as to 'regulate their own behaviour, transform their internal structure and even go so far as to remodel their fundamental goals'.[22] A system is simply 'any set of variables'[23] and a political system consists of 'those interactions through which values are authoritatively allocated for a society'.[24] There is little here that is different from the functionalist approach to social behaviour. The major difference is that it is applied to what Easton calls 'political life', and while he argues that his theory is a general systems theory, he also maintains that there is a distinctive political system. It is clear from his argument that he is concerned with a functional explanation of a polity which is not clearly defined but which is asserted to be distinguishable from an environment consisting of other 'systems'. The basis of this distinction is the notion that there is an 'authoritative allocation of values' in a society and that this is administered by concrete 'authorities'.[25] Such an idea is empirically derived.

To refer back to the earlier discussion of functional theory, we can see that the essential part of such a theory, if it is to explain, is the establishment of a causal proposition which determines the interaction between a system and its component parts. The notion of regulation, that is, the way in which the system is maintained or exists, and its adjustment to change, must also be related to some general normative principle against which change and systemic responses can be assessed or measured. This involves the problem of defining stability, equilibrium or the 'normal' state of the system. Such a definition, if it is to be more than an untestable assertion, should be part of a theory which establishes processes and enables predictive statements about future or sequential states of the system. Instead of elucidating such a theory, Easton turns to the notion of regulation without clearly defining what is being regulated. This is formulated as 'information feedback',[26] and it constitutes an interactive process between the system and its environment. He argues that this is not an automatic determinant but is 'consciously shaped'[27] by the members of a political system. As he puts it:

It is not likely that we can find a system the members of which permit themselves to be buffeted about helplessly by events in their environment. All systems seek to adapt continuously at least to some extent, by using, acting upon, and shaping the conditions to which they are exposed.[28]

Apart from the subjectivity of this generalisation, there is some ambiguity in the distinction between 'members' and the 'system', for the system is no more than the activities of its members. But what Easton seems to be saying is that interactions take place but that their nature is indeterminate. This avoids the problem of making a general proposition either about individual behaviour or systemic behaviour.

The actual regulation of the system is conducted by what are termed 'authorities', which seek to maintain a 'goalorientation'.[29] This is done by translating information (conceived of as an input into the system) into responses and action (conceived of as outputs into the environment) which seek to maintain specified ends. This process of information–action–regulation between the system and its environment is termed 'feedback loop'.[30] Thus the idea of function as purposive action is merged with the conception of the functional needs of the system. An authority must exist in order to interpret the information and to make the necessary adjustments and responses which maintain the system and which constitute 'feedback'. It is thus functional for the system. But so is 'feedback' itself, for Easton argues: 'If feedback – both information and responses – did not exist, the system would find itself utterly exposed to the vagaries of chance'.[31] The idea of 'feedback' here appears to subsume that of 'authorities'.

It is not clear whether his system is a formalisation of a governmental–state relationship, whether it exists in its own right as a 'living reality' or whether it is entirely hypothetical and abstract. The principle of feedback, which Easton considers 'the most dominant and most fertile innovation of our own age'[32] since Newton and Darwin, appears to be merely a synonym for interaction rather than an explanation of it.

From this we can see that the application of this kind of systems analysis to the field of international politics has certain difficulties. The construct of system we have considered above is derived partly from a mechanical hypothesis and partly based on empirical generalisations about a particular kind of polity. If Easton's conceptual scheme did not depend upon such referents, then it might be useful in an explanation of international political behaviour. As it is, his assertions that there is an international society, an international economy and an international culture[33] are not supported by any evidence and amount to little more than an expansion of notions derived from specific national or social contexts. Such a conceptualisation of a body politic translated into the terms of a mechanical system may or may not be appropriate to national politics as an explanation of 'political life', but it is inappropriate when it is applied to an area lacking in the institutions and normative elements necessary to support such a scheme. The attempt to project it in statements such as that there is 'an international political community', or that 'the members of the international society seek to resolve some of their problems through the authoritative allocation of values',[34] are not empirically convincing in the absence of an 'authority' which is necessary for the existence of such a system. What Easton appears to be saying is that if international politics corresponded to his idea of political life, then his conceptual scheme would be appropriate to it.

A distinction can be made between a general systems theory of this kind and systems theories which are relevant only for particular phenomena. We might ask ourselves two questions at this point; firstly, is there a valid systems theory of international politics which corresponds to the systems theory considered above? and secondly, is there a valid systems theory of political and social behaviour within the terms of scientific explanation? To take the first question, the most developed systems theory of international politics is that of Morton Kaplan, although a number of writers have applied a systems approach to this field.[35] Kaplan sought to use the basic systems argument, but in application to an area of phenomena which differed in certain respects from that found within the boundaries of a nation-state, or a national or primitive society.

An international system of action,[36] he asserts, constitutes a set of related variables which has behavioural regularities or characteristics. Each such system has an identity in time and maintains itself according to some regulatory process.[37] In the terms used by systems analysts, it has inputs and outputs, that is, contributions made to the system, and contributions made by the system. These imply the existence of a systemic environment, and this is conceived of as consisting of other systems, the inputs of one being the outputs of another. Certain distinctions are made between functions. Some inputs are positive, some are negative and some are 'step-level'.[38] By this is meant that some relationships maintain the *status quo*, some change parts of it; a negative feedback counteracts change but a positive feedback creates a new component. This follows the distinction made earlier by Merton, between interactions which are functional, that is, system-maintaining, and interactions which are dysfunctional, that is, which are system-changing. A step-level function is one which affects the system as a whole and completely changes its characteristic behaviour, that is, changes it into something else, either a new system or some kind of systemic limbo.

There is little in this which differs from the schemata produced by other systems theorists in other fields, except for Kaplan's conception of an international system as a 'null political system'.[39] By this he means that, since no institution comparable to that of government exists in international politics, it is consequently not a *political* system. An international system is therefore composed of interactions *between* political systems which function as 'sub-systems' for it. A specific international system consists of a set of related variables which interact so as to induce a particular behaviour pattern from the participating sub-systems. These last do not consist solely of national political systems, but include some institutions, such as international and supranational organisations, and also relations between individuals such as ambassadors, businessmen, politicians, heads of state, etc.

In spite of the absence of an institutional structure in international politics, comparable to that of the nation-state, the international system is conceived of as an integrated entity of various degrees of cohesion. The nature of this entity is not clearly defined, but it is maintained by a regulative process[40] in which the component elements are functional (or dysfunctional) for the system as a whole. Such a system has both capacity and also needs: The first is defined as the number of responses which the system is capable of making when faced with disturbances, and the latter, rather more vaguely, as what is necessary to the system to permit it to remain in being. It is clear from this outline that this concept of system is ambivalent in that it is not wholly organic but nevertheless assumes some degree of integral unity for the system. As Kaplan puts it, his notion of system is that of 'an analytic entity'[41] which consists of variables and which has an 'identity over time'.[42] It is problematical whether 'system' in this sense means an aggregate of variables or some describable concrete entity which is empirically derived.

What are these systemic variables? According to Kaplan there are five: 'the essential rules of the system, the transformation rules, the actor classificatory variables, the capability variables and the information variables'.[43] The first specifies a norm and describes the characteristic behaviour of the system, the second constitutes the 'laws of change' for the system, the third classifies the actor according to the kind of political system it comprises, the fourth category specifies the physical capacity of actor relative to specified kinds of action, and finally the information variable refers to the degree and content of the knowledge possessed by the actor. These five variables constitute the basic elements of the system, and the nature of their relationship determines the type and behaviour of the system. Subsequent modifications made by Kaplan[44] deleted the rather tautologous 'systems rules' and placed more emphasis upon the attributes of the actors: their capabilities, motivations, goal orientations, and their 'style' of strategic and political activity. Perhaps the actor variables could be expressed in simple terms as a set of questions: What 'kind' of actor is he? What function does he have in the system? What is his normal or characteristic behaviour? What does he know? And how does he use his knowledge and capacity?

Using these variables, Kaplan adduces six international systems. These are not, he says, actual historical examples but heuristic models. Two of them, the 'balance of power' and the 'loose bipolar' systems, have what he calls 'historical counterparts'.[45] Two others, the 'tight bipolar' and the 'unit veto' systems, do not appear to be systems at all since their main characteristic is that of a progressive disintegration. The remaining two, the 'hierarchical' and the 'universal' systems, seem to infringe the distinction made between an international and a political system, since they appear to possess some structural or institutional features akin to those of governments. As will be seen subsequently, there is some confusion over the structural element present in the international system, particularly with regard to the regulatory functions of 'decision-making units' and system maintenance.

These six international systems can be simply described as corresponding, firstly, to a situation in which states move into and out of alliances in a continuing attempt to prevent any one state from achieving hegemony; secondly, where two groups of allied states confront each other without the alliances precluding other forms of inter-relationships entered into by individual states; thirdly, where the same situation exists but with the alliance placing a strong constraint upon the independent action of its members; fourthly, where international organisations and co-operative bodies exercise some influence upon national behaviour; fifthly, where this influence assumes a supranational character; and sixthly, where each nation-state possesses weapons capable of destroying the other states. Most of these model situations or systems are interchangeable, that is, one system may be transformed into another with greater or lesser probability. Only one, that of the hierarchical system, is conceived of as incapable of trans-formation, and this closely resembles a polity or political system.

Such model systems remain static abstractions unless an explanation of their occurrence, maintenance and transformation is provided. A selection of a particular set of interdependent relationships at a given time does not constitute a system. The notion of a process or dynamic is a concomitant of a *causal* explanation. But a simple structural-functional model is clearly inappropriate for an international system which lacks an empirical focus and which consists of fluid political relationships. Kaplan's systems consist of a set of characteristic actions and these require, if explanation rather than hypothetical description is sought, both a normative principle and a causal law. The problem of establishing these is resolved by assuming that a specific system exists and then posing hypothetically necessary conditions for its continued existence. Ambiguities arise because a system is sometimes treated as if it were a concrete entity with a real existence, and sometimes as if it were a purely hypothetical type of behaviour.

Thus in his discussion of the process of regulation, Kaplan moves away from the notion of an international system as a null political system and draws most of his empirical references and his argument from the regulatory process of national political systems. He argues, for example, that integration occurs when 'units' find their system needs unsatisfied and consequently merge to form a larger 'unit' which can satisfy their needs.[46] 'Unit' and 'system' would appear in this context to be used as synonymous terms. Thus a unit has 'system needs' and, it is argued, 'without structure of some kind needs could not be satisfied, nor could they even exist'.[47] Yet the notion of international system contained in the argument denies it structure and it is therefore incapable of having 'needs'. There are no 'units' in an international system and hence it cannot be regulated in this particular way. The idea of regulatory units is derived from concealed assumptions about the functions of government in a political system which parallel those made by Easton in his systems analysis of political life.

A decision-making unit[48] is both a system in its own right and a sub-system for other systems. It is also an organisation which performs the important and theoretically necessary function of translating information and action into feedback processes which maintain the system. When this idea is applied to the international system, it is apparent that, unless it is argued that such units exist, the system is essentially directionless. Or alternatively it may be argued, as Haas points out, that such a system has 'an autonomous will that determines in considerable detail the behaviour of the actors'.[49] Information feedback can take place only within the sub-systems themselves, since only these possess decision-making units. The structural-functional approach seems inappropriate for a system almost totally lacking in structural features. Again, this difficulty is skirted by arguing that the function of regulation is performed through the actors themselves: 'the foci of regulatory maintenance are the national actor systems'.[50] This is ambiguous to say the least, especially when it is reinforced by the suggestion that international and 'supranational' organisations and diplomats themselves constitute a vestigial international society with an institutional framework.[51]

There is a further difficulty in applying this conception of system to international politics, and that is the notion of successive states or sequences in it. This is difficult to reconcile with the idea of a system as having a finite identity in time and a characteristic behaviour capable of description.[52] If this last is the case, then which particular state is *the* system? According to the theory, when a disturbance occurs then the system either maintains itself, that is, it remains the same, or it changes into another system or disappears altogether. But each of these possible responses must be related to some norm for the system as a whole, otherwise all that is being examined is change itself. Any concept of balance, stability, equilibrium, state or needs is dependent upon some systemic norm. This ambiguity is apparent in these six systems, for it is uncertain whether they are states within a larger international system or whether they are systems in their own right. If the former, then the problem of defining an international system is left unresolved. If the latter, then a theoretical explanation is necessary to explain a particular sequence and the normative principle to which the sequence is related.

Objections may also be made to the variables which, it is argued, interact to form systems. If the analysis based upon these variables is to be more than subjective interpretation, some measure of recognition and quantification is necessary. The variable of capacity, for example, requires a focus. An actor has capacity for what? Capacity is relative to specific action and to certain other variables. Although this is accepted by Kaplan,[53] it is given a number of meanings in his argument. Thus 'capacity' subsumes a number of physical factors such as resources, territory and population, but it also includes other factors such as an actor's 'willingness' to undertake particular actions and 'the capacity to draw on aid from others'.[54] It is inseparable here from the variable of motivation and includes both questions of value and also psychological variables. Moreover, it is defined as a 'measure of the responses a system is able to make that compensate for potential disturbances of the system',[55] and as a capacity 'to receive information corresponding to the significant variety possible in its environment'.[56] These definitions are open-ended unless the dynamics of the system are explained in such a way as to establish testable propositions about systems behaviour. Otherwise all that is being said is that certain optimum conditions are necessary for a given action, not that such an action would actually occur given these conditions. It may be of practical importance to know that the Swiss are unlikely to challenge American naval power, but this hardly constitutes an advance in our explanation of an international system.

Capacity as a variable suffers from the same weaknesses as those of the concept of power, that is, it cannot be expressed as a measurable quality but only as part of a *post facto* argument. The notion of a theoretical capacity involves postulating a complete knowledge of all alternatives and contingencies relevant for a given action. It is perhaps possible to argue that success or failure in governmental activities may be retrospectively explained in terms of power or capacity, but a prediction of this cannot be made unless certain theoretical conditions are met. If the variable of capacity is incapable of precise definition, then it is unlikely that a valid theory which is based upon it will ensue.

Perhaps an example might help to clarify some of the points made in this analysis of systems theory in international politics. The notion of the balance of power has a considerable antiquity, as is indicated by this quotation from Francis Bacon. He said of the 'triumvirate of kings', Henry VIII, Francis I and Charles V, that 'there was such a watch kept, that none of the three could win a palm of ground, but the other two would straightways balance it, either by confederation, or if need were by a war; and would not in any wise take up peace at interest'.[57] According to Kaplan, this notion can be expressed in systemic terms as a balance-of-power *system*, one of the two systems out of his six which have actual historical counterparts.

We may recognise a balance-of-power system through its three main characteristics; these are, firstly, it is an international social system without a political sub-system; secondly, there must be five or more participant states; and thirdly, the participants must conform in their behaviour to certain rules.[58] Observance of these rules is essential to the system, for if they are not observed then the system ceases to exist. Briefly, rule 1 states that the participant states seek to increase their capabilities; rule 2 that, rather than lose an opportunity to do so, they will choose to fight; rule 3 that, nevertheless, they will cease to fight if there is any danger of destroying one of their number; rule 4 that each state will try to prevent any other state or coalition from becoming too strong; rule 5 that each state will try to prevent any one of their number from attempting to create a supra-national organisation; and finally, rule 6 states that defeated states are allowed to climb back into the fold and rejoin the system.

In other words, these rules describe a situation in which a number of states seek to obtain advantages, but restrict their use of violence and alter their political and military relationships, in order to prevent any one state from becoming dominant. Hence they act in order to preserve a 'balance' between them.

But are these essential rules more than historical generalisations based upon what statesmen apparently did at various times in European history? In what sense are these 'rules' rules? It would appear that Kaplan conceives of them in systemic terms as conditions, or relationships between variables, which determine the process which, in turn, maintains a balance of power. Moreover, as he puts it, 'a high correlation between the pattern of national behaviour and the essential rules of the international system would represent a confirmation of the predictions of the theory'.[59] What does this mean? The pattern of national behaviour clearly constitutes the essential rules, that is, these *are* the behaviour. Behaviour, in the terms of the argument, is rules and rules are behaviour. This is to reassert generalisations as conditions for the generalisations themselves and to produce a tautology. The point is, that to express historical generalisations about 'characteristic' behaviour is simply an exercise in description unless it is possible to make predictive statements and, as we know from our earlier argument, these depend upon a verifiable hypothesis. If the concern of the theorist is more than the appendage of labels to a particular historical situation in international politics, then a theoretical explanation is required. A description or definition of a 'balance of power' situation does not provide this.

It is also apparent from these 'rules' that some of them depend upon supporting concepts such as 'capability' and 'power'. These, as we have seen, require a supporting hypothesis. Does the rule which stipulates that all states seek to increase their capabilities mean an attempt to engage in a number of unspecified actions or to accomplish some defined objective? Are these concepts related to prediction or can they be applied only retrospectively to national policies? It seems clear that if a rationalist or 'external' objective position is rejected, we cannot separate capacity from motivation. Do all statesmen seek to expand their 'capabilities', however these may be conceived, or is this simply a *post facto* judgement upon what they actually did in a balance-of-power situation? If capacity is used as a variable in systemic terms, then it is open to the major objection that it involves postulating a complete knowledge of all alternatives and contingencies open to the actors. If it simply means that the actors seek to obtain power or other objectives in international politics, then it is open to the charge of vagueness. The point here is that such generalisations themselves depend on the assertion of hypotheses related to assumptions about the nature of power and capacity which need to be made explicit and which can be tested.

From the assertion of essential rules for a balance-of-power system, Kaplan goes on to examine the problem of regulation and system maintenance. The question, why does a balance-of-power system come into existence, is answered by stating that *if* it exists then it must observe these rules. We have seen that this is tautological, in that these are not rules in the sense of behavioural laws but simply another way of describing behaviour itself. But how does the system persist or change? How is it regulated? The terms used to explain this process are exceedingly ambiguous. Kaplan argues that in order 'to account for change from one system to another it is necessary to isolate the critical conditions for the maintenance of the "balance of power" system'.[60] In other words, the central problem is in establishing which conditions are sufficient as well as being necessary for the existence of such a system. It is thus a theoretical problem directly related to causation. But nowhere in the argument is this problem resolved.

The sources of regulation, according to Kaplan, lie within the nation-states themselves. Diplomacy consists of an informal decision-making system, although *alliances* constitute the formal decision-making bodies. Nevertheless, these are simply the instruments of the nation-states who move into and out of alliances as they observe the essential rules of the system. When they do not, the system ceases to exist. In short, regulation was as regulation did and no general behavioural law is adduced to explain the process within the system. We are back to the historical generalisation: that a balance-of-power system consists of states which seek to prevent any one of their number from dominating the rest.

It should be apparent by now that although the language of systems 'theory' is employed, this type of system is a descriptive model which is derived from a number of historical generalisations. The level of historical judgement itself is open to question, on historical grounds. For example, in order to support a generalisation about goal objectives to the effect that 'supranationality is inconsistent with the exclusive values of nationalism',[61] Kaplan cites the 'self-imposed' limitations on German demands after her victory over France in 1870. He argues that because Germany was 'nationalistic' at this time, this precluded the absorption of France into a German

Empire. It is debatable whether nationalism inhibited Germany at the time, but no such inhibition existed in later wars, although German nationalism, if anything, waxed rather than waned. The real distinction which is made between the notion of supranationality and the notion of nationalism is one of definition, and not of historical instance. The point is that, on historical grounds, as we shall see subsequently, such an interpretation is incapable of empirical validation, and conflicting interpretations are possible. Yet here it is used to support part of an argument which is itself incapable of verification.

So far as the claim of this kind of systems analysis to be scientific is concerned, it would appear that what is meant is a reduced kind of predictive explanation. As Kaplan puts it, his concern is with 'what kind of coalition patterns, and goal objectives and limitations go along with given kinds of nations, capability ranges, economic and political systems, military forces and so forth', and from this to develop a theory which 'predicts what kind of coalition should occur, and how its objectives should be limited if certain interests of the member states are to be protected, but does not predict which particular nations will be members of which coalition'.[62] Clearly, an explanation which can do this must be empirically testable if it is to be more than a description of the past or a tautology. If the six systems cannot be tested, then all that can be said of them, *if* their internal arguments are considered coherent and logical, is that they are simply models which cannot explain empirical reality, in the sense of scientific explanation. It is not possible to deduce from them a general proposition about international political activities which advances a theoretical explanation. It may be true, as Kaplan says, that the individual paths of molecules in a tank of gas cannot be predicted by scientists,[63] but his contention that this reduces the explanatory force of scientific argument ignores the fact that even limited scientific propositions are testable, whereas his own, when he makes them, are not. If the system under analysis is dependent upon empirical assumptions which are neither made explicit nor are capable of verification, then there is the danger of a circular argument in which the assumptions become the conclusions.

Hence there is an ambivalence between such a conceptual scheme laid down as an abstract system, and empirical references which depend upon generalisations made about actual behaviour, and which themselves require an explanation. It is not clear what is really being explained – behavioural reality or the conceptual scheme? The reduced claim that propositions made in systems analysis concern statements which 'represent only potential rather than actual observations'[64] make it difficult to devise a means of validating them. Such a systems theory assumes that a particular system exists with its own distinctive characteristics and concludes that its existence depends upon certain necessary conditions being fulfilled, without providing any means of establishing the nature of this necessity, or of the systemic reality.

In short, these six systems are really models of an ideal world rather than the component parts of an empirical explanation. They are, as their author states, not intended to explain actual international behaviour. Consequently it is difficult to treat them as part of a theory of action which has scientific validity. If their propositions were capable of an empirical test, a critique would be possible. Similarly, if they were exercises in historical interpretation, other tests might be applied. As it is, neither of these two forms of validation is wholly applicable or relevant to this kind of theorising. It would appear to be neither science nor history. Its historical or empirical content may be treated as analogous or illustrative, and the scientific element as being formal rather than explanatory.

What, then, is the theoretical nature of systems analysis? If it is claimed to be scientific, does it explain why things happen in such a way so as to be able to say that, given the same conditions, factors, variables and relationships, the same phenomenon will recur? As we have seen earlier, such an explanation would provide a theory of action, events and behaviour which permits predictive statement. There is no historical time outside the chain of relationships and the sequence of processes. Once a process has been identified and explained by a scientific theory, then, wherever and whenever that process occurs, it will do so in the same way and with the same effects. Variations or deviations from empirical reality will give the theorist an indication that his assumptions or his arguments are faulty and that his explanation is consequently inadequate. If the objective of the political theorist is to find a theory which can say that 'given knowledge of the present state of a system and of the value of its parameters, the future states of the system are, in principle, predictable – whether with certainty or with some degree of probability is not at issue – if the changes in parameter values are given',[65] then this has not been achieved in systems analysis.

Why is this the case, after so much effort has been made in an attempt to achieve an adequate theoretical explanation of human behaviour? One major problem is that human behaviour is interdependent. This is both obvious and true of material or physical behaviour. But selection appears to have been possible in the natural sciences without invalidating the general propositions derived from the field. The variables in scientific explanation are isolable and can be defined precisely. The interdependence of human and social behaviour appears a more intractable problem; causes and effects, processes and phenomena, appear to be inextricably interwoven. An analysis based upon selected variables and problems seems to create more complexity than it resolves. Most of the categories in common use in political science are either borrowed from other disciplines or are analogous in some way. The terms balance, stability, equilibrium, force, power, pole, sphere, influence and system are borrowings from science, while democracy, anarchy, chaos, polity, state and so on are culled from the writings of philosophers or classical historians. Their use as categories or as variables in a theory of human behaviour is lacking in precision. They are really synthetic terms and, when an attempt is made at definition, are usually found to be the tip of some dialectical iceberg. In defining the term 'power', for example, subordinate concepts are required to give a more precise meaning. A choice is posed between a conception of power as an essence or quality – in which case it can be used as a measurable variable – or as part of a relationship – in which case it cannot. If the former conception is used, the yawning gap between empirical verification and theoretical conclusions appears and the concept becomes purely hypothetical. In refining terms of common usage in this way in order to fit them into a theory, the danger exists of producing a purely abstract argument which is really a kind of scientific metaphysics.

Variables in human behaviour are thus very difficult to isolate without engaging in preconceptions which invalidate the theory in which they are incorporated. The kind of rationalising assumption made in science can also be made in the social sciences, but without the same utility because of the problem of different levels of meaning. Moreover, not only is recognition difficult, but such variables are impossible to quantify with any theoretical success. In explaining why a phenomenon occurs, it is necessary to place a value on specific variables if anything other than description is to emerge from the analysis. Given conditions and quantifiable variables enable propositions to be elucidated and then verified. In the case of human phenomena, it is not yet possible to assert that in a specific situation one factor will have one value and another factor a different value.

If systems analysis is rejected as being unscientific in this sense, what value has it as an explanation of international politics? As was seen earlier, its chief failing as a method of analysis is that, in order to achieve logical coherence within the terms of its own assumptions and definitions, the enquiry becomes an examination of purely hypothetical systems with little empirical reference. It is the system itself which is being explained and not international politics. Like Tolstoy's clock in *War and Peace*,[66] the analogy is too mechanistic for it to do otherwise than illustrate the interconnectedness of things. But if the analogy is taken too literally, then the danger exists of attributing to reality the attributes of the image. It may of course be argued that both image and reality are the same and that systems analysis provides a view of the world which renders it intelligible within its own terms, but this is to anticipate the arguments of the following chapter.

A further danger is that of implicitly assuming a form of determinism in which all phenomena are interpreted as being functionally necessary to the system. A normative element may be introduced into the analysis, in that stability and adaptation to change are conceived of as occurring in relation to some desirable social or political state. Underlying the mechanics of systems theory may lie a conceptualisation of international politics which is Hobbesian, or of the modern state which is essentially Aristotelian. It is this element which has led some critics to comment on the conservative bias of structural-functional analysis. Such a bias is reinforced by the static nature of the systems model, for although change is a postulate, it is the self-maintaining regulatory process which assumes prominence in the explanation. A systems approach is not therefore as neutral as may be assumed, since it can contain assumptions which are derived from historical generalisations, more implicit than explicit, and which are not subjected to the same rigorous analysis as the hypothesis which they support. To be fair, this criticism is more relevant to systems theories outside the field of international politics where a particular institutional structure is assumed.

Another objection is that, as Valéry said, 'toute politique tend à traiter les hommes comme des choses'. Systems analysis in international politics pays only lip-service to individual behaviour and motivation. The actors are not aggregates or institutions, but people. But statesmen and diplomats are too often treated as the unwitting puppets of a structural-functional process which determines their actions. They are either subsumed within the category of the systemic environment or treated as separate psychological or cultural systems which act as sub-systems for the international system under consideration. Rational behaviour is assumed as corresponding to the rules and processes of the system as laid down in the abstract argument, and the arbitrary and irrational elements in human behaviour are either ignored or discounted. The problem of cognition, that is, the individual's own awareness of his social or political situation, is not resolved in this type of explanation.

It is sometimes said by advocates of systems theory that, although the level of a valid scientific theory has not been achieved in extant theorising, nevertheless such an approach has a heuristic value.[67] By this is meant an educative or intellectually stimulating effect. This may well be true, but such a claim cannot be the subject for critical evaluation since heuristic criteria are impossible to establish. An argument is either intellectually stimulating or not; if it is, then the response is purely subjective and individual. The reverse may be equally true. It is of course possible to establish conventions which may be accepted as criteria for critical judgement in a particular field, but heuristic argument in its educative sense can be judged only on aesthetic grounds, and these are not susceptible to scientific treatment.

The other point most often made in justification of the use of scientific method in political science is that a beginning must be made somewhere, especially in view of the inadequacy of other kinds of explanation. It would be arrogant to dismiss such a claim, but, as will be seen in the following chapter, while the possibilities of achieving a valid scientific explanation of political behaviour cannot be precluded, neither can it be said of a particular 'pre-scientific' explanation that it constitutes a step in this direction. Such an assertion can only be made retrospectively when it is possible to relate to a valid theory all that preceded it.

There is a value in isolating relationships and in stressing the point that human action often has unintended consequences. The reciprocal and inter-dependent nature of international politics has long been noted as a historical generalisation, and the conception of an international system provides a framework for the examination of specific historical situations in which relationships are indicated which might otherwise have remained undetected. Such an approach perhaps provides a useful corrective to that of projecting specific national policies into international politics and regarding the latter exclusively from the national level. A systems approach asserts a dimension of interactions with cross-related effects within particular temporal situa-tions. The balance-of-power system may or may not have had an actual material existence, but the interactive effects of particular national actions can be said to have had a balancing effect and to have prevented any one state from achieving hegemony over the others at various times in the past. Such a generalisation, however, is essentially historical and not theoretical. The effort to isolate factors relevant to a historical situation, and to establish clearly the criteria of relevance, at least asserts the complexity of history while seeking to make it intelligible. But if such a selection becomes part of a transplanted mechanical hypothesis, then this is as much of an over-simplification as any idiosyncratic or nationalist history.

Although the objective of a valid scientific explanation seems to have eluded the grasp of systems theorists, it may be the case that a different, but equally valid, type of explanation has been achieved. This possibility will be examined in the next chapter. It may also be the case that there is a distinction between a theoretical explanation and an explanation which confers meaning upon its subject. As J. David Singer puts it: 'Models, paradigms and conceptual schemes are merely intellectual tools by which we order and codify that which would otherwise remain a buzzing welter.'[68] Reality, in this sense, consists of our world-view and does not exist as some external empirical world to which our theories relate. Thus validity, if this argument is accepted, cannot consist of a correspondence between theory and reality, but is to be found in the world-view itself. But, as we shall see, the implications of this argument deny the force of the model of scientific explanation which has been used in this chapter to provide the criterion on which to evaluate 'scientific' theorising. If empirical verification or falsifica-tion is rejected as a test of explanatory validity, how can we choose between arguments which create 'reality' rather than correspond to it? What means have we of choosing between arguments once we have identified them as explaining through their internal coherence? Are such arguments equally valid? Is there a distinctive sense in which 'meaning' can be distinguished from explanation? The following chapters of this study will seek answers to these questions.

REFERENCES

1. Karl R. Popper, *The Logic of Scientific Discovery* (London: Hutchinson, 1959) p. 42, and *Conjectures and Refutations* (London: Routledge and Kegan Paul, 1963) pp. 223–50. For a countering argument, see Carl G. Hempel, *Aspects of Scientific Explanation* (New York Free Press, 1965) p. 106.
2. See Hans Reichenbach, *The Rise of Scientific Philosophy* (Berkeley: Univ. of California Press, 1968) pp. 236–49; and Carl G. Hempel 'Explanation in Science and in History', in P. H. Nidditch, *The Philosophy of Science* (London: Oxford Univ. Press, 1968) p. 59.
3. Reichenbach, op. cit., p. 231.
4. R. B. Braithwaite, *Scientific Explanation* (Cambridge Univ. Press, 1968) p. 9.
5. David Easton, *A Systems Analysis of Political Life* (New York: Wiley, 1965) p. 9.
6. W. G. Runciman, *Social Science and Political Theory* (Cambridge Univ. Press, 1965) p. 109.
7. Karl W. Deutsch, *The Nerves of Government* (New York: Free Press, 1966) esp. pt. III, 'Communication Models and Political Decision Systems', pp. 145–61.
8. Carl G. Hempel, 'The Logic of Functional Analysis', in May Brodbeck (ed.), *Readings in the Philosophy of the Social Sciences* (New York: Macmillan, 1969) pp. 179ff.
9. Robert K. Merton, *On Theoretical Sociology* (New York: Free Press, 1967) chap. iii, 'Manifest and Latent Functions', pp. 73ff.
10. Pitirim A. Sorokin, *Contemporary Sociological Theories* (New York: Harper, 1928) pp 207–18.
11. Bronislaw Malinowski, *A Scientific Theory of Culture* (London: Oxford Univ. Press, 1969) p. 158.
12. Daniel M. Taylor, *Explanation and Meaning* (Cambridge Univ. Press, 1970) esp. chap 4, 'What-Explanations', pp. 32–9.
13. See Runciman, op. cit.; Alan Ryan, *The Philosophy of the Social Sciences* (London: Macmillan, 1970); Peter Winch, *The Idea of a Social Science and its Relation to Philosophy* (London: Routledge and Kegan Paul, 1958).
14. Emile Durkheim, *The Rules of Sociological Method,* trans. Sarah A. Solovay and John H. Mueller, ed. George E. G. Catlin (New York: Free Press, 1964) Preface to the Second Edition, p. lvii.
15. Malinowski, op. cit., pp. 52–66.
16. Talcott Parsons, 'Order and Community in the International Social System', in Rosenau (ed.), *International Politics and Foreign Policy,* pp. 120ff.
17. See David Easton, *The Political System* (New York: Knopf, 1953); 'An Approach to the Analysis of Political Systems', *World Politics,* vol. IX (1957) pp. 383–400; *A Framework for Political Analysis* (Englewood Cliffs, N.J.: Prentice-Hall, 1965); and *A Systems Analysis of Political Life.*
18. Easton, *A Systems Analysis of Political Life,* p. 13, n. 12.
19. Ibid., p. 13.
20. Ibid., p. 17.
21. Ibid., p. 12.
22. Ibid., p. 19.
23. David Easton, 'Categories for the Systems Analysis of Politics', in *Varieties of Political Theory* (Englewood Cliffs, N.J.: Prentice-Hall, 1966) p. 147.
24. Ibid.
25. Easton, *A Systems Analysis of Political Life,* p. 24.
26. Ibid., p. 28.
27. Ibid., p. 345.
28. Ibid.
29. Ibid., p. 346.
30. For a discussion of the notion of 'feedback loop', see ibid., pp. 363–81.
31. Ibid., p. 267.

32. Ibid.
33. For a discussion of the international aspects of this systems approach, see ibid., pp. 484–8.
34. Ibid., p. 487.
35. See Richard N. Rosecrance, *Action and Reaction in World Politics* (Boston: Little, Brown, 1963); Klaus Knorr and Sidney Verba (eds.), *The International System* (Princeton Univ. Press, 1961); Andrew M. Scott, *The Functioning of the International Political System* (New York: Macmillan, 1967); C. A. McClelland, 'Applications of General Systems Theory in International Relations', in Rosenau, op. cit., pp. 412–20, and *Theory and the International System* (New York: Macmillian, 1966); R. D. Masters, 'World Politics as a Primitive Political System', *World Politics,* vol. XVI (July 1964) pp. 120–36; George Modelski, 'Agraria and Industria: Two Models of the International System', *World Politics,* vol. XIV (1961) pp. 118–43.
36. Morton A. Kaplan, *System and Process in International Politics* (New York: Wiley, 1964); see also 'Balance of Power, Bipolarity and Other Models of International Systems', in Rosenau, op. cit., pp. 343–9.
37. Kaplan, *System and Process,* pp. 4–8.
38. Ibid., p. 5.
39. Ibid., p. 14.
40. Ibid., pp. 7, 89–145; see also Appendix 1, pp. 253–70.
41. Ibid., p. 18.
42. Ibid., p. 4.
43. Ibid., p. 9.
44. See Morton A. Kaplan, 'Problems of Theory Building and Theory Confirmation in International Politics', in Knorr and Verba, op. cit., pp. 6–24.
45. Kaplan, *System and Process,* p. 21.
46. Ibid., p. 89.
47. Ibid., p. 253.
48. Ibid., p. 99.
49. Ernst B. Haas, *Beyond the Nation-State* (Stanford Univ. Press, 1964) p. 5.
50. Kaplan, *System and Process,* p. 120.
51. Ibid, p. 113.
52. See Kaplan, 'Problems of Theory Building and Theory Confirmation', p. 14 and n. 4.
53. Kaplan, *System and Process,* p. 11.
54. Ibid.
55. Ibid., p. 89.
56. Ibid., p. 103.
57. Francis Bacon, 'Of Empire' in *Selected Writings* (New York: Random House, 1955) p. 53.
58. Kaplan, *System and Process,* p. 23.
59. Ibid., p. 24.
60. Ibid., p. 26.
61. Ibid., p. 28.
62. Kaplan, 'Problems of Theory Building and Theory confirmation', p. 17.
63. Kaplan, *System and Process.* Preface, p. 7.
64. Ibid., p. 245.
65. Ibid., p. 10.
66. L. N. Tolstoy, *War and Peace,* trans. Rosemary Edmonds. London (Harmondsworth: Penguin Books, 1957) vol. I, p. 298.
67. This claim is made by Kaplan throughout *System and Process;* see, for example, p. 21, and 'The New Great Debate: Traditionalism vs. Science in International Relations', in Knorr and Rosenau (eds.), *Contending Approaches to International Politics,* pp. 39–61.
68. 'The Incompleat Theorist: Insight without Evidence', ibid., p. 76.

CHAPTER 3

Middle-Range Theories, Methods and Techniques

IN the last chapter, systems theory was criticised on a number of grounds, the most important concerning its status as a theoretical explanation of human activities. It was argued that such a theory is not a scientific explanation in any empirically meaningful sense. Nor is it internally logically consistent; it is abstract, with its categories based upon definitions. Its hypothetical argument is not so organised as to explain human behaviour in terms of (1) a set of explanations asserting the occurrence and time of the phenomenon which is the subject of explanation; (2) a set of universal hypotheses or laws which is related empirically to the phenomenon; and (3) the logical deduction of the phenomenon from these two sets. It enables neither prediction nor retrodiction, nor is it capable of empirical verification or falsification. Thus, in terms of their logical structure, their explanatory form and their criteria of validation, such 'theories' are non-scientific.

Nevertheless, it is sometimes argued by social scientists that while their arguments do not meet the requirements of a valid scientific theory, their method or approach is scientific. In this sense, systems theory constitutes not a theory, but the application of scientific method to the study of human activities. It is at the same time a way of ordering the world to make it intelligible in some meaningful sense. A distinction is thus made between a mode of enquiry and the explanatory results of enquiries. It would appear that the former may be judged on different criteria from the latter.

There are, however, a number of confusions in this concern with theoretical procedures. Scientific method is taken by some scholars to mean techniques of enquiry which are formally systematic, organising and categorising data on a quantitative or categorical basis. For others it means the creation of what are termed 'conceptual' or 'analytic' schemes which serve as a general framework of explanation conferring meaning on empirical data. Another approach is concerned with 'middle-range' theories which offer only partial explanations but serve as a guide for enquiry and can be linked together to create more general theories. Finally, it is argued by some writers that theoretical approaches should not be judged by criteria which properly belong to scientific argument, but should be considered as a form of explanation which is *sui generis*. Although such approaches are broadly called 'scientific', the notion of science implicit in this claim does not coincide with that discussed in the preceding chapter.

What all these various methodological positions have in common is a concern with theory as an approach rather than as an explanation proper. In a sense they are conceived of as being necessary preliminaries to achieving genuine theories. Even here, as we shall see, there is confusion arising out of the ambiguity surrounding the notion of theory. Easton, for example, argues that although

> one of the major tasks of theory has been to identify a set of behaviours that it could describe as political and in the process, to construct an analytic system or a theory that would help to explain the behavioural reality. A political theory is but a symbolic system useful for under- standing concrete or empirical political systems.[1]

Clearly, the level of meaning associated with 'understanding' is not the same as that related to scientific explanation and knowledge. Moreover, this argu- ment blurs the relationship between the explanation and 'reality'. In other words, if a theoretical approach is intended to elicit an explanation, what sort of explanation is being sought? Is it the kind of explanation found in science, in which an 'external' reality is posited? Or is it to be found in the kind of reality which is conceptually coherent and which is created by the argument? A theoretical approach which seeks the latter objective is not only concerned with a different notion of meaning from the former, but may turn out to be not a mode of enquiry but an explanation in its own right.

Thus in seeking to make distinctions, for example, between a conceptual scheme, an analytic system, a model, a hypothesis, a middle-range theory, and a meta-theory or macro-theory, we must not only relate the various kinds of activity undertaken under one or more of these labels to the kind of empirical explanation said to be characteristic of science, but we must also consider them as attempts at explanation subject to different critical criteria. There are two broad questions which will be considered in this analysis: firstly, what is the relevance of 'conceptual schemes' and theo- retical approaches to the establishment of empirically testable explana- tions? and secondly, do they have any value or relevance outside this asserted function? This second question concerns their status as arguments and involves the relationship between various techniques of analysis and theoretical procedures, and policy-making and political prescriptions.

There is a major problem associated with the first of these questions. In order to answer it adequately we have to produce and validate an explana- tion of explanations or a theory of the provenance of theories. This poses fundamental epistemological problems. Moreover, how can we relate the mode of enquiry under investigation to a particular explanatory category without examining the notion of knowledge to which this category belongs? In a sense, we have begged this question in using the model of scientific explanation in this analysis. The justification for doing so lies in the fact

that, although the philosophical problem of the nature of scientific knowledge is left unresolved, there is a commonly recognised test of validity
within the framework of scientific explanation. This, it must be admitted,
is a convention or a rule and, as was argued earlier, does not constitute
a universal canon of truth.

However, the general philosophical problem of knowledge is beyond the
scope of this anaylsis. The more immediate problem which concerns us here
is that, although we know what a valid scientific theory is when we get one,
can we have a theory which can be used to guide us in the right direction?
When the 'pre-Galileans' in the social sciences assert that their theoretical
approaches are milestones on the path to scientific truth, how can such an
assertion be validated before we have the equivalent of a Galileo as a
landmark in this field?

Any account of the provenance of scientific theories reveals a large
number of what, viewed retrospectively, we might term misdirections before
a generally acceptable level of theoretical explanation was achieved. As
Kuhn points out, 'an apparently arbitrary element composed of personal
and historical accident is always a formative ingredient of the beliefs
espoused by a given scientific community at a given time'.[2] But whether
we regard the history of science as a process of changing theories, each
superseding its predecessor, or not, it is clear that the 'scientific community'
possesses standards of evaluating such explanations which it generally holds,
and which apply to whatever theory is currently orthodox. The replacement
of one theory by another might be fraught with difficulties, as Kuhn has
shown,[3] and involve a conflict between 'conservative' scientists and proponents of the new school, but both have in common a recognition of the
way in which their explanations may be tested. It is possible for them to
agree and to disagree because they have this common ground. The point
was made earlier that a process of validation, that is, a means of *defining*
knowledge and its truth, was the central characteristic of scientific explanation, rather than its logical structure or its *modus operandi.*

While scientific knowledge depends upon an ordering of the empirical
world through concepts and 'all empirical observation is in terms of a
conceptual scheme',[4] scientific explanation does not stop at a point when
logical coherence is obtained. The level of empirical observation provides
a number of presuppositions which are then organised and defined so as
to be logically consistent. Empirical assumptions are made abstract and the
level of *this* argument is essentially non-empirical. But while scientists
assume or make presuppositions which render their world coherent, they
also possess a means of retaining or rejecting those which are useful or not
through a process of hypothesis and falsification. The presuppositions are
not reified in their argument, either in its form or in its validation. If this
last were the case, then it is hard to sce how anything other than a tautology could emerge from their enquiry. Thus scientific explanation makes

the 'world' intelligible in a particular way, but it does not consist solely of a conceptual scheme which derives its integrity from its coherence. As we have seen, the notion of explanation in science consists of posing general propositions *about* something. Although 'facts' are elicited by 'theory' and cannot be separated from the conceptual judgement which selected and interpreted them, there is a relationship between the two in which both coexist. In this sense scientific 'facts' are neither created nor invented, and science is not science fiction.

If we turn to the notion of conceptual scheme in the social sciences, we are faced with the problem of relating it to explanation. Is it an 'explanation' in terms of making the world 'real' through the concepts which confer reality upon it? If this was the case, then we should judge it on different criteria from that appertaining to empirical falsification. If we regard a conceptual scheme as a logically connected set of ideas and propositions which are based upon initially defined categorical assumptions, then such a scheme may be far removed from the level of empirical explanation. We might conceive of the relevant criteria as appertaining to its internal logic, to the consistency of its argument, or to its overall coherence and comprehensiveness as a system of related ideas, but such criteria have little to do with whether it 'explains' in an empirical sense. It may have 'meaning' and it may make the 'world' intelligible in some way, but the criteria proper to its evaluation do not belong to the field of science. Alternatively, is a conceptual scheme a means of achieving the kind of theoretical explanation which is characteristic of science? If this is the case, then we need to examine the relationship between method or theory construction and theory proper.

If we look at usage, we shall find that the term 'conceptual scheme', as employed by Parsons, Easton, Kaplan and others, contains an ambiguity in that, while the *results* of their work may take the form of a logically ordered world in which the categories of a system or of a theory of action are internally consistent and externally coherent, the *purpose* of such a scheme is to achieve a valid empirical explanation. We are thus forced to apply two different sets of criteria to an evaluation of their schemes. The first conceives of a conceptual scheme as a different kind of explanation from the second. The ambiguity arises out of a confusion between two radically different kinds of explanation. This stems from the notion, prevalent in this kind of theorising, that an empirical explanation can be achieved through 'more precise and explicit conceptualisation of the components of action and of the ways in which they are interrelated'.[5] But is the notion of concept here that of an abstract or idealised category into which must fit observed social phenomena? Or does it mean simply that, since ideas precede observation, the more precise the ideas, then the more precise the observation?

Perhaps an example will serve to clarify some of these points. The example taken is that of Talcott Parsons's general theory of action, since in many ways this has been of considerable influence upon attempts at theory construction in the field of political science, including the general systems theory discussed in the previous chapter. Parsons states that his intention is

> the exposition and illustration of a conceptual scheme for the analysis of social systems in terms of the action frame of reference. It is intended as a theoretical work in a strict sense. Its direct concern will be neither with empirical generalisations as such nor with methodology, though of course it will contain a considerable amount of both.[6]

What is meant by 'strict' theory in this context? It would appear that a distinction is made between 'scientific theory' as an empirical explanation and a level of abstraction which constitutes a frame of reference or a conceptual scheme. Although Parsons accepts a view of science which postulates an 'immediate correspondence between *concrete* experienceable reality and scientific propositions',[7] he rejects this as being the only form of 'valid knowledge'. Theoretical systems, according to his argument, are equally valid, although they do not explain empirical reality in the same sense as scientific explanation. As he puts it: 'It is fundamental that there is no empirical knowledge which is not in some sense and to some degree conceptually formed'.[8] Thus a conceptual scheme enables the selection, description and definition of social phenomena and makes the world intelligible. But it would appear from this that such a world is not an external concrete reality, for it is created by the theory. It is therefore an ideal world.

The general theory of action was devised as such a scheme, and is an attempt not at explaining the act of an individual or his perception of action *per se,* but at explaining human acts in a societal context. This follows Weber's view that

> The action of each [actor] takes account of that of the others and is orientated in those terms. The social relationship thus *consists* entirely and exclusively in the existence of a probability that there will be, in some meaningfully understandable sense, a course of social action.[9]

Such courses of action constitute modes which can be recognised and explained in terms of the subjective understanding of the actor's awareness of his social situation, his expectations and his goals. Weber cited as examples of these modes of behaviour, conflict, sexual attraction, friendship and economic exchange. Sociology is, on this argument, concerned with the elucidation of these 'typical modes of action'.[10]

Such an argument leads on to the notion of type or ideal and to the idea of role. As Schutz puts it: 'There is a certain conformity in the acts and motives of priests, soldiers, servants, farmers everywhere and at every time'.[11] An explanation of action is thus an explanation of a class of action conceived of as a type. But each term used in a scientific system referring to human action must be so constructed that a human act performed within the life world by an individual actor in the way indicated by the typical construction would be reasonable and understandable for the actor himself as well as for his fellow men.[12] Hence the action theorist must be in a position to make a generalisation about rational behaviour in a social situation which is not imposed upon the situation and on the actor, but which is derived from an understanding of the motives, objectives and the cognition of the nature of the situation itself, on the part of the actor. In short, there must be a conformity between the social mode and the social act, that is, between the theorist's explanation of typical action and the actor's understanding which prompted his action. Otherwise the theorist is imposing a rationalisation upon the social action which he is seeking to explain, rather than advancing an empirical explanation.

Yet this is in fact what is actually done in the general theory of action. There are obvious difficulties in the notion of action, notably arriving at an understanding, empathetic or otherwise, of the motivation and cognition of the actor and in making a clear distinction between his understanding and the conditions of the situation in which he acts. Do we consider the latter in terms of constants, or as 'objective' circumstances, so that, given the actor's precognition and goals, we can say that he will invariably undertake the same action? Are we explaining an individual act as a unique event or as one of a number of acts within a class of action? Or are we explaining the act-situation itself, that is, the relevant circumstances and the participant's motives, goals and understanding, in order to make the act 'intelligible'? These are problems which arise out of the ambiguity of this type of argument, and some of their theoretical implications will be considered at length in the following chapter.

To sum up so far: action is considered in this argument to be the behaviour of an individual in a social context, seeking to fulfil some purpose. The nature of this purpose and of the means chosen to fulfil it are determined by his perception of the behaviour and purpose of other people, that is, in terms of his expectations. Hence what he actually does is explicable in terms of the nexus between his perception and the context in which he perceives. From this, the theory of action asserts that such an influence may transform an individual's pursuit of his objectives into activity which fulfils some social purpose. Whatever the ostensible purpose or the specific perceptions of the individual, his acts perform or fulfil some societal function. Thus the individual acts according to the roles which he performs within a particular social context, and in so doing he enters into, and helps to create, a functional set of social relationships. The explanation moves away from an understanding, empathetic or otherwise, of the individual within society, that is, to a concern with what might be called the inter-act.

According to this argument, the main concern of the enquiry is with the role-functioning of individuals conceived of as types or classes within a social system, in terms of their contribution to the maintenance and regulation of that system. Social interactions composed of individuals fulfilling their roles constitute systems of relationships which in turn relate to and maintain other systems. On this argument a polity is a particular type of social interaction which constitutes a 'primary functional sub-system'[13] of a society, and it consists of the collective behaviour of people seeking to achieve specific goals and, in so doing, creating a largely unintended mode of behaviour which in turn contributes to the social system in a particular way. A polity is functional to the social system because, firstly, this collective mode of behaviour[14] legitimises goals and authority within a social system and thus integrates it. Secondly, a polity is an agency for mobilising resources, and thirdly, it also mobilises support for the implementation of a goal necessary to the system. There is little in this which differs from the general systems theory considered in the last chapter.

The dichotomy between the individual's rational pursuit of his own objectives and the perceived environment, which both influences his choice and provides the means of fulfilment, is resolved by an emphasis on role. This last is defined by Parsons as 'that organised section of an actor's orientation which constitutes and defines his participation in an interaction process'.[15] The freedom of the individual to choose and to define his objectives within the limits of his perception is restricted by what are termed

> functional imperatives limiting the degree of incompatibility of the possible kinds of roles in the same action system; these imperatives are ultimately related to the conditions of maintenance of a total on-going social system of this type in which the more constitutive of these roles are found . . .[16]

It is thus not possible for the choices of the actors to fall at random and still form a coherently organised and functioning system.

What keeps the actor from acting in disconformity to the functional requirements of his social system is the presence of values and norms which condition him. What is being said here is that an individual behaves according to his expectations of proper action: so, for example, a soldier behaves like a soldier in so far as he is acting as one – he can also be a devout Christian, or a lover of poetry, or invest his pay and loot in a building society. In other words, his acts conform to the roles appertaining to characteristic social interactions. He is induced to remain within these roles by the fact that he would not succeed in attaining specific goals, i.e having a successful military career, believing in God, obtaining aesthetic satisfaction or increasing his wealth, if he stepped outside them. Moreover, to step out of these roles would not only be irrational but would also be socially disintegrative. If the soldier disliked killing or military discipline and acted on his dislike, then clearly he would be acting outside his role as a soldier and would be pursuing some other objective, which may or may not be compatible with the social system, but is not compatible with the particular system in which he plays the role of a soldier.

Parsons, like Easton and Kaplan, creates out of this basic argument a conceptual scheme which is dependent upon the concepts of act, role and structure. The scheme is full of categories which are analytic rather than empirical, and which are based upon definitions. For example, in explaining how all systems maintain themselves, Parsons asserts that they must fulfil the four major functions of pattern maintenance, integration, goal attainment and adaptation.[17] These are defined as adherence to the basic principles of the system, adjustment within it, collective action designed to bring about relations between the system and its environment, and the development of disposable resources. The polity, as we saw earlier, consists of a sub-system which performs the necessary function of goal attainment. How is this done? According to Parsons it is done through the medium of power. 'Power in a collectivity is a means of effectively mobilising obligations in the interest of collective goals',[18] and 'At various points in the societal system, power is exchanged both for other generalised media, notably money and influence, and for intrinsically significant rewards (services and support) and factors of effectiveness'.[19] The subordinate concept of power is thus highly important in this analysis.

But what is power? On this argument it is an entity which can be exchanged, transferred and accumulated. Thus there is an allocable power potential within a polity, and it can be increased by obtaining more of it from the external environment. Yet the definition of power as a medium of exchange begs the question as to what is actually being exchanged. It is purely a definition and not an empirical referent. Of course, it is not lacking in meaning; and Parsons makes distinctions between various notions of power as well as between the notions of 'influence' and 'authority',[20] but the meaning is analytic and *a priori* in nature. Such an argument does not provide us with any general propositions or laws relating to social behaviour.

A mode of behaviour or set of social interactions are purely abstract categories if there is no means of explaining their causes through a testable hypothesis. The roots of social behaviour, according to Weber, lie in the individual's motivation, and he was careful to point out[21] that an external observer must enter into an understanding of the individual before he is in a position to explain what he does. The jump from motivation to roles (and ideal types), of course, gets over the difficulty of actually doing this, but in so doing imposes a rationalisation which asserts two things: firstly, that a pattern can be discerned in human behaviour, and secondly, that the main concern of the enquiry is with the effect of human behaviour on systems entities. The emphasis is thus switched from human behaviour itself to the role-functioning of ideal modes of behaviour in terms of their causal influence on an assumed social structure. For it should be stressed once again that the argument does not get out of the difficulties of requiring general propositions by substituting function for cause. The general theory of action, like general systems theory, is really a causal explanation by removes.

Although the emphasis is placed upon the structural basis of the argument, that is, upon systems, nevertheless we should be aware that the focus of explanation is human activity, albeit conceived in collective terms. Each system is a category of human behaviour with its own autonomous processes, its own objectives or goals and its own distinctive features. Even if the reduced view is taken that what is being asserted by such a conceptual scheme is that specific conditions are necessary but not sufficient for the survival of a system, and that the functions of its components are necessary for its existence, but do not of themselves explain it, then some general proposition must be established for this assertion to be more than tautological. An optimal theory, as we have seen earlier when functional theory was examined, which states a number of preconditions that must be satisfied for a phenomenon to exist, is under the theoretical obligation of providing an argument which generalises to the effect that every example, or a stated proportion of examples of the phenomena, has satisfied these preconditions. Such an argument would not be a scientific argument, but at least it would be an explanation, although the question of what sort of explanation must be left open at this stage.

Now in what sense is this argument, and the systems analysis which stems from it, a conceptual scheme? Its proponents do not claim for it the status of an empirical explanation. Yet it is not entirely abstract, since it is concerned with the way people actually behave. Moreover, it is claimed that such an analysis provides the basis for a successful explanation of human activities. It is an explanation in its own right and also constitutes an approach to scientific theory. We are faced with the twin problems of deciding what is the nature of a conceptual scheme as an explanation and whether it is a precondition for an explanation of a different order.

Taking the first question: if we accept that a conceptual scheme based on the notion of role-functioning is really a theoretical explanation of the type found in science, then we can apply to it the critical criteria which properly belong to such an explanation. It stands or falls as an explanation on these grounds. But it is clear from the argument that the level of empirical observation provides a number of presuppositions which are then organised so as to be logically consistent. In other words, empirical assumptions are made abstract but the level of this argument is essentially non-empirical. The notion of concept is that of an abstract or idealised category, such as act, role, function, goals, norms, power, etc., into which must fit empirically derived facts. If a category is ambivalent in empirical terms, then it is refined so as to resolve the ambivalence in systemic terms. This is really a semantic or logical exercise; and the kind of propositions contained in the argument are really little more than self-evident or tautologous propositions. This is not to say that they have no meaning, but that they are irrelevant to scientific enquiry.

It seems to come to this; there is no way of validating conceptual schemes of this kind, in the sense of seeking to refute them in terms of a correspondence between conclusions and observations. No propositions are formulated which enable us to attempt the kind of process of falsification asserted by Popper[22] as being characteristic of scientific explanation. Since this test is regarded as being central to the evaluation of scientific explanation, as has been argued throughout this work, conceptual schemes are non-scientific. Indeed, this is supported by the actual claims made by proponents of conceptual schemes. If we accept this, we must consider their arguments as being of a different order. They 'explain' solely in terms of their internal argument. The world of human activities is a world not of observation or of a kind of empirical reality which is 'out there', but a world of concepts defined and related within the framework of the scheme. Such an explanation is closely related to the notion of experience as a mode which is maintained by Oakeshott,[23] and it is idealistic in nature. It can only be evaluated in terms of its coherence. If this argument is accepted, this still leaves us with the problem of establishing criteria for evaluating its coherence as an explanation. We are thus left with three main questions: in what way is such a conceptual scheme coherent? in what sense is it communicable as an argument? and how can we distinguish one conceptual scheme from another? These questions will be considered at length in the following chapter.

What of the claim that conceptual schemes of this type constitute an *approach* towards scientific explanation? Can a clear distinction be made between a mode of enquiry and an explanation? So far as this kind of theorising is concerned, what is being asserted is that an ideally conceived world can be used to 'explain' an external empirical reality in the same sense as a scientific theory explains physical phenomena. Yet as Parsons himself points out: 'The scheme can only be of empirical significance so far as it is possible to devise observational operations in terms of which these problems can be answered'.[24] In other words, the scheme must produce hypotheses which are empirically testable. This is put more forcefully by Hempel, who asserts that

> an ideal theoretical system, as indeed any theoretical system at all, can assume the status of an explanatory and predictive apparatus only if its area of application has been specified; in other words, if its constituent concepts have been given an empirical interpretation which directly, or at least mediately, links them to observable phenomena.[25]

But as we have seen earlier, this major theoretical condition is not fulfilled by general systems and action theories.

We are thus forced to choose between the position that such schemes are really implicit untested or untestable empirical explanations, and the position that they represent simply a means of ordering the world and making it intelligible. If the former is the case, the argument must be made more rigorous for it to 'explain'. But if we accept the latter, then there is no logical connection and certainly no theoretical connection between such a scheme and the kind of argument which states categorically, in a hypothetically deductive form, that given the same conditions, factors, variables and relationships, the same phenomenon will recur according to a stated statistical regularity or in terms of general occurrence. The use of conceptualisations and analytic schemes would appear to be the application of an explanation rather than a means of deriving one. In order to achieve logical coherence within the terms of its own assumptions and qualifications, the enquiry becomes an examination of the compatibility of abstractions, with very little empirical reference. It is the abstract system which is being explained, not human activities. Of course, the implication in this approach is that if human behaviour were like the system, then the system would 'explain' it. But this is not an empirical explanation. Whichever position is adopted, the main point here is that a conceptual scheme is not a mode of enquiry – that is, a means of achieving an explanation; it is an explanation in its own right. In other words, a conceptual scheme is not an operational guide to enquiry, for it prescribes the enquiry in such a way as to determine what its conclusions will be.

An alternative to general theoretical systems has been suggested by Merton, who argues that what he terms a 'middle-range theory'[26] can provide both an operational guide to research and an adequate explanation of human phenomena which falls short of 'all inclusive systematic efforts to develop a unified theory that will explain all the observed uniformities of social behaviour, social organisation and social change'.[27] He suggests that a theory of 'role-sets' constitutes a suitable example of such an approach. A middle-range theory, in this view, differs from the kind of conceptual scheme considered above, since it deals mainly with lower-level propositions which are capable of 'a measure of empirical confirmation'.[28]

Before examining this claim the question might be asked, what is a 'role-set'? According to Merton,[29] the central assumption of the concept of role-set is that social status is organised within the social structure. People who enjoy 'status' possess attitudes which are responsive to those who do not. A role-set consists of a complex of 'social relationships in which people are involved simply because they occupy a particular social status'.[30] It is distinguished from a status-set, that is, a number of different statuses occupied by one person, in that it is conceived of as a complex of roles related to a single status. The concern of a theory of role-sets is with the problem of reconciling the various role components of each role-set with one another, in order to avoid conflict and to achieve 'social regularity'.

The idea of status and of role prescribes a sociological problem, thus establishing the phenomenon to be explained. As Merton puts it:

> It raises the general but definite problem of identifying the social mechanism – that is the social processes having designated consequences for designated parts of the social structure – which articulates the expectations of those in the role-set sufficiently to reduce conflicts for the occupant of such a status. It generates the further problem of discovering how these mechanisms came into being so that we can also explain why the mechanisms do not operate effectively or fail to emerge at all in some social systems. It also provides an operational guide to relevant empirical research.[31]

What is the conception of theory contained in this approach? According to Merton:

> . . . such middle-range theories have not been logically derived from a single all-embracing theory of social systems, though once developed they may be consistent with one. Furthermore, each theory is more than a mere empirical generalisation – an isolated proposition summarising observed uniformities of relationships between two or more variables. A theory comprises a set of assumptions from which empirical generalisations have themselves been derived.[32]

In other words, such a theory seeks to provide an empirical explanation identical in nature to that provided by scientific explanation. Concepts, such as that of role, 'constitute the definitions (or prescriptions) of what is to be observed; they are the variables between which empirical relationships are to be sought. When propositions are logically interrelated, a theory has been instituted'.[33]

There is little here which differs from the action theory discussed above, except for the insistence that a theory of role-sets is an empirical explanation and therefore susceptible to an empirical test. Middle-range theory purports to be applicable to human activities and is not a conceptual scheme in the ideal sense. It is an explanation, not a mode of enquiry. Without embarking on a detailed analysis of the theory of role-sets, it is admitted in the argument that general testable propositions are not in fact derivable from such explanations.[34] In other words, they do not satisfy the criteria of validation proper to scientific explanation. But it is none the less claimed that they can serve as a guide to empirical resarch in the hope of achieving such an explanation. The distinction between an explanation proper and a mode of enquiry is thus maintained.

What is involved in this claim? As was pointed out earlier, to assert that a mode of enquiry leads to the establishment of a specific type of explanation poses fundamental epistemological problems. Either a theory of the provenance of theories is implicit in this assertion, or what is being said is that particular approaches, methods or techniques may have a heuristic value. This should be distinguished from the argument that an extant and validated theory may be applied to phenomena not originally included in its area of explanation. But explanation in this sense is not a method. An explanation (E) of X phenomenon may be extended to explain phenomenon Y, but this can only be validated by the same criteria appertaining to E's explanation of X. It is not axiomatic that this is the case. Hence we cannot say in advance of such a test that the application of E to Y class of phenomena will be fruitful. It may be, but the grounds on which such an extension is justifiable depends upon the test applicable to this type of explanation. A theory either explains or it does not; and while a particular theory may be applied to a range of varying phenomena, the validity of this application being subject to an empirical test, this does not constitute a method. In any case, the position in the social sciences is that of seeking a valid theory, in the scientific sense of theory, rather than applying one.

There is some confusion in methodological discussion in the social sciences between the notion of methodology as the study of methods or techniques and as the nature of truth or knowledge specific to an explanation. In the first instance a concern for procedures appropriate to an enquiry raises the question of the nature of the explanation sought. Thus a clear distinction between method and theory is not possible, since any kind of analysis is subject to theorising assumptions whether these are made explicit or not. Moreover, as we have seen earlier, the use of a specific method implies certain assumptions properly belonging to an unstated hypothesis. Consequently the investigation is likely to be conditioned by the theory. The use of a method may in reality be the application of, rather than a means of deriving, a theory. While in science it is possible to examine what has been called 'the logic of discovery'[35] and to explore the relationship between explanations and their procedural antecedents together with their logical structure, this is difficult to do in the social sciences in the absence of validated or generally accepted explanations. It is clear, from what has been said, what kind of explanation is being sought, but it is impossible to state what mode of enquiry or technique of analysis is appropriate to this activity. We may conclude by saying that all extant procedures are inadequate, since they have not succeeded in bringing an enquiry to a successful theoretical conclusion – but this is to anticipate later arguments.

The point can thus be made that it does not matter much what means are used in a particular enquiry provided that the results are good. By good is meant where the explanatory level is more than a reification of the problem or a circular argument, and where some clearly recognisable test of validation is possible. An experimental technique may be fruitful or prejudicial; the only test of this lies in the explanation to which it is related or which is derived from it. If by scientific method is meant the use of mathematical techniques, analysis, experiment or the construction of a logical argument, then so far as human activities are concerned all these are related to some assumption made about the problem under investigation.

Clearly, in certain fields, as for example, economics, such implicit assumptions do not seriously affect the argument advanced. Idealisations such as the maximisation of satisfaction or of profits may be assumed within the limits of the argument. This is not to say that economic theory can satisfy the conditions for a valid scientific explanation. As we shall see, the case for international politics is rather more difficult.

There are two main aspects of the use of various methods, techniques and procedures in the field of international politics which will be examined in this study. The first is that of the relationship between methodology and the establishment of various types of theory concerning conflict, crisis behaviour, decision-making and negotiation. These are essentially 'middle-range' theories in the sense used by Merton. Secondly, the notion of a policy science will be considered, that is, the relationship between various analytic techniques and models to political prescription such as bargaining and communication theories, game theory, simulation and cost–benefit analysis.

It was argued in a previous chapter that Kaplan's application of systems analysis to international politics led him not to the deduction of a theory positing laws which govern the behaviour of actors, but to the creation of a number of models based upon capability and other variables. Each of these variables, it was argued, required a supporting hypothesis or further theoretical clarification before this type of systematic analysis could be considered as being rigorous. Such models were really hypotheses which were incapable of any empirical test. In scientific argument the use of models is a valued technique. Although, for example, a mathematical model constitutes or incorporates a set of assumptions referring to an idealised situation, it is the relationships within the model itself which are important. Such relationships within the confines of the premises may yield knowledge of relationships which were not discernible through observation. The model itself is not an explanation, that is, a theory, but an untestable hypothesis. It is thus a technique. Nevertheless, from it theoretical deductions or inferences can be made which assist in establishing general propositions which are testable. Now in science this is possible, for reasons which have been given previously, namely because variables can be identified and measured. As we shall see, attempts at quantifying variables in international politics have not been very successful.

The essential feature of a model is that deductions can be made on a narrower basis than another approach would permit. A limited number of variables are selected, defined and, where relevant, quantified, and propositions governing their relationship are then formulated into a deductive argument from which further propositions are elicited. Its correspondence to empirical 'reality' rests on the general laws which emerge from the model. To put it another way, if a model simply correlates variables or factors without producing a level of generalisation about behaviour which is empirically testable, it is irrelevant to an explanation of behaviour. Such a model is an academic exercise in the pejorative meaning of the term. When conclusions derived from a model cannot be related to 'real' behaviour, the model does not advance explanation. If it does no more than assert relationships between loosely defined factors, then what has been achieved is a restatement or a description of a problem, not an answer to it. In other words, whether a model is a good or a bad one depends on its relationship to a valid theoretical explanation. It is not a substitute for theory.

It will be apparent from this that the postulates of a model and its variables require precise definition. It should not be a theory in disguise. Consequently the variables themselves should be capable of quantification; they should not require supporting hypotheses. Assumptions are made which are idealised or *a priori* in nature and factors introduced as constants, but whether this is a meaningless exercise depends on the level of theoretical generalisation which is elicited from the model. If it is really a set of untestable hypothetical arguments, it is hard to see how anything useful in the way of an explanation can emerge from it. In such a case the 'model' may be an 'explanation', albeit not of a scientific type.

Perhaps an example will serve to illustrate this point. It has been argued by C. A. McClelland[36] that 'acute crises are concrete phenomena of international history with distinct time and place boundaries'.[37] Such crises mark 'the time of a turning point in a conflict and a period when major decisions are likely to be made'. From this postulate he seeks, in Deutsch's words,

> to identify generally those conflict situations and states which are likely to lead to war; to evaluate particular conflict situations and the probable lines along which they are likely to develop if left to themselves; and to suggest further possible techniques for controlling such conflict situations so as to prevent them from breaking out into war.[38]

The main task is therefore the establishment of a theory of crisis behaviour which explains it in such a way as to enable prediction and, from this, prescription.

A major rationalising assumption is made, in that international crises are considered to be neither unique events, nor peripheral to the causation of war, but to reveal a process which is repeated in subsequent crises. If each crisis, it is argued, can be studied for its interaction sequences, a pattern might emerge suggesting the dynamics of crisis behaviour and from which predictions can be made about the course of future crises. The 'events' of a crisis are 'coded' in order to make 'possible the identification of patterns and the comparison of forms of crisis behaviour'.[39] Thus each selected historical crisis is systematised in terms of an action–reaction hypothesis which assumes that each action is a consequence of its predecessor. From this interaction a pattern emerges and crisis pattern is compared with crisis pattern. As McClelland puts it, 'in the course of an analytic study a mapping of the complete crisis from its initial dramatic input point to its tailing off into the normalcy of routine international relations becomes possible'.[40] Such a sequence is represented by block diagrams.[41]

It is clear from the argument that the notion of 'system interaction analysis'[42] is based upon a systems theoretical approach of the kind considered earlier. Briefly, the national actors in a crisis receive information as environmental and interaction 'outputs', and translate this into action, conceived of as 'inputs' into the 'system of action'. Thus our familiar concept of 'information feedback' makes an appearance as the linkage between actor and system. From this McClelland argues that it is unnecessary to consider decision-making in detail, but merely to regard national behaviour as evidence of the 'active traits of participating actors'.[43] Hence questions of motive and of policy are considered irrelevant since these can be inferred from actual behaviour itself. It is assumed that decisions taken by an actor are generally conditioned by its type of social organisation. This leads to a major supporting hypothesis, namely that a 'modernising society' is primarily concerned with problem-solving and consequently is 'inward-looking'.[44] Therefore external distractions are progressively reduced. The most 'desirable international situation would be one in which all goes smoothly, with minimum effort, minimum cost, minimum attention and maximum national benefits'.[45]

This supporting hypothesis contains three important assumptions about national behaviour and international crises. Firstly, it is assumed that modernising societies, however these are defined, act conservatively in international politics: secondly, that if existing or future political situations are similar to past situations, then national responses and behaviour will be equally similar; and thirdly, that crises are isolable phenomena.[46] These are incorporated into an argument which states that the major national actors wish to avoid wars, so that when they become involved in a conflict they seek to find a way of avoiding violence. If all past crises are examined in terms of a systematic interchange between these states, then a process of crisis management can be detected as they learn from participation and devise techniques for restoring 'normalcy'. Moreover, 'repeated exposures to acute crises may reduce the probabilities of an outbreak of general war',[47] because of this process of learning how to manage crises.

It is difficult to conceive of this argument as a model in the sense used above. It would appear to be a form of explanation. The only variables referred to in the exposition are those associated with an international system, that is, the nature of the actors, 'the effects produced by their contacts and interactions', and the 'environment'.[48] These are not given any precise definition. The central hypothesis is simply that modern states seek to avoid violent conflict because of their nature as modern states. If there is evidence that the 'interaction patterns' indicate 'bids countered by bids, claims countered by claims, stalemates, standoffs, postponements, and no-win, no-solution outcomes', then, 'barring upheavals in the system or environmental innovations, the general trend should be towards repetitions of such patterns of action but with a decreasing volume of interaction in succeeding crises'.[49] Thus, from the assertions that modernising states are inward-looking and therefore act conservatively in international politics, the argument goes on to state that evidence of conservative behaviour in international crisis situations, that is, the avoidance of violence and an attempt to achieve a diplomatic solution, will be 'taken as evidence in support of the hypotheses of the conservative behaviour, the routinising tendencies and the spill-over effects of crises in advanced modernising nation-states'.[50] This would appear to be a circular argument. 'Conservative' states behave conservatively; if there is evidence of conservative behaviour in international politics, then this proves that states are conservative.

The hypothesis that 'modernising states' behave in a particular way because of their internal political processes would seem to require closer and more precise examination. It will be noted that one major constant is assumed here, that of environmental stability. It can be argued that the international environment, however this is conceived, is not a constant and that change and innovation, far from being rare, are in fact its main characteristics. Past crises are unique in the sense that their environment is; if the latter changes, how can symmetry be assumed as a basis for the prediction of future crises when their contextual relationships are unknown? Such an argument is rather like saying that history repeats itself without being able to state general historical laws. The implicit assumptions might also be challenged. Do nation-states 'learn' from their experiences? Is domestic political change irrelevant? Are the actors a constant? Can rationality on the part of politicians and statesmen be assumed? Do all nation-states share a common conception of stability and normality in international politics? And so on.

Such a construction is termed by its author a model of international behaviour, and not an explanation of actual historical events. Nevertheless, it is expected to be helpful in the study of international behaviour during major crises. But it is clear that it is not a model in the sense used above. It is not a construction of an argument based on selected and precisely defined variables which are placed in various relationships in order to deduce propositions which may then be included in a hypothesis capable of an empirical test. But if it is not a model in this sense, neither is it an adequate theoretical explanation. Although the method adopted is the systematisation of past crisis situations on the basis of a sequence of actions and responses, represented in diagrammatic form in order to reveal their 'pattern', there is nothing to suggest that this is anything other than a way of describing them. There is no general proposition which explains why states are expected to behave in the way postulated by the argument other than the assertion that if they do, they are acting 'conservatively'. While McClelland admits two possible criticisms,[51] namely that historical situations may be unique in essential respects, and that relationships are variables in international politics that cannot be quantified, both these admissions would seem to invalidate the claims of this kind of model-making to be theoretical, since the major problems in creating a theoretical explanation are evaded.

It appears from this examination that such an argument is a model only in the sense that it is an idealised picture of international relations in a particular context, that of a major crisis. It is neither derived from historical 'reality' nor is it applicable to it. It is a substitute for it. We are back to the fundamental problem of evaluating a theoretical approach which cannot be related to a validated theoretical explanation. If model-making of this kind is asserted to be a method of achieving such an explanation, then such a claim can only be supported by results. These are conspicuously absent. The question as to what sort of explanation it is – if it is accepted that it is neither a model nor a scientific hypothesis – will be examined in a later part of this study.

McClelland argued that his 'model' of the acute international crisis was a viable approach towards an explanation of international politics. Nevertheless, he accepted that alternative approaches existed.[52] Although he rejected decision-making processes as being appropriate to an explanation of crises, he asserted that the 'conceptual framework of decision-making' constituted a viable 'mode of analysis'. We turn now to this aspect of the theoretical study of international politics. Here again we find an ambivalence between the notion of explanation and a mode of enquiry leading to explanation. Decision-making theory is conceived of by some writers as an explanation of political behaviour which must

> expound the rules that govern the shift and persistence of attentions on the particular issues that occupy the political arena. It must state the principles that govern the intention or design of potential courses of political action. And it must set forth the conditions that determine which actions will be chosen.[53]

Thus the central aim of this type of theory is the explanation of why a particular decision was taken in such a way as to establish 'simple invariant relational principles that will predict the actor's *next* decisions as a function of the situation as it has developed up to the given moment'.[54]

In spite of the fact that this particular writer takes as his point of departure an extant decision as an antecedent for what he seeks to explain, he nevertheless accepts the argument that 'If exactly the same antecedent conditions will produce any one of several decisions, attempts at prediction are futile'.[55] Proponents of this approach are therefore seeking the type of explanation in which antecedent, necessary and sufficient conditions for a decision are clearly stated. Thus, in their view, 'case studies of decisions made after the fact will contribute to the formulation of predictive hypotheses that can be tested in evolving situations'.[56] A distinction is made between this overtly theoretical aim and the type of decision-making theory which is concerned with the choice of an optimal course of action which maximises satisfaction in a situation which poses a number of alternatives. In this sense, as we shall see later, 'theory' is really a technique rather than an explanation.

If, however, we consider the broader sense of decision-making theory, we can see that its focus is the process by which decisions are taken. If past decisions are studied, it is argued, then this process can be analysed in order to derive from it general propositions governing all decision-making which will enable not only the prediction of future decisions but also their prescription. Thus while the elaborate 'frame of reference' devised by Snyder, Bruck and Sapin,[57] which will be considered here, does not constitute an explanation, it is considered to be a means of achieving one. These three writers assert that their main concern lies in the perceptions of those engaged in making decisions. Here they follow the argument, referred to earlier, of Weber, who insisted that the emphasis in sociological explanation should be placed on the understanding of the individual in terms of his perception of his social situation. They argue that the external observer should not impose his own rationalisation upon the actors, but should reconstruct their view of the political situation in which they are engaged in taking a decision. In other words, the aim is to find out what are the perceptions of the decision-makers, in terms of what they want, why they want it, what they are prepared to do to obtain it, and what they consider to be viable or legitimate alternative courses of action,

The frame of reference provided by this argument, in an attempt to answer these questions in terms of a theoretical explanation, begins with a set of definitions.[58] Decisions are taken by 'states', which act in a 'setting', more specifically in a 'situation', in pursuit of an 'objective'. The 'state' is defined as being composed of decision-makers holding an official or governmental position; 'setting' is defined as consisting of what they consider to be important or relevant within the state and outside it; 'situation' is defined as constituting the focus of interest of the decision-makers, and 'objective' as an image of a future state of affairs or, more simply, as what is desired by the decision-makers. These basic definitions are related to the concept of system. This is presented as an organisational unit. Such a unit is conceived of as a 'system of activities' and a 'structure of relationships' which are the 'outcome of formal rules governing the allocation of power and responsibility, motivation, communication, performance of functions, problem-solving and so on'.[59] Each identifiable decision has its own decisional unit. The three major determinants of action, or categories of 'factors which determine the choices made by the decision-makers',[60] are spheres of competence or role, communications and information, and motivation. These constitute the major variables of the system.

According to the argument, decision-makers are subject to certain limitations which arise outside the decisional system. In considering the nature of these limitations, the authors assert that judgements as to their relevance are made 'from a vantage point not shared necessarily by the actor'.[61] This gives us the clue both as to the nature of the argument and its central weakness. Although the point that any analysis of decision-making must include the perceptions of those making them is continually stressed, it is clear that a distinction is made between the analytic categories of the argument and what amounts to a historical reconstruction of particular decisions. If the 'search for explanation of why states behave as they do leads ultimately, according to our argument, to the factors which determine the choices made by the decision-makers',[62] are these factors perceived by those making decisions? Are they conditions which exist regardless of such perception, or do they exist solely as perceptions? In other words, are all decisions influenced by factors of which the decision-maker is unaware and which are thus external to his judgement, or are we concerned only with those perceived conditions made explicit by him? If the former is the case, then clearly the external observer is imposing his own rationalisation; if the latter, then these perceptions must be organised as to exist in all decisions, if any general proposition is to be made. The notion of limitations is ambiguous in this sense, for although the actor is asserted to be more than a passive agent, the implication of categories said to influence his choice tends to deny this.

Thus on this argument, 'given identified, authoritative decision-makers, an organisational system and a communication network (internal and external) decision-making consists of the combining of values plus attitudes plus information plus perception plus situation into the choice of a course of action'.[63] But in what sense are these categories distinctive and meaningful? Are they meaningful in terms of the understanding of the participants? Not according to this argument, for it is asserted that

> An observer cannot predict decision-making behaviour on the basis of knowledge of the actor's values alone. Values have to be operationalised in terms of the situation confronting the actor, which means that objective properties of the situation (information) and the relevancies surrounding it (perception) must be determined.[64]

The explanation, although including the actor's understanding of his situation, conditions and choices, poses a relationship between this and the 'objective' situation, conditions and choices. The problem of rationality is thus bound up in this argument. As it is, the authors of this frame of reference assert that 'the reasons for a decision given by the participants are not sufficient to explain why a particular decision was made – provided evidence of the relevant values and other data are available, the decision can be accounted for, regardless of reasons advanced by the decision-makers'.[65] The theorist can impose his own conception of 'reality' upon that of the decision-maker. This is to assert a criterion of rationality external to that employed by those engaged in making political decisions.

If, then, we examine the major variable of motivation, we can see that it is given a special meaning. The participants in decision-making are considered as *'actors'* (an analytical concept), *not as discrete 'real' persons,*[66] by the authors, so that motivation is also an analytical concept. In other words, what is examined as 'motives' or as 'motivation' in this analysis is a category which is defined as a 'process of mediation between organic factors and social factors operating within the individual which results in some form of observed behaviour'.[67] Here the three authors adopt a number of terms used in psychological theory relating to an innate propensity to act in a particular way. Actors have 'needs' and 'tensions' which 'impel' them to 'seek satisfaction and release'.[68] Such notions constitute subordinate hypotheses about human behaviour which require some validation in their own right before they can be used as assumptions for an argument of this type. Yet they are considered to be appropriate since they represent 'the consensus among scholars as to the essential nature of motivation as an analytic tool'.[69]

The insistence that motives can be inferred from behaviour itself is, of course, important if the problem of ascertaining 'real' motives is to be avoided. Thus the assertion that X motive exists is inferred from the activities of those to whom X motive is attributed. As it is put: 'Clues to the existence of motives are to be sought in consistency of direction.'[70] Yet while it might be possible to say what an objective is, that is, what is considered to be desirable by those seeking it, this would appear to be different from explaining why it is desirable and, hence, why it is being sought. 'Motive' in this sense appears to be used as being synonymous with 'objective'. To take the case study undertaken by Snyder and Paige as an example,[71] the decision made by President Truman to use force in Korea in 1950 might be explained by his desire to prevent South Korea from falling under communist rule. His 'motive' was thus his 'objective'. But what explains his desire? We can infer from a series of decisions and actions that President Truman consistently acted in order to preserve the 'free world', and that this was his objective, but this tells us nothing as to his motives for doing so. In short, only in a very limited sense can a decision be explained in terms of the objective sought.

Hence the assumption that behind every act and every decision exists a motive, and that the nature of this motive can be inferred from the activity itself, means that the notion of motive is prone to a number of possible interpretations, none of which can be established without further evidence of the reasoning of the participants. The argument of the logic of events is clearly dubious. A distinction is made by the authors between motives which are purposive, i.e., 'in order to' and motives which might be termed causal or genetic, i.e., 'because of'.[72] The former are those which are deemed to be central to the concept of motivation used in this frame of reference. The latter are rejected because, as it is put, 'If we had to trace every act back to an ultimate cause our task would be impossible'. Thus the concept of motive is further refined to constitute 'acceptable justifications for present, past and future programmes of action',[73] that is to say, the reasons given by the participants for their actions. Moreover, perception is part of this concept of motivation. 'Motive determines what one selects in perceiving and how one organises and uses it'.[74] Motivation also includes what are termed valuation and evaluation, that is, the choice of preferences and their revision, and the 'appraisal of the relationship between specific acts and the state of affairs envisaged as well as the immediate target'.[75]

What can be said of this notion of motivation as an analytic category? It is asserted in the argument that what is desired constitutes a motive; what is done to obtain it, i.e., perception and action, is also motive, and what is preferred, given various alternative choices, is also part of motivation. And all these terms are to be understood as reasons given by the participants for their action, or as inferences which can be made about them from their behaviour. It would seem that there is considerable ambiguity in the meaning of this category. We can see this ambiguity more clearly, together with the non-theoretical nature of the argument, if we examine how it is used. In answering the question, how does the frame of reference determine behaviour? The authors state that it is operative only after 'an attitude or attitude cluster has been triggered by a stimulus'.[76] By this is apparently meant that a predetermined propensity to act in a particular way, or 'need-disposition', is translated into a decision-making process leading to action when some external event occurs. If a decision occurs, then a stimulus must also have occurred, and the nature of the decision implies the propensity to make it and its motive. From this it is argued that once stimulated, the decision-makers, using a decisional process which operates as a systemic unit, create a frame of reference which constitutes a view of reality related to an objective, and to the means of achieving it. Hence the frame of reference is really the way in which the decision-makers view their world; so that we are back to the problem of establishing what this is, without being in the position of using the concept of the decisional unit, and the three variables of competence, communication and motivation, to elicit a theory of decision-making. It appears that these categories or analytic concepts are attempts to break down the constituent 'parts' of a decision. But does such a systematisation constitute a mode of enquiry likely to lead to a theoretical explanation, not simply of particular decisions taken in the past, but of decisions, past, present and future, as a class of phenomena? Even if we ignore the confusion between the rationality of the observer and that of the participants, the heterogeneity of categories such as motivation, or the dubious terms borrowed from psychological theory, such as 'drive' or 'needs', it is clear that the variables used in this analysis are not capable of precise definition. Nor are they capable of quantification. It is hard to see how they can be used in a testable hypothesis in the absence of such precision.

We may agree with the authors that 'the attitudes, perception, valuation, and evaluation of the decision-maker – as parts of his motivational structure – will be expressed in certain intellectual operations',[77] although we might quarrel with the formal definitions of these categories, but this amounts to a common-sense and rather general statement loosely applicable to those engaged in international politics. However these terms may be defined or refined so as to be logically compatible with one another – or to fit in with empirical assumptions – they amount to no more than a formal way of describing what happens when a group of people decide on something. Such a method of description is directly related to assumptions about international politics made by those using it, which are untestable in any empirical sense. For example, it is asserted that values which exist in society may exert an influence on the decision-makers of that society. This amounts to what is termed a 'cultural bias', and to exemplify this the authors state: 'It seems perfectly obvious that the extremely high value placed on human life and the great respect for the individual as a moral being in American society limit the ends and means which United States decision-makers can seriously consider'.[78] Even when this was written there seemed little empirical justification for this assertion of such a value inhibition on American policy-makers. Even if we agreed with this generalisation, it would seem incapable of any empirical proof. We are left with the specific questions as to which 'attitudes', which 'perceptions', which 'valuations' and which 'evaluation' are related to which 'decision' and which 'situation'. In other words, while these categories might constitute pertinent questions about the interpretation of particular political decisions, they are not theoretical categories which enable us to transcend the particular in order to arrive at a general explanation of all political decisions. They may help us to organise the reconstruction of a specific political situation by clarifying the stages of its development and establishing a sequence of events. However, there is nothing intrinsically 'theoretical' about such an approach.

Most historians would probably agree with the authors that a reconstruction of a past political situation should be done in terms of the participants' perceptions and understanding, and that this is central to an explanation. But, as we shall see, such a reconstruction is fraught with difficulties, and in any case it cannot be presumed that this type of analysis will lead to a theoretical explanation in advance of such an explanation. In this sense, the method is the theory. In examining decision-making in this formal and systematic way, breaking it down into its component 'parts', we are achieving a form of explanation which, as will be argued subsequently, is historical and not scientific in nature.

It was said earlier in this study of decision-making theory that a distinction can be made between a general theory of political behaviour in a decision-making situation and a more limited approach which is concerned with the choice of a course of action, out of a number of alternatives, in a conflict or bargaining situation. Perhaps what is called game theory, or 'the theory of interdependent decisions',[79] is the most prominent example of this latter approach towards an explanation of international politics. Game theory is concerned with the maximisation of gain in a conflict situation. In the case of economics, from which game theory has been borrowed,[80] this notion is quantifiable in terms of money or supporting concepts such as profits or utility. But in politics, gain is not so easily measurable. The purpose of the theory is to enable decision-makers to make the right choice of strategy in order to maximise gains at the lowest cost, or to achieve a given object in the face of opposition. The maximisation of satisfaction is expressed according to a stated scale of preferences and is quantified. Hence the object of the 'game' is to obtain the highest score.[81]

To translate this into more concrete terms, we might express the desired outcome of the Cuban missiles crisis, so far as President Kennedy was concerned, as a range of preferences with the restoration of a capitalist regime in Cuba at the top of the scale, and a withdrawal of Soviet missiles without disrupting the *status quo* outside the Caribbean at the bottom. In order to do this, the *actual* preferences of those participating in a conflict must be precisely identified and separated one from the other. Multiple or conflicting preferences pose problems in formulating such a scale. In a simple two-party conflict the winner takes all, one either wins or loses, and this is called in the language of the game theorist a minimax situation. But international politics, or indeed any situation of political conflict, is rarely so simple, and there are other more complicated games in which the object is mutual accommodation, or the avoidance of undesirable outcomes, and which involve several players.

The choice of an optimal strategy is dictated not only by what is preferred but also by the limited courses of action open to the players. Again, these require precise definition. But the difficulty arises not simply in establishing what the players conceive of as viable courses of action open to them, but in separating means from ends. Neither are fixed or isolable categories, for they are so related in a developing political situation as to involve changes of objective, or the selection of a course of action, producing unintended consequences affecting both the original objectives and the available course of action. This is to say that the fixing of ends and means as two categories capable of quantification produces a static rather than a dynamic model. Thus in the example cited, President Kennedy could conceive of a variety of actions which he could take, but all of which were fraught with the possibility of unintended consequences which might affect other interests and other objectives. In order to appraise his actual decisions involving Cuba in 1962, it is necessary to place these in the context of his world-view. Such a construction transcends the notion of the Cuban crisis as a game even if the world-views of the other participants, allies and opponents, are omitted.

Nevertheless, once quantities related to the scale of preferences and to the course of action open to the contestants are given, a mathematical model in which an optimal strategy is postulated, is then constructed by game theorists. In what sense is such an approach to decision-making in international politics 'theoretical'? Clearly, there are major empirical assumptions contained in this procedure, which range from estimations of capacity and optimal conditions to the rationality of the players. It is assumed that the rules of the game are perceived by them and that perfect information prevails throughout the game. We can see that it is not a theory of behaviour, since it is primarily concerned with the problem of rational choice, once ends and means have been defined. Problems of motivation and of the kinds of categories central to the theory of decision-making considered earlier are irrelevant. Once an objective has been defined and a number of alternative courses of action postulated, then game theory, using mathematical models, seeks to indicate what a rational decision would be, given these terms. It is not a theory which explains behaviour, but one which prescribes it on the basis of implicit assumptions about human action. In a sense it is dependent upon an *unstated* behavioural theory.

As we shall see in a later part of this study where actual examples of this type of theory are considered, the chief use of game theory has been in analyses of policy alternatives involving the use of nuclear weapons which assumed clearly definable limits on the behaviour of those states engaged in conflict. If we consider international politics from the point of view of a practitioner, we can perhaps say that game theory is on the same level as psephology in studies of domestic politics. Its utility is of a practical rather than a theoretical nature. But its use as such could be criticised on the grounds that it creates the danger that a policy based upon a game might become self-fulfilling. An opponent's reaction is induced by the principal's first move, and the second move induced by this reaction. There is no real knowledge of the motivation, and the range of his possible behaviour is based upon an assessment of his rationality and his resources. Moreover, choice is seen in terms of specific alternatives, and if they are inseparable then the game disintegrates as a logical exercise. The opponent may change the rules or act irrationally. Such a game is played in the dark. Perhaps this kind of analysis has a practical utility both in clarifying what is really desired, in order of priority, and in establishing some of the possible courses of action open to the policy-maker or strategist. This is more a question of subjective value than anything else. But whatever the merits of game theory as a technique, it is clearly not a theory in the sense of explanation. It depends upon assumptions and generalisations which are derived from historical situations and historical interpretation, and which constitute an implicit non-theoretical explanation. Game theory is useless as a tool for empirical study since it contains presuppositions about international politics on which its internal argument depends. Rather than eliciting an explanation, it imposes its own conditions upon the study of international politics. It is therefore an applied theoretical argument. If we reject the implicit theory with its assumptions of rational behaviour and its parameters, all that is left is a technique which may or may not be useful to politicians engaged in making decisions in situations of international conflict. If game theory is used in this way, then of course it becomes another subject for investigation, as an influence upon decision-making, that is, as a political phenomenon in its own right.

Throughout this study it has been argued that there must be precise definition of the variables which are asserted to be relevant, in any attempt at constructing scientific models, hypotheses or theories. The direct implication of this requirement is that quantification is a necessary concomitant of theoretical explanation. A variable must be identified and related to some unit of measurement before it can be used in explanations of this type. As we have seen, this condition has rarely been fulfilled in the various approaches considered so far, with the exception of game theory. This last, however, turns out to be a technique rather than an explanation. There is one major exception involving an attempt to provide what might be termed a mathematical theory of international politics, and that is the quantitative analysis of the relation between arms races and wars made by Lewis F. Richardson.[82]

Earlier in this study, reference was made to an explanation of war which attributed its cause to international competition in armaments. It argued that one nation's security always implies another nation's insecurity because the notion of security depends upon the possession of sufficient armaments to deter possible aggressors, or to defend national interests. But, paradoxically, the attempt to create the margin of armaments considered necessary for national security provokes a similar policy on the part of other nations, and hence a competition known as an arms race results. The armaments of one state represent a menace to the security of other states.

Richardson examines this idealised situation and, with the aid of equations, analyses the reciprocal relations between national armament programmes. According to his argument, a nation is represented as a 'single variable, its outward attitude of threatening or co-operation'.[83] It coexists with other nations and they all share common attributes, being motivated by resentment, suspicion, dissatisfaction, fear, rivalry, etc. Now at some point in time these nations may be supposed to be in an unstable equilibrium, that is, with a constant level of armaments expenditure but still retaining grievances and demands on one another. If one nation, acting on one or more of the psychological motives mentioned above, begins to increase its armaments in order to achieve security or to fulfil a demand, then this produces a chain reaction in which the initiating state A induces an increase in armaments expenditure in state B (or C, D, E, etc.), and in turn responds to this development by making further increases which produce further effects. In other words, a disruption of an unstable equilibrium in armaments expenditure, defined as a fixed rate over a period of time, produces an arms race which grows at an exponential or geometrical rate of progression, ultimately culminating in violence. Clearly, this is a description or a definition of an arms race.

The point which Richardson wishes to emphasise is that such a process of 'schismogenesis' or 'symmetrical reciprocity'[84] will lead to war unless steps are taken to stop it. The international world, given this process, is inherently unstable unless a condition of permanent peace is achieved through general disarmament and satisfaction. The converse of war is thus not a 'balance of power' through parity in armaments or alliances, but a combination of disarmament and increased co-operation between nations. Such co-operation is conceived of as taking the form of a growth in trade relations which exercise a restraint on competition. Armaments, in this view, equate with international hostility, and trade with international friendship.

The method of analysis which is adopted consists firstly of the selection of arguments from various statements made by politicians and commentators which relate armaments and security, refer to the armaments of other countries as menaces, and suggest that there are limits to the level of armaments expenditure. Such selection is made unsystematically and without reference to political or historical context. The statement 'When one cannot find statistics it may be permissible to quote the experience of a leading man; for the fact that he is a leader implies that his sentiments were probably typical of an important part of the nation'[85] is typical of this highly impressionistic approach. Secondly, from these statements are derived the terms armaments, menaces, grievances, rates of change, economic limitations and time, which are then incorporated into a set of equations which represent reciprocal processes.

The basic equation is one which correlates the armament expenditures of two countries, and states that where $t=$ time, $x=$ defences, $y=$ menaces, and k and $l=$ 'a positive constant which will be named a defence co-efficient',[86] then for nation A, $dx/dt=ky$, and for nation B, $dy/dt=kx$. If x and y, defences and menaces, are 'ever more positive, they then (according to these two equations) will become more positive and go on increasing faster and faster without any end to the process'. Ultimately war between these nations will occur. In order to meet the objection that the mere existence of armaments, coupled with a rate of change in one country's armament expenditure, is an over-simplification of an arms race because it does not take into account economic limits on national expenditure, or the actual content of national foreign policies, two further terms are added to the equations. These are grievances and ambitions, g and h; and economic limitations, a and b. Thus the equations are refined for nation A to $dx/dt = ky - ax$ and for nation B to $dy/dt = lx - by$, representing the economic limitations factor, and to $dx/dt = ky - ax + g$ for nation A and to $dy/dt = lx - by + h$ for nation B, to include the factor of grievances.

Using these basic equations, Richardson then proceeds to examine the actual historical record of armaments expenditures and trade figures preceding the two major wars of this century, in order to see how this evidence 'fits' his theoretical process. The unit of measurement employed is the 'money value of arms expenditure' divided by some 'average wage' which is expressed by the neologism 'warfinpersal'.[87] A fairly close fit is found between the model and the arms race preceding the First World War, but a less satisfactory correlation exists for the Second World War.

What can be said of this mathematical theory of arms races? It should be apparent that it is not an explanation at all but a description of an idealised phenomenon. The fundamental 'causes' of war, according to the argument, lie in the psychological condition of nations, although at the same time it is asserted that the actual theory is concerned with 'politics without personalities'. Fear, it is argued, inspires an increase in armaments which triggers the arms race. This is one of the motives asserted to be part of the 'general tendencies common to all nations',[88] including resentment, suspicion, feelings of revenge, dissatisfaction and rivalry, etc. But although these are alleged to be the basic causes of arms races, they are not given any precise definition, nor is a supporting explanation provided. Instead they are lumped together in the category known as 'grievances' and included as a constant in the equations. Causation is thus ignored and the argument concerns itself solely with the process generated by these causal factors. In so doing the major assumption is made that armaments expenditure is the product of reciprocal responses. Whatever the ostensible purposes of a defence policy or the interpretations and vision of politicians, or indeed the actual domestic and international political situations, the determining factor in international politics is the existence and rate of change of defence expenditures in the major nations. Assuming this to be the case, the consequences of such reciprocity are expressed in mathematical terms.

But this is no explanation, since the central question, why this mutual stimulation should occur, is simply assumed and not explained. Not all arms races result in war, nor are all wars preceded by arms races of the kind postulated in the theory. The phenomenon of exponential growth in armaments expenditures is comparatively rare. Even where the basic model is modified by the inclusion of the category of 'grievances', the lack of precise definition militates against its usefulness as a qualification of the simple argument that armaments create wars. How can a 'grievance' be quantified or even identified without some degree of specificity or relation to a unit of measurement? How can it be regarded as a constant in an equation? According to Richardson, *g* and *h*

> represent any motives which, while affecting warlike preparations, remain constant independently of the amount of such preparations at home or abroad. From the psychological point of view such motives could include deeply rooted prejudices, standing grievances, old unsatisfied ambitions, wicked and persistent dreams of world conquest or, on the contrary, a permanent feeling of contentment.[89]

Such an argument not only makes a number of presuppositions about the 'psychological state' of nations which require explanation, but also totally ignores the factor of change in attitudes and the nature of politics and diplomacy in international relations. This objection is not met by the countering argument that, although *g* and *h* may be 'imponderables', nevertheless their products, *x* and *y*, can be counted in terms of men and money.[90] The notion of 'grievance' remains an imponderable and the question of its relation to armaments and menaces is begged.

It was said that this theoretical model best fitted the arms race preceding the First World War, covering the period 1908–14. The reason for this lies in the treatment of the competing states as two groups, thus corresponding to the relatively simple linear model of a two-nation arms race. As we have seen, the reciprocal effects of an arms race must occur as a result of a specified relationship between the armaments expenditures of specified competitors. Hence the actual rivalry between nations must be identified, if the theory is to have any empirical application. If this is not specified, then it is impossible to argue that mutual stimulation occurs, other than as part of an abstract relationship. The model does not provide us with a means of predicting the competitors, or of stipulating which nation will engage in violence with which opponent. Thus the model can describe only in terms of an asserted symmetrical schismogenetic relationship. While it may be true that such a feedback sequence has sometimes occurred in the armaments expenditure of particular nations in the past, there is no means of predicting this for the future. The theory is unable to predict political alignment in the event of war. Retrospectively, of course, we know what alignments took place before and during the two major wars of this century, but the mathematical theory of arms races does not enable predictions based on the interaction of resources, grievances and levels of armament, since it postulates the competitors as given.

For example, it was not axiomatic that Britain or Italy would fight Germany, Austria-Hungary and Turkey in 1914, nor could it have been argued prior to the event that Germany would both ally with and fight the Soviet Union in 1939 and 1941, and declare war on the United States. Nor could it be predicted that Japan would choose to go to war with the United States and Britain rather than with the Soviet Union. The political and diplomatic record reveals a complexity which is not resolved or explained by the simplistic argument that increased armaments expenditures produce an arms race which leads directly to war. The central theoretical question is, what is the nature of such a process in terms of an explanation of war? – not how it can be defined or described in abstract terms. Certainly, wars cannot occur without weapons, and international competition and violence are relatively common phenomena in international politics, but an explanation of such phenomena must do more than express in mathematical language a description of one highly idealised aspect of such conflict. Political alignments and disputes are not fixed in any deterministic sense, and diplomacy and foreign policy are not determined, although they may be influenced, by defence expenditure.

There are other objections to this argument, notably the major assumption that trade 'is the most extensive form of international co-operation'[91] and constitutes a limiting factor to the development of hostilities. The notion of 'co-operation' is vague and, like that of 'armaments', grossly oversimplifies the complexity of international economic and commercial relationships. But the principal objection, so far as this examination is concerned, is that the attempt at 'quantitative history' fails mainly because there is no unit of measurement which can be employed with any validity in such a theory. Even if we disregard the various assumptions and implicit interpretations underlying the mathematical arguments, we may question the treatment of the categories of warlike preparedness, co-operation or negative preparedness for war, grievances, ambitions, defences, menaces, suffering and economic limitations on armaments expenditure as measurable entities. In short, can the friendship or hostility of a nation be measured? Certainly, as this theory demonstrates, they can be given a magnitude and incorporated into equations which may then be used to indicate the consequences of their relations; but in what sense does this advance an empirical explanation of conflict in international politics?

It would appear that Richardson himself regarded his theory as being descriptive rather than explanatory. As he put it: 'The equations are merely a description of what people would do if they did not stop to think. . . . It is what *would occur if instinct and tradition were allowed to act uncontrolled.*'[92] But the 'real' explanation of war, in his view, lies in the 'great instinctive and traditional tendencies which are formulated in my description'.[93] What we have, therefore, in this mathematical theory is not an empirical explanation but a highly abstract hypothetical description, couched in symbolic terms, of a process which has no empirical application other than as of a non-theoretical and individual interpretation of international politics. It may be, as one critic argued, that 'What the model gives us that common-sense conclusions do not is a neat quantitative way of expressing these results'.[94] But this is to express a preference for style or for language rather than for a mode of enquiry which leads to fruitful results. The apparent precision of such an argument masks the imprecision of its assumptions and its categories.

We have seen from this examination of an attempt to explain international politics using mathematical terms, that there is a need for a measurable unit before measurement can take place. Until this is established beyond cavil, there is no means of engaging in a quantitative explanation of international politics which is empirically valid. For example, the statement that X nation is a great power implies both a universally accepted standard of power and some basis for comparison between the 'power' of various countries. Of course, we can give notional quantities to this concept, or perhaps conduct an enquiry into the various weightings given to this proposition by various commentators or politicians. In general terms, any explanation of foreign policy or of national attitudes will include an interpretation of assessments made by participating statesmen of the 'power' of other countries. But such an evaluation, although it might take the form of a survey of public opinion and express its findings in quantitative terms, is not a quantitative theory.

If we approach the problem of quantification more narrowly and examine attempts at measuring a factor or variable commonly asserted to be central to political activity, then perhaps we can see more closely the difficulties involved. The notion of power has a long history in explanations of politics and has found particular expression in the field of international politics. According to Morgenthau, 'whatever the ultimate aims of international politics, power is always the immediate aim'.[95] There is a well-established school of thought which regards political activity as being essentially a struggle for power. This is to suppose that a distinction can be made between power and aims, and that power has some definable quality. Thus the most common definition of power asserts that power is the capacity to achieve objectives, without these objectives being modified, or formulated, under conditions of opposition and where the only restriction which applies to the fulfilment of a desire is the imagination or will of those holding it.

But since a condition of absolute power, such as that implied in this definition, can hardly be said to have existed in the 'real' world, it is more commonplace to talk of 'degrees' of power, or to make statements which imply that power can be shared, obtained or transferred. For example, earlier in this analysis reference was made to the notion of a polity contained in the general theory of action of Parsons, which was dependent upon a concept of power. It was argued that

> we may regard a polity as maintaining its power potential through continual interchanges with its environment. On the one hand it 'exports' power in the form of opportunity for effectiveness, and gets in return power in the form of commitment of services. On the other hand, it 'exports' power in the form of policy decisions, and gets in return power in the form of political support.[96]

The question concerning us here is, in what way can such a notion of power be used quantitatively in a theoretical explanation of international politics? Is it, as Russell maintains, a 'fundamental concept in social science in the same sense in which Energy is the fundamental concept in physics'?[97] Can it be treated as a 'major intervening variable between an initial condition defined largely in terms of the individual components of the system and a terminal state defined largely in terms of the system as a whole'?[98] In other words, when the term 'power' is used, does it have the same implications in an explanation of politics as it does in an explanation of mechanics? Can it be measured?

In a critique of attempts at using a power model to explain situations of 'social choice', James March asserts, albeit with some reservations, that a 'simple force model . . . represents a reasonable approach to the study of social choice'.[99] If, then, we examine this claim, we find that the central concept of power in such a model is that of 'a quotient of the maximum force which b can induce over a and the maximum resistance which a can offer'.[100] Translating this into more concrete terms, this means that change in a social situation involving choice, or decision-making, is produced by a force which is the product of the individual powers possessed by the participants. Thus, assuming an initial condition to be constant, any change which occurs is the product of the exercise of power. It is also assumed in this argument that 'social choice will be a predictable extension of past choices *unless* the power is exerted on the choice.'[101] The bigger the change, then the bigger the power, is the concomitant of this proposition. Thus a measure of power can be obtained through the extent of the changes which occur from one optimal condition to an end-state. The notion of power as a force is also related to that of power as a valuation, that is, as an estimate of what people consider to be a powerful position in a given social context. Participants in a situation of social choice may each be allotted an 'amount' of power on this basis.

According to this argument, given an initial state, in which if no power is exercised a continuum of action is postulated, and given a number of participants each with an allocation of 'power', desiring to make changes according to their individual preferences or choices, the degree of change which results from their interaction, and the degree to which the change corresponds to the preference of one of the participants, constitute a measurement of the power utilised and of the power of the individuals engaged in the situation. It would appear from this that the notions of change and direction are written into the model rather in the same way as force is related to mass and velocity in mechanics. The measurement of power in this sense depends on the recognition and definition of some optimal state to which change is related. Clearly, in such a model this condition is assumed as a constant rather than explained. Can we regard 'social choice' situations as axiomatic in this way, and extrapolate from them verifiable statements about power? The basis for quantification depends upon the assertion of some normative condition for each such situation. But if the amount of power is the amount of change produced by its exercise, then we must first establish what it is which is changed in quantitative terms before we can engage in measuring power. Degrees of change and hence degrees of power can then be quantified.

However, the 'simple force model' avoids this problem by assuming that all situations of social choice are essentially the same and that initial conditions to which subsequent changes are related can be considered as 'given'. It would appear that the use of concepts derived from mechanics, in explanations of political relationships, is analogous rather than explanatory. The notion of change would seem to be an imponderable in human relations, unlike physical behaviour which can be explained using precisely defined terms such as mass, velocity, force, etc., related to an empirically testable theory. Thus this particular notion of power in politics begs a number of theoretical questions relating to the type of explanation to which it properly belongs. It is yet another example of the use of concepts borrowed from one validated theoretical field, in which the form rather than the substance is taken over.

An alternative method of using the concept of power as a measurable variable is that put forward by Deutsch. Although he accepts that power cannot be measured exactly, nevertheless

> it can be estimated in proportion to the power resources or capabilities that are visibly available, such as the number of countable supporters, voters or soldiers available or required in a particular political context. Levels of intensity of support, of morale, of skills and resourcefulness, in so far as any or all of these can be estimated, may also be taken into account by appropriate weighting, much as man-power budgets or estimates of military forces can be at least roughly calculated.[102]

Such indices are, of course, subjective and refer to power as an unrealised potential. A well-filled war chest and a standing army, to paraphrase Frederick the Great, are tangible evidence of military strength and certainly can be counted. But although men and money are quantifiable, does this help us to quantify power? We know on commonsense grounds that the Swiss navy is no potential challenger to British naval power or, perhaps more pertinently, that it would be extremely difficult at present for the Chinese People's Republic to mount a naval invasion of the Philippines, Indonesia and Malaysia, but as we have seen in another context, estimates of capability without some definition of aims or of political context are mere exercises in abstraction. If power is a synonym for capacity, then we are entitled to ask: capacity for what?

It would appear that while we may define power as the capacity to compel or persuade an opposition to accept the national will in international politics (a distinction sometimes made between power and influence is that the latter does not involve the use of force or coercion), there is no possibility of incorporating it into a predictive empirical explanation unless such a capacity can be quantified. Hence while the term 'power' is frequently used as a descriptive expression conveying this meaning in politics, it refers to an activity rather than to a state or condition. Power is really a relationship. By this is meant that we cannot know whether a nation was powerful until we can relate its actions to the ends which it sought, to its resources and capacity, to the existence of opposition and to the perceptions of the policy-maker. Modest aims may be framed by those responsible for political decisions, and achieved, while those more ambitious may only achieve a proportion of their objectives. Both cases involve the exercise of political judgement based upon an awareness of the international context and national resources, together with some idea of what is considered desirable. But only when such ends are clearly stated and achieved (or not) can any evaluation of power have any meaning.

Power is as power does, and cannot therefore be considered more of an aim than the aim itself. A distinction between the achievement of power and the achievement of a specified objective cannot be made because, in the absence of a means of measuring power, the two are essentially the same. It is insufficient to state that the primal national interest is the pursuit of power, because this is a necessary precondition to the achievement of any objective. We know that a state has been 'powerful' because it has achieved something. We can only speculate about whether a state will achieve its objectives and thus be 'powerful'. Thus our common-sense judgements about the relative 'power' of states are based upon past achievement, combined with a rough notion that there must be some relationship between capacity and objective if the latter is to have some chance of fulfilment. As we shall see later in this study, the attempt to use the concept of power as an explanation rather than as a descriptive term has been notably unsuccessful. The point here is that, despite its frequent use in political analysis, it remains either descriptive or analogous in the absence of a means of relating it to a unit of measurement.

From this examination of attempts to explain international political phenomena in quantitative terms, we can see that in most cases, rather than being a mode of enquiry designed to elicit a theoretical explanation, they prescribe what sort of explanation is actually achieved. In other words, the apparent precision of quantitative definitions and hypotheses usually conceals implicit assumptions concerning the subject of the explanation. Such arguments are really applied theories. Of course, as we have seen earlier, assumptions which are speculative in nature are made in science, and these may prescribe the mode of the field of enquiry, but the theories which are derived from them are susceptible to some empirical test. When attempts are made to apply the same *modus operandi* to explanations in international politics, the resultant hypotheses either reify the assumptions, become abstract exercises in mathematical or symbolic reasoning, or are simply analogous to established explanations in science.

It is sometimes argued that the attempt to produce a valid theoretical explanation in this field should be preceded by the establishment of 'hard' data. As Singer puts it, 'we cannot explain and we cannot predict until we can describe and . . . satisfactory description in turn requires relatively systematised procedures'.[103] This argument places emphasis on the search for 'statistical regularities' in human activities and seeks to place facts or 'data' on a quantitative footing so that they can then be used in a theory. There are indeed a number of quantitative techniques used in international politics which seek to elicit 'hard' data from 'large and unassorted heaps of facts'.[104] Such techniques imply the kind of argument discussed earlier in this analysis, which asserts some kind of pattern in human affairs so that 'once a process gets underway or a system begins to take on structure the effects of conscious human intervention upon any future state of affairs are apparently reduced'.[105] This type of quantitative analysis is seeking to place 'observational' data in the field of international politics on the same basis as that of observation in the natural sciences. Thus factor analysis, content analysis, cost–benefit analysis, the measurement of communication flows, public opinion polls and the analysis of voting and simulation are all techniques involving measurement which are used to enable the establishment of some standard of valuation or of comparison.[106] Of course, certain of these techniques are closely related to what is termed 'operational research' and are used as guides to policy rather than as a method of producing a theoretical explanation. Polls and surveys may be used in attempts to formulate marketing policy – whether for soap or for politicians would appear to be theoretically immaterial. They are thus closely related to the decisional or policy process and are part of the repertory of political practice properly belonging to the politicians. But in any case, surveys and other methods of assessment of attitudes and opinion can only be applied to the living, and this excludes their use for the study of past international political behaviour. Other techniques are dual in nature; for example, cost–benefit analysis, with its related theories of value and opportunity costs, is both a means of guiding choice and a part of extant theoretical explanation in the field of economics.

But other techniques appear to be more germane to our concern with theoretical enquiry, involving the creating of 'hard' or 'objective' data as a necessary preliminary to the formulation of valid theories. Content analysis, for example, consists of the examination of selected writings, diaries, letters, speeches, diplomatic papers, etc., in order to determine the perceptions and values of their writers or to formulate categories for comparison. The purpose of this technique is to obtain data which can then be used in quantitative analysis. As it is put by one writer: 'The objective of content analysis is to convert recorded "raw" phenomena into data which can be treated in essentially a scientific manner so that a body of knowledge may be built up.'[107] Thus the frequency of particular expressions and arguments can be expressed statistically and compared from one source to another. This is to assert some level of meaning present in the 'manifest' content of the source or independent of it which can be used as a referent. The method adopted is that of establishing key variables as 'types of attributes' and using these as categories for the analysis of a range of writings. It is clear that, if it is not purely arbitrary, this method contains theorising presuppositions which prescribe the type of analysis and its findings.

This is also true of factor analysis, which consists of the reduction of a number of hypothetically posited processes or variables in a social or political situation to a set of factors which are then mathematically correlated. The point of this exercisce is to reduce the number of variables in the analysis of human activities in order to discover their relative significance. But as in the case of content analysis, such an approach is dependent on the nature of the assumptions which it makes about the selected variables.

Communication-flow analysis, or the measurement of communication between states or other entities, is concerned with relationships rather than with variables, but it too seeks to establish 'hard' data. The procedure adopted is the selection of a number of 'indicators', and the quantification of their incidence in communications, as a means of eliciting facts about international relations which can then be incorporated into testable hypotheses. For example, information can be measured in terms of the frequency or volume of interchanges between governments or individuals. It would seem that such a technique is limited by the assumptions which are made about the nature and type of indicators selected as the basis for quantification. Moreover, it is difficult to see what value this technique has in advancing an explanation. The cessation of exchanges between the Wilhelmstrasse and the British Foreign Office after September 1939 might indicate a breach of diplomatic relations between the United Kingdom and Germany; but this does not tell us much.

Finally, simulation[108] has been considered by some scholars to be a fruitful method of eliciting data about the actual processes of international politics. This approach posits the notion that there is an 'external' reality which can be replicated in a simpler form as a game or laboratory exercise. The point is that, by playing a game, processes which are not directly observable in the 'real' world may be discovered. Thus a simulation is a model based upon assumptions made about the external world of international relations, in which a small number of fixed variables and rules are established. The relationships between these are then acted out by the participants and the outcome of the game is then compared with reality. This technique differs from the others referred to above, since it is an explicit hypothesis rather than a quantitative mode of enquiry. Its assumptions are explicit. It is clear from this that such a model can only imitate international politics and thus simply replicates what is already known. In short, it postulates the kind of knowledge which it is supposed to discover.

All these techniques proceed on the basis of making assumptions about the nature of the phenomena which they are investigating. The assumptions guide the selection of the 'key' variables in social or political activity and, whatever the refinement of the mathematical techniques used in the analysis, the results are no more precise, so far as a theoretical explanation is concerned, than the assumptions on which they are based. Karl Deutsch puts this succinctly in his assertion that 'nothing can be counted that has not been recognised; counting is repeated recognition'.[109] This is indeed an unresolved problem, not simply in international politics but in the social sciences as a whole. But such recognition clearly depends upon the achievement of a valid theoretical explanation. Yet, as was argued earlier in this study, in the absence of such an explanation it is difficult to evaluate modes of enquiry which seek precise formulation of the factors asserted to be important in political activity, through the medium of mathematical and statistical analysis. It is true that none of these theoretical approaches has led to any fruitful results. Consequently we might feel entitled to dismiss them as irrelevant to attempts at explaining international politics. But it was also argued throughout this study that certain of these modes of enquiry can be considered to be explanations in their own right. Let us return therefore to the notion of explanation in order to examine this possibility.

At the beginning of this study a distinction was made between a mode of enquiry which is both an explanation and a means of achieving an explanation, and one which is simply the latter. It will be recalled that the proponents of conceptual schemes urged the necessity of formulating concepts and hypotheses which would enable more precise observation. The underlying notion of this argument is that theory precedes observation. In other words, an explanation is achieved through the creation of hypotheses which are then tested against the empirical data. But this would appear to contradict the view discussed above, that before any theory can prove fruitful, it is first necessary to define in precise terms the facts which the theory seeks to explain. The first position asserts the primacy of conceptualisation while the second stresses the importance of factual observations which are unprejudiced by hypothetical presuppositions.

So far as the achievement of a scientific explanation is concerned, it can be said that the former argument is more soundly based than the latter. What are the grounds for this assertion? A mode of enquiry proceeds by making assumptions which prescribe or define the phenomena to be explained. As we have seen, the various attempts at establishing 'hard' data discussed above were in fact riddled with theorising assumptions. In what sense then can a fact be considered to be 'objective' and independent of any evaluation or assumption? This question will be considered in more detail in the following chapter; but the point here is that the selection and perception of facts are based upon the entity observed. If particular facts are selected as part of the quest for a theoretical explanation, then this implies some criterion, which may be implicit or explicit, of relevance or of significance. Even attempts to place empirical observation on a quantitative basis contain assumptions relating to some measurable entity which can be distinguished from the actual procedures of measurement.

Thus while it is true that, in the absence of a validated or confirmed theory, there is no means of establishing which of these initial assumptions has explanatory value, nevertheless some assumptions are a prerequisite of any enquiry or attempt at explanation. Hence the notion that a mode of enquiry is concerned not with the establishment of hypotheses but with the establishment of 'objective' data is mistaken, firstly, in thinking that a clear distinction can be made between theorising assumptions and the facts to which they are related, and secondly, in believing that such an approach is characteristic of scientific method. Unrelated or 'objective' facts are simply irrelevant to explanation, for it is the explanation which confers significance and meaning upon them. Thus a mode of enquiry which postulates as its main purpose the establishment of facts, even if it could be shown to be completely void of evaluation or of theorising assumptions, cannot be said to be a means of achieving an explanation. It is the explanation and not the 'mode' of investigation which determines the nature of the phenomena to be explained, unless this last is really an implicit theory.

Now it was argued that certain of the modes of enquiry considered in this analysis were explanations in their own right. Although their relationship to theoretical explanation was shown to be tenuous, nevertheless they created a meaningful and intelligible world. The implications of this argument led to a notion of explanation radically different from that of science which has prevailed in the discussion so far. These will be considered at length in the next chapter. We may conclude this examination of middle-range theories, methods and techniques by saying that method is intimately related to explanation, in such a way as to make it extremely difficult to assert that a particular explanation is the fruit of a particular method. Experimental techniques and analytic procedures go hand in hand with theoretical advances, but until a theory of the provenance of theories is formulated and confirmed, the connection between the two will remain ambiguous. In the absence of any theoretical advance in the field of international politics in particular and social sciences in general, it is impossible to assert any direct connection between method and explanation.

REFERENCES

1.   David Easton, 'Alternative Strategies in Theoretical Research', in *Varieties of Political Theory,* p. 5.

2.   T. S. Kuhn, *The Structure of Scientific Revolutions,* 2nd ed. (Univ. of Chicago Press, 1970) p. 4.

3.   Ibid.; see esp. chap. vii and viii.

4.   L. J. Henderson, cited in Talcott Parsons, *The Structure of Social Action* (New York: Free Press, 1966) p. 28.

5.   Talcott Parsons and Edward Shils (eds.), *Towards a General Theory of Action* (New York: Torch Books, Harper & Row, 1962) p. 27.

6.   Talcott Parsons, *The Social System* (London: Routledge & Kegan Paul, 1970) p. 3.

7.   Parsons, *The Structure of Social Action,* p. 23.

8.   Ibid., p. 28.

9.   Max Weber, *The Theory of Social and Economic Organisation,* trans. A. M. Henderson and Talcott Parsons (New York: Free Press of Glencoe, 1947) p. 118.

10.   For a discussion of ideal types, see ibid., pp. 115–18.

11.   A. Schutz, 'The Social World and the Theory of Social Action', in *Collected Papers,* vol. xi of *Studies in Social Theory,* ed. Arvid Brodersen (The Hague: Nijhoff, 1964) p. 13; see also 'The Problem of Rationality in the Social World' for a discussion of ideal types and rational action.

12.   Schutz, 'The Problem of Rationality in the Social World', p. 85.

13.   Talcott Parsons, 'The Political Aspects of Social Structure and Process', in Easton (ed.), *Varieties of Political Theory,* p. 71.

14.   Ibid., p. 93.

15.   Parsons and Shils (eds.), *Towards a General Theory of Action,* p. 23.

16.   Ibid., p. 25.

17.   For an exposition of the theoretical significance of these functions, see Parsons, 'The Political Aspects of Social Structure and Process', pp. 104–12; also footnote to p. 105 for further references.

18.   Ibid., p. 85.

19.   Ibid., p. 96.

20.   Ibid., p. 79.

21.   Weber, *The Theory of Social and Economic Organisation,* pp. 88–124.

22.   Karl R. Popper, *Conjectures and Refutations,* 3rd rev. ed. (London: Routledge & Kegan Paul, 1969) pp. 39–41.

23.   Michael Oakeshott, *Experience and its Modes* (Cambridge Univ. Press, 1933) p. 34.

24.   Parsons, *The Structure of Social Action,* p. 38.

25.   Carl G. Hempel, 'Typological Methods in the Social Sciences', in M. Natanson (ed.) (New York: Random House, 1963) p. 228.

26.   Merton, *On Theoretical Sociology,* chap. ii, 'On Sociological Theories of the Middle Range', pp. 39ff.

27.   Ibid., p. 39.

28.   Ibid., p. 43.

29.   Ibid., p. 42.

30.   Ibid.

31.   Ibid.

32.   Ibid., p. 41.

33.   Robert K. Merton, *Social Theory and Social Structure,* rev. ed. (New York: Free Press, 1964) p. 89.

34.   Merton, *On Theoretical Sociology,* p. 140; see also chap. iv, 'The Bearing of Sociological Theory on Empirical Research', pp. 139–55.

35.   See Popper, *The Logic of Scientific Discovery;* and Kuhn, *The Structure of Scientific Revolutions.*

36. C. A. McClelland, 'The Acute International Crisis', in Knorr and Verba (eds.), *The International System,* pp. 182-204.
37. Ibid., p. 189.
38. Cited in ibid., from Karl W. Deutsch, 'Mass Communications and the Loss of Freedom in National Decision-Making: A Possible Research Approach to Interstate Conflicts', *Journal of Conflict Resolution,* vol. I (June 1957) p. 200.
39. McClelland, 'The Acute International Crisis', p. 193.
40. Ibid.
41. Ibid., p. 192.
42. See ibid., pp. 191-4.
43. Ibid., p. 194.
44. Ibid., p. 198.
45. Ibid.
46. Ibid., p. 199.
47. Ibid., p. 201.
48. Ibid.
49. Ibid., p. 200.
50. Ibid.
51. Ibid., p. 204.
52. See ibid., pp. 189–91.
53. Herbert A. Simon, 'Political Research: The Decision-Making Framework', in Easton (ed.), *Varieties of Political Theory,* p. 21.
54. Ibid., p. 17.
55. Richard C. Snyder and Glenn D. Paige, 'The United States Decision to Resist Aggression in Korea: The Application of an Analytical Scheme', p. 194, reprinted in Rosenau (ed.) *International Politics and Foreign Policy,* pp. 193–208.
56. Ibid., p. 194.
57. Richard C. Snyder, H. W. Bruck and Burton Sapin, *Foreign Policy Decision Making* (New York: Free Press of Glencoe, 1962).
58. Ibid., pp. 60–7.
59. Ibid., p. 95.
60. Ibid., p. 105.
61. Ibid., p. 101.
62. Ibid., p. 105.
63. Snyder and Paige, op. cit., p. 206.
64. Ibid.
65. Ibid., p. 198.
66. Snyder, Bruck and Sapin, op. cit., p. 138.
67. Ibid., p. 139.
68. Ibid., pp. 140–3.
69. Ibid., p. 141.
70. Ibid.
71. Snyder and Paige, op. cit., pp. 198–200.
72. Snyder, Bruck and Sapin, op. cit., p. 144.
73. Ibid., p. 146.
74. Ibid., p. 150.
75. Ibid., p. 151.
76. Ibid., p. 152.
77. Ibid., p. 162.
78. Ibid., p. 157.
79. See T. C. Schelling, *The Strategy of Conflict* (New York: Galaxy Books, Oxford Univ. Press, 1963) p. 16.
80. See John von Neumann and Oskar Morgenstern, *The Theory of Games and Economic Behaviour* (Princeton Univ. Press, 1947).
81. For a critical discussion of game theory in international politics, see Nigel Forward, *The Field of Nations* (London: Macmillan, 1971) pp. 24–52.
82. Lewis F. Richardson, *Arms and Insecurity,* ed. N. Rashevsky and Ernesto Tucco (Pittsburgh: Boxwood Press, 1960).
83. Ibid., p. 13.

84. Ibid., p. 65.
85. Ibid., p. 235.
86. Ibid., pp. 15–17.
87. Ibid., pp. 134–5.
88. Ibid., p. 13.
89. Ibid., p. 16.
90. Ibid.
91. Ibid., p. 19.
92. Ibid., p. 12.
93. Ibid., p. 227.
94. Anatol Rapoport, *Fights, Games and Debates* (Ann Arbor: Univ. of Michigan Press, 1960) p. 29.
95. Hans J. Morgenthau, Jr., 'Politics among Nations', in Stanley Hoffmann (ed.), *Contemporary Theory in International Relations* (Englewood Cliffs, N.J.: Prentice-Hall, 1960) p. 64.
96. Parsons, 'The Political Aspects of Social Structure and Process', p. 98.
97. Bertrand Russell, *Power* (London: Allen & Unwin, 1938) p. 9.
98. James G. March, 'The Power of Power', in Easton (ed.), *Varieties of Political Theory*, p. 40.
99. Ibid., p. 70.
100. Kurt Lewin, cited ibid, p. 41.
101. Ibid., p. 43.
102. Deutsch, *The Nerves of Government*, p. 120.
103. J. David Singer (ed.), *Quantitative International Politics: Insights and Evidence* (New York: Free Press, 1967) p. 1.
104. Ibid., p. 2.
105. Ibid., p. 3.
106. See, for example, John E. Mueller, *Approaches to Measurement in International Relations: A Non-Evangelical Survey* (New York: Appleton-Century-Crofts, 1969); Robert C. North *et al.*, *Content Analysis: A Handbook with Application for the Study of International Crisis* (Evanston, Ill.: Northwestern Univ. Press, 1963); J. David Singer, 'Content Analysis of Elite Articulations', *Journal of Conflict Resolution*, vol. VIII (1964) pp. 425–85; Alain C. Enthoven and K. Wayne Smith, *How Much is Enough? Shaping the Defense Program 1961–1969* (New York: Harper & Row, 1971); James M. Buchanan, *Cost and Choice* (Chicago: Markham, 1969); Walter Phillips Davison, *International Political Communication* (New York: Praeger, 1965); Karl W. Deutsch, 'Shifts in the Balance of International Communication Flows', *Public Opinion Quarterly*, vol. xx (spring 1956) pp. 143-60; James N. Rosenau, *Public Opinion and Foreign Policy* (New York: Random House, 1965); Richard Fargen, 'Some Assessments and Uses of Public Opinion in Diplomacy', *Public Opinion Quarterly*, vol. xxiv (1960) pp. 448-57; Thomas Hovet, Jr, *Bloc Voting in the United Nations* (Cambridge, Mass.: Harvard Univ. Press, 1961); Richard A. Brody, 'Some Systematic Effects of the Spread of Nuclear Weapons Technology: A Study through Simulation of a Multi-Nuclear Future', *Journal of Conflict Resolution*, vol. VII (Dec. 1963) pp. 663-753. See also R. N. Rosecrance and J. E. Mueller, 'Decision-Making and the Quantitative Analysis of International Relations', *Yearbook of World Affairs* (1967).
107. Aaron V. Cicourel, *Method and Measurement in Sociology* (New York: Free Press, 1964) p. 435.
108. Harold Guetzkow *et al.*, *Simulation in International Relations: Developments for Research and Teaching* (Englewood Cliffs, N.J.: Prentice-Hall, 1963).
109. Karl W. Deutsch, 'Towards an Inventory of Basic Trends and Patterns in Comparative and International Politics', in Rosenau, op. cit., p. 452.

CHAPTER 4

Historical Interpretation and International Politics

IT should be apparent from the previous chapters that part, at least, of the work done in the social sciences in general, and in the study of international politics in particular, is concerned with establishing theoretical explanations which are scientific in nature. Such an emphasis on scientific method and the consequent quest for theory arose out of dissatisfaction with the traditional historical approach towards explanation of human behaviour and institutions. As will be seen subsequently, this notion of historical explanation is an over-simplification which glosses over a number of different historical approaches. However, this dissatisfaction expressed itself in two main objections; the first was that historical interpretations were theoretically unstructured, although they contained concepts and assumptions which were theoretical in nature. The second objection was that historical narrative was subjective and based upon value judgements and assumptions. In other words, traditional historical explanations are not the same as scientific explanations which, as we have seen, are based on rigorous deductive arguments, from which theoretical conclusions may be derived, and which are capable of being verified empirically.

Of course, to say that historical explanation is different from scientific explanation is not to assert that it is necessary invalid, although this is often implied by critics. A particular explanation may be non-scientific and yet be valid within its own terms. It is only if validity is closely defined as corresponding to a specific form of explanation that it becomes a universal model against which all interpretations are measured. The claims for this kind of certainty in scientific explanations of international politics were examined earlier and found to be exaggerated. If this claim is rejected, then the problem remains of establishing the nature of a historical enquiry and its criterion of validity. The central question in answering the objections of those who urge the scientific approach as a means of explaining human behaviour lies in its relevance to historical explanation. Should the criteria used in validating scientific theory be applied to historical explanations, and should this mode of enquiry seek to meet the theoretical requirements of that of science? Or alternatively, should we apply other criteria, and if so, which?

There are some historians who claim that they are concerned with explanations which correspond to those in science, and there are others who do not make this claim explicit but who nevertheless seek the same thing. They are concerned with explanations *of* history rather than with explanations which are historical. That is to say, the establishment of general laws of behaviour is sought, which not only explain what has happened in the past, but which also explain the present and the future. Such explanations are causal in the sense that some law of behaviour is adduced which states that, given the same conditions and relationships, the same event or phenomenon will recur. An explanation which seeks to generalise about future as well as past human activities is dependent upon propositions which extend across time. But the 'historical' nature and content of such an explanation is fortuitous, and it is temporal only in the sense that past events are subsumed in a theory which explains the past and the future. As in science, sequences of events or phenomena are significant, but in a theoretical rather than a historical sense.

Such an explanation differs from that found in science, and attempted in the social sciences, only in its subject-matter, that is, in its particular application. Its validation, as in science, takes the form of empirical verification. Clearly, a purely 'historical' predictive theory is unverifiable unless recourse is made to the future. Such a theory would be timeless and empirical verification could take place only in the present. Although past behaviour is not accessible to direct observation, nevertheless, as in science, recourse can be made to the observation of evidence from which one can infer behaviour. Direct observation of the individual behaviour of specific phenomena is not necessary in order to verify conclusions about the behaviour of the class of phenomena of which it forms a part. In other words, a scientific explanation is not invalidated because the behaviour of a single molecule cannot be either observed or predicted; and neither would a scientific explanation of historical phenomena be invalidated because the actual behaviour of an individual human being could not be observed or predicted. Empirical verification in this sense is concerned with classes of phenomena. As Danto puts it 'what scientists can directly observe may stand in no more intimate a relationship to their subject matter that what historians can observe – medals and manuscripts and potsherds – stand to theirs'.[1] In short, a scientific explanation of history is not made impossible because of the historian's inability to resurrect the past.

Nevertheless, some historians, including Weber, considered that a scientific explanation, although possible, would necessarily be limited because of the historian's concern for 'unique' events and for individual behaviour. While a scientific explanation provides a general theory and hence a structure for particular enquiries into historical phenomena, it does not go further. As Weber argued, 'the knowledge of causal laws is not the end of investigation but only a means. It facilitates and renders possible the causal imputation to their concrete causes of these components of a phenomenon the individuality of which is culturally significant.'[2] According to this argument, the historian is concerned with making an interpretation of individual and specific phenomena within a general theoretical framework. This would seem to avoid the major problem of relating theory to explanation and begs the question of 'causes'. The point about unique historical situations will be taken up later in this analysis; the question which will be considered at this stage is whether historical explanation is causal explanation and, if so, whether it corresponds to the kind of causal explanation found in science. This is not simply a question of urging a particular mode of explanation upon the historian, but one of evaluating the kinds of general propositions found in historical narratives.

The argument that history is a science is based on the assumption that a historian is concerned with explaining the occurrence of past events in terms of their origins. This concern may be explicit or implicit in historical argument. On this assumption the theoretical task of the historian is the isolation of causes from effects and in establishing the precedent conditions for particular historical phenomena. If terms such as 'causes', 'origins', 'influence', 'course', 'development', 'growth' or 'decline' are used in historical narratives, then implicitly, or explicitly, some causal hypothesis is implied in the argument. By cause is meant a statement of relationship between phenomena, such that X action resulted in Y event, and which also implies that Z action or N result would not have stemmed from the same interaction. More specifically, a causal argument is one which establishes not simply that Y existed, or occurred, but that it was a necessary consequence of X. In other words, such an assertion states that the necessary precondition for the occurrence of Y constituted the category X. The nature of this necessity implies the operation of some general law or proposition contained in the causal hypothesis. A full causal explanation would be able to establish the sufficient conditions for the event Y and thus establish a general proposition, governing not merely that particular event but all other occurences of that class or type of event. Such an explanation would be validated by empirical verification and would enable predictive statement.

Clearly, if these criteria apply, there is little or no difference between historical and scientific explanation: both can be judged on the same grounds. It has indeed been argued by some writers[3] that historical enquiry is not intrinsically different from scientific enquiry, because historians always assume a causal relationship when they are explaining specific phenomena. Even when historical enquiry is concerned with singular events, it 'aims at showing that the event in question was not "a matter of chance", but was to be expected in view of certain antecedent or simultaneous conditions'.[4] Thus Reichenbach argues that 'the logic of explanation is the same for historical and for physical events, historical explanation, like physical explanation consists in showing that the individual occurrence is of a pattern for which a general relationship can be established'.[5] According to these arguments, any statement about a particular historical situation which has implications beyond that situation or contains presuppositions governing it, requires a generalisation to support it, of which such a situation is only an instance. If it can be shown that these implications or conceptual presuppositions exist in historical narrative, then, of its nature, it falls into the category of explanation typified by science.

To refer back to the proposition that this kind of historical argument is really a genetic or causal argument, we can see that it is based on the notion that some relationship is presumed between events and their preconditions. The major question here is whether a statement of causes, or assumptions which presuppose causes, can be made, without it becoming necessarily subject to the criteria of validity for a fully predictive scientific theory. If historical explanation is indeed concerned with causes, is it necessarily concerned with achieving the theoretical criteria for genetic explanation in science?

It is asserted by some historians that while there is indeed a concern with causes in historical argument, it is not the same concern which is found in science. The historian asserts that there are relationships between historical events and phenomena and that some of them are necessary to the particular events which are the subject of an explanation. But necessity consists of no more than stating that they are precedent conditions for the events explained. In short, where some general causal argument is being advanced in historical narrative, all that is being said is that some phenomena were necessary preconditions for other phenomena. The sufficient conditions and the general law are not stated in this kind of argument. Any statement of optimal conditions for the existence of a phenomenon implies the kind of causal theory found in science. But the historian, it is asserted, does not need to go beyond this point in rendering the past intelligible.

Perhaps an example of a scientific approach towards historical phenomena might illustrate some of these theoretical problems. The most outstanding example, both in terms of its complexity and level of argument, and also in terms of its influence upon historians and social scientists, is the materialist theory of history propounded by Karl Marx.[6] This theory claimed to be a universal explanation of history which explained reality and not appearances. According to the argument, the objective conditions of a particular mode of production, which determined the nature of a particular society, were both created and dissolved by a historic process.[7] The nature of this process and its laws were left vague, and the distinction between the description of a specific state within the historical process and the process itself was left undetermined in the explanation. It is never clear, for example, whether Marx was describing the relationship between monetary capital and free labour in feudal society,[8] or whether he was stating a particular historical law which dissolved this relationship and produced a completely new state, that of capitalism. There is a constant ambiguity between the description of the operation of relationships within a historical situation and the working-out of a dynamic process of change which transforms it. Within a particular historical 'state' there is a causal hypothesis in which material factors and conditions determine human activities.

Nevertheless, implicit in this apparent ambivalence between the elucidation of a historical situation and the forces which created it, there is a conception of an underlying historical process which leads to generalisations about human behaviour which are empirically verifiable and thus scientific. The argument itself is founded upon premises which Marx considered to be axiomatic: for example, the premise that a condition for man's existence is a mode of production, however 'primitive'.[9] This leads to the assertion that 'the nature of individuals thus depends on the material conditions determining their production'.[10] The ensuing explanation is concerned with elucidating these conditions and revealing the various gradations and processes which led to the contemporary state of capitalism. As Marx put it:

> Empirical observation must in each separate instance bring out empirically and without mystification and speculation the connection of the social and political structure with production. The social structure and the state are continually evolving out of the life-processes of definite individuals, but of individuals not as they may appear in their own or in other people's imaginations, but as they really are: i.e. as they operate, produce materially and hence as they work under definite material limits, presuppositions and conditions independent of their wills.[11]

In his view, it was the task of the historian to elicit from history these conditions, not merely to provide an objective explanation of history, but in order to change it. The place of the individual and of his beliefs and values is subordinated to the material conditions of his productive system which create him. 'Conceiving, thinking, the mental intercourse of men, appear at this stage as the direct efflux of their material behaviour. The same applies to mental production as expressed in the language of politics, laws, morality, religion, metaphysics, etc., of a people.'[12] One is inclined to wonder how Marx succeeded in emancipating himself, and his own arguments, from the operation of this dictum.

The root cause of human behaviour, according to this argument, is not found in human consciousness or in the socio-political situation in which men find themselves, but in their objective material conditions. In order to exist, man is compelled to satisfy his material needs. In doing so he creates the conditions of production which then exert a compulsion on him. Social and political relationships are thus determined by human needs and the mode of production created to satisfy them. This mode of production has an objective existence over and above men's perception of it. The nexus between needs and their satisfaction 'is ever taking on new forms and thus presents a "history" independently of any political or religious nonsense which would especially hold men together'.[13] The point is not so much that Marx emphasised the importance of material conditions in shaping human beliefs and activities, as that he clearly believed that he had devised an explanation which explained almost everything in human existence, which corresponded more closely to reality than any other explanation, and which was also capable of empirical verification.

Relationships between men and the condition necessary for their existence are seen not in static terms, within the framework of the particular historical model, but as a process of transformation or 'dissolution'. Each generation inherits a mode of production,

> a mass of productive forces, capital funds and conditions, which on the one hand, is indeed modified by the new generation, but also on the other, prescribes for it its conditions of life and gives it a definite development, a special character. It shows that circumstances make men just as much as men make circumstances.[14]

From this it would appear that the historical process is not completely deterministic but permits particular societies to modify the conditions for their existence in various ways. In developing this argument, however, Marx did not make clear the distinction between the notion of successive historical stages governed by a specific process and the notion of free will in human choice. The latter is essential to any idea of men changing the conditions which determine the society in which they live. Revolution is immanent in successive societies but is not inevitable until certain necessary preconditions are met. One of these conditions is the creation of a conflict between labour and capital. Such a conflict was itself the product of a particular historical process.

This ambivalence is most clearly revealed in Marx's analysis of the pre-capitalist stages of history. Marx conceived of the 'Asiatic, the ancient, the feudal and the modern bourgeois methods of production as so many epochs of the economic formation of society'.[15] These stages, as Hobsbawm points out, are in the 'outcome not of theory but of observation'.[16] Marx continually asserts in his analysis that both his premises and his facts are observable and empirically testable. The question here is, how hypothetical are the successive stages of history which he describes? Or, to put it another way, was Marx concerned with the establishment of theoretical models loosely based upon actual historical situations but which were designed to illustrate a hypothesis rather than explaining the past? It must be admitted that there is considerable difficulty in establishing either position. Certainly, it can be shown that Marx's interpretation of primitive or feudal society is historically inaccurate in so far as the secondary sources from which he drew much of his material have been superseded by later discoveries and other interpretations. But does this necessarily invalidate his theory? If his argument is a theory of history, it ought to be testable in some acceptable way. If it is a historical explanation which does not claim to be scientific, then the question is one of which criteria are applicable to its evaluation. If it is purely hypothetical, the problem still remains of relating the historical content to the hypothesis. It is not possible to examine these questions in detail in this study, but the point here is that if Marx's argument is regarded as a theory of history, that is, as a scientific explanation of human behaviour, then the only acceptable test of its validity lies in its empirical verification. If it can be shown to be invalid in this sense, then it may have value in other terms, but not as a scientific explanation.

The difficulties involved in evaluating Marx's theory of history can perhaps be indicated by examining the notion of change and the historic process contained in it. This is the dynamic part of the argument and forms the very basis of the theory, for while the historical stages themselves may be only models or hypothetical illustrations, the idea of process itself depends on a level of generalisation and of abstraction, corresponding to theoretical behavioural laws. A dynamic law, as was shown in the earlier discussion of structural-functional theory, implies a normative entity to which change is related. This entity is provided in the form of a historical model. Its basis is a universal generalisation which establishes both the norm and the process of change related to it. Such historical models may be coeval or successive; the point is that they possess innate characteristics and are maintained by the operation of a process which also transforms them. The question is, how are these models related?

So far as Marx's conception of historical stages is concerned, does capitalism develop out of feudalism, or feudalism from primitive communalism? Or are these models illustrations of the working of a particular hypothesis which could produce any number of specific historic situations unrelated to each other? It is clear that the models actually described by Marx are both distinctive and dependent upon a common hypothesis which relates a mode of production to behaviour; but are they stages in a historical process? Moreover, within the models themselves, does the hypothesis constitute a theoretical explanation? Marx himself denied that he was concerned with a 'historico-philosophic theory of the general path that every people is fated to tread'.[17] In support of his position he cited the distinction between the dispossessed peasant of ancient Rome and that of post-feudal Europe. Although monetary capital appeared as a phenomenon in both cases, the peasants became, in the former case, a 'mob of do-nothings', while in the latter case they were transformed into the type of free labour characteristic of capitalist society. As he put it: 'Thus events strikingly analogous but taking place in different historical surroundings led to totally different results.'[18] Although this would suggest that Marx did not conceive of an inevitable progression from one particular historical stage to another, it leaves open the question of the relationship between them and, in particular, the question of 'successive' stages is begged. To sum up, it is not clear whether Marx conceived of the historical situations which he explains as stages or states.

Marx argues that the appearance of free labour, a necessary condition both for capitalism and for revolutionary situations, occurs because of a transformation process. As he put it:

> For the fact that the worker finds the objective conditions of his labour, as capital, and the fact that the capitalist finds the workers property-less as abstract labourers – the exchange as it takes place between value and living labour – assumes a historical process, however much capital and wage labour themselves reproduce this relationship and elaborate it in objective scope as well as in depth. And this historic process, as we have seen, is the evolutionary history of both capital and wage labour.[19]

The emergence of this situation is thus the consequence of a particular process in history. This suggests two things: firstly, that 'pre-capitalist economic formations' or stages are necessary in creating the conditions for capitalism; and secondly, that within the state of capitalism itself, as with its previous stages, the more a society seeks to maintain or preserve itself and its 'objective conditions of production', the more it accelerates the process itself and the transformation of society. In other words, the particular models or stages are not important in themselves but only in so far as they represent this dynamic of change.

The argument thus asserts that an entity capable of description exists which is composed of a specific form of community and property. This entity has its reality in a specific mode of production which determines, *inter alia*, social relationships. It seeks to perpetuate itself but in doing so brings about its dissolution, or transformation into a different form, and so on. Marx put this hypothesis explicitly by saying: '. . . the relationship of labour to capital or to the objective conditions of labour as capital presupposes an historic process which dissolves the different forms in which the labourer is an owner and the owner labours'.[20] Such a process is therefore one of dissolution and, more specifically, the transformation of primitive and feudal stages of society into capitalism. 'The historic process was one of the separation of hitherto combined elements'[21] and was 'not the result of capital but its prerequisite'.[22] In Marx's view, monetary capital is both an agent of dissolution but dissolution is also a condition of the transformation of monetary wealth into capital; it is therefore not a causal agent but acts as an accelerator or catalyst.

Thus Marx is not so much concerned with describing the appearance of capital and free labour in terms of their 'history', as with explaining them as phenomena. Such an explanation is both causal and universal in the same sense that, as we have seen, all aspects of human behaviour – politics, law, culture, ideology, social institutions, etc. – are created by the mode of production which prevails in a particular economic stage or state. The explanation profferred by Marx is a total one. Historians who do not accept this view of history 'have consequently only been able to see in history the political actions of princes and states, religions and all sorts of theoretical struggles and in particular in each historical epoch have had to share the illusions of that epoch'.[23] Reality for Marx lay in the recognition of a process of interaction between the material conditions of a mode of production and society and, as he put it: 'Life is not determined by consciousness, but consciousness by Life.'[24] An objective history is one which places its emphasis upon the influence of production upon society and in particular recognises capitalism as the culmination of a historic process.

It seems clear from this that Marx conceived of certain preconditions as hypothetically necessary for the appearance of capitalism. Hobsbawm cites these as being found in feudalism and consisting, firstly, of 'a rural social structure which allows the peasant to be "set free" at a certain point; second, the urban craft development which produces specialised, independent non-agricultural commodity production in the form of the crafts; and third, accumulations of monetary wealth derived from trade and usury'.[25] These phenomena constitute the necessary but not sufficient conditions for the appearance of capitalism. Their interaction brings about the process of dissolution which transforms feudalism into capitalism. The problem with this notion is that it is not clear whether Marx was seeking to explain a particular historical phenomenon, that of European capitalism in the nineteenth century, and was therefore primarily concerned with its 'history', or whether he was advancing a general hypothesis which explained human behaviour, past, present and future, in terms of 'the material conditions determining their production'. It would appear that he does both. Marx's conception of 'feudalism' is one which views it retrospectively as a necessary precursor to capitalism. In this sense it is not a state but a stage. But the implication contained in this argument is that there are specific necessary and sufficient preconditions for the appearance of capitalism. When these are satisfied, then the phenomenon will appear. This is a theoretical argument which implies a causal relationship between phenomena. It is one thing to say that there is a relationship between man and his environment, however these last may be defined, but the assertion of a particular relationship requires some general proposition to sustain it which is capable of validation. As Popper and others have pointed out,[26] a reference to determinism by needs ignores the purely idiosyncratic or individual aspect of social situations and in particular the possibility of the unintended consequences of human action. If the argument depends upon the assertion that 'objective material conditions', although created by man's activities, nevertheless exert a compulsion on him he does not control, then there must be some means of establishing the truth of this proposition which is itself immune from 'the illusions of the epoch'.

Thus although Marx believed that his material facts were 'definite' and concrete in a way which ideas were not, his analysis of human behaviour based upon 'objective reality' remains vague. It may be true, as Hobsbawm argues, that even if Marx's history is factually inaccurate or wrong in interpretation, his 'theory of historical materialism would remain unaffected',[27] but this is to beg the question as to the nature of such a theory. It may be criticised on the grounds of its vagueness, on the validity of the historical 'facts' selected as 'evidence', or on the level of historical generalisation derived from such facts, but the main criticism is levelled at its explanatory power. If it was a theory in the sense used in the previous chapter, that is, as a scientific theory, then it could be verified and would enable general and predictive statements about human behaviour. As it is, the argument makes the development of socialism from capitalism and capitalism from feudalism dependent upon the assertion of the prior existence of conditions which makes such a change possible. It thus falls into the category of hypotheses which assert optimum conditions for an activity or for a phenomenon, without explaining how these conditions come about or how they produce the phenomena which are being explained.

Thus while this argument is one which is both coherent and general, it is not empirically verifiable, nor does it in fact depend upon such verification in spite of Marx's contention that it is derived from observation. Of course, recourse may be made to 'facts' and phenomena which appear to confirm Marx's generalisations, but, as will be seen later in this study, this no more amounts to verification than the same recourse in support of a totally contradictory argument. If it is considered as a historical interpretation and not as a scientific theory, then it appears less coherent, and this not only because of the weakness of the actual historical models, but because the link between the general hypothesis and empirical 'reality' is diffuse. It is one thing to assert that social life is conditioned by material needs, and another when, for example, concrete evidence of what Hobsbawn calls the '*modus operandi* of feudal agriculture'[28] and its relationship to feudal society is lacking. The generalisation appears plausible but its application reveals a number of contradictions, especially in the areas of human motivations and beliefs.

It is possible to accept the distinction made by Avineri,[29] that a historical situation or 'state' such as capitalism can be used both as a theoretical model and as 'reality', but the difficulty arises when conclusions derived from the hypothetical model are applied to empirical reality. The hypothesis 'explains' only in very general terms, and while it may have heuristic or other value, it cannot be said that it explains any specific historical event or situation. In general terms, the comprehensiveness claimed for it by Marx does not hold good in practice, and the emphasis in it on economic or material causation is, as Weber said, 'one-sided'.[30]

So far as international politics is concerned, Marx accorded a specific significance for war,[31] in that the omnipresence of violence in human life acted as a social integrator for primitive communities and was thus a causal factor in creating early social organisations. It is also suggested that organisation for war was a major factor in establishing feudal society. Outside this special case, Marx regarded international conflict and politics as being simply extensions of national politics themselves stemming directly from the prevailing material conditions. The view of war as an economic force will be considered later in this study, as will the general theory of imperialism propounded by Hobson and Lenin.

Karl Marx was not alone, of course, in advancing a general theory of history which subsumed both past and future. Oswald Spengler[32] and Arnold Toynbee[33] both produced general explanations of the course of history which correspond in scope at least, if not in intellectual rigour, to that of Marx. These explanations are not strictly causal theories, although a cause is implied, nor do they claim the same kind of objectivity or empirical reality as that made by Marx. They are, however, intrinsically the same kind of theories, that is, they are theories *of* history. Other writers have offered similar teleological explanations of human history based not on the operation of general laws as such but on the innate natural or ethnic characteristics of man. Alfred Rosenberg, for example,[34] conceived of race, while Konrad Lorenz[35] and other ethologists conceived of instinctual aggression, as providing a partial explanation of human behaviour.

The main point about such explanations is that they impute a general proposition or law governing human behaviour, the operation of which explains the course of history. In this sense they are really implicit causal explanations which explain why events and activities have taken place in the past, which occur in the present and which will recur in the future, although for the most part they lack theoretical rigour in that the basic hypothesis is rarely clearly stated. The notion of objectivity in this type of argument consists of the recognition of the causal law to which all the behaviour which forms the subject of the explanation is related. Whatever the particular hypothesis, the purpose is the same, that is, to provide a single true explanation of complex human behaviour which excludes other more partial explanations. They are thus reductionist in nature. Such an explanation can be validated only on the same criteria as that of scientific argument. If validation through empirical verification is not possible, either because of the lack of rigour in the theoretical argument or because of the nature of the general proposition which is being advanced, they are not objective in the scientific sense of objectivity, or true, unless some alternative criterion for establishing their validity is advanced. Such explanations have the form but lack the substance of scientific argument.

If it is argued that causal propositions, although inseparable from historical narrative, do not constitute its chief characteristic, and that they cannot be made explicit and validated without the explanation changing its nature, then on what basis can historical argument be validated? If two conflicting explanations of the same phenomena, or two contradictory generalisations, are advanced, then how can they be reconciled or refuted? It would appear, as Danto argues,[36] that unless there is common agreement on the criteria used for validation, there can be neither agreement nor disagreement between proponents of conflicting explanations of the past. Such arguments are valid only within their own terms and are therefore incommunicable either as explanation or as knowledge. They may be communicable on other levels, that is, as aesthetic experience or through intuitive or emotional responses. This question of which criteria are relevant for historical truth is the most crucial theoretical problem, for on its solution depends the notion of history as a coherent and specific explanation. If it is not answered satisfactorily, then what is termed 'historical argument' either forms part of some other form of explanation subject to its particular critical criteria, which is what is claimed by some social scientists, or else it constitutes purely subjective and idiosyncratic narrative. In the absence of such a test, historians lack the common ground necessary to engage in 'genuine agreements or disagreements'[37] about the nature and validity of their arguments. It may be, as Danto has argued, that since no absolute standard exists even in scientific explanation, then historical argument is not in this sense different from any other form of argument. But as was pointed out earlier in this study, while empirical verification in science is not an absolute test of validity, it constitutes a commonly recognised test of scientific hypotheses. It may be true, as this writer avers, that 'History is no more and no less subject to the relativist factors than science is',[38] but this is not the main point, since in the latter case there is a clear notion of truth, even if this is a negative one, in that a contrary instance invalidates a theoretical conclusion, rather than that conformity between conclusions and empirical reality 'proves' a hypothesis to be true. In this sense there is no 'objective' standard of validity in the scientific argument which is clearly recognisable by scientists.

A different notion of objectivity has been adopted by some historians. This is based on the idea of the totality of past experience and asserts that the historian's main task lies in its reconstruction. All partial or general historical explanations are both parts of such a reconstruction and may be assessed in terms of their relationship to this objective reality. It therefore constitutes a purpose and a goal for historians, as well as providing a standard for evaluation. Thus the difficulty of establishing a specific criterion such as that of empirical verification, or of providing a causal theory, is avoided.

It can be said, if this notion of historical objectivity means the achievement of a generally true explanation of the totality of the past, then, as in the case for scientific explanation in the social sciences, no such explanation has yet been achieved. Whether it can be attained, or how it would be recognised and validated on its attainment, are questions best left open at this stage. What can be said is that a historian's factual knowledge of the past, as opposed to his conception of meaning or significance, is necessarily limited. His substantive data or material consists of 'evidence' of past events in the form of artefacts and records and other histories. These are incomplete in a way which cannot be established with any certitude. The total past, in the sense of its survival into the present, cannot therefore be known. In practice the historian selects from the historical record, and the basis of his selection has no theoretical or objective justification unless it is related to some hypothesis or theoretical explanation which is itself subject to validation. The question as to what constitutes evidence is one which can only be answered in terms of the argument to which it is related. Only in a very loose sense can the selection or treatment of such evidence be conceived of as part of an attempt to reconstruct the 'total' past.

As we have seen in the case of Marxist explanation, the material conditions of life and the hypothesis related to the mode of production determine the major categories of data which are selected and used to support the hypothesis. Furthermore, the hypothesis itself is applied to the total past and thus used to explain as well as to determine what is 'evidence'. Similarly, in Toynbee's hypothesis of the growth and decline of civilisations and the general law of challenge and response,[39] the argument itself determines what is selected as evidence in its support, as well as 'explaining' the past. Yet some historians have asserted that arguments stem from the facts and that it is possible to conduct an investigation into the past without any presuppositions or distorting hypotheses. We may reject the over-simplifications of the historicists without accepting this argument. Unless the historian has a positively omnivorous appetite for everything

which is recorded of the past and which exists in his present – and, as we
have seen, such a record is incomplete in a way which is unknown – then
he must perforce select. It may be that certain historians have engaged in
a kind of academic coal-mining for facts, and that their activities correspond to those described by Roy Campbell in his famous quatrain:

> You praise the firm restraint with which they write
> I'm with you there of course.
> They use the snaffle and the curb alright
> But where's the bloody horse?[40]

But however arid the researches of such scholars appear to be, they are not
totally devoid of some assumptions about the subject of their enquiries or
of its value in terms of general interpretation.

Moreover, it can be argued that the establishment of facts about the past
does not distinguish historical explanation from any other kind of exercise
in 'fact-gathering', even if such an activity can be conceived of as void of
any presuppositions about the relationship between fact and argument.
Thus the geologist and the archaeologist are equally concerned about the
past in this sense, although their activities amount to considerably more
than establishing facts. If it is retorted that the historian, unlike the
geologist or botanist, is concerned with the establishment of facts about
past *human* activities, then this in itself presupposes some criterion of
selection. However, few historians seek to maintain this distinction and
the writer shares the common assumption that history is concerned with
aspects of human behaviour in the past, and not with the 'history' of ideas,
art, music, literature, etc., except in so far as these phenomena are related
to behaviour itself. Thus social, economic and cultural, as well as political,
histories are all part of a common concern with man and his past. Nevertheless, it is as well to be aware that 'events' in history are no more (or less)
concrete than 'ideas', and in a general sense a historian is concerned with
man's perception and experience, not with tangible objects.

Thus one may agree that the discovery of facts is necessarily part of a
historian's activity, but also recognise that the nature of historical explanation lies in the interpretation of facts, not in their exposition.[41] This is to
say that a collection of facts, however apparently miscellaneous, implies
some criterion of selectivity, but that such a collection in itself does not
constitute history. The distinction between history and chronicle which is
sometimes made is not a very clear one, for even the dreariest catalogue of
'facts' related to the early Church, for example, implies some organisation,
even if its purpose is that of the glorification and vindication of the ecclesias-
tical institutions to which the chronicler belongs. The past in such accounts
was not studied for its own sake but for the sake of some presently held
belief. In this sense such a chronicle is an interpretation, and it is this
interpretation which constitutes history. If it is urged that the 'objective'

truth in historical explanation consists of stating a kind of total reality for the past, and that this consists of a reconstruction of the total past, then this poses a number of problems which are left largely unanswered. The total past cannot be known either in the sense of complete knowledge of the facts or in the sense of historical experience. Such a goal, in view of the incompleteness of the surviving evidence and the subjective nature of the criteria used to select, define and interpret 'evidence', appears to be unattainable.

An alternative view has been put forward, which seeks to avoid both the theoretical problems of advancing general explanations and also the difficulties of the notion of the 'totality' of the past. According to this argument, a historian is concerned with the reconstruction of unique events. This is perhaps a variant on the notion that history is concerned with elucidating facts from the past, and it can be criticised on the same grounds. But as was pointed out earlier, any statement about a particular situation which either has wider implications or contains presuppositions implies some generalisation to support it, of which such a situation is only an instance. The selection of the event in question, together with its antecedents and its consequences, contains such implications, however restricted the historical focus may appear to be. It may of course be advanced that the historian is not concerned with pursuing these implications or indeed with formulating broad general propositions which apply to all such situations, but again this is to avoid the central theoretical problem of establishing both the nature of his enquiry and the acceptable criteria for its evaluation. Without doing this, each such 'reconstruction' is equally valid or invalid. Few historians would accept this in practice. Since the totality of the past cannot be known and thus used as a criterion of 'objectivity', any attempt at reconstructing part of it is both selective and dependent upon theorising, conceptual or organising criteria. Such criteria may be implicit in the narrative or defined and made explicit, but even if they are not so systematised they exist none the less.

Following from this it has been argued that while the past in the sense of an external total reality is unknowable, ' "the past" is a construction we make for ourselves out of the events which take place before our eyes'.[42] Historical knowledge, in this view, consists of the historian's creation of the past rather than his discovery or reconstruction of it. The position that the historical past is an unknowable constitutes scepticism, and the position that all historical judgements are innately based and equally subjective in their nature constitutes relativism. Now while we may agree that the past is indeed unknowable, it can be argued that this in any case does not consist of history, for historical knowledge consists of a construction, either of thought, or of what is termed experience, and consequently is not subject to an external objective test derived from the notion of correspondence between the explanation and an external past reality. We can see from this that historical knowledge and explanation in this sense are radically different from the notion of scientific knowledge and explanation discussed in earlier chapters. Of course, this leaves open the problem of making evaluations of constructions of thought and experience. In other words, the argument that there can be no true knowledge of the past, while sceptical about the possibility of *discovering* history, does not invalidate a notion of history which conceives of the past as something which the historian *creates*.

Historical knowledge, according to this view, consists of a re-experiencing of the thought of historical agents or, alternatively, the establishment of a coherent world of ideas. Collingwood,[43] the proponent of the first notion, asserts that the historian is concerned with events, not in the sense that a scientist is concerned with phenomena, that is, as a concrete and, in principle, observable happening, but with the thought which is asserted as being always present in events representing human action. An event consists of an external and internal dimension, the former category constituting material, circumstantial, descriptive, referential and contingent elements, and the latter of intention, motivation and purpose, intimately connected with the material factors.[44] The historian is concerned with both, in the sense that he is concerned with the unity between the corporeal nature of an event and the thought to which it is related. To understand, or to explain, history means establishing the connection between thought and action, and consequently the special concern of the historian is always with thought in this relationship. It is important to point out that Collingwood is not concerned with thought alone, any more than he is solely concerned with the external nature of an event. He is concerned with a relationship between the two, and when he is in a position to say what this relationship is, then he has explained not only what has happened but also why it has happened. It will be seen from this that there are close similarities with the notion of sociological knowledge propounded by Weber, discussed earlier.

Now the historian is not merely re-enacting the past, that is, discovering what X agent thought in connection with Y event, but with re-enacting this 'in the context of his own knowledge, and therefore in re-enacting it, criticises it, forms his own judgement of its value, corrects whatever errors he can discern in it'.[45] This activity, which Collingwood calls criticism, is not merely a secondary but an 'indispensable condition of the historical knowledge itself'.[46] Historical knowledge is thus a process of understanding which consists of a re-thinking of the thoughts-in-connection-with-events of the past (taken from present evidence), but in the light of the historian's own intellectual context. Hence history is not reconstruction but construction or creation, and one component of it is the individual historian's psyche. Not only will each such historical recreation differ from historian to historian, and from generation to generation, but the same historian can have different creations, during his lifetime, of the same thoughts-in-events of a historical agent. As he put it, 'the historian's thought must spring from the organic unity of his total experience and be a function of his entire personality with the practical as well as its theoretical interests.'[47]

Thus the historian is his own authority for historical explanation,[48] and his criteria for selecting and interpreting evidence are based upon his experience of the world. It is not possible to assess his arguments on the basis of past facts or evidence because they are defined by the historian's own selection and usage. A challenge from one historian to another on these grounds is simply a challenge of differing experiences, and the notion of evidence as a criterion of validity is thus itself invalid. What then is the criterion for historical truth if this idea of historical knowledge is accepted? It is found in the argument itself. The historian himself decides whether his argument 'gives him a coherent and continuous picture . . . which makes sense. The *a priori* imagination which does the work of historical construc- tion supplies the means of historical criticism as well'.[49]

This argument leads on to the view propounded by Oakeshott that historical knowledge consists of experience, or rather can only consist of experience. By experience is meant thought, or judgement, which also includes sensation, reflection, volition, feeling and intuition.[50] While these elements can be defined and made distinct, they cannot be separated from experience, which alone constitutes a unity. Thus unity is a world of ideas created through the transformation of the given into a coherent whole. Such a world is absolute in the sense that it must contain no ambiguity or alternatives, that is, it 'requires neither modification nor supplement and it is operative always and everywhere . . . it is alone and complete in itself'.[51] This is clearly a theory of knowledge proper and is not simply confined to history. Two aspects only will be considered here, the first being the notion of historical knowledge as a mode of experience, and the second the grounds of validation which Oakeshott terms coherence. In his view historical argument is what he called an 'arrest' of experience.[52] By this he means that a mode of experience falls short, or is arrested, of the absolute coherent unity which is experience itself. Nevertheless, it is in itself coherent. The truth of a mode of experience is thus always relative, relative to the degree of completeness which belongs to its world of ideas and its organisation of reality.

Like Collingwood, Oakeshott argues that the past is unknowable except in the sense of the historian's own constructions. History is the historian's own experience and is not 'the correspondence of an idea with an event for there is no event which is not an idea . . . there is no fact in history which is not a judgement, no event which is not an inference'.[53] How may such constructions be judged? Since the absolute criterion of coherence can- not apply to a mode of experience which is itself arrested, the judgement must be confined to the construction itself. It must be coherent, but such coherence is a relative and therefore imperfect coherence. Truth is defined as 'the coherence of the world of experience; a world of ideas is true when it is coherent and because it is coherent'.[54]

What can be said of this argument so far as historical knowledge and its evaluation are concerned? It provides us with a means of distinguishing between types of explanation and it also provides us with a definition of the proper subject-matter for history. It is not past facts or past evidence; it is rather the experience of the historian in terms of his thought or his world of ideas. But there is clearly a problem in relating this to the notion of the past. History, in Oakeshott's words, 'recognises an obligation to what actually happened or it becomes indistinguishable from fiction'.[55] In Collingwood's words, the historian's construction must be true, 'that is he must construct a picture of things as they really were and of events as they really happened'.[56] But reality for these arguments consists not of facts, or of events or their relationships, but in the historian's conception of reality. We are faced with the same problem as that found in the evaluation of the conceptual schemes discussed in the preceding chapter, that is, what is the test of reality? If it is to be found in the historian's own construction, then clearly reality as an external objectivity does not, and indeed according to these arguments cannot, exist. The only test of a true fact or of a true reality lies in what the historian conceives of as being true, and the test for this lies in the coherence of the world of ideas which he has created, not in the external reality of his facts.

It is clear that there is a notion of a relationship between thought and events in these arguments. While a fact cannot be separated from the judgement which selected and interpreted it, nevertheless there is a relationship between the two in which the fact and the judgement coexist. If history is not fiction, then one of these elements – the fact – must be attestable in some way outside the context of the argument. There must be a criterion for distinguishing between the real and the imaginary other than simply a definition of reality, if historical arguments are to be communicable. If we return to the Collingwoodian conception of history, we can see that thought was part of an event. The corollary of this is that where there is no evidence of thought, the event is of no historical significance. If we do not know what was in William the Conqueror's mind, then we cannot offer an adequate explanation of the Battle of Hastings or of the Norman Conquest. Only past events which possess the internal dimension of intentions and purpose belong properly to historical explanation. Even if we accept this, there are certain difficulties in establishing the relationship between expressed thought and the external dimension of the event. We cannot make any meaningful statement other than that of describing what the expressed thought was, unless we are also in a position to establish what the external dimension was. We cannot simply assume this to be given. We may, for example, have the surviving record of William the Conqueror's thought, but if we are unable to relate it to events then we are not able, in these terms, to undertake a historical explanation.

In short, on this argument, the external dimension of events is necessary to such an explanation, and if we know nothing of it then we cannot engage in historical argument. Consequently it is a necessary and legitimate part of the historian's task to seek to reconstruct or to discover this dimension, since, unlike thought, it cannot speak for itself. The historian cannot *create* facts, for if he does then they become fiction. Certainly, not all past facts are necessarily historical facts; they become so in the sense that it is the historian's own interpretation which makes them historical, but they must exist in a sense which is distinguishable from interpretation, and it must be established that they exist before the historian can interpret them. As Collingwood recognised, a historian's concern with facts is to discover something: 'His business is not to invent something, it is to discover something.'[57] Unlike the constructions of the historian, which are valid in their own terms, it would seem that common agreement is necessary on 'facts' if history is not to be historical fiction. We may agree that the nature of historical explanation lies in the interpretaion of facts, but recognise that the discovery of facts is a necessary part of this activity and that this will include not only the intentions and purposes of the historical agents, but the external dimension and its context also. There is clearly a dilemma here, for even if inference is used to induce facts where there is no direct evidence for them, such induction depends upon other facts for which there is such evidence.

However, if we leave the general sceptical position – that is, that the past is unknowable – aside for the moment, and beg the question as to whether there is a particular form of historical knowledge which is not concerned with a knowable past, we shall find certain difficulties in the kind of relativism, implicit in the argument above. Truth, as we have seen, for both Collingwood and Oakeshott, consists of the coherence of the world of ideas, of the experience, or of the argument, in historical explanation. In the case of the latter the truth lies in an absolutely coherent experience which constitutes a unity. Modes of experience cannot therefore be judged other than in terms of this absolute. Degrees of coherence would thus appear to be a logical impossibility, and the argument that historical explanation should be judged on the basis of its coherence would seem to avoid the problem of defining coherence outside its absolute form. If incomplete worlds of ideas can exist, in what way can they be evaluated other than by asserting that they are incomplete? If it is accepted that coherence neither requires, nor recognises, any external test or guarantee, and that arguments should be judged on their own terms, this leaves open the question as to what these terms might be. In short, while we might accept the distinctiveness of historical explanation or understanding in terms of other kinds of explanation, we are unable to make critical judgements about particular historical explanations without common agreement of criteria for such judgements. Either we share the same experience or we do not, and if we do not then we are unable to disagree or to agree.

Collingwood appears to be more aware of this critical difficulty, probably because he was also concerned in writing history. For him, while the historian is his own judge in the sense that his criteria of selection and his interpretations are 'on his own authority'.[58] and that the judgements of other historians, past or contemporary, should not be accepted as evidence, nevertheless he argues that 'it is only by his peers that any claimant to knowledge is justified'.[59] Yet almost in the same breath he advances the rather arrogant claim that 'the only way of knowing whether a given type of argument is cogent or not is to learn how to argue that way and find out'.[60] One must be a believer first before one is competent to judge. Thus even if we agree that historical understanding takes the form argued by Oakeshott and Collingwood, we are unable to communicate beyond this recognition, for we are each locked in our own experience.

Yet while this idealist view of the nature of historical knowledge has found little support in contemporary historical writing, the assertion is often made that part, at least, of a historian's interpretation consists of intuitive judgement. In this view a historian should have a 'feel' for the period of time or the society or institution which he studies. It is urged that presently held beliefs or values should not intrude into the interpretation of the past as anachronisms. But if interpretation in history is to be dependent in some way on an intuitive understanding, then some criteria for evaluating such arguments should be established by historians, if their explanations are to be communicable on a non-aesthetic level. Even if the idealist position is rejected, any notion that history is dependent upon the understanding of the historian poses this problem of critical criteria.

Moreover, it is possible to argue that the intuitive understanding of a historian is as much a product of his own psychology and his own personal values as a reconstruction of the values, experience and motivations of those engaged in past events, even where evidence exists for this kind of reconstruction. There are clearly great difficulties in meeting the requirement that the 'thought' of historical agents should be elucidated or 'experienced' by the historian without prejudicing the interpretation by the introduction of his own beliefs.

As will be seen later when the question of 'contemporary' history is considered, there are fundamental difficulties in establishing a connection between experience, motives and actions in human behaviour, even where sources of information exist. The major problem in this conception of historical understanding appears to be not so much that the anachronistic application of presently held values and beliefs to the past cannot be avoided, as that, in the absence of any acceptable criteria for the evaluation of intuitive argument, it is impossible to distinguish between one interpretation and another *except* in terms of one's own values and beliefs. Criticism and judgement are no less subjective in this sense. Such interpretation does not constitute an explanation in the sense used earlier in this study, unless there are such criteria. Thus while the subject–matter of the historian, or even the central problem which faces him, might include the evaluation of motivation and reasoning in past human behaviour, it cannot be said that this excludes other considerations, nor that the empathetic relationship between the historian and the participant in history does not require adequate definition. One man's understanding may not be another's, and this view of history poses problems similar in nature to those found in establishing criteria for aesthetic judgement in art and literature.

It could also be argued that such an intuitive understanding implies the existence of a rational or hypothetical argument, in that the inference is that if the historian were so motivated or subjected to the same contextual circumstances or conditions, he would act in a particular way; or, conversely, that this hypothetical reasoning can be deducted from the action. Such an argument is a rationalist explanation by removes. This is not of course an inevitable concomitant of an emphasis on 'understanding', but this implication exists in any assumption of motives which cannot be directly attributed to an actor in a historical situation. As will be seen later in this study where political decisions are considered in the context of international politics, this type of argument is based on the notion of rational behaviour or of the rational observer, i.e. the historian or commentator, without establishing the theoretical basis of the explanation or the criteria on which rationality may be judged. The main problem involved in the consideration of the 'feel' of a historian as a characteristic of the explanation which he offers is that it cannot be evaluated or tested in any meaningful sense. It may be true, as Collingwood asserted, 'that the only way to tackle any historical question, such as the tactics of Trafalgar . . . was to see what the different people concerned were trying to do',[61] or, to be more precise, what they thought they were doing. But this raises questions of even greater magnitude than those arising out of the assertion of causation or of a continuum or process in history, which this particular view of history rejects, on the grounds that it ignores the human element in explanations of the past.

We can say perhaps that the factor of 'thought', conceived of as motivation and experience related to action, is relevant to any explanation of the past, but that this is not the historian's exclusive concern. The main point here is that an explanation which does not state the terms of its argument and the criteria on which it is based is not an explanation in the sense used in the earlier part of this study. The major theoretical problem raised by Collingwood and other exponents of the 'understanding' of history is not answered. This is the definition of what it is which constitutes 'experience' in terms both of the participant's and of the historian's understanding, and how it may be evaluated.

This leaves us, however, with the same questions with which we began this study. In the absence of the kind of test referred to earlier in this discussion when scientific explanation was considered, we are forced to accept the subjective judgement of historians. But what is the nature of this subjectivity? Is it susceptible to tests of any description? If 'objectivity' in historical explanation consists of the discounting of particular elements, then clearly what is discounted, or rather the grounds for discounting, will constitute a rule or convention which can be applied to historical narrative. This is a reduced view of the notion that objective truth in historical explanation can only be achieved by the historian making a conscious effort, as Beard put it, to 'divest himself of all taints of religious, political, philosophical, social, sex, economic, moral and aesthetic interests[62] as an influence upon his enquiry. If this view is accepted, then 'objectivity' in this sense really means the discounting of value, prejudice or ideological elements from a historical explanation.

Yet it is difficult to see how this kind of emancipation from values is possible, and, as we have seen earlier, some historians, at least, hold the notion that historical judgement consists of a 'reliving' of the past in the sense of understanding the experiences of those engaged in past events. It is hard to conceive of this without reference either to shared experiences or feelings, or to some recognition founded upon the historian's own extant awareness of his own society. A historian must himself be able to relate to the past, and in doing this he runs the risk of anachronistic judgement, or of attributing thoughts and feelings to the past, in rational or general terms, which are not supported by evidence. The key to a historical know-ledge, in this sense, lies in the historian's *own* experience.

A distinction can be made between the view that contemporary beliefs and values should not obtrude upon this understanding, and the view that history consists of their application to the past. This last argument was advanced by Meinecke,[63] who asserted that the value element in historical interpretation was not merely implicit and ineradicable but was a pre-requisite. In his view a historian should not seek to conceal or deprecate value judgements, but should conceive of his task as being their vindication. This point of view is put neatly by Dray, who said:

> . . . historical enquiry might thus be said to employ two standpoints; it seeks to understand past ages as far as possible in their own terms, but it does this preparatory to judging them in broader terms. Since the standards employed at the second level will be those which the historian believes in the present to be valid it might be said that present values ought to enter historical reconstruction.[64]

'Significance' and 'meaning' in historical interpretation are thus intimately related to the present. While historical anachronisms should be avoided in reconstructing the past, the reconstruction itself will always be both influenced by, and relative to, the historian's present. The historian is concerned not only with explaining present traces of the past, but also with his own experience in relation to this.

According to these arguments, a value-free history is not only impossible but should not be attempted by the historian. The question here, however, is, what are meant by values? Are values simply assumptions about the nature of things which constitute presuppositions about the phenomena being explained and which do not form part of an empirically testable argument? Are they ethical or moral judgements of good and evil containing prescriptions for human behaviour? Or are they concepts founded upon contemporary beliefs but which are anachronistic when applied to an interpretation of the past?

For example, the relationship between ethical or moral beliefs and the use of expressions in historical narrative such as 'peace', 'repression', 'atrocity', 'terrorism', 'purge', 'dangerous', 'aggression ','menace', 'success', 'failure', 'right' and 'wrong' can be established by reference to the context in which they are used. Words with pejorative or approbatory connotations can be related relatively easily to the user's values. But less obvious is the use of expressions such as 'race', 'state', 'liberty', 'freedom', 'rights', 'civilisation', 'culture', 'nation' and 'society', which may be used in the way indicated above, but which may also be derived from one historical context and applied to periods of time where they are either inappropriate, hold a different meaning, or simply did not exist as concepts. And less obvious still are the value or belief connotations of assumptions about normative behaviour, which are implicitly used in historical narrative, and which form the hidden theorising assumptions used to organise the argument. Examples of this category of value or connotative expressions are found in the use of terms such as 'growth', 'decline', 'origins', 'interests', 'essential' and 'significant'. Finally, there are those analogues or metaphorical terms borrowed from non-historical arguments which were referred to in previous chapters. These include many expressions culled from the physical and natural sciences such as 'organ', 'function', 'system', 'balance', 'power', 'energy', 'mass', 'catalyst', and so on.

Of course, such expressions may be defined and their meaning and usage made explicit within the terms of the particular argument. However, as will be seen later in this examination, it is doubtful if their meaning is solely confined to specific arguments. It is the contention here that while a historian may be able to make an explicit exclusion of specific beliefs from his interpretation, it is not possible to eliminate beliefs altogether or to restrict them in such a way as to confine their meaning to a particular argument. Such terms properly belong to areas of experience and meaning which transcend the specifically historical.

Clearly, there may be agreement among some historians that moral or ethical values should be discounted from historical narrative. It has been pointed out by many social scientists that in scientific explanation 'ought' questions or statements are neither relevant, nor present, in the argument. It may be true that the scientist is influenced by his own cultural or social environment and that he does not, as Danto puts it, 'go naked into the laboratory',[65] but the products of his researches and discoveries are, as we have seen, verifiable in a recognisable way, and the test itself is not subject to the influence of values. Objectivity in scientific explanation is no more than this; and while the selection of the problem may be subject to value or other objective influence, its answer is not.

Thus while contemporary historians are also agreed that 'ought' questions should be deleted from their arguments, there is no general agreement on criteria for establishing the relevance or validity of other kinds of pre-suppositions. For example, while it may be conventional at present to discount the notion of race or innate ethnic characteristics from historical interpretations, it is not possible to discount all value statements. A modern historian might perhaps criticise the following passage taken from a book which is still used as a text:

The Prussian is a distinctive European type. Goethe, who lived in Weimar and may be taken to represent the mid-German view of the Prussians, speaks of them as barbarians. There was an uncouth vigour and asperity about this remarkable people which jarred on the more refined susceptibilities of the Saxon, the Franconian and the Rhinelander. To what causes the special characteristics of the Prussian race are to be attributed, whether to the Slavonic blood which flows through their veins, or to the harsh north German climate, or to the stern military tradition which nature imposes on a state undefended by geographical frontiers or, if to all these causes, in what proportion: these are questions which admit of no precise answer.[66]

But while this set of undeveloped hypothetical propositions and its assumptions of racial characteristics might be attacked, either because of the absence of theoretical rigour, or because it implies hypotheses about human nature and behaviour which have been refuted by arguments outside the field of historical interpretation, few would criticise the assumptions contained in a more recent historical work which relate to the notion of power. For example, the statement 'In the 1440s there began to form in certain Italian minds a conception of Italy as a system of independent states, coexisting by virtue of an unstable equilibrium which it was the function of statesmanship to preserve',[67] contains certain conceptual generalisations. Of course, the notion of balance in this statement is attri-buted to the political practitioners of the time, but subsequent descriptions of Italy as 'an unstable balance of power, a precarious counterpoising of the conflicting interests of jealous sovereign states',[68] depend upon the general conception of 'dynastic power politics' advanced by the author as a coherent organising hypothesis for his narrative.[69] The point here is not that the use of such organising concepts in historical interpretation is in some way illegitimate, but that it is unavoidable. The use of general concepts depends upon the relation of historical interpretation to explanations in non-historical fields and to prevailing conventions in the area of historical writing. It may be possible to regard scientific explanation as being independent of other explanations and as being essentially non-conceptual in its approach, but historical interpretation is intimately related to concepts and attitudes which lie outside its immediate focus. As they change, so does the conceptual content of historical explanation. This does not necessarily mean that historical explanation lacks distinctive characteristics as an explanation, or that the existence and nature of these presuppositions determine its nature as an explanation, but that it is related to other forms of explanation so far as its concepts are concerned.

If it is accepted that agreement exists among historians to the effect that values and value judgements of a particular nature should be discounted, the problem remains as to which values should be excised, and which retained, in historical interpretation. Whatever is accepted or rejected in this sense depends upon the existence of some convention consciously applied by historians. Where there is common agreement on such conventions, it is possible to continue to the next stage of evaluative criticism. Thus the notion of 'objective' history takes on the meaning given to it by the specific convention prevalent in a particular historical school. This is, of course, already the case for historical schools which accept an ideological framework for their arguments. Such a convention is clearly neither universal nor permanent, but it has the virtue, such as it is, of being explicit and recognisable. This is to accept, moreover, that a total emancipation from the past is not possible and to argue, in E. H. Carr's words, that 'History acquires meaning and objectivity only when it establishes a coherent relation between past and future'.[70] The coherence, however, must be related to some accepted convention if it is to have meaning. It is clear from the example given above that historical explanations which are based upon the notion of innate racial characteristics are not currently in fashion with contemporary historians. Such a notion is derived from non-historical sources and indeed cannot be verified by any specifically historical test. Similarly, what Herbert Butterfield has termed the 'Whig interpretation of history'[71] is out of current fashion, although there are traces of this kind of implicit bias in the predilection of some historians for what has been called a Marxist approach. However, it is not proposed to examine changing fashions in historical interpretation, but to make the point that there is such a thing as historical fashion and that it stems from the major characteristic of historical argument. The reason why, as Collingwood put it, 'every new generation must re-write history in its own way',[72] is because of the intuitive or subjective element in it which is the major distinction between historical and certain other forms of explanation. From what has been said, the subject-matter of history is not its chief peculiarity, nor is the presence or absence of hypothetical or theoretical argument significant in this sense. History is subjective in that it consists of the interpretation of past events and experiences in terms of the historian's *own* predilections and intuitive judgements. It is this last, that is, the historian's own under-standing, which constitutes history.

It should therefore not surprise us to find that such an understanding will vary not only from generation to generation, but also from historian to historian. A multiplicity of interpretations of specific historical subjects, rather than orthodoxy, is a characteristic of historical argument, although it is generally true that each generation of historians has its own hallmark, its own characteristics which demarcate it from earlier generations and which perhaps constitute the main point of departure from them. This is not to say that 'history has no meaning, or a multiplicity of equally valid or invalid meanings or the meaning which we arbitrarily choose to give to it'.[73] Meaning in historical interpretation can be defined but not validated. There are, in this argument, no means of applying the same test of validity which is found in scientific explanation. In the absence of such a test we can judge historical arguments as being either untestable hypotheses, or as explanations of differing types of subjectivity. The choice between them, in critical terms, does not depend upon 'objective' criteria or upon 'validity', but upon their heuristic or their aesthetic qualities, or upon the temporal judgements of scholars, these last being no less subjective than the interpre-tations which they judge.

Thus we are faced in historical criticism with the application of criteria of judgement which are themselves subjective. The assertion of good and bad for particular historical interpretations will depend on values, on aesthetic grounds, on rationalist criteria and on logic. We can distinguish between an argument which is ideological, requiring a belief in something which cannot be established on a rational basis, or which demands the acceptance of a moral position or an ethic, from an argument which does not make such a demand. Similarly, we can distinguish between fact and fiction, and it is possible to say of an argument that it rests on insufficient grounds, or that alternative and conflicting inferences may be derived from the same premises, or the same evidence, or that the grounds are selected 'unfairly' in order to support a prejudiced conclusion. Thus although inter-pretations may differ, and a universal means of establishing validity may not exist, they are all related to the problem of establishing an argument and the selection of evidence, and to the question of how much strain this can take in supporting a case. But outside this critical activity the problem remains of validating or establishing the general hypotheses, the conceptual framework and the theorising assumptions which form an indispensable part of any historical argument. Unless the view is taken that more and more data about the past will mean better and better explanations in terms of their validity, we are bound to admit that historical judgement is itself temporal. The explanation of yesterday may be different from that of today, but that of today is no more valid. Since it is not possible to assert a criterion of objectivity, other than in the sense of historical conventions, we are forced to resort to relativist judgement related to some specific criterion. Such criteria are themselves subject to change, and therefore we shall have shifting standards of criticism from one historical school to another. The activity of historical writing and judgement is thus a continual critical exercise which does not lead to a finite or universal explanation of human behaviour in the past.

This does not mean that all historical writing is equally valid or invalid, for although we may not be able to establish an 'objective' standard for testing historical truth, it is possible to define a criterion for judgement as a set of conventions agreed on by writers of history. Good or bad historical writing is what historians themselves believe to be good or bad. Judgement is possible where the rules for historical writing are made explicit, and this implies a conscious effort on the part of historians to supply the critical criteria with their actual narratives. This would mean, *inter alia*, that Marxist history is as 'valid' as any other, but also that there is good and bad Marxist history, and that it should be judged on different criteria from the 'histories' of other schools. On this argument there are several sets of criteria which can be used for historical criticism, which should not be confused. Many of the major controversies between historians could have been avoided if the central issue was conceived of as which criteria were relevant to historical criticism. Clearly, in the absence of general agreement on the nature of historical explanation, there is likewise no agreement on a single set of criteria for judging historical interpretations. But the claims of particular historical schools that their forms of explanation pre-empt all other claims to historical truth are untenable in the absence of criteria for establishing the objective nature of this truth.

To return to the argument in the early part of this study, it was asserted that there is no theoretical division between explanation in social science and in history. Theories in the sense of untestable empirical hypotheses and conceptual schemes abound in both fields. As we have seen, the systematic attempt to explain social and political phenomena in terms of conceptual schemes led directly to the creation of an ideal world. Such a world constituted its own reality, and critical evaluation is consequently confined to its internal coherence as a 'world of ideas', rather than as an empirical explanation. The criticism of the notion of coherence as a criterion of historical truth made earlier is as appropriate to the general theory of action as it is to any similar attempt to transcribe the world of experience into conceptual terms related by definition and logical consistency. Such conceptual schemes, or modes of experience, are not scientific in the sense used at the beginning of this study, and are therefore not susceptible to the criteria of evaluation proper to scientific explanation. If this argument is accepted, we are then faced with the problem of using 'coherence' as a means of evaluation. But what is coherence? As was argued earlier, it can only have an absolute existence in terms of the unity of knowledge and experience. 'Arrests' or 'modes' are incomplete in a way which cannot be established, and so we have no criteria for evaluating partial explanations. An argument which defines, *inter alia,* the nature of historical truth, without providing the means of evaluating particular applications of it, thus hangs in a theoretical limbo. We are forced on to subjective criteria.

Where explanations in the social sciences are not solely imitative of scientific methods, it would appear that they are really forms of historical argument, dependent upon the same kind of unverifiable generalisation and intuitive judgement found in the latter. The dispute between those who believe that history is subjective and theoretically unstructured and those who believe that social science is unhistorical and non-scientific is really a false controversy. This does not necessarily mean that a historian is an unconscious theorist who theorises badly, while a social scientist is a theorist who consciously theorises badly, since this is to assume a common theoretical standard to which this judgement can be related. The point is that such criticisms together with the debate between the traditionalists and the scientists, rest on invalid assumptions, since an 'objective' history does not exist and neither does a scientific explanation of human activities. Those who seek these are seeking something other than history or social science. Those who are content to leave this theoretical and methodological controversy alone are still left with the problem of clarifying the terms of their own interpretations, and establishing the criteria on which they may be judged. Such criteria cannot depend upon superior insight or on the assertion of an authority. This is a problem which cannot be avoided if there is to be any meaningful communication between scholars about the nature of their activities.

Perhaps the main requirement, both in the social sciences and in history, is for some kind of explicit statement of intentions and assumptions to be included in an interpretation. If this were generally done, then part of the process of evaluation would be simplified. The social scientist, for the most part, has been judged on his intentions which, to his credit, have usually been explicitly stated. One may be properly critical of his performance but at least a critical standard exists, albeit, as was argued earlier, an inappropriate one. Much of the criticism of 'traditional' history could be made more profitable if its relativistic and non-scientific basis was made clearer. In criticism the easiest kind of judgement consists of asserting that the argument criticised does not meet the criteria found either in a model explanation or in some other kind of explanation. To say that history is not science is one thing; to say that social science is not science is another. But this begs the question as to what these studies represent. What if both are really forms of historical explanation, equally relativistic and subjective, and each with its own autonomy? If the kind of model explanation discussed in the first part of this study is not applied as a critical touchstone to extant explanations in the social sciences, then it must be admitted that much of the criticism of historical explanation then becomes relevant to this field. In other words, those who have failed to establish a scientific theory but who claim to have provided an empirical explanation can be judged on the same grounds as those who have not sought such a theory but who also provide an empirical explanation of past human activities. A good theory in these terms is science, but a bad one is history. This leaves open the criteria for the evaluation of historical explanation. It was argued earlier that such criteria are essentially critical and not theoretical, and depend upon accepted conventions rather than on a notion of validity related to a verifiable hypothesis.

This is to reject both the idealist notion of coherence and the notion of an external objective reality as providing criteria for the judgement of historical argument. Neither its logical structure nor the implications of its presuppositions provide the grounds on which a philosophy of history may be asserted. But if this leaves us with a notion of history as some form of 'understanding', then such an understanding must be communicable and this excludes any mystical, metaphysical or psychological basis. Moreover, such understanding is not an understanding of the past, but constitutes a construction based upon 'present traces of the past'. History, in this sense, is created by historians. Yet this does not mean that history is fiction. Characters in historical novels do not require external evidence for their substantiation; only the awareness or perceptions of the author and the reader are necessary for their communication. The novel has its own autonomous truth. But historical explanation does require evidence which is external to the argument, albeit selected and interpreted by the historian. Consequently the internal coherence of the argument is insufficient to provide a validation of historical truth, since appeal must be made to external sources, if there is no objective standard of coherence which can be applied. Nevertheless, the nature of such an appeal is not the same as that which takes the form of an empirical test in science. Historical narratives cannot be falsified *in toto* but only in part, and this in turn depends upon the nature of the facts, events or documentary sources employed in the argument, as well as on the internal argument, its assumptions and its logical consistency.

Thus, ideally, a historical narrative or interpretation is a process of reasoning based upon a selection from surviving evidence of past events or 'facts' which is organised into a logically consistent argument, rendering its subject both intelligible and communicable. It is not value-free, since it is dependent upon what the historian conceives of as significant or relevant, nor can the extent of its bias be established, since in the absence of any external criterion there is no means of doing so. Nevertheless, it has its own explanatory autonomy, and the grounds for its evaluation are best expressed by Berlin, who said:

> We know what we mean by disparaging a judgement or method as subjective or biased – we mean that proper methods of weighing evidence have been too far ignored; or that what are normally called facts have been overlooked or suppressed or perverted; or that evidence normally accepted as sufficient to account for the acts of one individual or society is for no good reason ignored in some other cases similar in all relevant respects; or that canons of interpretation are arbitrarily altered from case to case; that is, without consistency or principle; or that we have reasons for thinking that the historian in question wished to establish certain conclusions for reasons other than those justified by the evidence according to canons of valid inference accepted as normal in his day or ours and that this has blinded him to the criteria and methods normal in his field for verifying facts and proving conclusions; or all, or any, of these together; or other considerations like them.[74]

It is clear from this that such standards are both normative and subjective and are prone to change. Yet they exist, and historical truth or 'objectivity' consists of agreement on such conventions, which then provide the common ground for agreement and disagreement necessary to the pursuit of any enquiry. An examination of this argument in terms of extant writings which claim to be 'historical' is a historiographical exercise which is beyond the scope of this study, but such an examination should elicit the actual criteria used at various times and by various schools of historians.

This analysis has been concerned with the nature of historical explanation in general rather than with any particular aspect of actual historical writing. The study of international politics is not, in this context, different from other historical fields. It has, as was pointed out in the introduction to this study, certain peculiarities, but these do not, phenomenologically or theoretically, make it a discipline with its own explanatory autonomy. The recent past is as much a historical field (or scientific field) as the remote past. It is worth pointing out in this context that the first 'modern' history, that of Thucydides' account of the Peloponnesian war, was a contemporary history. He said of his method:

> And with regard to my factual reporting of the events of the war I have made it a principle not to write down the first story that came my way, and not even to be guided by my own general impressions; either I was present myself at the events which I have described or else I heard of

them from eye-witnesses whose reports I have checked with as much thoroughness as possible.[75]

The immediacy of this long-drawn-out struggle, as well as the political significance of the defeat of Athens, did not prevent him from achieving a level of detachment which has been considered worthy of emulation by scholars ever since. But clearly, in the absence of conflicting or alternative explanations of the same events, and of direct evidence of the events themselves, we are unable to evaluate it as an explanation other than in terms of its internal argument or where partial evidence has survived. The point here is that the immediacy of events need not blind the contemporary historian or prevent detachment.

Such a detachment is sometimes called a historical sense, that is, an awareness of the historical context of the events which form the subject of an explanation. It is often urged against some contemporary historians and social scientists that, because of their concern for questions and problems relevant to their own times, they lack this sense. It is important to realise that the contemporary historian, like the historian of the remoter past, is concerned with reconstructing events in terms of the participant's own perceptions, motives and understanding. He therefore faces the same problem of anachronistic argument in the sense of attributing to an agent thoughts and motives which he could not or did not have at the time. The difficulty is not, however, the transference of presently held values and concepts to the past, where they are inappropriate, but the involvement in decisions and policy-making, which may lead the contemporary historian into making prescriptions rather than judgements.

For example, the attack on what has been termed 'appeasement'[76] often takes the form of criticising British politicians for conciliating the German government over the period 1935 to 1939 and thus allowing Germany to regain her former military capacity, enabling her to challenge the international *status quo*. The implication of this criticism is that Britain should have intervened while Germany was weak. This is, of course, to posit foreknowledge on the part of the historical agents, in the period before Munich and the subsequent German occupation of Prague, and also to assume a policy on the part of Hitler which was unchangeable and inexorable, and which directly challenged British interests. Such an argument is essentially *ex post facto*, and ignores the context in which historical events take place. They are assumed to be changeable in some way and alternative 'histories' are postulated, in which the outcome would have been more favourable from some specified point of view, in this case the maintenance of British influence and power. But the reasoning of the politicians themselves changed from the attitudes adopted over the period 1933 to 1936, and different assumptions were made in the later thirties. The use of the situation of 1938 in order to argue about the situation of 1933 or 1936 is unhistorical. In this sense history is concerned with what happened and not with what might have happened. The confusion between the two occurs in contemporary history because of the involvement of the historian with policy and events which have a continuing significance, and which extend from his present into the immediate future. It is consequently often difficult to make a distinction between interpretation and speculation, and it probably explains why 'modern' history is usually considered by 'traditional' historians to end some two or three decades before the period of their existence or their social and political awareness. This problem is especially true for the historian of international politics, who is concerned with the level of decision- and policy-making which involves motivation, and the selection of one out of a choice of a number of possible courses of action. He has to explain not only why this choice was made, but he has to do this in terms of rejected alternatives and their hypothetical consequences.

The danger of rationalising in an unhistorical way thus exists; firstly, in the assertion of motives held by the historical agents, based upon conceptions of the international and domestic political environment which did not exist during the events and actions forming the subject of the explanation; and secondly, in explaining these actions and events in terms of a superriding hypothesis which establishes motivation by making the agents prisoners of the hypothesis. A distinction can be made between two levels of generalisation contained in this form of argument. The first is that of the concepts which influenced the participants, and which must therefore be reconstructed as part of an explanation of their actions. The second consists of those concepts which properly belong to the hypothesis which is itself being advanced as an explanation. Both are found in explanations of contemporary political events, and the relationship between the two requires very careful consideration in evaluating particular interpretations.

The next chapter will seek to clarify some of these problems of historical enquiry by examining a number of interpretations of the origins of the Cold War.

REFERENCES

1. A. C. Danto, *Analytical Philosophy of History* (Cambridge Univ. Press, 1968) p. 95.
2. Max Weber, *The Methodology of the Social Sciences,* trans. E. A. Shils and Henry A. Finch (New York: Free Press, 1949) p. 79.
3. For example, see Carl G. Hempel, 'The Function of General Laws in History',

in *Aspects of Scientific Explanation*, pp. 231ff; and Ernest Nagel, 'Problems in the Logic of Historical Inquiry', in *The Structure of Science* (New York: Harcourt Brace & World, 1961).

4.   Hempel, op. cit., p. 235.

5.   Hans Reichenbach, 'Probability Methods in Social Science', in David Lerner and Harold D. Lasswell (eds.), *The Policy Sciences* (Stanford Univ. Press, 1951) p. 123.

6.   Strictly speaking, Friedrich Engels and Karl Marx; see *The German Ideology* (London: Lawrence & Wishart, 1964); but see also Karl Marx, *Pre-Capitalist Economic Formations*, trans. Jack Cohen, ed. E. J. Hobsbawm (London: Lawrence & Wishart, 1964).

7.   *The German Ideology*, p. 49; see also *Pre-Capitalist Economic Formations*, p. 86, 106.

8.   *Pre-Capitalist Economic Formations*, p. 110.

9.   *The German Ideology*, p. 31.

10.   Ibid., p. 32.

11.   Ibid., p. 36.

12.   Ibid., p. 37.

13.   Ibid., p. 41.

14.   Ibid., p. 51.

15.   See Shlomo Avineri, *The Social and Political Thought of Karl Marx* (Cambridge Univ. Press, 1968), chap. 6, pp. 150-84, for a discussion of these stages.

16.   *Pre-Capitalist Economic Formations*, p. 19.

17.   Shlomo Avineri (ed.), *Karl Marx on Colonialism and Modernisation* (New York: Anchor Books, Doubleday, 1969) p. 469.

18.   Ibid., p. 470; see also Avineri, *The Social and Political Thought of Karl Marx*, pp. 151-3.

19.   *Pre-Capitalist Economic Formations*, p. 86.

20.   Ibid., p. 97.

21.   Ibid., p.106.

22.   Ibid., p. 109.

23.   *The German Ideology*, p. 51.

24.   Ibid.,p. 38.

25.   *Pre-Capitalist Economic Formations*, p. 46.

26.   See Karl R. Popper, *The Poverty of Historicism* (London: Routledge & Kegan Paul, 1961) and *The Open Society and its Enemies*, vol. II: *Hegel and Marx*, rev. ed. (London: Routledge & Kegan Paul, 1966).

27.   *Pre-Capitalist Economic Formations*, p. 20.

28.   Ibid., p. 43.

29.   Avineri, *The Social and Political Thought of Karl Marx*, p. 158.

30.   Weber, *The Methodology of the Social Sciences*, p. 69.

31.   *Pre-Capitalist Economic Formations*, p. 71.

32.   Oswald Spengler, *The Decline of the West*, trans. C. F. Atkinson, special ed., 2 vols. (New York: Knopf, 1939).

33.   Arnold Toynbee, *A Study of History*, 10 vols. (Oxford Univ. Press, 1934–54). See *A Study of History: Abridgement of Volumes I-VI* by D. C. Somervell (Oxford Univ. Press, 1946), and *Abridgement of Volumes VII-X* (Oxford Univ. Press, 1957).

34.   Alfred Rosenberg, *Selected Writings*, ed. Robert Pois (London: Cape, 1970).

35.   Konrad Lorenz, *On Aggression* (London: Methuen, 1963).

36.   Danto, *Analytical Philosophy of History*, pp. 88-111.

37.   Ibid., p. 108.

38.   Ibid., p. 110.

39.   Toynbee, *A Study of History: Abridgement of Volumes I-VI*, pp. 60-79.

40.   Roy Campbell 'On Some South African Novelists', *Collected Poems* (London: Bodley Head, 1949) p. 198.

41.   On this point, see Oakeshott, *Experience and its Modes*, pp. 96-101.

42.   Oakeshott, 'The Activity of Being an Historian', in *Rationalism in Politics and Other Essays*, p. 146.

43.   R. G. Collingwood, *The Idea of History* (New York: Galaxy Books, Oxford

Univ. Press, 1956); see also *An Autobiography* (London: Oxford Univ. Press, 1970).

44. See *The Idea of History*, pp. 213-17, and *An Autobiography*, p. 127.
45. *The Idea of History*, p. 215.
46. Ibid.
47. Ibid., p. 305.
48. Ibid., p. 236.
49. Ibid., p. 244.
60. Oakeshott, *Experience and its Modes*, p. 10.
51. Ibid., p. 37.
52. Ibid., p. 71.
53. Ibid., p. 99-100.
54. Ibid., p. 48.
55. Ibid., p. 39.
56. Collingwood, *The Idea of History*, p. 246.
57. Ibid., pp 251.
58. Ibid., p. 236.
59. Ibid., p. 252.
60. Ibid., p. 263.
61. Collingwood, *An Autobiography*, p. 58.
62. Charles A. Beard, 'That Noble Dream', in Fritz Stern (ed.), *The Varieties of History* (New York: Meridian Books, 1956) p. 317. It should be noted that Beard criticises this view and argues in favour of a relativist approach towards history.
63. Friedrich Meinecke, 'Values and Causalities in History', ibid., pp. 268-88.
64. William H. Dray, *Philosophy of History* (Englewood Cliffs, N.J.: Prentice-Hall, 1964) p. 38.
65. Danto, *Analytical Philosophy of History*, p. 101.
66. H. A. L. Fisher, *A History of Europe*, vol. II (London: Collins, Fontana Library, 1960) p. 831.
67. Garrett Mattingly, *Rennaissance Diplomacy* (Harmondsworth: Penguin Books, 1965) p. 77.
68. Ibid., p. 85.
69. Ibid., p. 154-62.
70. E. H. Carr, *What is History?* (Harmondsworth: Penguin Books, 1964) p. 130.
71. Herbert Butterfield, *The Whig Interpretation of History* (London: Bell, 1931).
72. Collingwood, *The Idea of History*, p. 248.
73. Carr, *What is History?* p. 109.
74. Isaiah Berlin, *Historical Inevitability* (London: Oxford Univ. Press, 1954) p. 59.
75. Thucydides, *The Peloponnesian War*, trans. Rex. Warner (Harmondsworth: Penguin Books, 1954) p. 24.
76. For the debate on appeasement, see Esmonde M. Robertson (ed.), *The Origins of the Second World War* (London: Macmillan, 1971); Lord Avon, *The Eden Memoirs: Facing the Dictators* (London: Cassell, 1962) and *The Reckoning* (1965); Winston S. Churchill, *History of the Second World War*, vol. I: *The Gathering Storm* (London: Cassell, 1948); Tom Jones, *A Diary with Letters* (London: Oxford Univ. Press, 1954); Martin Gilbert and Richard Gott, *The Appeasers* (London: Weidenfeld & Nicholson, 1963).

CHAPTER 5

The Origins of the Cold War

IT was argued in the last chapter that critical judgement often contained criteria which imply an alternative hypothesis against which the interpretation criticised is being assessed. The evaluation proceeds on inappropriate grounds, since the interpretation is being judged for what it is not rather than for what it actually is. Consequently the first task of a critic of historical writing is to establish the criteria on which his judgement is to be based. As we have seen in the preceding discussion, this is a difficult problem, since there is no common agreement on such criteria other than in a very general sense. Indeed, the essence of historical explanation is the subjective nature of its argument. Thus while we can agree on a distinction between fact and fiction and between the historical novel and history, the evaluation of good and bad history, the relevance of facts and evidence to an interpretation, and their significance, contain problems which are more complex. The following analysis of the origins of the Cold War will seek to examine differences between various interpretations and attempt to establish evaluative criteria.

The intention, as with the earlier discussion of apparently conflicting approaches towards the study of international politics, is not to pose a choice between orthodox and revisionist histories, but to reveal their common ground as historical arguments. As was argued earlier, all history is revisionist history, in the sense that historical interpretation has a relativist and subjective basis. If this view is taken, the claims of one school of historical argument to pre-empt historical truth cannot be justified. Clearly, as we shall see, there are substantive differences between historical explanations, but this is to assert alternative evaluatory criteria. A reductionist or historicist interpretation cannot be refuted by posing its theoretical 'opposite' or by an appeal to the available 'evidence'. Such arguments must be criticised on their own grounds. In short, this study will be concerned with elucidating the distinctions between interpretations, rather than with imposing a single set of critical criteria upon them. Where an attempt is made to provide an interpretation of events independent of those criticised, either as part of the descriptive narrative or as an alternative, it should be borne in mind that this too is subject to the same general criticism. It is difficult, however, to sustain a critique of a critique, as well as to present a coherent exposition both of events and their explanation.

Before undertaking such an examination, some elucidation of its subject is necessary, together with the questions with which any enquiry begins. Of course, the question 'What was, or is, the Cold War?' is answered by the interpretation itself, and we must not beg this by assuming some common definition, with its implicit assumptions, which most historians accept. In this particular case, however, it is generally agreed that the empirical focus for an enquiry into the origins and nature of the Cold War is found in the political relations between the United States and the Soviet Union. Some historians have conceived of the Cold War as consisting simply of the mutual hostility of these two countries. Linked with this view is that of a transcendental conflict which has divided the world into two groups of states. For the first time in international history, it is argued, two states have emerged with antagonisms which embrace not merely Europe or Asia but the whole world. The conflict is thus a global struggle dominated by two countries. These powers are able to influence the pattern of international relationships because of a qualitative discrepancy in military capacity and resources between the most powerful states and the rest of the world.

Moreover, this struggle is seen as being transcendental because it involves a conflict of ideologies. It is argued that the existence of a strong Marxist state, which cannot accept permanent relations with non-Marxist states, and which believes in their eventual self-destruction, makes a stable international political system impossible. Such an attitude, combined with military and political strength, presents a challenge to other states with different values and socio-economic organisations. Conversely, the Marxist view asserts that the problem of international instability and violence is caused by the instabilities of capitalist society and imperialistic competition between capitalist countries, consequent on this internal instability. Conflict between Marxist and non-Marxist states is thus viewed as inevitable, so long as these states conceive of their external relationships in ideological terms. Thus the Cold War has been seen by some commentators as a twentieth-century war of religion.[1]

Without making any criticism of these views at this stage, it can be said that the historian, in selecting his problem, is concerned with what is significantly different from preceding events and actions. He is of course aided in this sense by his capacity to select from a historical context, looking backwards as well as forwards. This is not to say that all historians are concerned with turning-points in history, but that the notion of significance very often means significantly *different*. This is itself a subjective judgement, given the relativity of the notion of significance, and it may be that future generations of historians will not consider those political relationships which constitute our focus as being the most significant events of the latter part of the twentieth century. In this sense the selection of subject and focus is arbitrary. Who is to say that the study of great-power relationships is more important than the study of constitutional relationships in the Swiss Republic? Nevertheless, accepting the subjective nature of our selection, we must make some preliminary assumptions before beginning any enquiry. The narrower these assumptions, the easier the task of historical interpretation becomes. But the corollary, that the narrower the assumptions then the narrower the interpretation, must also be accepted. The value of these tentative steps in defining our subject will be established by the interpretation to which they are related. In other words, they are confirmed or rejected by the enquiry itself.

The difficulty with the transcendental view of the Cold War is that it is too general and contains a number of circular arguments. It becomes, in effect, the history of the world since 1945 – or from 1917, in the view of some commentators. Such a focus really avoids the problem of selection, and our understanding of the nature of the Cold War is not enhanced if it is simply conceived of as a situation in which a major war has not been fought, or as some ill-defined omnipresent struggle between nations. A definition of Cold War should include what is significantly new in relations between states. All relationships are unique in some sense and change is normal in human affairs, but some changes are more significant than others. The notion of significance here is related to some evaluative principle or judgement which is contained in the interpretation itself. In this case a major alliance, which emerged victorious after a long and costly war, turned into a major conflict which, although stopping short of actual violence, was also long and costly. This conflict itself changed in its nature and significance over the post-war period. In short, there were a number of conflicts and political relationships over this period of time and only one of these constituted the Cold War. Its essential characteristic was a complete breakdown of relations between former allies, a breakdown so complete that although each responded to, and paralleled, each other's actions, there was no attempt to achieve a political dialogue and to reach an accommodation of their conflict. Such a breakdown is relatively rare in international politics, for, as Clausewitz pointed out in his study of war, even in cases where states actually fight each other, they do not cease to communicate.[2] Thus the novel feature in post-war international politics was the almost complete absence of a political dialogue between two conflicting groups of states, each engaged in preparing for a major war. This situation persisted for a number of years and then changed, as will be seen in a later part of this study, into a new pattern of relationships dominated by strategic considerations influenced by the development of nuclear weapons technology.

The concern of this study is not with the Cold War proper but with its origins. Yet some definition of the Cold War is necessary, for otherwise such an enquiry becomes chimerical. We may thus regard the Cold War as being a period in which two groups of states engaged in conflict, with no direct diplomatic or political contact with each other, and committed to a struggle which could only be resolved by war, by the surrender of one side of its position, or by mutual recognition of each other's positions. It was both a deadly quarrel and a kind of hiatus in international politics. At the height of the Cold War both sides attempted, without direct negotiation, to apply pressure on each other in order to achieve success. Each such attempt was interpreted by the opponent in the light of its own policy and led to retaliation, which in turn provoked further hostile responses. The unusual aspect of this competition was that, although an arms race developed, and although war strategies were prepared, with their concomitant alliances, neither side pressed its position to the point of war. This is in itself a historical judgement, that is, a retrospective description of great-power relations in the immediate post-war period, and it does not purport to be related to an abstract definition of conflict, nor does it necessarily reflect the attitudes of the participants towards their disputes. There are various assumptions and interpretations involved in this notion of the Cold War, but it may serve as a preliminary and tentative focus for our enquiry into various explanations as to how this conflict came about.

If, then, we regard the Cold War as an international conflict of an unusual nature, one of the major questions is why such a conflict developed between allies so soon after their alliance had triumphed over their enemies. Was the conflict latent and only temporarily obscured by the pressing need to bring the war to a successful conclusion? What was the nature of the conflict? Was it an inherent incompatibility of interests between the allies, or the product of a power struggle brought into being by the collapse of two world powers, Germany and Japan? Before examining various interpretations which seek to answer these questions, some exposition of Soviet policy over the period from 1939 to the closing stages of the war would seem appropriate, since the attitudes adopted by the allies were, apparently at least, responsive to Soviet demands. Without assuming that this was actually the case, the major diplomatic overtures, concerned with what may be called political rather than military questions, are clearly important to any explanation of the divisions between the allies which came into prominence at the end of the war.

From the very beginning of the war the Soviet Union appeared to be seeking control over certain East European, Baltic and Balkan countries. The nature and degree of this control varied, and while the Soviet Union actually occupied parts of Poland and the Baltic states and thus pursued a policy of territorial expansion, in other cases the central problem was the nature of the governments of neighbouring countries and their attitudes to the Soviet Union. In dealing with the growing menace of Germany, Stalin was not merely concerned with ensuring Soviet neutrality in the struggle between the major capitalist powers, but with strengthening his position in his border areas. The Molotov–Ribbentrop Pact of 23 August 1939 restored to the Soviet Union the territory which had been lost to the Poles after the Soviet–Polish war of 1920.[3] On the German invasion of Poland, the Soviet Union occupied the part of Poland ceded to it in the secret protocol to the treaty. In addition to this territorial gain, Germany recognised Soviet influence as being predominant in Finland, Estonia, Latvia and Bessarabia. After the successful invasion of Poland, the Germans agreed in a supplementary protocol[4] of 28 September that the greater part of Lithuania should fall under Soviet influence and that all German citizens living in the Baltic states should be transferred to Germany. In October the Soviet Union demanded territorial concessions from Finland. Negotiations broke down and the Finns proved more obdurate than the Balts. Nevertheless, they were forced after a bitter struggle to cede to the Russians Petsamo, the Karelian isthmus and the lease of the port of Hangö.

After the defeat of France, the Soviets made further demands for German recognition of Soviet influence in the Persian Gulf, for a land and naval base in the Dardanelles, for northern Sakhalin and for Bulgaria as a Soviet sphere of influence. Earlier in March 1940 the Soviet government signed a pact of neutrality with Japan in which they recognised Manchuria as part of the Japanese Empire in exchange for recognition of Outer Mongolia as a Soviet area. Thus by the time of the German invasion of Russia in June 1941 the Soviets had acquired the Baltic states, concessions from Finland, Bessarabia and northern Bukovina from Romania, part of Poland and a sphere of influence in the Balkans, while maintaining a state of neutrality in the war waged by the major capitalist powers.

Of course the German invasion, with its initial victories, changed the whole situation, and the Soviet government found itself fighting for its existence. But in spite of these immediate difficulties, the Soviet Union sought to turn an alliance with the United Kingdom into a British recognition of her territorial and political interests in these areas. In December 1941[5] Stalin urged British recognition of the gains in Poland which the Soviet Union had achieved through the Molotov–Ribbentrop Pact. Poland, he argued, should be compensated with territory taken from Germany. Territory north of the Tilsit should go to Lithuania. To this list of Soviet requests was added Bessarabia, northern Bukovina and the recent gains in Finland. It was clear from the very beginning of the wartime alliance with Britain that the Soviet Union wished to retain all the gains which had been made through her neutrality pact with Germany, although in 1941 the prospect of victory must have seemed very remote. Indeed, the measure of importance accorded to these demands by Stalin can be estimated by the fact that they were made when the Soviets were engaged in a life-and-death struggle with Germany, and when the need for material help from the British was desperate. The Anglo-Soviet Treaty of May 1942 did not resolve the question of frontiers, or include any accommodation of these Soviet demands, apart from a general recognition by the British government of Soviet authority in the Baltic states.

But whatever agreements could have been reached on the question of territorial changes in Europe after the war had been won, the fortunes of the war itself, and the continuing reluctance of the United States to negotiate political questions during it, were the two major factors which eventually strengthened the Soviet bargaining position. Sooner or later the allies would have to come to terms with a victorious Soviet Union on the subject of post-war Europe. Although no agreement was reached at the Teheran Conference of 28 November – 1 December 1943 on the Soviet demand that Poland be reduced to its 'ethnographic' frontiers, with the Oder constituting its western frontier, nevertheless it was agreed that the Soviet Union would undertake the liberation of Eastern Europe. Thus Soviet influence, given military success, would inevitably extend to cover at least the area which the Red Army occupied, just as British and American influence in Southern and Western Europe and in Asia would extend to the area of their conquests. The nature of this influence, and the degree of agreement on it among the allies, were of course open questions. But it was apparent that some kind of accommodation would have to be reached if there was to be a general settlement of the major political questions arising out of the defeat of the Axis powers.

On 9 October 1944 Churchill went to Moscow to negotiate with Stalin. The war situation had changed very much to the allies' advantage and the Soviet Union had been able to advance into Poland and the Balkans. Further concessions had been obtained from Finland as the price for her support of the German invasion. During the talks with Stalin, Churchill proposed that spheres of influence in the Balkans be divided between the allies on a percentage basis. He suggested that the Soviets should enjoy 90 per cent of influence in Romania, 75 per cent in Bulgaria, 50 per cent in Yugoslavia and Hungary, and that the British should enjoy 90 per cent of influence in Greece.[6] Given the American refusal to conclude political and territorial agreements during the war itself, this was only an indication of attitudes which would be adopted in post-war negotiations. It did indicate, however, that whatever 'influence' meant, the British government accepted that both countries would enjoy some measure of political influence in the Balkans after the war. Churchill had already conceded much of the Soviet position in the Baltic.

Thus although this agreement was couched in very general and ambiguous terms, it indicated that an extension of Soviet influence was acceptable to the British government. Although Churchill in his account of this negotiation tried to suggest that it applied to the immediate wartime situation only, it appears clear, both from his argument and from the events themselves, that Britain obtained a free hand in Greece in return for some recognition of Soviet interests in the Balkans. Such interests[7] did not cease with the defeat of Hitler. It was, however, Poland which constituted the major contention between the allies. The problem here was that not only were there two rival governments, but that the territorial changes advocated by the Soviet Union largely affected this country. The Lublin government, which came into being in Soviet-occupied territory and which was supported by the Soviet government, accepted the proposals of the latter in respect of the territorial area of post-war Poland. The London government-in-exile did not. This government was antipathetic to the Soviet Union and, in particular, refused to accept the Curzon Line as Poland's eastern frontier. The central question for the Soviet Union was not simply a matter of resolving the frontier question but of the nature of the post-war Polish government, and its attitude towards the Soviet Union. The problem of the existence of two groups of political leaders, each claiming to represent their country, and each supported by a foreign power, appeared intractable. As will be seen later on, a great deal depended on the policies and attitudes adopted by the allies on this question. The *de facto* situation, from 1944 onwards, was that the Soviet Union had effective control over Poland and sought to persuade the allies into accepting her position on the questions of frontiers and the government. The allies, although helpless to intervene in Poland, sought to apply pressure on the Soviet Union to achieve a Poland which was independent and amenable to western influence.

In short, the situation in Europe was very different from that following the First World War, when self-determination really meant the dismantling of the Austro–Hungarian Empire and the creation of a number of succession states, nominally free to relate to other countries, but whose existence was primarily designed to weaken the defeated countries as well as to satisfy the demands of ethnic minorities. The question of free elections, which was to assume prominence in the later stages of the war and in the immediate post-war period, really meant, given the predominance of Soviet military forces in Eastern Europe, whether an East European or Balkan government would be free to ally with, or relate to, Western European governments, or whether its international relations would be controlled by the Soviet Union. In the case of Poland, if the London government had been installed in power, then it would be free, theoretically, to relate either to the East or the West. It would be in the same position as pre-war Polish governments which first allied with France, then with Germany and finally with Britain, but which consistently refused to ally Poland with the Soviet Union.[8] Since this particular political faction opposed ceding the territory east of the Curzon Line to the U.S.S.R., and since its erstwhile enemy, Germany, was on the point of defeat, it did not take a politician of genius to predict which political relationship it would seek in the post-war world. And conversely, it was equally easy to predict which relationship the Lublin government would choose once it had achieved power.

Of course, there was no question as to a 'free' choice for either faction, and their fortunes were bound up in the overall political situation and, more precisely, with the direct control exercised over their national territory by foreign governments. The point here is that the disputes between the allies over the question of 'free' elections, and the competition of the provisional governments in the liberated or conquered areas of Europe, were directly related to a demarcation of their respective influences in these territories. This was as true for the British and American governments as it was for that of the Soviet Union, and the armies of the former states exercised a considerable influence in determining the governments which were to emerge in Italy, Greece and in the ex-enemy states which were under their exclusive control. Put simply, so far as Poland was concerned, the real issue was whether Poland should be considered as being exclusively within the Soviet sphere of influence in Europe, or whether Poland would be free to choose her future political relationships for herself. Britain and the United States clearly favoured the latter, while the Soviet Union insisted on the former.

Thus at the Crimea Conference at Yalta in February 1945,[9] the Polish question constituted the most important and controversial issue on the agenda. The Soviet Union had recognised the Lublin faction as the provisional government of Poland in the previous December, and the British government had accorded the London government-in-exile some measure of support and represented its interests in negotiations with the Soviet Union. The debate on the frontier question resulted in the acceptance by Britain and the United States of the Curzon Line as the eastern frontier of Poland, although they demurred at the Oder–Western Neisse line as the western frontier. Nevertheless, they agreed in principle that Poland should be compensated for her losses in the east with territory taken from Germany. The difficult question of government was skated over with the Soviet Union agreeing to reconstitute the Lublin government, by including in it representatives from other political factions, and to hold free elections as soon as possible.

The Crimea Conference considered other questions relating to Soviet demands, notably that of reparations, and the price for Soviet entry into the war against Japan. The reparations question was particularly delicate because of the former unhappy experience of the allies after the First World War with Germany. The United States did not want to bear the burden of reparations by providing Germany with capital and materials, which would then be transferred to the Soviet Union. Similarly, the British government, already preoccupied with serious economic problems, was very reluctant to assume the burden of supporting the most densely populated industrial zone of Germany, while the Soviets simply took what they wanted from the defeated country. Yet both countries recognised that the Soviet Union had suffered more losses in men and material than any other country as a consequence of German aggression. The United States accepted in principle that the Soviet demand for $10 billion compensation from Germany should form the basis for future discussions, although the British dissented.

The agreement on the Far East was perhaps the most important indication of the future objectives of the allies. The Soviet Union agreed to break its neutrality pact with Japan and enter the war 'two to three months' after the defeat of Germany. In return for this the allies recognised the *status quo* in Outer Mongolia which had been agreed with Japan in 1941. Furthermore, they agreed that southern Sakhalin and the Kurile Islands should be annexed by the Soviet Union and that the latter should have a joint share with China in the Chinese Eastern Railway and the South Manchurian Railway. The Soviets bound themselves to accept Chinese suzerainty over Manchuria, and also agreed to co-operate with the Kuomintang government. These provisions were to be the subject of negotiations between the U.S.S.R. and China.

Finally, the division of Germany into zones, and of Berlin into sectors, established by the Protocol of 12 September 1944 of the European Advisory Commission, was accepted at Yalta. An addition was made to this by giving France both a zone and a place on the Control Council.

It was, however, the Potsdam Conference of 17 July–2 August 1945,[10] after the defeat of Germany, which established the main political settlements in Europe, although the negotiators at the time believed that these were interim agreements to be refined on by later negotiations, conducted by the Council of Foreign Ministers. The Polish question, after prolonged and controversial discussion, was resolved by the western acceptance of the Oder–Western Neisse line as the *de facto* frontier between Poland and Germany. Poland was to administer this area 'pending its final determination'. The difficulties over the composition of the government were again avoided by the Soviets agreeing to the reconstitution of the Lublin faction and to 'free elections'. This in effect reaffirmed the Yalta agreement and represented a moderation of the Soviet insistence on a friendly government in Poland.

The allies accepted four main principles in respect of Germany; firstly, that Germany should pay reparations; secondly, that she should be disarmed and demilitarised; thirdly, that she should eventually have a democratic constitution; and finally, that she should be administered as an economic unit. These were principles which depended for their fulfilment, with the exception of that relating to reparations, on the negotiation of a peace treaty. So far as reparations were concerned, the agreement finally reached stipulated that the U.S.S.R. would compensate herself from her own zone of occupation and in addition would receive from the western zones

> 15 per cent of such usable and complete industrial capital equipment . . . as is unnecessary for the German peace economy and should be removed from the Western zones of Germany, in exchange for an equivalent value of food, coal, potash, zinc (etc.) . . . and 10 per cent of such industrial capital equipment . . . to be transferred to the Soviet government . . . without payment or exchange of any kind in return.[11]

In this connection it should be remarked that the German 'peace-time economy' was established by the levels of industry agreement, negotiated by the Level of Industry Committee, which was set up in September 1945. This fixed German steel capacity at 7·5 million tons, although actual production was pegged at 5·8 million tons. German steel production in 1929 had been 18 million tons, and this agreement in effect, gave Germany an industrial capacity of half that of 1938. While this did not amount to the 'pastoralisation' of German industry,[12] it meant that a considerable amount of surplus capital goods could be transferred to the Soviet Union without radically disturbing this notional 'level of industry'. It should also be noted that, while France was not represented at Potsdam, the attitude of the French government on this question can be seen in its refusal to accept the proposal that there should be central administrative units for Germany, in its proposals that the Saar should be annexed to France, that the Rhineland should become a separate state, and that the Ruhr should be placed under an international administration.[13]

The acceptance of reparations by the allies can thus be regarded as a concrete agreement emerging out of the Potsdam Conference and one which, in spite of considerable western reluctance, in large measure accepted the Soviet demands. Another concrete result, although one not ratified by formal agreement, was the transfer of the German populations of the Sudetenland, and from the territories transferred to Poland and Hungary, to the truncated Germany. Whether this is regarded as a political 'settlement', or as a *de facto* consequence of the agreements reached at Potsdam, it was an act which even to the most sanguine of politicians could not be regarded as being easily reversible. Indeed, since Churchill, for one, argued against the additional burden upon the western zones of the German émigrés, as a consequence of the frontier changes, it can be assumed that an acceptance of the changes themselves was also an acceptance of the population transfer.[14]

Finally, the conditions for Soviet entry into the Japanese war were discussed and Stalin reaffirmed his determination to participate in the war. According to Truman: 'There were many reasons for my going to Potsdam, but the most urgent, to my mind, was to get from Stalin a personal reaffirmation of Russia's entry into the war against Japan, a matter which our military chiefs were most anxious to clinch.'[15] This he succeeded in obtaining. Yet, ominously, Truman also recorded that

> the experience at Potsdam now made me determined that I would not allow the Russians any part in the control of Japan. Our experience with them in Germany and in Bulgaria, Rumania, Hungary and Poland was such that I decided to take no chances in a joint set-up with the Russians. . . . I made up my mind that General MacArthur would be given complete command and control after victory in Japan. We were not going to be disturbed by Russian tactics in the Pacific.[16]

Clearly, whatever agreements had been made at Potsdam were based on very shaky foundations. While the Soviet Union was to expend life and resources in the fight against Japan, her claim to influence in the Pacific was to be resisted.

The Potsdam Conference was the last major conference to be held between the allies, and although negotiations continued between the foreign ministers, relations continued to worsen. It had been increasingly clear from early 1945 onwards that the British and American governments were antipathetic to the expansion of Soviet power in Eastern Europe as a consequence of the fall of Hitler. Their central difficulty was that the Soviet Union enjoyed *de facto* control over this region, and the only bargaining power which the West had lay in the possibility of extending economic assistance to the U.S.S.R., or in areas where they possessed influence, such as in Western Europe itself, the Mediterranean and in Asia. Their stronger position in these areas could be used to apply pressure on the Soviet Union in order to obtain concessions in Eastern Europe. But as will be seen subsequently, any attempt to force a relinquishment of the Soviet position in Eastern Europe in exchange for an accommodation elsewhere raised the question of the western motivation for such a move, and ignored the primacy of Eastern Europe in Soviet policy. Moreover, the allies were bedevilled, at least until the successful testing of the atomic bomb,[17] by the need to have the Soviet Union participate in the war against Japan and, as Truman put it, 'to neutralise the large Japanese forces on the China mainland and thus save thousands of American and Allied lives'.[18] Similarly, the need to have Soviet participation in the newly created United Nations Organisation helped to inhibit any attempt to apply pressure on the Soviet government. After the defeat of Germany and Japan, however, the differences between the western attitudes and the Soviet position came out into the open and the earlier attempts at accommodation withered away.

It is not proposed to trace every instance of Soviet and western disagreement over this period, but to point out that the central issue was the Soviet position in Europe after the defeat of Germany. The period between April 1945 and March 1947 was a time of mutual hostility, culminating in the acceptance of political commitments and relationships which delineated the conflict and which established the two groups of opposed states to be aligned subsequently within NATO and the Warsaw Pact. Both sides followed unilateral policies in the areas under their control. The British and American governments merged their zones of occupation on 1 January 1947, and the Soviets went their way with the fusion of the German Communist Party and the Social Democrat Party into the Socialist Unity Party in April 1946. One by one the governments of the Eastern European countries and the Balkans became communist.[19] Most historians are agreed that the Truman Doctrine declaration of March 1947, and the concomitant offer of Marshall Aid to Europe made in June 1947, constituted both a definition of the conflict and the beginning of the Cold War. Perhaps more to the point, the participants themselves considered them to be a turning point also, for as Truman put it: 'This was the time to align the United States of America clearly on the side, and at the head, of the free world.'[20]

This brief survey of the major territorial proposals and changes which occurred during the war, and immediately after the German surrender, is intended to provide a context for the consideration of interpretations which now follows. Yet such a survey is in itself a partial interpretation, since it consists of a selection of facts which cannot be divorced entirely from evaluation. There are assumptions involved in their selection, and in their presentation as a coherent narrative, which ought to be examined. Moreover, there are omissions in this survey. Why, for example, is there no mention of the negotiations of the United Nations Charter and of the various international organisations set up to promote international economic and social co-operation? Why is there no mention of events such as the Katyn massacre, or the various manoeuvrings of the communist parties and the resistance organisations in the liberated countries? Similarly, the progress of the war itself, and the relationship between military and political objectives, have not been discussed. It must be admitted that this recital of facts is neither comprehensive nor free from interpretation. It is related to the interpretation of the post-war disagreements which led to the total breakdown of diplomatic relations between the Soviet Union and her allies. Consequently it was felt necessary to delineate the area of controversy between them, in terms of the main territorial and political questions which formed the subject-matter of their negotiations. This is of course to assume that these constituted the real area of disagreement. A Marxist historian, however, would not accept this, and perhaps neither would an idealist western historian. However, without necessarily accepting this assumption, we can begin by examining those interpretations which focus upon the various conflicts over territorial influence which, for them at least, constitute a cause rather than an occasion of the Cold War. But it is necessary to emphasise that such a narrative is essentially subjective in nature and that other assemblages of facts and judgements could be made with equal validity.

In a number of different explanations of the origins of this conflict[21] we encounter the type of argument which seeks to attribute blame or responsibility. Even where such an attempt is not outwardly partisan, espousing one 'side' or the other, it assumes that there is an alternative to what actually happened in history and, more specifically, that there exists a level of behaviour in international politics which is in some way legitimate. A good deal here depends upon what assumptions are made about the nature of international politics and, more particularly, whether values are being injected into the interpretation. It may be appropriate to say that one particular act influenced a subsequent event or provoked a particular response, but not to depict the initial act as being immoral. This last implies that there is such a thing as a generally recognised standard of morality for political behaviour. While individual politicians may have their own notion of what is legitimate, or proper behaviour, in a particular political context, we must beware of substituting for this our own view, or of presuming that a politician necessarily acts upon his. Putting it more concretely, a view which swings away from the notion of the Soviet Union as being the chief architect of the Cold War, to one which stigmatises the United States, is no less prejudiced than the interpretation it condemns. Such a revisionist 'history' is not really historical, but is concerned with moral or ethical questions related to the responsibility of certain politicians for the alleged effects of their action.

We may distinguish between such an approach and the notion of cause which is implicit in any discussion of origins. We must be careful to separate the tautology of confusing cause and effect in explaining conflict in terms of conflict, from general causes conceived of as theories of international political behaviour. We have not explained the Cold War by describing its peculiarities in terms of action and reaction, or as sequences of events which are linked in some unexplained causal process. Such explanations are usually reinforced by general hypotheses relating to concepts of security and power, or the conflict of national interests or of ideologies.

However, leaving these general considerations aside for the moment, we can examine the view that there existed a fundamental hostility between the Soviet Union and the major western powers, which was concealed temporarily by the exigencies of their joint war against Germany and Japan. This broad view is shared by those who stress the ideological aspect of this conflict, but who nevertheless draw different conclusions from it. Thus, in the view of Marxist-Leninist historians,[22] the conflict between capitalist states is explained by reference to a theory of imperialism. This theory will be examined in some detail in a later part of this study, but the point here is that it regards war as inevitable between capitalist states because of innate characteristics in their economies. Consequently the position of a communist or socialist state in international politics is one in which its security may be endangered by such conflicts and it is therefore compelled to adopt a defensive policy. In less ideological terms, the chief danger for such a state is the possibility of a hostile coalition between capitalist states. The 'correct' policy is thus to take advantage of the inherent divisions between capitalist states, and to allow them to destroy each other, while avoiding any involvement in their quarrels. This is the usual justification for the Soviet negotiation of the Molotov–Ribbentrop Pact and of the neutrality agreement with Japan, as it is, of course, for the alliance with the West after the German invasion. In the event of such an involvement, the most expedient course of action, designed to preserve both the state and its ideology, should clearly be followed. Once the danger has passed, then whatever post-war commitments were adopted should be designed to protect the state from a recurrence of the original threat. A Soviet state, in this view, exists in a hostile and dangerous world and consequently needs to be constantly on its guard against the repercussions of inevitable conflicts between powerful capitalist states. Essentially, this view places great emphasis upon the defensive aspects of Soviet policy and makes no clear distinction between one capitalist state and another.

The mirror-image of this view is one which recognises the ideological basis of the social and political structure of the Soviet Union and other socialist countries, but concludes that *they* constitute a danger to the existence of non-socialist states because of the revolutionary nature of their ideologies. Moreover, since it is assumed that their political behaviour is determined by their values and beliefs, no agreement can be regarded as binding with states which regard all capitalist countries as temporary political systems brought about by the same historic process which will eventually sweep them away. Consequently no international agreements can be concluded with socialist countries, other than those which can be maintained by force rather than through mutual interest or reciprocal relations. Such views thus conceive of the struggle between the Soviet Union and the United States as being a conflict of conceptions about the ordering of society which are extended beyond the boundaries of the nation-state. It is essentially a war of absolutes, since it can be won only when the ideological opponent is either converted or destroyed. In this respect such a conflict is different from the model of power and security competition, which will be discussed later in this study, where the contest takes a tangible form, in terms of relative capacities to wage war, and where, although war is regarded as being endemic, the actual alignments and policies pursued are *ad hoc*, with friends becoming enemies and enemies friends. The issue, or occasion, of conflict in this latter case is the existence of differential war capacities and the consequent fears of states for their existence as inviolable territorial entities. As will be seen later, this view of international politics is concerned with a number of factors related to international violence, technological, organisational, logistical and material in nature, and asserts that these determine, if not the respective belligerents, the actual scale of the war itself. The modern age is regarded as an age of total war because of the vastly increased capacities of states to use violence against each other. Ideological conflict is, however, total in a different sense, since what is at stake here is the total destruction of the alien ideology and, given the absolute basis of such a struggle, such a conflict is not won or decided until this has occurred. The element of variability, or what might be termed the pragmatic nature of political activity, if not completely absent, is peripheral to this type of conflict.

Thus while political conflicts which are occasioned by national concerns for security, or by tangible or definable interests, can be resolved by means other than violence, ideological conflicts can only be resolved by violence itself, unless the opponent is willing to abandon its socio-political system. The view of the Cold War as being essentially an ideological conflict postulates an inherent incompatibility between socialist and non-socialist states. Hence an explanation of the struggle between the Soviet Union and the United States, in terms of their competing socio-political systems, contains this assumption of total war as the means of resolving their conflict. The military and diplomatic aspects of the early stages of the Cold War simply reflect this fundamental incompatibility between these states. Before examining some of the implications of this argument, a distinction should be made between an ideological explanation which purports to be a universal explanation, and an interpretation which asserts idealogical causes for a particular conflict, but which does not claim that these afford an explanation for all international political behaviour. In short, this distinction exists between those who accept the kind of Marxist explanation of history discussed in the previous chapter, and those who proffer a more limited interpretation, which stresses the importance of values and beliefs in motivating human action.

The former position has been criticised on theoretical grounds and a discussion of the Hobson–Lenin theory of imperialism will be found later in this study. The point here is that the Cold War can be seen in ideological terms without accepting a Marxist explanation of historical process. Clearly, a Marxist historian is forced to advance an interpretation of the Cold War which can be subsumed within the framework of his general theory of human behaviour. To this extent such an interpretation *is* an ideological explanation and can be refuted or verified only within its own terms. However, we are concerned here with the argument that the statesmen of the period 1945 to 1947 were primarily motivated by values and beliefs about their own political systems, and about the world, which were irreconcilable, and which influenced their actions and decisions. It cannot be assumed, because politicians habitually express their policies in terms of values, or because there is a conscious attempt to relate ideologies to practice, that an explanation of their behaviour can be grounded on an ideological position. A historical interpretation which makes such an assumption is under the obligation of providing evidence for it.

If, then, we look again at the international politics of this period, we may find evidence that behaviour bore some relationship to values and beliefs. For example, according to Milovan Djilas, Stalin expressed the view that the Second World War was 'not as in the past: whoever occupies a territory also imposes on it his own social system. Everyone imposes his own system as far as his army has power to do so.'[23] This would appear to recognise the political significance of changing the internal political conditions of an occupied country and also the major condition for doing so. But it does not provide an explanation of motive. As we have seen, Stalin did impose new political conditions in all the countries which were occupied by the Red Army. In his diplomacy he advocated territorial gains for the Soviet Union and a recognition on the part of his allies of parts of Europe and Asia as being within the Soviet sphere of influence. He was willing, in exchange, to recognise western influence in other areas.[24] Yet his motives and his intentions were open to speculation, and it is significant that his actions and diplomacy were not divorced from an attempt to reach an accommodation with the major capitalist powers. Moreover, the pursuit of unilateral policies in the area of Soviet interests paralleled those of the western powers and cannot be explained without reference to the policies of the latter states. The Cold War was defined earlier as a complete breakdown in relationships, in which two hostile alliances developed, each extending its own power within its own capabilities, but avoiding violence against each other. Such a breakdown must be described in terms of *both* sides and their respective diplomatic positions and interactions.

In the case of the United States and her allies, reference to values certainly existed in their political statements and explanations of policy. Some commentators[25] have treated the Truman Doctrine as direct evidence of ideological motivation. Passages from this speech which assert an American concern for the free world have been cited in support of this view. For example, the following passage:

At the present moment in world history nearly every nation must choose between alternative ways of life. The choice is too often not a free one. One way of life is based upon the will of the majority and is distinguished by free institutions, representative government, free elections, guarantees of individual liberty, freedom of speech and religion and freedom from political oppression.

The second way of life is based upon the will of a minority forcibly imposed upon the majority. It relies upon terror and oppression, a con-

trolled press and radio, fixed elections, and the suppression of personal
freedom . . . [26]

is taken to represent a declaration of ideological war by the United States.
The major motivation in American policy, in this view, is based upon
democratic values and a rejection of communism.

There is a major problem in historical interpretation when the question
of motivation arises. This is particularly true when values are alleged to
be the basis of political decision-making. But while political statement and
political action are linked, the latter cannot be explained solely by the
former, especially in the field of international politics, given the heterogeneity of the environment. The nature of the link requires careful
examination. A universalist or reductionist explanation of history avoids
this problem by the assertion of general causes, or by stating the conditions
for specific types of political behaviour, and thus reduces the irrational
factor in human choice. But the politicians themselves are also apt to
present the reasons for their actions in general terms, or in such a way as
to indicate their control over international situations. There is a language
of politics as well as conventions which govern what politicians can admit
to their public. The level and nature of political statement such as the
Truman Doctrine varies according to the socio-political system in which
it is made, or to which it is directed, and one can explain the discrepancies
between them in terms of the different audiences which receive them. It is
clear from what has been said that the Soviet Union and the United States
came to regard each other as enemies, but the fact that they separately
described their mutual hostility in ideological terms does not mean axiomatically that the basis of their conflict was ideological. It could mean
that the ideological language in which it was expressed represented a
dialogue between rulers and ruled, and that the non-ideological nature of
international relations is translated into other terms for domestic political
purposes. We may take the interpretation of the world situation offered
by party leaders at Soviet Party Congresses as being intrinsically of the
same nature as presidential messages to Congress, that is, as part of the
domestic politics of the U.S.S.R. and the U.S.A.

Nevertheless, foreign policy consists of choices of objectives which may
or may not be fulfilled or capable of fulfilment, but which are conceived
of as being desirable by those in power. In this sense they may condition
judgement and decision in specific international situations. If these
objectives are based upon ideological premises, then the influence of values
may be felt in international politics. To return to the international situation
just after the Second World War, it is possible to construe Soviet foreign
policy as being opportunist, but in a way which was related to the desire
to extend socialism beyond the U.S.S.R. Similarly, the United States chose,
out of several possibilities, to extend economic and military support to

Western European and Mediterranean countries. Yet the choices of these two states may have been ideologically conditioned but not ideologically directed. For example, Stalin agreed to give Britain a free hand in Greece, although there was a promising situation there from the point of view of the promotion of an indigenous communist movement into power. He also advised the Yugoslav communists[27] to compromise with the royalists, and similarly advised Mao Tse-tung to collaborate with the Kuomintang.[28] Even in the area actually occupied by the Red Army, the notion of a popular revolution was not encouraged, although the allegiance of governments to the Soviet Union was based upon the careful packing of regimes with members of the indigenous communist party. There is little evidence of a concern with world revolution or the promotion of specifically ideological goals in Soviet foreign policy at this time. The ideological content of Soviet policy statements became more apparent when hostility deepened to the point that any accommodation with the western powers became extremely unlikely. It was therefore a reflection of the worsening relations with the capitalist countries and was not of itself a cause of this deterioration.

This was also true of western policy, and the height of the Cold War was marked by the assertion of ideological, rather than political, differences between the contenders. When attempts at compromise had been abandoned, then nothing was lost by such posturing, and indeed it can be argued, particularly in the western case, that the assertion of the Soviet threat in ideological terms was necessary, in order for governments to obtain the necessary legislative and financial support for the new foreign and defence policies. Truman and his advisers were aware that popular sentiment at the closing stages of the war was not hostile to the Soviet Union, and that some preparation of public opinion was essential,[29] in order to obtain both bipartisan support for the new policy and Congressional approval of the new commitments which the United States was about to undertake. The emphasis on both sides was on the need for defensive measures to be taken against what was represented as being an aggressive and powerful state bent on territorial expansion, and with an alien ideology. Rearmament and the maintenance of conscription were not popular measures, especially after the heavy burdens of the war itself, and some political justification had to be found for them. This argument of itself would appear to explain why public explanations of policy were couched in language which was intended to appeal to the susceptibilities of the audience to which they were directed. The question as to whether values and ideology were actually relevant to motivation will be left open for the moment.

The problem of defence and national security is closely related to an alternative explanation of the origins of the Cold War. This is bound up with what has been called the security dilemma, which will be discussed at length later in this study. Essentially, the explanation is based on the assumption that the primary objective of a state in its external relations is the preservation of itself as a state, that is, with its security. The threat to its political integrity is interpreted in terms of the capacity to use violence possessed by other states. Consequently, security is achieved only where the state possesses a superior military capacity and is therefore capable of waging a successful war. If all states share this concept of security, then the result is a perpetual competition between them, in order to achieve the decisive superiority which alone will make them secure. Thus the Second World War ended in the destruction of those states which sought to achieve this superiority, but left the problem of security to the victors. All they had achieved was the removal of one specific threat, they had not resolved the central problem of security in international politics. The United Nations has been regarded by some commentators as being an attempt to change the competitive nature of international politics much as its predecessor, the League of Nations, had been. This aspect will be considered in another part of this study. However, the point is that in terms of its peace-enforcement function the United Nations consisted of the great powers themselves. Those states most capable of breaking the peace were in effect charged with keeping it. The United Nations could only therefore be effective if these powers were in agreement. Given this condition, it is difficult to conceive of a political conflict in which the United Nations could be effective, other than one which involved the smaller powers only. Should the great powers themselves be in conflict, then the *United* Nations did not effectively exist, and should they be in harmony then a condition of peace already existed. The point is that the victor powers created an organisation which symbolised their war-time agreement but which did not, and could not, resolve their respective security dilemmas. Once the war was over, these states were forced by this dilemma into regarding each other as a threat, actual or potential.

It is important to point out that this argument does not place its emphasis upon intentions but rather upon the relative capacities for violence which coexist in any given international situation. A nation-state treats as a potential enemy those states which are in a position to deal it a grievous blow, regardless of any clear intention to do so, or any overtly hostile policy. It can be seen that ideology is irrelevant in this interpretation of international political behaviour, for the enemy is defined not in terms of a hostile socio-political system but in terms of resources, geography and weapons technology. There are a number of factors, such as the nature and strength of a government, the degree of organisation of its resources, its economy and the level of its technology, etc., which, as will be seen later in this study, act as variables in the international environment and make it, from the point of view of the state, chaotic. The consequence of this unstable environment is that it presents a permanent threat to the states existing in it, and so that pursuit of security extends into an attempt to control it. This attempt is usually termed the pursuit of power, and security competition turns into a power struggle between states, each endeavouring to achieve weapons superiority and to control the factors which appear to be decisive in determining victory. These factors are variables and consequently the conditions for this struggle, and its specific form, are constantly changing. The invention of new weapons or the discovery of new industrial or technological processes may be as important to a nation's security as a change of government or of an alliance.

On this argument, alliances are merely temporal arrangements designed to forestall any hostile coalition from forming, and to prevent isolation. Such arrangements are prone to constant change as the major factors in the overall political and strategic situation change. There are, given certain stable factors such as spatial relations between states, and a weapons technology which is not subject to qualitative changes, constants in a nation's defence policy, in the sense that a government is concerned with a continuing strategic problem. Certain neighbouring states may be 'hereditary' enemies, for example. However, the relationship between war, foreign and defence policies and the international environment will be discussed at length in a later part of this study; the point here is that the emergence of two opposed alliance systems in the immediate post-war world can be explained by the exigencies of national security, and the responses made to them by the participants, without recourse to other interpretations such as that based upon ideological conflict discussed above.

To return to the post-war situation, it is true, as we have seen earlier, that the Soviets emphasised their security needs in demanding territorial concessions in their frontier areas and in extending their spheres of influence in Asia and in Europe.[30] Certainly, this was the justification made by Stalin and his representatives on presenting their demands to the western allies. In two major wars the Soviet Union had suffered German invasion, although their defeats could be attributed more to internal military and political weaknesses than to their lack of adequate buffer zones between a major potential aggressor. The evidence in support of this assertion is found in such factors and events as the purges of the Red Army in the late 1930s, the disaffection and pro-German sentiments in White Russia and the Crimea during the initial stages of the German invasion, the reverses in the Winter War with Finland and those in the fighting with Japanese troops in 1938 and 1939, and the general military unpreparedness revealed at the beginning of the war with Germany, with the subsequent heavy reliance on Lend-Lease for war material. Nevertheless, the instability of Eastern European and Balkan politics over the inter-war period had been a source of considerable anxiety to the Soviet government, especially after the German treaty of friendship with Poland in 1934. Poland, in particular, was conceived of as a major weakness on Russia's western frontier. In April 1945

Stalin reacted to American pressure on him to implement the terms of the Yalta agreement by broadening the provisional Polish government, saying: 'But you demand too much of me. In other words you demand that I renounce the interests of security of the Soviet Union, but I cannot turn against my country.'[31]

Thus the defeat of Germany and of Japan had profound political significance, not only because two of the major threats to security had been removed, but also because of the release of those countries which had been dominated by these two powers from their influence. The situation was what has been described by some commentators[32] as a 'power vacuum' in Central Europe and in the Pacific. The areas over which these states had held sway were either occupied by their opponents or were 'liberated' and nominally independent. In political terms this meant that the German and Japanese losses were the allies' gains, and this was clearly understood by the latter states. In terms of security, however, what was the significance of this changed situation? Soviet forces in Eastern Europe were as supreme there as American forces were in Japan and the Pacific. No challenge could be made to either position in terms of conventional weapons without embarking on another world war. The United States' insistence on its monopoly of control in Japan, in the conquered Pacific territories and in South Korea, and her alliance with Chiang Kai-shek, were the political concomitants of her position as the largest naval power in the Pacific and a concept of security through dominance over this area. The Pacific was a vital interest to the United States, and the Japanese attack on Pearl Harbor may be considered as traumatic an experience to the Americans as the German invasion was to the U.S.S.R. Thus both states placed considerable importance on their control over the areas which they considered important to their security. If this could be achieved by mutual accommodation, then a diplomatic settlement was obviously preferable, but if not, then both were prepared to pursue unilateral policies in areas which directly involved their security.

Retrospectively, it was ironic that such a security interest had become invalid with the advent of nuclear weapons. It is clear, using hindsight, that the security situation had changed radically after the Second World War. The most important invention in weapons technology since the discovery of gunpowder had occurred with the creation of the atomic bomb. The significance of this weapon, and its effect on international politics and national defence and foreign policies, will be discussed later in this study: the point here is that with its invention a new arms race began between the victorious allies. Even those states which were to be most closely related to the United States, Britain and France, in spite of their alliance were not content to allow the former country to retain its monopoly in the nuclear field, and developed nuclear weapons programmes of their own. The subsequent arms race appears to bear out the point made earlier, that defence policies are largely a response to the capacities, and not to the intentions, of other states. At this time, however, since strategy was based on relatively short-range aircraft, a territorially orientated defence policy effectively masked the revolutionary nature of these weapons. The United States needed foreign air bases, and the Soviet Union needed a neutral insulation around its borders composed of states under its control.

What were the attitudes of the other major powers towards security questions and the changed situation in Europe after the Second World War? Britain from the beginning of its wartime alliance with the Soviet Union had resisted the territorial demands of the latter state.[33] In traditional terms, British policy was concerned with preventing any one European power from dominating the continent and thus being in a position to control the Channel ports and thus challenge British security. The defeat of Germany and Italy, given the weakness of France, made it clear that the Soviet Union would emerge as the most influential power in Europe. Consequently, British policy sought to counterbalance this extension of Soviet influence. There were a number of difficulties in doing this, not the least being the initial reluctance of the United States to agree to any wartime negotiations over political questions.[34] It was not clear, in any case, that American interests were bound up in supporting British policy. Moreover, the declared intention of Roosevelt to remove American troops from Europe within two years of the cessation of hostilities seemed to confirm the lack of American interest in European politics.[35] On the grounds of security alone, it can be seen that Britain had a clear interest in checking any extension of Soviet influence, particularly in areas adjacent to the Channel and the North Sea. This reflected a British concern for security which was related to traditional naval strategy and also to the new weapons of aircraft and long-range rockets. Thus British policy not only opposed the Soviet attempt to gain territory and influence in Europe, but also played on American fears and suspicions in an attempt to obtain support from the United States. It was very much in the British interest to drive a wedge between the U.S.S.R. and the United States at this time. There were other factors, in addition to that of security considerations, which urged British policy in this direction.

For example, Britain was absorbed with serious economic problems which precluded any major commitment, either to the economic recovery of Western Europe or to its defence. A major loan from the United States was in the course of negotiation in the period immediately following the war. As Churchill put it: 'If the Americans left Europe, Britain would have to occupy single-handed the entire western portion of Germany. Such a task would be far beyond our strength.'[36] This situation was exacerbated by British imperial interests outside Europe. The situation in the Far East after the defeat of Japan would require a considerable expenditure of resources in order to restore the pre-war situation. Hence the existence of a large overseas empire, part of which had been overrun by the Japanese, constituted a major preoccupation for the British government, and a diversion from European questions. Nevertheless, security considerations appeared to be the major motivation for British policy towards the Soviet Union, and these established the latter state as being hostile, not on the basis of its actual demands, some of which were acceptable to Britain, but because of her capacity to expand even further, and more directly, against British interests. It should not be forgotten that British policy in 1939 challenged Hitler, not because his political demands were made directly against specific British security interests, but because of the German capacity to make and implement them by force, and because of the inability to trust German agreements which was revealed after the German occupation of Prague in March 1939. In 1945, so far as the British government was concerned, the size of the Soviet armies in Eastern Europe, and the weakness of the Western European governments, indicated a capacity of which Stalin could take advantage, as Hitler used the political divisions in Europe to further his own ends. There also existed the same doubts as to Stalin's intentions and his desire to keep agreements once they had been negotiated. In short, British policy placed numerous obstacles in the way of the Soviet Union and sought to establish an Anglo-American coalition. In order to achieve this last, Churchill tried to extend the area of western influence in Europe by urging Eisenhower to continue his advance as far beyond the designated western zone of occupation as possible.[37] He sought also to hold the major negotiations between the heads of state before the general withdrawal to the allocated zones, in order to be in a position to put pressure on Stalin. The former was against the spirit, and the latter against the letter, of the agreements between the allies. This move reflected the attitude taken towards the Soviet Union by Britain and the security fears which prompted it.

France was much less suspicious of the Soviet Union and much more concerned with internal political problems stemming from the occupation and the liberation. It could, in any case, be argued that her exclusion from the diplomacy and negotiations at the closing stages of the European war not only isolated her temporarily from international politics, but also bred in her political leaders a conviction that the divisions between the allies could be exploited to the French advantage. Moreover, given a continuing American presence in Germany, the French were able to adopt an independent line in policy, which took advantage of the new situation. Thus in spite of internal political difficulties and the presence of a large communist party with representation in the government, the French disagreed with British and American attempts to fuse the western zones of Germany and sought an accommodation with the Soviet Union.[38] It was clear in this early period that security questions were not predominant in French policy, except in so far as it was committed to preventing any future German military revival. So far as this last was concerned, French policy was much more in line with the Soviet position than with that of Britain or the United States.

This ambivalent attitude was dropped during the European economic crisis of 1947, and the French moved rapidly with the British to an acceptance of the Marshall Plan and to the negotiation of NATO. The point here is that the French initially sought to exploit a bargaining situation, implicit in the Soviet–Western conflict, which was emerging from 1945 onwards. The abandonment of this attempt for a policy of alignment was really the product of economic problems, combined with domestic political factors, rather than of a desire for security. It could of course be argued that this last question was in any case resolved by the continuing presence of British and American forces in West Germany, since this commitment provided an implicit guarantee of French security almost regardless of the French government's attitude.

However, the security interpretation of the origins of the Cold War appears to break down when the policy of the United States towards Europe is considered. As was noted earlier, President Roosevelt had declared his intention of withdrawing his troops from Europe, yet some two and a half years later the American government was not only consolidating a position in Western Germany which implied an indefinite commitment of troops in Europe, but was also extending material support to governments outside Europe itself and in areas remote from former American interests, in order to allay their fears of their communist neighbours. Clearly, a major change in American policy had occurred and it is this change which lies at the root of any explanation of the origins of the Cold War. The question here is, in what way was this profound shift in American policy related to security questions? The statement made by Truman to Congress, known as the Truman Doctrine, said that 'totalitarian regimes imposed upon free peoples by direct or indirect aggression, undermine the foundations of international peace and hence the security of the United States'. He went on to argue that if Greece and Turkey fell under communist domination, then 'Confusion and disorder might will spread throughout the entire Middle East'.[39] If this statement is taken at its face value, then such a notion of security was related to an ideological challenge which operated very indirectly, and which affected the United States only in terms of its relationships with the non-communist world. In this sense security was intimately connected to the form of government, or the socio-political system, found in the United States, and did not take a tangible military form. Such a concept of security contains a number of uncertainties and paradoxes. The point here is that it was a new concept, and the traditional concern with relative military capacities as the major factor involving national security was subordinated to a concern with the nature of governments in other countries. In other words, the position of the Soviet Union in Eastern Europe may have been a threat to British or French security, conceived of in military-political terms, but it could not have been a threat to American security in the same terms unless the Soviet Union possessed nuclear weapons, and a navy equal or superior in strength to that of the United States in both the Atlantic and the Pacific.

We may thus rephrase our question by asking, why did the United States conceive of the Soviet position in Eastern Europe, which on this argument was undoubtedly a threat to Western European countries, as a threat to itself? It would appear that such a question can be answered only on ideological or other grounds and not in terms of national security. The American commitment to Europe was undertaken in order to prevent the expansion of communism, and the danger to Western Europe was conceived of as being as much from indigenous European communist parties, exploiting post-war economic difficulties, as from the presence of the Red Army on the Elbe. Given the nuclear monopoly enjoyed by the United States at the end of the Second World War, it was inconceivable that a direct military threat could be posed against either the United States, or an ally, without a devastating response. Once the United States undertook the major responsibility for the security of Western Europe, the major problem was not from without but from within. Yet this concern for the domestic politics of non-communist countries represents a concern with the tactics of a containment policy and, so far as motivation or its premises are concerned, is not very revealing. A European security threat, and the notion of an ideological menace from a revolutionary political faction, supported by a major power, could coexist in terms of a common tactic without anomalies arising out of their inherent incompatibility. Western European politicians could accept, and indeed encourage, the American concern for the spread of communism, while maintaining their own preoccupation with political and security questions. It was only when the nuclear arms race reached a new stage of development, and when the conflict moved to areas outside Europe, that the latent divisions between the allies, arising out of their different policy premises, became overt. But in the period immediately after the war the security element and the ideological element were fused in the notion of the Soviet Union as the common enemy. It should be clear from this argument that Britain, France and Italy were not obsessed by fears of communist ideology, except in so far as these could be related to the exploitation of domestic political situations by various parties and factions seeking power, but that their real concern was with obtaining economic aid from the only country capable of conferring it, and with transferring the burden of providing a guarantee for European security on to a power which at that time enjoyed a monopoly of nuclear weapons.

Why the United States undertook such a burden is inexplicable on general grounds. Such a commitment to European security meant providing a guarantee to the Western European states against external aggression, providing them with large amounts of capital, and the permanent occupation of West Germany. All this was a radical departure from previous American foreign policy. The only security gain for the United States would appear to be the agreement with Britain for the leasing of strategic air bases.[40] It could be argued that such an agreement could have been achieved on the basis of a 'special relationship' without involving the United States in a major commitment in Europe.

If we return to the problem of motivation, we can see that general hypotheses such as the notion of power and security competition, or of ideological war, do not provide an adequate explanation for the breakdown in relationships between the former allies. It has been maintained in this discussion, and in the chapter which preceded it, that recourse to general hypotheses is a characteristic of historical interpretation. Any analysis of ideological or security interpretations of international political behaviour implies certain concepts and theorising assumptions, if only to give coherence to a narration of selected political events. Such an explanation implies some form of generalisation. Yet it should be remembered that the events which form the subject-matter of this analysis were the consequences of human decisions. Thus a reconstruction of the situation, and an explanation of it, should consider the beliefs and attitudes of the participants. What is important, if this approach is taken, is not the assertion of the dynamics of a security competition as an explanation of political decisions, but establishing whether the participants themselves accepted this argument and, if so, whether they extended it into action. The theoretical incompatibility of rival ideologies, or the inexorable nemesis of an arms race, may be adequate or consistent as hypotheses but inadequate as an explanation of the past, if the participants themselves were totally ignorant of these arguments. Certainly, many of the terms and concepts. belonging to the level of hypothetical reasoning in international politics are commonly used by politicians. Terms such as 'power', 'security', 'the national interest', 'the rule of law', etc., abound in the speeches, statements and writings of those involved in the major decisions of this period. What they meant by them, and how they influenced their actions, are difficult questions to answer and yet they are essential to any non-mechanistic explanation.

In the case of the Soviet Union, the evidence for Stalin's motivation, or of the reasoning which underlay his decisions, is virtually non-existent. Any attempt at reconstruction must depend upon what evidence exists for Soviet diplomacy and on Soviet action itself. Interviews with journalists, and the various indirect sources used by some commentators, are difficult to evaluate and would appear to support any hypothesis, provided it is sufficiently broad or ambiguous. The picture obtained of Stalin in Milovan Djilas's book, for example, cannot be disassociated from the hypothesis of Soviet expansion or 'imperialism' also contained in that work.[41] This argument is clearly related to a very small part of Soviet diplomacy, namely that concerned with Yugoslavia. If it is accepted, then Stalin was not ideologically inspired in his policy but was simply a modern Tsar, governed by a conception of *Realpolitik* shared by his western opponents, and concerned for the acquisition of territory for the sake of Soviet aggrandisement. Such a view cannot easily be separated from the author's own perception and his own ideological presuppositions.

Thus an explanation which is founded upon the operation of some external hypothesis unknown to the participants, or one which presumes upon attitudes and knowledge which did not exist or could not have existed at the time, is not a historical interpretation. For example, recent 'revisionist' historians[42] have sought to explode the 'myth' of Soviet expansion in the immediate post-war period by pointing out certain inconsistencies in this argument and the unreasonableness of such a policy. They argue that Stalin tried to reach agreement with his allies and did not conceal his demands from them, that agreements actually reached through negotiation were broken by the western governments which participated in their negotiation, and that in any case the Soviet Union was too weakened by her war losses to embark upon any major territorial expansion. The point is, of course, that what appears reasonable to later commentators is not relevant to a historical interpretation. A historian is concerned with reconstructing the attitudes, etc., of the participants, not with imposing his own on them, or relying on later reappraisals based upon changing political attitudes. It is clear from what evidence we have that the Truman administration believed that the Soviet Union was an expansionist power, however irrational such a belief might appear *post facto*. Some members of the administration, notably Henry Wallace, thought otherwise, but the policy premise which was actually adopted was that which was embodied in the Truman Doctrine. It is possible for latter-day revisionists, such as George Kennan himself,[43] to say that American policy was misguided, or resulted in self-fulfilling prophecies, but while the implications of a policy can be pointed out in historical terms, that is, as they actually evolved on the level of action and behaviour, the 'rightness' of a decision or the rationality of a policy cannot be established except in terms of the attitudes and behaviour of the participants themselves. These questions are really related to the world of practice, rather than to historical analysis. We are not concerned with the 'responsibility' or 'guilt' of the political leaders of the immediate post-war period for the Cold War. Such judgements contain moral or ethical standpoints rather than a concern for 'causes'.

While there is little evidence of the reasoning of the Soviet leaders, other than that which can be inferred from their diplomatic overtures, there is considerable evidence for the western side. Many of the participants subsequently wrote their memoirs and explained their policies, or their influence upon decisions and events. Obviously, these accounts should be approached with caution, especially where they are both partial and contain retrospective judgements. Nevertheless, there is a remarkable degree of agreement in them in treating the Soviet Union as an expansionist power which endangered western interests. It was the Soviet Union, in these arguments, which initiated the Cold War by breaking agreements and making demands on the western states which, if they were accepted, would result in a considerable extension of Soviet power. Some writers stressed the argument that the chief danger to Western Europe was from its own internal weakness and the activities of its indigenous communist parties,[44] while others have emphasised the danger of direct Soviet aggression.[45] It seems clear from the Truman Doctrine and the Marshall Aid programme, as well as from the available evidence, that the American government leaned more in the direction of the former argument than the latter. The point is, however, that from early 1945 onwards the Soviet Union was treated as a hostile state by the British and American governments and consequently all agreements, both tacit and formal, which had been concluded during the closing stages of the war were revised and negotiations ceased to be important, since a genuine accommodation to the Soviet position was not sought. The early part of this period was complicated by the rapid advance of Soviet troops into Germany and by the priority of military requirements. Since the allies had agreed on the unconditional surrender of Germany as their prime objective, and on the division of Germany into occupation zones,[46] it was difficult to introduce political considerations into the strategy for the final German collapse without running the risk of creating a major rift in the alliance. Churchill's attempt to counter the advantage provided by the Russian advance, by extending the area of western conquest and using this as a means of putting pressure on the Soviet Union during the negotiations of the European settlement, was eventually rejected by the United States.[47] Moreover, the desire of the United States for Soviet entry into the war against Japan, and for Soviet participation and acquiescence in the United Nations negotiations, further weakened the Western bargaining position. Once Germany and Japan had been defeated and the United Nations was a *fait accompli,* these inhibitions on western policy were removed and a confrontation with the Soviet Union could then be sought.

Thus once the end of the European war was in sight, the two western allies tried to restrict Soviet influence in Eastern and Southern Europe. Soviet responses to this were initially to try to obtain Western agreement on her predominance in this area in exchange for Soviet acquiescence to the Western position in other areas. Linked with this were other demands, some of which appear to be made for bargaining purposes, rather than as substantive proposals. When it became apparent through the negotiations on Poland that the Western powers were uncompromising on this question, then the Soviet Union adopted a unilateral policy in order to consolidate her gains. The period from April 1945 to May 1946 was largely a time of diplomatic manoeuvring, with the western powers, initially handicapped by the factors referred to above, seeking to apply pressure on the Soviet Union. The point when this manoeuvring ceased and co-operation with the Soviet Union was abandoned probably occurred some time in 1946, although the cessation of reparations deliveries from the western zones to the Soviet Union, which occurred in May, could be interpreted as being yet another attempt to put pressure on the Soviet government.[48] Other hostile acts, such as the support given to Turkey in resisting the Soviet proposals for the revision of the Montreux Treaty, could be considered in the same light. There was evidence that Soviet intentions, although profoundly mistrusted, were still considered as being in doubt by the United States. Thus Forrestal describes the President's reaction to the Soviet proposals on the Dardanelles made in August 1946 in the following terms: 'The President replied that he was perfectly clear that we should take a firm position both in this instance and in China; that we might as well find out whether the Russians were bent on world conquest now as in five or ten years.'[49] Truman then took the unprecedented action of establishing a permanent Mediterranean squadron with the full approval of the British government.

Thus, on the American side, the documents published by the State Department and by the Senate Foreign Relations Committee on this period, as well as the various memoirs and diaries written by the participants, give a coherent picture of a growing hostility to the Soviet Union dating from April 1945, that is, from the time Truman came to power. Up to this time individual voices had been heard, warning policy-makers as to danger from the Soviet Union, but these were tempered by the pragmatic and flexible policy pursued by President Roosevelt, concerned in the main with war aims and which leaned in the direction of co-operation with the U.S.S.R. In any case, policy-making was firmly in the hands of the President, and there was no official or quasipublic debate on its objectives. The death of the President created a major hiatus in American foreign policy at a most critical stage in international politics. President Truman, although having acted as Vice-President, was not privy to policy-making and was not informed as to the current situation when he came to office.[50] It is noteworthy that those who had been prominent as critics of the Soviet Union in the previous administration became most influential as advisers or officers in the Truman administration. Those who believed that some form of agreement with the Soviet Union was possible, or desirable, were either forced to resign, as was the case with Henry Wallace, or were removed to less prominent positions. Such a leading advocate of a firm policy as Averell Harriman moved from the ambassadorship at Moscow, from which position he had urged the administration as early as April 1945[51] that 'unless we and the British now adopt an independent line the people under the areas of our responsibility will suffer and the chances

of Soviet domination in Europe will be enhanced', to the key ambassadorship in London. From this position he was promoted into the Cabinet as
Secretary of Commerce in place of Henry Wallace. Similarly, James
Forrestal, himself an active critic of the U.S.S.R., moved into the foreign
policy-making circle and was promoted from the Secretaryship of the Navy
to become Secretary of Defence, George Kennan likewise moved from a
subordinate position in the Moscow embassy to become chief of the central
planning group set up in 1947. This body was to implement Forrestal's
proposal, made to the Cabinet after the Truman Doctrine had been
declared, that 'in view of the feeling that our support for Greece and
Turkey might be the forerunner of many other and very much larger
economic political actions in other parts of the world we should make a
study of what may confront us in the next eighteen months'.[52] Kennan
had been responsible for a number of memoranda[53] as well as for the
'Mr X' article, in which he urged a policy of containment of the Soviet
Union permitting the Soviets to have freedom of action in the areas which
they actually controlled, but which refused to accept this control in terms
of formal diplomatic recognition, and was aimed at preventing any future
expansion.

The policy-makers of this period were thus moving away from a policy
of accommodation to Soviet interests, to a position which not only refused
to accept Soviet demands as being negotiable, but which rejected those
agreements which had already been made. By December 1946 Byrnes, then
Secretary of State, said of his private meeting with Molotov earlier that
month that he had taken the position that the Kuriles and the Sakhalin
question had not been finally decided by the Yalta agreement.[54] This was
in response to the Soviet demand for involvement in determining the fate
of the former Japanese possessions in the Pacific. According to Forrestal,
he said to Molotov that 'he regarded nothing as being subjected to
previous agreements'.[55] The American tactic was to reopen all partially
resolved disputes since Yalta itself, and was clearly an attempt to bring the
Soviets to accept the American positions on the peace treaties with the
former enemy states, on the government of Poland, on the administration
of Germany as an economic unit, and on reparations. The advocates of
'firmness' had won the day. The American government argued that the
Soviet Union had itself violated the agreement to hold free elections in
the occupied territories and to treat Germany as an economic unit. Hence
it was free to interpret such agreements as had been concluded as it wished,
and to take reprisals in response to Soviet failure to abide by decisions
which had been reached by prolonged and controversial negotiations.

It is of course possible to regard these differences between the Soviet
Union and the two western allies as more the product of misunderstandings
than of a fundamental clash of interests. It appears clear from the extant
evidence that both the British and the American governments realised

that the Soviet desire for security was the basis of the demands which they were making as part of the post-war settlement. Byrnes himself said, apropos his negotiations with the Soviets over the composition of the governments of Romania and Bulgaria in December 1945: 'It must be recognised that the Soviet government has a very real interest in the character of the governments of these states.'[56] The dilemma appeared to him to be the problem of reconciling conflicting security interests. As he put it in the following May: 'Security is the concern of every nation. But the effort of one nation to increase its security may threaten the security of other nations and cause them in turn to try to increase their own security. The quest for security may lead to less rather than more security in the world.'[57] In his argument, the American offer to guarantee German disarmament, and consequently Soviet security, for twenty-five years should suffice to allay Soviet fears. But such a proposal was itself disingenuous, since it arose out of a speech made by Senator Arthur Vandenberg in January 1945[58] and was considered by Forrestal to be a device for keeping the Soviet Union out of the border states. With an independent Poland, Soviet occupation forces in Eastern Germany would be isolated and could not then pose as a threat to Western Europe. The notion that this situation, or that American power itself, could be conceived as a security threat by the Soviets does not appear to have been seriously considered by American policy-makers. Byrnes's clear statement of the security dilemma did not consider the qualitative changes in the notion of national security caused by the development of nuclear weapons, nor did he see that the argument could be applied to the United States as well as to the Soviet Union.

Nevertheless, this reference to the mutual security problem highlights the central difficulty in the negotiations of 1945–6. It is a difficulty which has bedevilled American policy-makers ever since, and it hinges on the relation-ship of power to policy, that is, of war or military capacity to intentions. The United States moved into a position of support for the British policy of opposing the Soviet demands in Eastern Europe. As we have seen, this policy was based upon a traditional conception of national security. Yet while the Churchill government was apparently prepared to compromise on the relative degree of influence which would be enjoyed by the contend-ing powers in this area, the United States was not. British policy was designed to obtain the support of the United States, but having obtained it, it then ceased to be the major influence in Europe. This was the price paid for what amounted to an Anglo-American alliance and it was closely bound up with Britain's economic difficulties and the need for financial aid from the United States. American policy thus became dominant and was based on 'firmness'. In Truman's view, success in negotiation with the U.S.S.R. rested ultimately on American power. As he put it: '. . . Russia's ambitions would not be halted by a friendly reminder of promises made. The Russians would press wherever weakness showed – and we would have to meet that pressure wherever it occurred, in a manner that Russia and the world would understand.'[59] The problem with this approach was that understanding turned on the intentions behind the respective pressures and counter-pressures. From the Soviet point of view their security needs appeared to have been understood by the West, but after tentative agreement were then denied fulfilment. Consequently they moved, as did the West, into the pursuit of unilateral policies in the areas which they controlled. It is this movement which the West termed expansion. But the United States also expanded in this sense. The power and influence of the United States were exerted in areas which had formerly been free of American interest. In September 1946 Byrnes made an important speech in Stuttgart in which he said: 'Security forces will probably have to remain in Germany for a long period. I want no misunderstanding. We will not shirk our duty. We are not withdrawing. We are staying here. As long as there is an occupation army in Germany, American armed forces will be part of that occupation army.'[60] In the following December agreement was reached with the British government on the merger of the British and American occupation zones of Germany.[61] At the end of 1946 the United States was committed to a military presence in Central Europe until agreement was reached with the Soviet Union on a German peace treaty. But such an agreement appeared to be purely academic once this position was adopted.

At the same time, American expansion occurred in the Pacific as a consequence of the Japanese collapse. With the exceptions of the small gains made by the U.S.S.R. in North Korea and north of Japan, and the European colonial territories, the United States reigned supreme in this area. A close involvement in the internal affairs of China, together with the presence of occupation forces in South Korea, extended American influence even further. If the possession of the largest naval forces in the world and a monopoly of nuclear weapons is added to this situation, it is not surprising that Soviet reactions to American 'firmness' were sharp. In April 1946 General Bedell Smith, the American ambassador to the U.S.S.R., had an interview with Stalin in which he asked the latter whether he thought the United States and Britain were 'united in an alliance to thwart Russia.' Stalin is reported to have 'replied in the affirmative'.[62] Certainly, in the Soviet view the United States was a potential, if not actual, security threat.

But from the American and British views during these two years, Soviet demands for more territory and influence appeared to be insatiable and, what was perhaps more disturbing, related to some long-term objective which threatened Western interests. What President Truman called 'pressures' not only amounted to a virtual monopoly of influence over Eastern Europe and the Balkans, but also consisted of the refusal to co-operate in treating Germany as an economic unit and to agree on a common policy as to its post-war future, the prolonged negotiations over Trieste and the Italian peace treaty, the continued presence of Soviet troops in Iran and the attempt to create a pro-communist state in northern Iran, the demands for a joint Russian–Turkish defence force for the Dardanelles and the revision of the Montreux Treaty, giving the Soviets a base and predominant influence in this area, the demand for a Soviet trusteeship in Tripolitania, the presence of Soviet troops in Manchuria, the demands for a say in the administration of Japan and in the negotiations over the former Japanese territories, the Soviet presence in North Korea, and a number of other annoyances over the administration of Berlin and the occupation of Austria. All these were considered to be objectionable by the Western allies, not to mention the actual territorial gains made by the Soviet Union in the Baltic and in Finland. Stalin appeared to be following a policy which at the least claimed a share in world influence, and perhaps was intended to challenge Western interests directly in the near future.

The response to these 'pressures' was, however, not an attempt at accommodation but, as was noted earlier, a repudiation of extant agreements and a show of force to meet what was considered a Soviet challenge. The question is, was this show of force and hostility towards the Soviet demands an attempt to reach agreement with the Soviets through 'firmness', or did it represent a fundamental division between the former allies? In other words, did the Cold War conflict arise out of a misunderstanding as to the intentions of the contenders, or did it arise out of this incompatibility and, if so, what was the nature of this incompatibility? In seeking to answer these questions we come back once again to the problem of motivation and its interpretation referred to earlier in this analysis of the origins of the Cold War. It should be apparent that there is no simple explanation.

It was said earlier that American security was not at stake in Europe, although it can be said that American economic and political interests in Britain and Western Europe would be seriously eroded if the Soviet Union became the dominant power in Europe. Most of the post-war economic and financial organisations, which were being negotiated at this time, posited a heavy American involvement in post-war economic co-operation. Yet the Soviet Union was also involved in these negotiations and had indeed made a request to the United States for a substantial loan.[63] The argument that the United States was interested in countering Soviet influence in Europe for economic reasons would appear to be more than doubtful, given the preponderance of American financial resources and her participation in the world economy. Such an argument is related to the notion of economic imperialism, referred to at the beginning of this study of the origins of the Cold War, and a detailed criticism of it will be found later on. It is true that a close economic relationship existed between the United States and Britain, and that the latter country was in the process of negotiating a major loan during this period.[64] Moreover, economic assistance was extended to various countries by the United States even before the massive commitments incurred through Marshall Aid.[65] But these may be regarded as a concomitant of political acts, and the Soviet Union in no sense represented a major economic rival to the United States. Trade with Eastern European countries was not significant, and American concern with the rehabilitation of the Western European economies stemmed from the problem of their internal political weaknesses, rather than from any desire for economic dominance.

In other words, while economic factors are certainly relevant to the American relationship with Western Europe, these are largely subordinate to, or consequential upon, the political relationships which developed out of the change in American policy. The broader economic arrangements for international co-operation shrank into a regional and capitalist system, but this reflected the political divisions of the Cold War itself. An explanation of American foreign policy on the basis of economic motivation tends to confound effects with causes.

However, it was extremely unlikely that the Soviet Union had the capacity or the intention to invade Western Europe, and there is no evidence that American policy-makers considered that this was a serious possibility. The main problem was seen as being the product of internal economic and political weakness in Western Europe which might provide a favourable opportunity, particularly in France and Italy, for a communist *coup*. Even this was considered as doubtful during the period 1945-6, largely because of the presence of American troops in Europe. Thus, when the question was raised of a possible communist *coup* in France during the referendum for the new constitution in 1946, President Truman adopted a wait-and-see attitude, against the suggestion that the 30,000 American troops then present in France might be used to forestall such a development.[66] It should be noted that at this time there were communist members of the French government.

There was an element of pragmatism in this attitude, which suggests that ideological factors were also peripheral to the motivation of the policy-makers. In any case, direct intervention in the domestic politics of the major Western powers was not possible without the co-operation of the governments in power. The threat from the Soviet Union was seen as being in direct proportion to the strength of indigenous communist parties in other countries, but this itself was a variable. It was the Red Army which had been the decisive factor in Eastern Europe, and this factor was absent in Western Europe. It was of course easy to say that the United States was 'dealing not only with Russia as a national entity but with the expanding power of Russia under Peter the Great plus the additional missionary force of a religion',[67] but the ideological element in the situation contributed to the uncertainty as to Soviet intentions, rather than convincing American policy-makers that they were countering an attempt at world revolution. Hence, while Soviet intentions were certainly distrusted, they were not conceived of in purely ideological terms. The United States government in this early period was concerned with more limited tactical problems relating to the respective diplomatic positions of the contending states. The immediate conflict itself, and not its long-term implications, dominated American responses to the Soviet attitudes and demands. The problem was seen as that of the effective use of American power to repulse Soviet 'pressure' in order to offset a relatively weak bargaining position vis-à-vis Eastern Europe.

The attempt made by the United States government to solve this problem was the new factor in the immediate post-war situation, which brought about the total breakdown in relations with the Soviet Union and her allies known as the Cold War. It rested upon the effective use of threats and counter-pressures, designed to elicit a more reasonable response from the opponent over the question in dispute. In this sense it was a tactic, not a strategy. The dilemma was that such a tactic is dependent upon a strategy, since, in the absence of the latter, that is, some conception of a mutually acceptable international political situation, a permanent contest was the result, which could be resolved in the long run only by the use of violence. This is the negation of diplomacy, in which the threat of force or an attempt to coerce by the prospect of inimical action is indeed present, but which nevertheless holds out the prospect of some accommodation. The Soviets pressed for advantages as a consequence of their victory on a number of different fronts, and in so doing they exploited their improved bargaining position during the German collapse. This was, of course, no more than the Western allies were doing. Yet the Soviet position was not acceptable to these states, and the United States embarked on a course of action which was construed by the Soviets as being so hostile as to preclude any prospect of agreement, although their demands did not appear to conflict with any tangible American interest. They had shown that they were prepared to co-operate on a division of interests in Europe with their support for Britain in Greece. It was, in the Soviet view, for the United States, from its vastly superior position in the post-war world, to make concessions and to demonstrate its willingness to co-operate.

On this argument, the Cold War arose out of a confusion between power politics and diplomacy rather than out of a conflict of interests or of ideology between the Soviet Union and the United States. Thus politics became subordinate to the use of threats and coercion, in an attempt to persuade the opposition to concede. Any concession on the part of the coercing state was construed as appeasement, that is, as an abandonment of a position out of weakness. From this, the definition of national interests as part of a coherent policy ceased to be a prominent issue in decision-making, and the immediate exploitation of advantages dominated. Thus the assumptions of Soviet hostility, and of Soviet 'expansion', constituted general premises in American policy, without any clear conception of what the major issues were. The struggle was conceived of solely in terms of capacity. Soviet power was thus opposed by a corresponding extension of American power in order to achieve a superior bargaining position in the long term. Such an extension was resisted because it was dangerous to the security of the U.S.S.R., and this resistance similarly reinforced the American belief that the Soviet Union was an aggressive and expansionist state. Out of a tactic designed to improve the American bargaining position sprang a power conflict which was to be finally resolved by the consequences of a nuclear arms race between the contenders. In other words, a concordat with the Soviet Union over Eastern Europe was rejected by the United States, because of the belief that it would not be respected, and because of the relative weakness of the United States and Britain in negotiating on European questions. The Soviets were in position and could not be dislodged without another world war.

In rejecting accommodation with Soviet demands, the United States was in effect turning a political dispute over the question of relative influence in Europe into a dispute which was irreconcilable so long as the Soviet Union maintained its position on the question of its security. No compromise could be made over Poland which surrendered Russian influence over a Polish government. The point here is that the use of threats, or the development of a situation in which the intentions of states become subordinate to their capacities to use violence, leads to a trial of strength, and is the negation of political accommodation. So far as the Soviets were concerned, their security interest was tangible and could be expressed in concrete terms. But the United States could not so define its interest in Europe. What then was the motive for American opposition to Russian interests? Given the fact of opposition, the situation resolved itself into a contest which could not be resolved short of war. The policy of firmness adopted by President Truman, and advocated by his advisers, was instrumental in bringing about this situation. As Forrestal said, 'power is needed until we are sure of a reign of law'.[68] The central problem in this view of international politics is that such an attitude rejects diplomacy and places the rule of law in the utopian future. In short, there was no inherent incompatibility between the Soviet Union and the United States in terms of their joint interests in Europe, or indeed in their extra-European interests. In this argument, the Cold War came about because of the United States' refusal to accept Soviet dominance in Eastern Europe. We are still left with the problem of explaining why President Truman adopted this attitude, although the interpretation given above would indicate that, far from constituting a policy, this American opposition to the Soviet Union was based on a short-term tactic and that Soviet responses to this, together with their repercussions in the United States, produced the Cold War conflict.

If we turn away from this general interpretation of the origins of the Cold War to a reconstruction of the context of decision-making in the

United States during this early period, we may find another explanation for the American attitude towards the Soviet Union. This places the emphasis upon the political situation when Truman came to power in April 1945. The argument runs that a number of American politicians and advisers were committed to the view, on various grounds, that the Soviet Union should be treated as a hostile power. Their common ground in promoting this view was that they could use it as a means of improving their political fortunes, or of sharing in decision-making. Reference has been made earlier to a number of these politicians who emerged from relatively subordinate positions in the political hierarchy, and who succeeded in advancing to Cabinet posts and to the innermost circles of policy-making. In other words, the shift in American policy and the new attitude can be attributed to a number of men who were politically ambitious and who sought to use an international situation in order to gain prestige and power. This argument is what is rather loosely called a conspiratorial view of politics.

The problem with this type of explanation lies in its simplicity and in the difficulty of separating causes from consequences. Inevitably in policy-making, those associated with taking decisions gain or lose influence as their views are rejected or adopted by those in power. Some political situations permit changes of position without serious consequences for the political careers of those whose views are not adopted. But in others – and the immediate post-war situation may be regarded as one of them – a conflict may arise in which the victorious party in effect purges the losers. This had, of course, happened in Britain with the purge of the 'appeasers' on the accession of Winston Churchill to power.[69] In the context of American politics at this time, Truman achieved power by inheritance, not as the result of a presidential election. He had neither been accepted by his party as a presidential nominee, nor had he been voted into his position. Although he had his own supporters, he could not be said to have achieved the support of all his party.[70] Roosevelt had, of course, been in power for a very long time by American standards, and was certainly master both of his party and of policy-making. The point here is that foreign policy-making cannot be divorced from domestic political considerations, or from Truman's own conception of his role and of his political future. He became President at a very critical time in international politics when he was largely ignorant of most of the political issues and diplomacy between the allies. While he was in a position to exert great influence upon the world, his own domestic political position was relatively weak. It is difficult to avoid interpreting his policy of firmness towards the Russians as an expression of an intention to gain domestic prestige in order to improve his political position.

Certainly, the assertion that his decision to challenge Stalin was based upon his desire to be considered as a 'great', and not as an interim, President, and to obtain a personal victory in the post-war presidential elections, cannot be substantiated by anything which he has explicitly said. Very few politicians are frank about their own ambitions or about the context in which they may be realised. Yet it is possible to infer from Truman's own account of his political career his concern that his record at least should be comparable to that of his predecessor. Of course, his memoirs may be regarded in the same light as those of any other retired politician, that is, as a vindication of a political record. What is revealing about this particular account is that it was made so close to the events and decisions which it describes, and its consequent reflection of the prevailing sentiments of the time. It was written at the height of the Cold War. In it Truman presents an interpretation of his part in international politics which reveals very little of his reasoning or motivation, but which makes his attitude towards the Soviet Union explicit. He argues that the Soviet Union was bent on world conquest and was ruled by a dictator governed by a belief in world revolution and practising *Realpolitik*.

There are a number of inconsistencies in this attitude. Truman himself could be accused of the same aggressive diplomacy as that of Stalin. It does not strike Truman, for example, that his action in persuading Stalin to join in the Japanese war, but denying him any part in the peace-time settlement after Japanese defeat, could be interpreted by Stalin as duplicity.[71] In his account of the Polish negotiations,[72] Truman makes full play of Stalin's treatment of the Polish politicians who belonged to the Polish government-in-exile and his intervention in Poland itself, but he does not do justice to the security argument which Stalin offered as a justification for his attitude, nor, except on moral grounds, does he explain why he opposed the Soviets on this question. The difficulty in interpreting such an account is that there is no coherent explanation as to why Truman believed the U.S.S.R. to be hostile to the United States. Was this belief genuinely held or was it window-dressing for a credulous audience? Certainly, part of Truman's account is an explanation as to why he was forced to make concessions to the Soviet position, and why he could not adopt a stronger attitude from the beginning of his dealings with Stalin. This appears to be very much a *post facto* rationalisation, intended for a particular audience.

Certainly it is true, and it was acknowledged as being true, not only by Truman's advisers but by Truman himself, that the American public did not conceive of the Soviet Union as being either a danger to the United States or as a menace to the free world in 1945 and 1946.[73] It was necessary for the Truman administration to prepare the public through speeches and press conferences and meetings with journalists, businessmen and trade union leaders, in order to launch the policies associated with the Truman Doctrine and Marshall Aid. Clearly, given the political process, the importance of the financial controls exercised by Congress and the magnitude of the measures contemplated in the policy, the administration had to provide credible reasons for the radical change in direction in the external relations of the United States. In establishing these reasons the administration became more or less a prisoner of public attitudes and its own persuasion. Such considerations created a rigidity in American policy and also meant that political opposition itself was polarised and isolated. The new policy was largely bipartisan and rested upon the fundamental premise that the Soviet Union intended to spread communism throughout the world. As Truman himself put it, he was 'afraid' that Henry Wallace, former Vice-President of the United States, then Secretary of State for Commerce, and a fellow Democrat, 'would lend himself to the more sinister ends of the Reds and those who served them'.[74] The message was clear for those who cherished political ambitions: opposition to the new line in foreign policy was politically disastrous, especially after public opinion swung around to endorse it.

To return to the argument that the antipathy of the Truman administration to the Soviet Union was the consequence of the political ambitions of Truman and his supporters, it must be admitted that this is an unprovable assertion. The conspiratorial view of politics ignores interactions between states and over-simplifies the complexities of international politics and foreign policy-making. It is certainly true that in this case foreign policy had an influence on domestic politics, and the later phenomenon of McCarthyism may be regarded as being one of its effects.[75] Moreover, while this interpretation may be rejected, it indicates that the most important factor in any interpretation of the Cold War was the attitude of the American government and of Truman in particular. We are left with the question unanswered as to why Truman adopted a position of hostility to the Soviet Union. What of the explanation proffered by Truman himself? This places the responsibility for the conflict solely on the Soviet Union. Truman explains his actions as a response to those of the U.S.S.R. and as being closely related to an ethical approach towards politics.[76] In his view, the Soviet Union sought to destroy democracy in Eastern Europe for dubious ends and he opposed this, not out of selfish national interests, but in order to defend the free world, and to preserve the values on which it was based. The very war itself had been a defence of democracy against the forces of evil. Such a simple morality does not sit easily with the political realism shown by Truman both in his actions and in his own account of his diplomacy. Yet on the face of it, how else can the attitude which he took towards Poland be explained?

Stalin was apparently baffled when, in response to his security argument in favour of Soviet dominion in Eastern Europe, he received the countering argument that this was undemocratic. The political implications of 'free elections' and of an independent Poland, and their international consequences, were readily apparent, but what was not so obvious was why the United States should be so interested in the promotion of democracy in a country which had never been democratic in any meaningful sense.

What American interest was at stake? The search for American motivation on this issue must have been a constant Soviet preoccupation during the protracted negotiations over the period 1945–6. Soviet negotiators constantly urged a *quid pro quo* on the American government in their willingness to recognise Western interests. They pressed the similarities between their interests in Eastern Europe and the Western interests in the Channel coast, in Spain, in Italy and in the Pacific.[77] The American response, which stressed the primacy of certain political values, appeared to be hypocritical and devious, in view of the realities of American power, and the actualities of world politics and of the political systems which prevailed in most countries, including those most intimately linked to the United States. Perhaps the Soviet conclusion was one of 'motiveless malignity' on the part of the United States, and of the declaration of a war which ultimately involved the very survival of the U.S.S.R., faced with a hostile capitalist coalition opposing any Soviet proposal on the grounds that it was inherently illegitimate. In the absence of any concrete evidence as to Stalin's reasoning, this is of course speculative. In the case of President Truman, we are left with the problem of deciding to what extent he was motivated by his values, that is, by his idiosyncrasies, by strategic and security considerations, or by the influence of his supporters; or whether he was swept along by circumstances which he influenced by using American power and resources in an effort to force the Soviet Union to be more reasonable in its attitude towards a European settlement, and thus provoked Stalin into a series of actions and responses which in turn created the political conflict known as the Cold War.

It should be clear from this discussion that such an evaluation is extremely difficult to make, and involves the assessment of a number of imponderables for which there is very little tangible evidence. But the intention here is not to present an unassailable explanation of the origins of the Cold war, even if this were possible. The purpose of this analysis is to indicate the wide variety of interpretations which are based upon the same historical materials. We may categorise these into those arguments which seek to reduce the causes of this political conflict to a single hypothesis, as for example the notion of ideological warfare or the power–security competition or economic imperialism; those arguments which are largely prescriptive or with an ethical basis, such as that which has been called the radical critique of American foreign policy; and those which are largely interpretative, placing greater or lesser emphasis on situational or circumstantial factors and on the personalities involved. So far as these last are concerned, their major differences turn on the question of the relative significance of particular events or decisions and on the perceptions of those engaged in taking or making them.

We may conclude by saying that there is no single hypothesis which, successfully and completely, explains the complex interactions which preceded the total breakdown of relations between the East and the West. But from this study of a specific historical problem, it can be seen that the central theoretical problem lies in the relationship between the hypothetical or conceptual referents, such as values or power, and the interpretation proper. It is clear that a historical interpretation is not devoid of theorising assumptions, but that nevertheless such an interpretation does not constitute a theory or hypothesis in the sense used in the first part of this study. What then is the part which the general hypothesis and the generalisation have in historical explanation? More particularly, since all interpretations of this kind contain them, how can an evaluation between different conceptual or hypothetical referents be made? As was noted earlier, certain of the various hypothetical arguments which 'explain' the Cold War are incompatible. It is not possible, for example, to reconcile the notion of security competition between nations with that of ideological conflict. In the case of the former, ideology is either irrelevant in explaining international conflict, or it consists of *post facto* rationalisation in the form of political persuasion. Conversely, an ideological explanation conceives of power politics as a symptom and not as a cause of such conflicts. Any attempt to synthesise these two levels of abstraction results in contradiction and they cease to be coherent arguments.

Most attempts at hypothesising in explanations of international politics, however abstract their terms, depend upon generalisations about human behaviour which are empirically derived. The level of these generalisations is historical in the sense that they are statements or propositions about how men behaved in certain situations in the past. The difficulty for the critic is that he may agree with the generalisation as a specific historical judgement applied to the situation itself, but not with the hypothesis and its conclusions to which it is related. There is an ambiguity between the hypothetical level and the level of historical generalisation in this type of argument. A historian seeks to qualify general statement by reference to specific conditions and factors unique to the situation which he is seeking to explain.

But a hypothesis, in this context, is a form of explanation which assumes a pattern in history. It is not an argument confined to a unique political situation but is applicable to all situations of the same kind. It takes the form of a logical argument which says that, given its premises, a rational progression of events may be deduced or inferred. If, then, as one historian puts it,

> like its predecessors, the Cold War has been a world-wide power conflict in which one expanding power has threatened to make itself predominant and in which other powers have banded together in a defensive coalition to frustrate it – as was the case before 1815, as was the case in 1914–18, as was the case from 1939–45,[78]

then a level of generalisation would be possible and a testable hypothesis, which explains the occurrence and the course of such situations, could be established. But are these situations really the same? And if so, which explanatory hypothesis is appropriate as a valid explanation? Or is the assertion of a historical recurrence simply a descriptive or analogous statement?

If we take the first question and apply it to our analysis of the origins of the Cold War, it is clear that part at least of our examination consisted of the reconstruction of the perceptions of the participants. The enquiry proceeded from the general to the particular, that is, from the hypothetical level to a study of the idiosyncrasies and understanding of the politicians involved in this political situation. In this sense we might agree with Arthur Schlesinger, in principle at least, that 'An analysis of the origins of the Cold War, which leaves out these factors – the intransigence of Leninist ideology, the sinister dynamics of a totalitarian society and the madness of Stalin – is obviously incomplete'.[79] We may not agree that these particular factors are either valid or relevant, but we are certainly concerned with factors which are equally idiosyncratic and unique to this particular situation. Thus unless it is argued that the decisions which the participants took, and their influence upon events, were themselves the product of factors which were beyond their control, and that, given a repetition of these factors, the same behaviour would be induced, it must be admitted that historical explanation conceives of a class of phenomena as being peculiar to each specific historical situation. To this extent the historian is concerned with the unique. He is concerned with explaining aspects of behaviour special to the situation which is the subject of his enquiry, as well as with those which may perhaps be found in other historical situations.

A distinction can be made between a hypothesis, which is really an untested theoretical argument, and one which is a more systematised form of description and is abstracted from historical interpretation itself. The former belongs to other forms of explanation which were discussed at the beginning of this study, while the latter is not an explanation at all. For example, if we take the hypothesis of power and security competition, we are bound to assume that the primary objective of a state in its external relations is its self-preservation. Yet, firstly, this is by no means historically true, and secondly, the notion of self-preservation, and the relationship between it and other objectives, are sufficiently vague, as well as being complex, so as to make the hypothesis an over-simplification of most international conflicts. It does not, as will be seen in a later part of this study, explain why particular wars have occurred in the past, nor can it be used to predict the occurrence of wars in the future. It is really a description of a specific kind of conflict. What then is the value of such a hypothesis in an interpretation of the kind of historical phenomenon considered here? As we have seen, it does not explain a number of actions and events which are germane to an explanation of the origins of the Cold War. Certain attitudes adopted by the participants are inexplicable in terms of the notion of power or security competition. Yet it is equally true that historical interpretation cannot proceed on the basis of an assertion of unique circumstances and factors. There is a level of generalisation contained in historical interpretation. It is not solely an individual politician's understanding of his resources, capacity and his political situation which is important, but also the capacity itself. Perception and material conditions, and their inter-relationships in international terms, are the focus of our interpretation, and they are intimately linked. To this extent we are concerned with the circumstances and conditions of a historical situation as well as with the participants' perception of them. The interactions between them are important to an explanation of the situation. The problem is that hypothesising tends to produce a dichotomy between the level of abstraction with its emphasis on the 'objective' conditions of the situation, and the level of idiosyncratic human behaviour which, to a historian, is of primary importance.

He is generally concerned, as in this case, with expressing all the relevant relationships between attitudes, events and factors in a given political situation, rather than with explaining these in hypothetical terms. He may be selective in emphasising certain relationships or factors as being, in his view, particularly significant in influencing the course of events, or the situation which he is seeking to interpret. But the point here is that his reconstruction is a general one, in which he seeks to render the complex intelligible. Thus it could be argued that the Cold War was 'caused' by a concatenation of circumstances, factors and attitudes, the relations between them being unique, but which does not lead to the conclusion that their repetition would result in a recurrence of the same phenomena. The assertion that history repeats itself is either a tautology or indicates a different kind of argument, and a level of generalisation, which is not historical. Such hypothetical argument is too much of an over-simplification of complex human behaviour to explain satisfactorily the origins of the Cold War. It omits the idiosyncratic and aims at making general propositions which transcend the particular and which sacrifice the detail for the sake of logical consistency. In the sense that this level of abstraction affords another perspective to historical understanding and. another means of evaluating political relationships, it is relevant to historical argument, but it is not a substitute for it. For, as we have seen earlier, it is incapable of verification and thus of emerging as a distinctive kind of explanation with its own validity. The closer the historian is to events, then the more complex is his explanation, and the less reducible to a set of generalisations about political behaviour it becomes. Yet a piece of historical writing which is devoid of concepts and abstractions would be arid indeed. In this, as in all historical argument, it is not possible to be dogmatic about the relationship between generalisation and interpretation.

The questions now arise as to which criteria are relevant to historical criticism and to what extent are they generally accepted by historians. It should be apparent by now that whatever they are, they are subjective in nature. There is no criterion of validity that can be used to determine the truth of one of two conflicting explanations. The kind of criteria with which we are concerned relate to the selection of facts and events, as well as of the questions which form the basis of any enquiry, to the available evidence or source material and their relationship to the argument, to the various conclusions which may be adduced from such evidence, to the values implicit in the interpretation and to the internal consistency of the argument itself. Most of these are critical standards which apply to any argument, historical or not. The most important to a historian is that which is concerned with evidence and sources, since this is at the root of an understanding of the past. Clearly, these are not absolutes and they admit of considerable variation between historians in their application to a historical argument.

If we return to the historical problem of the origins of the Cold War, we can see that most of the interpretations of this phenomenon were based on statements, narratives or personal accounts made by the participants. In evaluating this source in order to use it as the basis for a historical interpretation, a historian can compare one such account with another to seek confirmation or to establish inconsistency; he can compare it with the events themselves and with the subsequent behaviour of the writer; he can relate it to later explanations made in a different political context; or he can rely on internal evidence and on what inferences he can derive from this. But this critical exercise may not result in conclusive evidence for a particular interpretation, except perhaps in making one more probable than another.

For example, both Truman and Churchill wrote accounts of the Potsdam Conference,[80] but their respective versions of their negotiation with Stalin over Soviet participation in the Japanese war flatly contradict one another. Unfortunately we do not have Stalin's version as corroborative evidence. According to Churchill the advent of the atomic bomb meant that Soviet involvement in the war was no longer necessary. More to the point, he said that this was also President Truman's position: 'The President and I no longer felt that we needed his [Stalin's] aid to conquer Japan. . . . In our opinion they [Soviet troops] were not likely to be needed, and Stalin's bargaining power, which he had used with such great effect upon the Americans at Yalta, was therefore gone'.[81] But, as was noted earlier, Truman's own account of this negotiation stated that the most important single reason for his going to Potsdam was to obtain Soviet entry into the war.[82] Churchill emphasised the diplomatic and political significance of the new weapon, while Truman barely mentioned it.

How can this discrepancy be explained and which version corresponds most closely to the truth? It would seem from internal evidence that Truman, writing at the height of the Cold War when his political career was at an end, was seeking to explain why he made concessions to the Soviet Union and was therefore covering himself from charges of appeasement. In the public mind at the time these memoirs were written, the main question relating to the Cold War was, why had not the U.S.S.R. been challenged from the very beginning? The agreements made at Yalta were conceived of as a betrayal of American interests. Truman had to explain his negotiations with the Soviet Union in more ambiguous terms than Churchill, who could assert his early awareness of the Soviet menace without incurring any responsibility for Western relations with the U.S.S.R. after July 1945. According to Truman, the reason why he agreed to make the Soviet Union a number of concessions in the Pacific and on the Chinese mainland was because he wanted to save American lives through Soviet participation in the war against Japan. Yet his determination, at the close of the Potsdam Conference, that the Soviet Union would be excluded from any participation in the peace-time settlement with Japan, indicates that he was well aware that the war would be brief, and that Soviet advances into the war zone would therefore be limited. This attitude suggests that Truman understood the military and political significance of the atomic bomb during the Potsdam negotiations. His subsequent 'firm' line towards Soviet negotiations with Chiang Kai-shek and his refusal to permit any further concessions to the U.S.S.R., other than those agreed at Yalta by his predecessor, are further indications of his awareness that his bargaining position, so far as the Pacific and Asian war theatres were concerned, was very much strengthened by possession of the new weapon.

It would seem, on the face of it, that Churchill's version is the correct one and that Truman's emphasis on the need for Soviet entry into the war was specious, and intended to support a justification of his policy towards the U.S.S.R. which was perhaps open to criticism, given the later change in policy and in public attitudes. It might have been true before the successful test at Alamogordo, but it was not true afterwards when a speedy means of ending the Japanese war existed. Indeed, his reticence over the political significance of the American monopoly of the atomic bomb may be contrasted with Churchill's ready appreciation of the new strength which the United States had acquired through its possession.

This example illustrates the difficulty of taking at face value the explanations contained in accounts of this kind. The politician is concerned with explaining the 'rightness' of his decisions and his command of the political situation to an audience which largely shares his prejudices and predilections. The historian is not concerned with vindicating a political record but with the problem of explaining it. Consequently he has to try to disentangle the *post facto* justification from the actual motivation and reasoning which prevailed at the time when the politician made his decisions. There is clearly no rule of thumb, other than a sustained scepticism, which can guide him in this task.

We may conclude this examination of various interpretations of the origins of the Cold War by saying that the relationship of evidence to argument, of generalisation to facts, and of facts to their interpretation, is imprecise in historical argument. Except where a question of fact is involved, it is not possible to invalidate a historical interpretation other than to criticise it on the grounds referred to earlier, that is, on the use and the nature of evidence, its internal consistency as an argument, and on its general plausibility as a coherent and intelligible explanation of the events with which it is concerned – in short, on the general critical criteria discussed at the end of the preceding chapter. Where there is more than one such explanation which meets these criteria, then it would seem that preference is governed by aesthetic considerations, that is, it is then a matter of taste. In short, while there are critical standards which may be used to determine good or bad historical argument, these standards, like the interpretations to which they are applied, are subjective in nature. No explanation of a historical problem or situation may be considered as being either generally true or as being complete. It is in this sense that all history is revisionist history.

REFERENCES

1. For example, see P. A. Reynolds, *War in the Twentieth Century*, Inaugural Lecture (Cardiff: Univ. of Wales Press, 1951) pp. 24ff.

2. Carl von Clausewitz, *On War*, ed. Anatol Rapoport, trans. J. J. Graham, 1908 (Harmondsworth: Penguin Books, 1968) p. 402.

3. See Piotr S. Wandyz, *Soviet–Polish Relations 1917–1921* (Cambridge, Mass.; Harvard Univ. Press, 1969) map, p. 151.

4. *See Nazi–Soviet Relations 1939–1941*, ed. Raymond James Sontag and James Stuart Beddie (Washington: U.S. Department of State, 1948) pp. 76-85.

5. For an account of this negotiation, see Lord Avon, *The Eden Memoirs: The Reckoning*, pp. 271-303.

6. See Winston S. Churchill, *History of the Second World War*, vol. VI: *Triumph and Tragedy* (London: Reprint Society Edition, Cassell, 1956) p. 195.

7. See ibid., pp. 199, 274.

8. Poland adhered to the Little Entente after 1920, signed a non-aggression pact with Germany in January 1934 and allied with Britain in March 1939.

9. See U.S. Dept. of State, *American Foreign Policy: Papers Relating to the Foreign Relations of the United States. Diplomatic Papers: (a) The Conferences at Malta and Yalta, 1945* (1955).

10. See ibid., *(b) The Conference of Berlin, the Potsdam Conference, 1945* (1960).

11. See Wilfrid Knapp, *A History of War and Peace 1939–1965* (Oxford Univ.

Press, for Royal Institute of International Affairs, 1967) p. 79.

12.   For details of the Morgenthau Plan, see Senate Committee on Foreign Relations, *A Decade of American Foreign Policy: Basic Documents 1941–9* (Washington: U.S. Government Printing Office, 1950) pp. 502-5.

13.   See Alexander Werth, *De Gaulle* (Harmondsworth: Penguin Books, 1965) pp. 199-200.

14.   Churchill, op. cit., p. 309.

15.   Harry S. Truman, *Memoirs,* vol. I: *1945, Year of Decisions* (New York: Signet Books, 1965) p. 454.

16.   Ibid., p. 455.

17.   This was achieved at Alamogordo on 16 July 1945.

18.   Truman, op. cit., p. 444.

19.   Bulgaria in October and Romania in November 1946, Poland in January and Hungary in August 1947, Czechoslovakia in February–March 1948.

20.   Harry S. Truman, *Memoirs,* vol. II: *1946–52, Years of Trial and Hope,* p. 125.

21.   See for example, D. F. Fleming, *The Cold War and its Origins 1917–60,* 2 vols. (Garden City, N.Y.: Doubleday, 1961); Louis J. Halle, *The Cold War as History* (London: Chatto & Windus, 1970); H. Seton-Watson, *Neither War nor Peace* (London: Methuen, 1960); Gar Alperovitz, *Atomic Diplomacy: Hiroshima and Potsdam* (New York: Simon & Schuster, 1965); Robert Stover, 'Responsibility for the Cold War: A Case Study in Historical Responsibility', *History and Theory,* vol. XI, no. 2 (Middleton, Conn.: Wesleyan Univ. Press, 1972)

22.   This is admittedly a fairly rough-and-ready category, but see Gabriel Kolko, *The Roots of American Foreign Policy* (Boston: Beacon Press, 1969); David Horowitz, *From Yalta to Vietnam* (Harmondsworth: Penguin Books, 1967); and Harry Magdoff, *The Age of Imperialism* (New York: Modern Reader Monthly Review Press, 1966). For a critique, see Robert W. Tucker, *The Radical Left and American Foreign Policy* (Baltimore: Johns Hopkins Univ. Press, 1971).

23.   Milovan Djilas, *Conversations with Stalin* (Harmondsworth: Penguin Books, 1963) p. 90.

24.   See, for example, Churchill, op. cit., p. 244.

25.   For example, Horowitz, op. cit., p. 68.

26.   Cited in Richard D. Challener, *From Isolation to Containment 1921–1952* (London: Edward Arnold, 1970) pp. 147ff.

27.   Djilas, op. cit., pp. 53, 62.

28.   Ibid., p. 141. Also Stalin's comment: 'We told them bluntly that we considered the development of the uprising in China had no prospects, that the Chinese comrades should seek a *modus vivendi* with Chiang Kai-shek, and that they should join the Chiang Kai-shek government and dissolve their army', in Vladimir Dedijer, *Tito Speaks* (London: Weidenfeld & Nicolson, 1953), cited in David Floyd, *Mao against Krushchev* (New York: Praeger, 1964) p. 211.

29.   See James V. Forrestal, *The Forrestal Diaries,* ed. Walter Nillis (London: Cassell, 1957) p. 108.

30.   See Churchill, op. cit., p. 304, and Truman, *Memoirs* vol. I, p. 103.

31.   Truman, ibid., pp. 102-3.

32.   See, for example, the interpretation offered by Halle, op. cit.

33.   Lord Avon, *The Reckoning,* pp. 271-303.

34.   See Sumner Welles, *Seven Major Decisions* (London: Hamish Hamilton, 1951) pp. 126-45.

35.   See Churchill, op. cit., p. 291.

36.   Ibid.

37.   Ibid., pp. 374-5.

38.   For an account of de Gaulle's mission to the U.S.S.R. in December 1944, see Werth, op. cit., pp. 181-6, and Knapp, op. cit., pp. 91-3.

39.   Challener, op. cit., p. 150.

40.   See Herbert G. Nicholas, *Britain and the United States* (London: Chatto & Windus, 1963) pp. 50-1.

41.   Djilas, op. cit., p. 137.

42.   See in particular Horowitz, op. cit.,

43. See George Kennan, *Memoirs,* vol. I: *1925–1950* (New York: Bantam Books, 1969) pp. 378-87.

44. See George Kennan, *Memoirs,* vol. II: *1950–1963* (Boston: Little, Brown, 1972) Annex, 'The Soviet Union and the Atlantic Pact', pp. 327-51.

45. See, for example, Philip E. Mosely, *The Kremlin and World Politics* (New York: Vintage Books, 1960) pp. 425-37.

46. These were established at the second Quebec Conference in September 1944.

47. See Churchill, op. cit., pp. 374-5, 410. See also Truman *Memoirs,* vol. I, pp. 237-46.

48. On 3 May General Clay suspended all reparations deliveries from the American zone to the U.S.S.R.

49. Forrestal, op. cit., p. 193.

50. Truman, *Memoirs,* vol. I, pp. 67-71.

51. Forrestal, op. cit., p. 55.

52. Ibid., p. 258.

53. See Kennan, *Memoirs,* vol. I, pp. 309, 373-87. The 'Mr X' article was published in *Foreign Affairs* in July 1947 after having first been submitted to James Forrestal on 31 January.

54. Forrestal, op. cit., p. 232.

55. Ibid.

56. Cited in *A Decade of Foreign Policy: Basic Documents 1941–9,* p. 68.

57. Ibid., p. 76.

58. See Forrestal, op. cit., p. 40.

59. Truman, *Memoirs,* vol. II, p. 118.

60. Cited in *A Decade of Foreign Policy,* p. 522.

61. The Bizonia agreement was formally agreed in 2 December 1946; see Knapp, op. cit., pp. 90-1.

62. See Forrestal, op. cit., p. 149.

63. See Kennan, *Memoirs,* vol. I: p. 281. and also Truman, *Memoirs,* vol. I, p. 97, for the political implications of this request.

64. This loan was successfully negotiated on 6 December 1945 and amounted to $3·75 billion; see Forrestal. op. cit., pp. 182, 267.

65. See, for example, Werth, op. cit., p. 192; also Knapp, op. cit., pp. 559-62, and Forrestal, op. cit., p. 215.

66. Forrestal, op. cit., pp. 161-2.

67. Ibid., p. 149.

68. Ibid., p. 160.

69. See Harold Nicolson, *Diaries and Letters,* vol. I: *1930–1939,* ed. Nigel Nicolson (London: Collins, Fontana Books, 1969) pp. 371, 399, 411, and also vol. II: *1939–1945,* pp. 76-7; Henry Channon, *Chips: The Diaries of Sir Henry Channon,* ed. Robert Rhodes James (Harmondsworth: Penguin Books, 1970) p. 329.

70. See Truman, *Memoirs,* vol. II, p. 237.

71. Ibid., vol. I, p. 455.

72. Ibid., pp. 102, 379-457.

73. On this point see Forrestal, op. cit., pp. 192, 248.

74. Truman, *Memoirs,* vol. I, p. 613; vol. II, p. 216.

75. See Kennan, *Memoirs,* vol. II, pp. 190-228.

76. For a typical expression of this attitude, see Truman, *Memoirs,* vol. I, p. 482.

77. See ibid., pp. 102-3.

78. Halle, op. cit., p. 9.

79. Arthur Schlesinger, Jr, 'Origins of the Cold War', *Foreign Affairs,* vol. XLVI, no. 1 (Oct. 1965) p. 49.

80. See Truman, *Memoirs,* vol. I, pp. 379-457; and Churchill, op. cit., pp. 507ff.

81. Churchill, op. cit., p. 509.

82. Truman, *Memoirs,* vol. I, p. 457.

CHAPTER 6

War, Policy and International Politics

THE view that the world is an anarchy in which violence is the *ultima ratio* is, of all influences on international politics and on foreign and defence policy-making, perhaps the most pervasive. From it stems the notion that the basis of diplomacy and of all contractual obligations beyond the boundaries of the state rests on the capacity to use violence, both to protect the state and to promote its interests in the face of opposition from other states. Such a view is not confined to autocracies or totalitarian dictatorships pursuing imperial policies, but is found in a wide variety of political systems. For example, the statement made by Adolf Hitler in *Mein Kampf*, that 'We must clearly recognise the fact that the recovery of the lost territories is not won through solemn appeals to the Lord or through pious hopes in a League of Nations but only by force of arms',[1] may be compared with Winston Churchill's reflection that 'no foreign policy can have validity if there is no adequate force behind it, and no national readiness to make the necessary sacrifices to produce that force'.[2]

Most states, even those which pursue a policy of neutrality, have a defence policy and engage in contingency planning for the eventuality of war. Clearly, the nature of an actual war is determined by the policies and capacities of what are commonly referred to as the great powers, but in general all statesmen assume that international violence, if not normal, is at least endemic in the world at large. This study is concerned with two main questions; firstly, what is the basis for the view that the world is inherently anarchic and violent?; and secondly, what is the relationship between national security and the pursuit of national interests and violence?

The argument, which will be termed the power–security hypothesis in this discussion, begins with the premise that the world is composed of sovereign nation-states, each responsible for its own order, welfare and external relations. The state alone is the judge of its own interests and obligations. Yet while each state is responsible for its own relations with other states, the problem is that these relationships are fundamentally unstable and are subject to the influence of factors which elude control. Thus although the state exists in a network of relationships and obligations which appear to inhibit its independence, it is not only free in principle to decide for itself whether it wishes to maintain them, but this freedom is a necessity if its interests are not to be adversely affected by unforeseen changes in its environment. There is no international law, authority, or sanction capable of enforcing such law, to which recourse can be made if obligations are broken unilaterally.

Within the state itself, of course, there is a form of normative order. There is a legal system, a police force, and a notion of political authority embodied in government, which together provide a mechanism for inter- pretation as well as for changing the rules. The rules may be suspended and civil war or revolution create a legal or political hiatus, but the aftermath of violent political struggle within the state in historical times has been the reimposition of law and order. The citizen is not a free agent in the same sense that the state is.

Thus the only constant in international politics since the sixteenth century has been the persistence of the nation-state itself, with its own political autonomy. International relations are constantly changing and any attempt to find a pattern in them, as we have seen earlier, is fraught with difficulties. Descriptive terms such as 'the balance of power', which seek to characterise particular historical periods, tend to gloss over the dynamic factors and variables in international politics. Given this instability and uncertainty, statesmen are forced to participate in a chaotic world, since abstention from international politics is not possible without jeopardising the state. Neu- trality, in the sense of isolation from a specific conflict, is of course sometimes a viable alternative, but the moment the activities of other states present a threatening aspect, then the neutralist is forced to respond, and to adopt measures for the protection of his state and its interests. In this sense there are no neutrals in international politics and isolationism is possible only when circumstances permit it.

Yet the paradox is, as we shall see, that this very chaos is itself the product of the nation-state and, more particularly, of the notion of national security. Before discussing this last, let us examine the factors which contribute to international instability and to the uncertainties which beset statesmen. The first broad category is that of the domestic politics of the states participating in international politics. International agreements are negotiated by governments and no statesman can guarantee that a change of government in one related state will not affect that relationship directly, or have an indirect effect on the overall pattern of relationships in which his country participates. Although changes of government do not invariably produce adverse international repercussions, nevertheless there is always some uncertainty present as to the intentions of the new regime and its attitude towards the commitments which it has inherited. The frequency of pilgrimages of reassurance made by allied statesmen after a change of administration in the United States illustrates this point.

When radical changes occur, then this uncertainty is heightened. Revolu- tions and civil wars create a hiatus in international relations, as well as within the divided country, and few states are content to abstain from seeking to influence the struggle in an attempt to produce a settlement consonant with their interests. Foreign intervention, violent and non-violent, has been an important factor in the American, French, Russian and Chinese revolutions. The point here is that the political condition of the state itself is a factor which introduces a permanent uncertainty in the calculations and commitments of those responsible for foreign and defence policy. Those states which possess the requisite resources have an interest in seeking to counteract this uncertainty by imposing conditions on political change in their external environment. For example, in the post-Second World War period two powers, the Soviet Union and the United States, have sought to control domestic political events in other countries through intervention and through the substitution of their own authority. This, in its extreme form, is a type of imperialism, that is, the replacing of one political system by a metropolitan authority which alone legitimises change. Thus one characteristic of international politics is the propensity of certain major powers to control their unstable environment by imposing their authority upon it. As will be seen subsequently, this exacerbates the general condition of instability because of its competitive effects.

A second broad category of factors which make the international world chaotic and difficult to control is that of the values and ideas which influence political behaviour. Nationalism and social revolutionary ideologies have been perhaps the most influential political doctrines in the present century. No explanation, for example, of German, Japanese and Italian imperialism on the one hand, or of the collapse of the Western European empires on the other, would be complete without some attempt to evaluate them. One of the parameters in decision-making is that of what might be called the value environment. This has an influence in two ways: firstly, it is restrictive in the sense that it establishes premises which condition the interpretation of political behaviour. For example, the premise that communism is evil establishes a moral value which influences any judgement of the behaviour of communist governments. This is a fundamental in policy- and decision-making. Secondly, values of this type may proscribe rather than prescribe action, in that certain kinds of action may be considered to be illegitimate. This may therefore act as an inhibition on choice in a situation where several courses of action are open. The reluctance of the American government to use its nuclear monopoly can only be explained in value rather than rational terms. Similarly, values may limit choice in that an initial commitment to a moral position may determine subsequent action. Thus the British commitment to Poland in 1939, or the American commitment to Formosa in 1949, afford examples of this value relationship which coexists with the element of expedience and political calculation. While a more tenable generalisation about international politics is that amoral behaviour is characteristic, given the heterogeneity and competitive nature of the international environment, yet, as in domestic politics, where hypocrisy is the tribute which vice pays to virtue, it is not possible to exclude value influences altogether. Thus the presence of political doctrines with specific prescriptions relating both to objectives and behaviour, and the pervasive influence of values in domestic politics, tend to add to international confusion.

It can also be argued that nation-states have no interest in international stability as a value, unless they fall into E. H. Carr's category of the 'satisfied states',[3] and that there is a positive relationship between national interest and instability. States can, and frequently do, use the situation of international anarchy to consolidate themselves as nation-states. The ever-present possibility of war and the emphasis on the uniqueness of the nation encourage the national society to integrate. The fear of external danger, or the concept of national greatness, or sometimes both, have been used to validate particular regimes and have the general effect of acting as, what Talcott Parsons has called in another context, a normative component.[4] The stability of the state thus has a direct relationship to the instability of the international environment. Moreover, the nation-state can seek an extension of its national interests at the expense of other states and have this policy accepted by its society as a positive virtue. In this context there is some evidence that changing values have modified the extent to which a state can pursue its interests without justification, but this perhaps means more a change of argument than a change of behaviour.

Thus inequalities among states are acceptable to those more powerful and developed societies which would not accept the same inequalities within them. The national interest involves a conception of a value higher than peace or stability in international politics. Governments exist to do their best by the people they govern, and if this involves the perpetuation of economic, social and political inequalities in the rest of the world, this is unfortunate but irrelevant. Perhaps the reason why the phenomenon of war has received so much academic and public attention in recent times is because modern wars have directly affected peoples in their destructive effects, and not only governments and armies.

The third and last category of factors inimical to international stability is that of economic and technological variables. National security, as we shall see, involves the creation and development of an armaments industry and an economy which can support it. It also involves technological expertise and the ability to make productive use of this. In the field of weapons, long-term planning is essential. For example, although the first prototype Hurricane flew in November 1935 and the first prototype Spitfire in March 1936, by 1939 Germany had twice as many aircraft as Britain.[5] The element of competition is an important influence on weapons production, and one innovation in one country forces all other countries, which possess the requisite capacity, to follow suit. This kind of situation involves running on the spot to keep up. Moreover, no state controls its own economy in any absolute sense, except perhaps for those centrally planned economies able to pursue a policy of autarky. Thus a policy-maker must try to take into account a number of variables in this field when he is making forecasts, in order to plan a mutually compatible defence and foreign policy.

Such variables are related not only to domestic, economic or social priorities, but also to technological and military developments in other states. The phenomenon of an arms race consists not simply of a competitive attempt to achieve superiority over other nations in terms of military capacity, but occurs as a response to the creation of new weapons or techniques of war in one country. Given the secrecy surrounding military innovations in advanced industrialised states, no statesman can be certain that his own country's war capacity is either adequate for national security, or is not being superseded by developments elsewhere. Consequently there is a constant effort, in those countries with sufficient resources, to maintain a high level of research and development in weapons technology. If this is the case, it adds to the pervasive sense of international instability. In the effort to avoid pre-emption in the military field, a nation might create for itself a relative advantage in weapons technology which in turn exacerbates international competition.

From this general interpretation of the international environment as a political chaos, the power–security hypothesis proceeds to assert the omnipresence of violence. Since the world is made up of sovereign states, each responsible for its own security, the primary concern of the state, over and above all other interests, is the preservation of itself as a political entity. In order to provide this security, each state creates a military capacity for what is usually termed defence. Thus all statesmen prepare for the eventuality of war, and the history of the nation-state has also been the history of warfare. War thus appears not as abnormal but as being pre-eminently normal in international politics. However, the paradox which makes this apparently sensible policy create the condition which it most wishes to avoid stems from the notion of security. Security only exists when a state possesses the capacity to fight successful wars against any potential aggressor, and defence policy is concerned in the main with relative military *capacities* and not the *intentions* of other nations. Clearly, if all nations share this concern then the result is a condition of permanent insecurity in the world.

To refer to a point made earlier, the central problem is that one state's security is another state's insecurity. The consequence is a competition between states which takes the form of arms races, treaties for mutual defence, and social and economic preparation for war, which can only be finally resolved by war itself. In attempting to achieve security the nation-states of the world succeed instead in creating anarchy and violence. Yet war can decide the question of national security or, to be more precise, *which* nation is secure, only if that nation succeeds once and for all in monopolising violence in the world, in the same way as its government has monopolised violence within the state. In theory, security can be achieved through world hegemony, or empire, or by the creation of one world state. None of these possibilities has been realised. No state has ever won a war, for victories and defeats have never been total. The end of every war has seen the beginning of another power struggle.

According to this argument, the element and form of violence in international politics are brought about by the presence of different military capacities created on grounds of national security. Thus the main determinent of war is the material capacity of states to inflict damage on each other, rather than political limitations, or the nature of the issues in dispute. These are occasions rather than causes of war. War is rational to the extent that political objectives are realisable through the use of force, but the major objective, that of national security, is not realisable unless the consequences of victory are such that the victor power achieves world hegemony.

It has been argued by some commentators that the absolute nature of this competition is modified by the need for states to co-operate with each other in order to pose a viable threat to a potential aggressor. A defensive alliance may constitute both a form of security and a limitation on the consequences of war. Moreover, posing such a threat reduces the possibility of actual violence. But if security rests upon some notion of balance provided by allies, then clearly, it must be certain that the allies share the same interests.[6] Otherwise a change in the situation affecting the interests of one ally may mean the disintegration of the alliance. In both the world wars of this century, allies have found themselves fighting each other or withdrawing from the original conflict. In any case, as was pointed out earlier, the success of a particular alliance does not resolve the security dilemma, since the eclipse of the defeated states usually results in the aggrandisement of one or other of the victorious allies, and a change in relative military capacities, thus posing further problems.

The same point may be made about collective security and the attempt to eliminate war by collective action against an aggressor. The two examples of the League of Nations and the United Nations indicate that their main function was the legitimisation of a particular power relationship which represented the interests of victorious alliances. The forces which brought these alliances into being also destroyed them, and with them the notion of the legitimate use of violence in international politics. Such organisations are really constitutions without states. However, these considerations will be treated at length in another part of this study.

To return to the notion of national security, we can see that the power–security hypothesis postulates the pursuit of power as the major objective of the state. Hence the attempt to provide security for the state in an anarchic and violent world compels the state to try to control its environment. The argument that national security is guaranteed only by political suzerainty, and that this is the primal goal of all states, is a logical extension of the thesis that one state's security is another state's insecurity and that only dominion resolves the perpetual conflict which is international politics.

Control over the world, according to this argument, takes two forms: the first is the creation of a 'defence' capacity which is superior to that of a potential aggressor, and the second is an attempt to control those factors, referred to earlier, which contribute to international instability. This in effect means the pursuit of an imperialist policy. Now, put in this bald manner, such an argument does not explain adequately the course of international politics over the post-war period. It is really a rationalisation which stresses the logical concomitants of a security-based policy, given certain assumptions about the nature of the international world. As was pointed out earlier, statesmen have been influenced by considerations other than the dictates of *Realpolitik,* and those states which have attempted to apply this policy have come to grief. Yet the relationship between 'power' and policy has been a major preoccupation for statesmen.[7]

The central difficulty lies in the confusion between ends and means, that is, between the notion of power and the notion of the national interest. If power is conceived of as an end, then this is to suppose that a distinction can be made between it and some other objective, and that power has therefore some definable quality. But power is achievement, and the main question for the politician is what is to be accomplished before he can examine the problem of means. The point, as we have seen earlier when the notion of power as a theoretical variable was discussed, is that a meaningful distinction between the achievement of power and the achievement of a specific objective cannot be made, since the two are essentially the same. For example, the 'power' of the United States at any given moment is not a quality, or state, but is evaluated in terms of the achievement of specific aims. Hence an inability to secure policy objectives in Indo-China over the late 1960s is a better indication of its 'power' than a hypothetical capacity to destroy the world or its opponents. In short, power is as power does.

Thus the notion of power as a capacity cannot be divorced from the ends to which this capacity is related. It has been argued throughout this study that international politics is the politics of competition on various levels. So far as the pursuit of national interests is concerned, there is always a relevant opposition, but an opposition which is not defined in general terms but only in terms of specific issues. While it is true that ideological conflicts have appeared in international politics, and are transcendental, in that they cannot be resolved short of the extermination of the ideological opponent, nevertheless they are comparative rarities and in any case have so far stopped short of a final solution. Security competition poses the question of absolute power, since only when competing states are eliminated can the victor power enjoy complete security. But while this is a logical extension of the power-security hypothesis, it does not correspond to empirical reality. Absolute power seeks absolute ends, but our concern is with more relativistic notions of power.

Thus any discussion about capacity in this sense must be connected with the world which we are seeking to explain, that is, it must have a historical argument to support it. In practice the notion of national security is relative, not absolute, and the notion of power relates to the achievement of specific, although competing, ends. It is possible to make retrospective statements about power, but, as was seen earlier, prescriptive or predictive evaluations in policy-making lack theoretical rigour.

Nevertheless, the policy-maker is concerned with providing security for his state, as well as with providing the requisite military capacity to support other policy objectives. He is thus faced with the problem of matching threats of force to policy. We come now to the second question, that of examining the relationship between security, policy and violence in international politics. To what extent is war, as Clausewitz put it, policy by other means?[8]

It was argued earlier that there were variables in international politics, notably the relationship of resources and technology to social and economic organisation, which reduced the rationality of war by making it uncontrollable. War is rational only in the sense that destruction and violence are means to an end and not ends in themselves, except in certain cases. As Clausewitz argued, 'that the political point of view should end where war now begins is only conceivable in contexts which are wars of life and death from pure hatred'.[9] Total war in this conception was the destruction of the enemy's capacity to resist and not the destruction of the state itself.

Given limited military capacity and social and economic organisation for war on the part of the contending states, this could be achieved at a relatively low level of destruction. Even so, a war *à outrance* is always inherent in any violent conflict, and the level of force commensurate to the opponent's will or capacity to resist is a variable, with the upper limit being the complete annihilation of the state. The will to resist is neither quantifiable nor indeed isolable from the context of actual violence. Thus while the use of violence may appear rational, in terms of the optimal force necessary to make an opponent concede a limited political demand, it ceases to be rational if the objective itself changes and the struggle then becomes a question of national survival. The central problem for the policy-maker is that so long as war or the use of force can be controlled, then so long does it remain rational; when it ceases to be so controlled, then it becomes irrational. In other words, if a state resorts to war as a means of achieving limited political objectives which fall short of the preservation of its territorial integrity, then such a challenge may involve the integrity of its opponent and the conflict changes its character. The original aims are lost, since victory consists of breaking the opponent's will to resist and hence defeat becomes total. Any objective may be achieved at the expense of the defeated. The point here is that it is difficult to restrict the use of force, or to control an opponent's responses, in order to obtain a limited political objective through violence, or the threat of violence, without that objective becoming transformed into a life-and-death struggle for the conflicting states.

If the argument put forward by Clausewitz and others is accepted, then the main factor which determines the scale of war and its political consequences is the material capacity of states to inflict damage on each other. If this capacity confers upon its possessor the power to destroy its opponent completely, and is shared by the latter state, then it is difficult to argue that war is 'policy by other means'. There is clearly a paradox in that the creation of a capacity capable of providing both security, and the means to achieve other political objectives in the face of opposition, results in a situation in which any attempt to achieve the latter places the former in jeopardy. The point is that it is not the content of demands made by states on others in a conflict which is important, but their relative capacity to achieve them by force. All limited wars and conflicts thus carry within them the seeds of a total or general war, in which the political limitations which were initially conceived of as being rational cease to limit, and the struggle becomes universal (and irrational) in the sense that the original objectives are lost. This is not to say that such a struggle is wholly irrational, since its outcome might be the achievement of security for the victor. But as we have seen earlier, security is only obtained when one power establishes political hegemony over the rest of the world. Such a war, however, has not yet been fought to a successful conclusion, and we can regard all past wars as being unresolved, at least in this sense. Yet few political contests from the outset seek a final solution to the security dilemma, and no one state since Napoleonic France has sought the world hegemony which is its primary condition. Statesmen have been preoccupied with using force outside its defensive role in order to achieve more restricted policy ends.

The confusion between the notion of national security as a capacity to defeat *any* opposition or threat to territorial integrity, and the pursuit of more limited political national objectives through the use of force, weakens the rationality of war as an instrument of foreign policy. A clear separation between the two fields of activity is not possible because, as was seen, the ability to achieve an objective against the will of an opponent is also a threat to the opponent's security and is interpreted as such. In this sense all wars are wars of 'life and death', although not for emotional reasons. Consequently there is an inherent conflict between the defence and foreign policies of states, since they are concerned with the pursuit of incompatible objectives. The former seeks, as its primary responsibility, to create a military capacity capable of providing national security. Since this is relative to other national capacities, there is a constant pressure on resources and continual demands for technological innovations in weapons in order to secure a national advantage. Foreign policy, while it too is concerned with national security, and in providing this through alliances and treaties, is also concerned with the promotion of lesser objectives and with the maintenance of existing interests. In some cases defence and foreign policy are united in making a challenge to the *status quo* in order to effect a radical change in the distribution of international assets. But they are really only compatible when the situation is one of a direct threat to national integrity, or when an attempt at world or regional hegemony is being made. Essentially, diplomacy seeks to maintain some minimal form of order conducive to the protection of interests, as well as to promote those which conflict with other states. In this sense it is conservative, while defence policy possesses a radical element which militates against this order.

This ambivalent relationship between two policy objectives, the creation of national security, and the defence and promotion of other national interests, not only makes planning and decision-making difficult in the state itself, but also means that every dispute between states could be construed as an issue involving national security. As was argued above, in essence this means that a threat of force, or even the existence of conflict itself, is interpreted in terms of relative military capacity by the states involved, and the substance of the dispute is only the occasion and not the cause of international violence. However, without necessarily accepting the power–security hypothesis discussed at the beginning of this analyisis, we can accept, on the basis of past international conflicts, that the element of force contained in them was largely introduced by the various national responses to the security problem. But while this was generally true of an era in which capacity to fight total wars of less than total destruction existed, it ceases to be true of an age when weapons technology and defence policies have succeeded in creating weapons of absolute destructive capacity. If these weapons were actually used, then the result would not be the problematic question of the reduction of the enemy's capacity to resist, but the devastation of the contending states and possibly of life itself. With the arrival of nuclear weapons we come to the point when the rationality of war both as a means of providing security and as an instrument of national policy is in question. There are two aspects of this situation which will be considered here; the first is that of the development of the arms race and the various strategic arguments and defence policies related to it, and the second is the evaluation of the effects of these new weapons upon contemporary international politics.

First of all, what is the basis of the statement that nuclear weapons have made war between nuclear powers irrational? What is the nature of what has been termed the 'balance of terror'? Unlike previous innovations in weapons, such as poison gas, the aircraft, the tank and the submarine, the precise effects of thermonuclear explosions can be calculated, and it is clear that a few dozen bombs or missiles of megaton capacity would be sufficient to destroy all the major population centres in the world. Moreover, given a missile carrier, these weapons can be deployed against targets several thousands of miles from the launching-site with an accuracy of between five miles and a quarter of a mile. The nuclear stalemate itself arises out of a situation in which two or more states possess an invulnerable nuclear capacity and vulnerable territory. If these two conditions exist for a number of states, then a nuclear power cannot initiate a first strike upon another nuclear state with impunity. Although it could destroy territory and population, it could not destroy at the same time the opponent's capacity to retaliate. It is this capacity to retaliate, the riposte capacity as it is sometimes called, which forms the basis of the present stalemate. The invulnerability of this capacity is created in a number of different ways. The missiles may be protected from destruction by deep underground silos, by a ring of anti-ballistic missiles, by undersea or orbital launching-sites, by mobility, or simply by having such a preponderance of missiles that a first strike would be unlikely to destroy them all. The other condition, that of vulnerable territory, is essential for a stalemate, because if an opponent is able to protect his centres of population, or his economic and productive resources, then clearly a retaliatory strike against him ceases to have significance. Conversely, if a way was found to make territory invulnerable, then whichever state succeeded in doing this first would have the power to use its nuclear weapons without incurring destructive retaliation.

If we examine the notion of riposte capacity a little more closely, we can say that this constitutes the level of unacceptable damage which can be done by whatever is left over after suffering a first strike. In other words, for a first strike to be rational, the initiator would either have to destroy his nuclear opponent's retaliatory capacity completely, or destroy enough of it to make the level of damage inflicted by retaliation acceptable. What is considered acceptable will constitute a variable and is subject to a number of influences some of which, such as domestic political reactions, will not be easily calculable in advance. Generally, if all nuclear powers can protect sufficient of their nuclear weapons to provide retaliation capable of destroying an opponent's economic system, or millions of people, then this would constitute a deterrent against attack. Such a deterrence, it is important to point out, is purely defensive, since according to this argument the only sort of conflict which would justify the use of nuclear weapons would be one which directly threatened the territorial integrity of the nuclear powers. It is this type of conflict, therefore, which is inhibited by the possession of an invulnerable riposte capacity.

The present situation of nuclear stalemate is such as to give four states a defensive deterrence. Thus the United States, the U.S.S.R., France and the United Kingdom all have a retaliatory capacity capable of inflicting considerable damage on each other after suffering a first strike. The development of this situation, and the defence and strategic policies pursued by these states, will be examined shortly, but the point here is that war between these states can be considered irrational since it would entail their destruction as political entities. No one of these states could win such a conflict in any meaningful sense, given the conditions for mutual strategic deterrence.

Nevertheless, it has been argued by some strategicians[10] that a limited or controlled nuclear war could be fought, provided the question of total destruction or massive retaliation was not involved. A limited nuclear initiative could be made, keeping the massive riposte in reserve, and thus maintaining an inhibition on the scale of the opponent's response. If, as a means of resolving a political dispute, state A made a limited strike on another nuclear power, state B, then the latter state would be faced with the choice of conceding the issue or of making a suicidal nuclear retaliation. This argument, as will be seen, is at the root of most attempts to relate political power to nuclear capacity. There are a number of objections to it, the most obvious being of course that state B could simply reply in kind to state A and make a retaliatory limited strike. State A would then find itself in the same quandary, facing a general nuclear exchange which would destroy both of them. Other objections are concerned with the problem of controlling this kind of exchange. The politicians responsible would need to know very accurately what the intentions were behind this use of nuclear weapons. They would also need to control public responses. While hypothetically a strike on a minor city would not be a death-blow to the state, it would be for its inhabitants. Thus the government of a state which received a limited nuclear strike would have to know that such a strike was 'limited' and it would be in any case under political pressure to retaliate. The dangers of a general exchange of nuclear weapons, given such a situation, would be very much increased, even though this would be suicidal for the countries concerned. A further objection is that the nature of a response to a nuclear attack may be automatic and that, for example, a doomsday machine or trip-wire system may take the initiative. No state initiating such a strike could be certain that it was not committing suicide. It would seem from this that the risks of a limited nuclear war would far outweigh whatever political gains might be envisaged.

If a general nuclear war between nuclear powers, given the conditions for nuclear stalemate, is deemed irrational, what of general conventional war? The main argument against another world war fought with conventional weapons is that such a war could not be won. This is based on the view that if a nuclear power found itself being defeated, then it would use nuclear weapons in order to extricate itself from defeat. It is true that this would be the equivalent of suicide, but few people could say axiomatically that the choice between that and unconditional surrender would always be the latter.

What of other kinds of war? Following from the previous argument, it can be seen that war is possible between nuclear powers and non-nuclear states. Similarly, war is possible between non-nuclear powers. Such wars are, however, limited, in the sense that while the rationality of violence holds good in the non-nuclear area, it does not in the nuclear area. A violent conflict between non-nuclear powers, or between a nuclear and a non-nuclear state, cannot develop into a general conventional war for the reasons given above. Thus whatever the objectives of the major powers, or the degree of their involvement in the non-nuclear area, their commitments and their capacities to use violence in their pursuit are strictly limited. It is, of course, true that two of the four extant nuclear powers are also major powers in conventional terms and hence have a considerable range and flexibility in their capacity to use violence outside the nuclear area.

Nevertheless, the nuclear inhibition upon the unrestricted use of power exists even in this non-nuclear area. In postulating the use of nuclear weapons against a non-nuclear power, or the pursuit of a policy which would lead to its subjugation or destruction, the question of opposition from another nuclear power arises. Clearly, this opposition cannot take the form of a direct nuclear attack against the nuclear power initiating the policy. Yet it is possible to make such an attack against a non-nuclear ally. In other words, a countering or indirect strategy may be used against each other's *allies* without going to the irrational lengths of making direct nuclear attacks on each other. Such a strategy could involve the use of nuclear weapons, but only in the non-nuclear area. Faced with this possible development, it can be argued that the use of either nuclear or conventional force against a non-nuclear power is precluded by the capacity of the major ally of that power to do the same in retaliation. The overall nuclear inhibition on general war still applies, and an indulgence in limited war in the non-nuclear area may result in more loss than gain.

The key to rationality in such cases is in the nature of the relationship between the non-nuclear power and its ally. In the case of Europe, a nuclear or conventional attack against a non-nuclear state could result in unacceptable retaliation without the consequence of general war between the Soviet Union and the United States. No gain could be postulated for such a conflict other than the Pyrrhic victory of destroying each other's allies. The non-nuclear allies thus owe their security to their situation as nuclear hostages, not to any nuclear umbrella in the form of their nuclear ally's capacity to make direct nuclear attacks on its nuclear opponent.

However, the case is different where the relationship between non-nuclear and nuclear powers is tenuous. For example, the Soviet Union apparently does not regard North Vietnam as being as closely related to its interests as Czechoslovakia and Hungary. Whether this relationship, in the former case, inhibited an invasion by the United States of North Vietnam, or a nuclear strike, is an imponderable. But it serves to illustrate that rationality can still be postulated for the use of violence and that the politics of violence may still be viable in the non-nuclear areas. Fundamentally, the nature of an alliance, and the consequent protection afforded to the non-nuclear allies by the major nuclear power, lies almost entirely in the latter's conceptions of its own interests. Outside the alliance proper, no major nuclear power has declared the non-nuclear area to be inviolate or has identified its interests completely with the rest of the world; although it is true to say that both the United States with its policy of global containment of communism, and the Soviet Union with its historic mission of promoting world communism, have at times come near this. As will be seen later, great-power competition in a nuclear environment has become irrational, since ultimate objectives cannot be reached without the total destruction of the contending powers. Thus unless further technological innovation occurs, giving one state an advantage, the consequences of the nuclear balance would appear to result in a change of objectives rather than an attempt to create an increased capacity to achieve them. Of course, these restrictions upon the use of force in international relations are based upon the conditions for nuclear stability between the nuclear powers stated earlier, and upon their respective government's recognition of them. These arguments assume that technological factors will remain constant and that politicians will behave rationally within the terms of these conditions. The present state of nuclear stalemate is based upon the capacity of the nuclear powers to deliver strikes against each other's territory, after having suffered a nuclear attack. Before examining the relation between defence policy and the various strategic theories which seek to relate policy to this new capacity for mutual destruction, a brief survey of the arms race which produced this situation might be appropriate.

It was pointed out in an earlier chapter that the use of atom bombs to obtain the unconditional surrender of Japan by the United States resulted in her allies developing their own nuclear programmes.[11] The first successful nuclear test at Alamogordo on 16 July, 1945, was the product of the Manhattan Project in which British scientists had participated. This collaboration was based on the Quebec agreement of 1943 and the Hyde Park agreement of September 1944. However, the sharing of nuclear secrets was abrogated by the McMahon Act of August 1946 and, while the United states amended this slightly by the Blair House agreement of early 1948, which provided for the exchange of information on non-military subjects, in effect the two countries pursued their own security policies in the atomic field, independently of each other. In 1948 the Attlee government announced its intention to make nuclear weapons while at the same time accepting the establishment of American bomber bases in England. Like France, Britain was content to accept American leadership in this field, given the persistence of the nuclear monopoly, although their development of nuclear weapons continued in order to preserve an option in the event of its disappearance.

The arms race proper over the post-war period was between the United States and the Soviet Union, in that it was these countries which took the major initiatives in developing both a strategy and a nuclear weapons technology. The course of this competition represents a classic example of innovation, followed by response, followed by counter-response, or what has been called an action–reaction phenomenon. As was pointed out above, the initial response of the United States' two major allies was to embark upon their own independent nuclear programmes, and the Soviet Union itself succeeded in successfully exploding an atomic bomb in August 1949, exactly four years after the American attacks on Hiroshima and Nagasaki. Britain followed suit in 1952, the French in 1960 and China in 1964. The American reaction to the discovery that the Soviets possessed an atomic bomb[12] was the decision announced in January 1950 to proceed with the development of a thermonuclear weapon – the H-bomb. This weapon was successfully exploded in November 1952. Only a few months later a Soviet H-bomb was exploded, in August, 1953. This new weapon did not make a qualitative difference to the overall strategic situation. The United States, with its Strategic Air Command, established not only an extensive system of bases deployed around the Soviet Union, capable of reaching most major targets, but also maintained a permanent airborne force. The aeroplane and the bomb constituted the basis of the two powers' strategic forces, and the United States enjoyed a superiority in that an overwhelming attack could be launched at Soviet nuclear forces and population centres, without the United States herself suffering a major attack. In the terms used in this discussion earlier, the United States possessed both offensive and defensive deterrent capacity. While the former was difficult to apply in practice, nevertheless this situation was not radically different from that of 1945 and constituted a direct threat to Soviet security.

The Soviet reaction to American nuclear superiority was the development of an intercontinental ballistic missile (I.C.B.M.), and Sputnik was launched on 4 October, 1957. This innovation was of profound significance because it now became possible to strike at targets over several thousands of miles with very little warning. Moreover, the missile launchers could be concealed or protected in various ways much more easily than strategic bomber bases. It was from this point onwards that the situation of mutual strategic deterrence was to emerge. Not only did the United States react sharply, but so did her allies, and both France and Britain embarked on 'independent' missile programmes. The political effects of these decisions and the reasoning on which they were based will be discussed later, but the point here is that the United States became much more co-operative with Britain in the nuclear field than before. The initial American reaction was to embark on a greatly expanded missile programme and to begin research and development in the field of interceptive missiles. From these efforts the Polaris missile, which could be fired underwater, and the nuclear launcher fleet which carried it, emerged. In 1960 the United States decided that this missile would be the basis of the American defence programme. It became increasingly clear, however, that Soviet development in the missile field had removed the offensive capacity from the United States. The situation of mutual strategic defensive deterrence, described earlier, appeared by 1962. However, a further innovation, this time in the interceptive missile field, appeared to present an opportunity of breaking the nuclear stalemate. As was noted, both the United States and the Soviet Union had commenced research and development on these missiles, but the factor which changed the situation was the discovery in 1966 that the Soviet Union had actually deployed an anti-ballistic missile system (A.B.M.) around Leningrad. The significance of this step was that if a way had been found to make territory invulnerable, then the nuclear power which first achieved this would possess an offensive deterrent capacity, and would thus have broken the nuclear stalemate. The initial American reaction was to devise a means of nullifying the effects of an A.B.M. system by developing missiles with multiple warheads and combining these with decoys and independently targeted missiles, which could saturate any defensive system. In 1966 the development of the new missile Poseidon began. In order to counter the Soviet A.B.M., the United States also began to develop its own Safeguard system in 1968. The Soviets' counter to this was the SS-9, a missile of up to 25 megaton capacity, whose strategic significance was that it could destroy the Minuteman missile silos and thus reduce the net effect of the riposte capacity possessed by the United States.

The question of arms control should now be considered. Since 1963 three nuclear powers, Britain, the U.S.S.R. and the United States, have succeeded in negotiating a number of agreements designed to prevent their defensive and security policies from provoking an uncontrolled arms race. Although various proposals on arms control and disarmament had been made since the Baruch Plan of 1946, negotiations between the major powers had been more significant for their disagreement than for their awareness of what McNamara called in 1967 'the action–reaction phenomenon', in which a technological development in one country provoked a counter-development in another, and so on. It was the realisation that the arms race had resulted in stalemate, first apparent at the time of the Cuban missiles crisis in 1962, which brought these nuclear powers to find a way of preventing accidental strikes, of restricting their competition and controlling the spread of nuclear weapons to other countries. The difficulty in maintaining the nuclear *status quo* is that there is no central control or any guarantee that an opponent is not seeking to introduce another revolutionary change. Moreover, one of the effects of the nuclear balance has been to force other states to develop their own nuclear deterrents. As was pointed out earlier, defensive deterrence is provided by an invulnerable riposte capacity which need not in terms of size be as large as the capacity of a potential opponent, so long as it is capable of inflicting unacceptable damage. Such a deterrent is purely defensive since it only inhibits an attack on the homeland. Non-nuclear allies or allies which do not possess I.C.B.M.s cannot be protected by their major nuclear partners except in the indirect way described earlier. Consequently, when the I.C.B.M. entered into strategic calculations in 1956–7, Britain, France and China, all possessing nuclear capacity, were forced to embark on missile programmes independently of their normal allies. Thus the proliferation of nuclear weapons was a consequence of this development in the arms race and a further complication to it.

Both France and China have refused to participate in arms-control negotiations, or to accede to those agreements which were successfully concluded by the other nuclear powers. This is a reflection of their relative backwardness in the arms race, and of their desire to acquire the same deterrent capacity enjoyed by the negotiating powers. So far as Britain is concerned, while her missile programme was abandoned in 1960, largely because of its rising economic cost, she was able to use her relationship with the United States in order to obtain the Polaris missile. This relationship hinged on the base facilities granted to the United States at Holy Loch and was part of an agreement made at Camp David in 1960. This agreement gave the United States base facilities in exchange for the Skybolt missile, then under development. The cancellation of this missile by the United States in November 1962 caused a crisis in Anglo-American relations,[13] and negotiations at Nassau between Macmillan and Kennedy resulted in an agreement in which the British were given the Polaris missile, under very vague conditions related to its inclusion in a multilateral force within NATO. These conditions were open to various interpretations and depended upon future negotiations regarding the establishment of this force. While the Nassau agreement was between Britain and the United States, the offer of Polaris was also made to the French, subject to the same conditions. The offer was neither taken up nor taken seriously by the French government.[14] The point is that in effect an 'independent' deterrent was conferred upon Britain by the United States, albeit under pressure, and this appeared to nullify any attempt at reaching general international agreement on the non-proliferation of nuclear weapons. Nevertheless, these three powers, Britain, the United States and the U.S.S.R., succeeded in achieving a number of agreements. Only one agreement existed before 1963, and that was the Antarctic Treaty of December 1959, in which a number of countries, including France, accepted the South Pole area as a nuclear-free zone. This modest beginning was followed up by the partial test-ban treaty of July 1963, a treaty banning nuclear weapons from outer space in December 1966, and the non-proliferation treaty in January 1968. In August of that year the U.S.S.R. indicated its willingness to engage in strategic arms-limitation talks. In October 1969 a treaty banning nuclear weapons from the sea bed was successfully concluded. As early as June 1963 a 'hot line' had been established between Washington and Moscow as a precaution against misinterpretation in crisis situations. This line was used during the Arab–Israeli war of 1967.

All these agreements were peripheral to the central question of controlling the arms race through a voluntary restraint on technological innovation and an understanding of each other's interests and motives. Nevertheless, they constituted a considerable advance on the preceding period of unrestricted arms race. Most significantly, the deployment of an anti-ballistic missile system by the Soviet Union provoked, not a radical response from the United States, but an attempt to reach an accommodation. It is apparent from the speech made by the American Defence Secretary, Robert McNamara, at San Francisco in 1967[15] that the dangers in a hasty American response to the Soviet initiative were appreciated by the United States. 'We do not want a nuclear arms race with the Soviet Union', he said, 'because the action–reaction phenomenon makes it foolish and futile.' Given the resources and technical capacity of the Soviet Union, such an arms race would result, after the expenditure of vast sums of money, in the two states arriving 'at the same point of balance on the security scale that we are now.' Yet the United States began to deploy a limited A.B.M. system. In order to explain this development, as well as the negotiations which accompanied it, the effects of A.B.M. systems on the overall strategic situation must be examined.

It is clear from what has been said that there are limitations upon the number of countries able to develop a nuclear capacity. These limitations range from technological knowledge and scarce resources, to political considerations. For example, Japan and the Federal Republic of Germany possess both resources and technical and scientific skills but, for reasons which are in the main political rather than strategic, have refrained from producing nuclear weapons. Even in the case of those countries which have opted for an independent deterrent capacity, the problem exists of providing resources on a continuing basis in order to maintain their strategic position. Any quantitative change in the levels and types of nuclear armaments employed by the Soviet Union and the United States affects the smaller nuclear powers, who are unable to undertake the costs of developing and innovating their own nuclear programmes. Nuclear powers with relatively limited resources are forced to respond to the strategic and production policies of the two principal nuclear powers. Thus both the Soviet Union

and the United States, without changing their conditions of mutual deter-
rance, can render the nuclear capacities of the smaller powers obsolete and
redundant.

This possibility exists in the development of anti-ballistic missile programmes. If a nuclear power succeeds in making its territory invulnerable,
then it is no longer inhibited from using violence against other nuclear
powers. In the view of the United States after 1963, security has rested in
the possession of a larger number of I.C.B.M.s than the Soviet Union, and
this is clearly linked to expectations of a nuclear attack. Conversely, the
Soviet Union[16] appears to have been more concerned with creating a purely
defensive capacity, and in nuclear warfare this can be achieved at a
relatively low level. As we have seen, all that is required is sufficient
retaliatory capacity remaining after an attack, capable of inflicting unacceptable damage on the attacker. The deployment of anti-ballistic missile
systems in the Soviet Union appears to be linked to a defensive strategy.
This deployment, however, reduces the effectiveness of the American
nuclear strike capacity. In order to inflict the same level of damage more
missiles are required. Thus the initial reaction to the Soviet initiative was
the development of missiles with multiple warheads. The answer to anti-
ballistic missile systems was seen to lie in an increased production of missiles
in order to saturate the defensive system. But it cannot be assumed that
saturation will always work, and if the Soviet A.B.M. system is developed
to the extent that Soviet territory is made invulnerable to nuclear attack,
then the United States will have lost the nuclear arms race. The question is
therefore whether to embark upon a programme of anti-ballistic missile
development and begin another arms race, or to accept the limitations of
the present Soviet deployment and simply expand missile production,
adapting existing weapons to the changed situation. The short-term answer
has been to embark upon a pilot scheme, while opening negotiations with
the Soviet Union in order to avoid another uncontrolled arms race.

What would be the hypothetical consequences of such an arms race of
the establishment of two opposing anti-ballistic missile systems? Firstly,
what would be the effects on the other nuclear powers assuming that they
lack the resources to develop their own systems? It has been argued that
on technical grounds no A.B.M. system can be made operable in Europe
because of the factor of space relations. This would hold good for any
nuclear powers which were contiguous in territory, unless potential targets
were well within the national frontiers. The warning period of a nuclear
strike would be too short and an A.B.M. system could not be alerted in
time. On other grounds it can be argued that no single developed country
outside the United States and the Soviet Union could afford to develop
these systems. The cost of the pilot scheme in the United States is estimated
at $10·8 billion, and if past experience is any guide it can be said that
this is certainly underestimated. Thus if the two major nuclear powers

succeed in making their territory invulnerable to nuclear attack, their 'independent' nuclear deterrents then become useless, except against each other or against non-nuclear powers. Even here the offensive capacity would be strictly limited by the capacity of the major nuclear powers to threaten nuclear attack and thus prevent any infringement of their interests. This would mean a reversion to bipolar nuclear balance, with the small nuclear powers being totally dependent upon the policies of, and their relationship to, the major nuclear powers. In other words, they would revert to the situation which existed before they developed their nuclear deterrents. In the short term the effect of such a change would be to increase the so-called conventional threat in Europe. Neither of the major nuclear powers is likely to threaten the use of nuclear weapons in Europe, since both have something to lose in a general exchange in that area. A conventional threat will create similar risks but conflict could remain limited at this level. The nuclear forces of France and Britain could not be used against the major nuclear aggressor but could be used against a non-nuclear ally of the aggressor. Thus aggression in Europe could only be deterred by a threat to the interests of the aggressor and not, as is the present case, by a direct threat to his territorial integrity. Such a threat is obviously very much reduced in its force.

The major powers themselves, should they both succeed in creating effective anti-ballistic missile systems, would seem to have achieved the paradoxical effect of rendering nuclear weapons ineffective. Since they could not be used against each other's invulnerable territory, nuclear war would not merely be made irrational through deterrence but would be excluded absolutely. A nuclear exchange could thus take place only in third-party territory. In theory, a new situation, created by a bipolar balance in A.B.M. systems, reopens the possibility of general conventional war. Apart from war in third-party areas, direct hostilities of a conventional nature could take place, with nuclear weapons becoming relevant only if the A.B.M. systems were suspended. Ground warfare would thus reassume its traditional role. It is, of course, highly speculative to posit a general conventional war between the United States and the Soviet Union, but the paradoxical effect of mutually effective A.B.M. systems is to make such a war the only kind of war possible between these two countries. This is a reversal of the present inhibition on conventional war referred to earlier in this study,

A by-product of the development of A.B.M. systems would thus be an increased emphasis on non-conventional weapons and on land forces, since national security could no longer be guaranteed by the possession of nuclear weapons. Only security from nuclear attack would be provided by mutually effective A.B.M. systems. This would mean the restoration of the security dilemma referred to earlier.

However, without too much speculation, it can be argued that even a modest development of A.B.M. systems, while not affecting the strategic relationship of the two major nuclear powers, will have profound consequences for the smaller nuclear countries. As was pointed out earlier, their defensive deterrent capacity lies almost entirely in the level of unacceptable damage they can inflict, in the event of themselves suffering nuclear attack. If the principal targets in the major nuclear powers can be effectively protected by A.B.M. systems, then clearly the level of unacceptable damage will be reduced. The only response which can be made by the smaller nuclear powers, short of developing their own A.B.M. system, is to try to saturate the system of their potential opponents. This means, at the least, an expansion of their present nuclear forces, and possibly the development and production of more sophisticated missiles. At the time of writing, the British deterrent is based upon the supply of Polaris missiles from the United States in fulfilment of the Nassau agreement of 1963. The French and the Chinese are in the process of developing their own missile programmes, and the former relies at the moment on the survival of a percentage of its bomber force to inflict a level of damage which would have a deterrent effect. While it may be possible to adapt existing weapons to the changed situation, any further change would have more radical effects. If, for example, further technological advances are made, the smaller nuclear powers would be left very far behind in the arms race. The main point in nuclear weapons technology is that development and deployment of these weapons depends upon the amount of resources devoted to it. It would appear that only two powers, the Soviet Union and the United States, have the economic capacity to innovate in the nuclear field, and consequently control over weapons technology is vested in these two countries. Their main strategic problems lie not in nuclear proliferation but in an uncontrolled bilateral arms race.

It is this last which has brought both countries into negotiations over the limitation of strategic arms in 1969 and, significantly, no new development has occurred in their respective strategic postures. The American A.B.M. system Safeguard, which was commenced in August 1969, appears to be designed to counter the development of nuclear missiles by China, to act as a bargaining counter in negotiations with the Soviets, and to act as an insurance should 'the Soviets decide to expand their present modest A.B.M. deployment into a massive one'.[17] From this it would appear that the two major nuclear powers are willing to accept a form of nuclear stalemate which preserves their mutual defensive deterrents, but which enables them to curb other nuclear powers and leaves them free to pursue policies without the constant pressure of security fears. If this is the case, then it seems that a major change has occurred in Soviet–American relations. The nature and extent of this change, together with its effects on international politics, will be considered later; for the moment, the relation of strategic theories to defence policies and political decisions will be examined.

The central problem for the United States, and perhaps for the Soviet Union, has been the relationship of security policies, based upon nuclear weapons, to foreign policy objectives. As was noted earlier, defence policy has two major tasks: the provision of national security and the furtherance of foreign policy objectives. Defence and foreign policy may of course be closely linked in, for example, establishing alliance relationships in order to offset the superior military strength of a potential enemy, or in obtaining foreign bases in order to deploy forces and weapons as part of a national security policy. The diplomatic relations set up by the Attlee government between 1946 and 1949 were linked, *inter alia,* to the problem of providing a viable answer to what was conceived of as a potential Soviet threat to British security. Similarly, American relations with Britain were linked to the dependence on nuclear bomber bases as part of the American defensive system. Thus political relationships in international politics may be directly related to security questions, and NATO and the Warsaw Pact are examples of the conciliation of different national conceptions of security within an alliance framework. There are, additionally, other motives and interests which may be reconciled within this concern for security.

The difficulty arises when the notion of security itself changes and becomes incompatible, or conflicts, with foreign policy objectives. The central problem for the defence planner and for the foreign policy-maker is to reconcile their notions of security. Traditionally, this has consisted in the possession of a military capacity, alone or in alliance with other powers, which was superior to that of another power considered to be a threat to territorial integrity. But this meant, as we have seen earlier, that the provision of security created an offensive as well as a defensive military capacity and thus endangered the security of other nations. Arms races, wars and competitive diplomacy were the consequence of constant uncertainty and insecurity. The creation of a defensive capacity posed a threat to other countries. Moreover, a temporary superiority in armaments tended to induce an attempt to take advantage of it, in order to reduce the uncertainties created by the international environment. In other words, the quest for security produces a situation which not only creates hostility from other countries but which, from this, provides an inducement to try to control other countries in order to counteract their hostility.

However, given the possession of nuclear weapons, the security problem lies in the arms race itself and security in the absolute sense depends on the existence of a nuclear monopoly. Only one state has enjoyed this advantage, and that for a comparatively short time. The United States could deliver an overwhelming blow in response to any direct threat to its territorial integrity, or to any hostile action, between 1945 and 1956. After this last date, although an overwhelming blow could still be delivered, some retaliatory damage would be incurred. In 1967 it was admitted by McNamara that 'the blunt, inescapable fact remains that the Soviet Union could still, with its present forces, effectively destroy the United States, even after absorbing the full weight of an American first strike'. For the first time in international history a clear definition of security could be made, which was strictly defensive and which did not imply either aggression or superiority. This is, as we have seen, based upon the concept of defensive deterrence and rests upon the two conditions shared by the nuclear powers, of an invulnerable riposte capacity and vulnerable territory. It would appear from this that it has at last become possible for a state to separate its security policy from its foreign policy, provided it enjoys a defensive deterrent capacity. The creation of this capacity cannot be construed as a threat by a state which already possesses it, since the threat is only credible for a direct attack upon national territory. It cannot be used to deter a state possessing this capacity from hostile actions which fall short of this. The pursuit of foreign policy objectives can thus be related to the use of force, in a way which was not possible when national security was bound up with military strength, so as to present a state on which demands were being made with the prospect of a major war if these demands were rejected. The threat of major war between nuclear powers is, as we have seen, irrational.

The full implications of this change in relative military capacities took some time to be appreciated by both politicians and strategic theorists. Initially, the problem was seen to be the relationship between an overwhelming military capacity and political objectives which were not intrinsically related to national security. Clearly, the American nuclear monopoly, while it conferred a strong guarantee of national security, did not confer power and influence in areas where a nuclear military threat appeared either impracticable, or likely to lead to reactions which would be fundamentally self-defeating. This dilemma was illustrated by the Korean war, in which the American decision not to use the atomic bomb against either North Korea or China, or to fight a major war under its shelter, resulted in a humiliating stalemate. There were difficulties in relating a policy of global containment with that of strategic nuclear deterrence. If containment is taken to mean the delineation of spheres of interest beyond the frontiers of the nation-state, and the prevention of any invasion or alienation of these areas, then there are two broad aspects of this policy.

Firstly, the policy is offensive in that, to maintain inviolate the frontiers of the protected area, a superior war capacity is required. As we have seen, the possession of such a capacity is regarded by the deterred state not merely as an inhibition to agression, but also as a danger to its own territorial integrity. This is because while the intentions of the deterring power may or may not be limited, its capacity to wage war is not so limited if it possesses military superiority. Secondly, it is defensive in that, while having a sufficient deterrent capacity to deter external aggression as a condition of a containment policy, nevertheless another threat exists in the form of internal political changes occurring within the protected area, which may be favourable to the state which is being 'contained'. In effect, any political change in the *status quo* may be dangerous, especially in cases where the government is actually allied to the United States, since there is no guarantee that a new government will wish to maintain the alliance. In circumstances where political changes are violent the struggle may permit intervention from a hostile state, and in any case its consequences may result in an unfriendly government gaining power. Hence to avert these possibilities, a different capacity is required which complements the nuclear monopoly and which permits military intervention on the conventional level. The United States has accepted in its policy both these implications. However, given a nuclear stalemate, how may the non-communist area continue to be protected? Offensive deterrence directly against an aggressing nuclear power is not possible, nor for other reasons is it expedient, although it is possible to use nuclear weapons in the area itself. The problem then becomes one in which military capacity is closely related to political calculation and objectives and does not involve national security. In what may be called the non-nuclear area, war may be rational on the nuclear or conventional level, provided some notion of victory or success may be defined. Given the condition of nuclear stalemate between the nuclear powers, it would appear that calculations of profit and loss are at present the same for both the United States and the Soviet Union. Prospects of success must, however be strictly limited to definable objectives, and the whole rationale of containment disintegrates once the prospect of accommodation with a communist power appears as a consequence of the loss of an offensive deterrent capacity. Victories in the area 'contained' are indefinable in the Cold War sense of containment.

Turning from this general description of the change in the nature of war to the various arguments provided by strategic theorists, it can be seen that their main concern has been to try to get over the problems posed by the strategic deadlock. Their aim in this respect has been prescriptive. There are two concerns in this examination: firstly, to examine how far strategic theories are theoretical in the sense used in the early part of this study; and secondly, how far they have influenced or reflected actual decisions and political behaviour.

Essentially, these type of theories are concerned with making rational decisions in international politics which confer the greatest advantages on the decision-maker, without provoking a situation which is either uncontrollable or which results in direct or indirect losses. The assumptions on which they are based are derived from interpretations of contemporary international politics rather than being dependent upon a general theory.

Strictly speaking, bargaining and game theories are relevant to all cases where a choice of decisions exist, but those which are relevant to this study are termed variously conflict or deterrent theories, or the theory of inter-dependent decisions.[18] The difficulty in evaluating these 'theories' is that their proponents are in the main concerned with a view of strategy which seeks to advocate rational courses of action within the framework of their assumptions. In the case of T. C. Schelling, for example, the theory put forward is not a theory in the sense of an explanation of international politics, or of conflict, but consists of a series of hypothetical situations involving a range of alternative courses of action. This writer assumes the existence of international conflict as a phenomenon and states simply that his primary concern is with how people 'actually do conduct themselves in conflict situations'.[19] This implies a historical study of conflict behaviour, unless some general theory is established.

It is apparent from the analysis of bargaining contained in this work that Schelling is seeking to elucidate model behaviour, making as he does so the major assumptions of complete information between the participants, of rational behaviour, on the basis of 'an explicit and internally consistent value system',[20] and of the possibility of some form of non-violent accom-modation between the contestants. Other assumptions made in this type of theorising are that the participants in a conflict are aware of the 'rules' governing it, and that they can define closely their notion of gain and loss. They must also possess the capacity to engage in various forms of hostile or coercive action in order to make their threats credible. Using these various assumptions, a number of bargaining ploys are then outlined. As Schelling puts it, this theory

> takes conflict for granted, but also assumes common interest between the adversaries; it assumes a 'rational' value-maximising mode of behaviour, and it focuses on the fact that each participant's 'best' choice of action depends on what he expects the other to do; and that strategic behaviour is concerned with influencing another's choice by working on his expectation of how one's own behaviour is related to his.[21]

This is why he terms his theory 'the theory of interdependent decisions'.

To refer back to policy- and decision-making in the general areas of defence and foreign policy, it is worth remarking that the notion of 'inter-dependence' between states engaged in conflict, violent or non-violent, has long been held by politicians and indeed, as will be seen subsequently, is implicit in the notion of global containment. In reference to nuclear strategy, McNamara in his San Francisco speech said:

> What is essential to understand is that the Soviet Union and the United States mutually influence one another's strategic plans. Whatever be their intentions, whatever be our intentions, actions or even realistically

potential actions, on either side, relating to the build-up of nuclear forces, be they either offensive or defensive weapons, necessarily trigger reactions on the other side. It is precisely this action–reaction phenomenon that fuels an arms race.

The trouble with the general theoretical approach towards international relations in terms of conflict and bargaining is that the hypothecating is not important. What is important is the foundation on which model 'bargains' are struck. In other words, we are concerned with the premises and the generalisations which are essential parts of any theory, and not with the much more limited hypothesis which stems from this. A hypothesis is not an explanation and consequently is remote from the 'real' world of political behaviour.

To illustrate this point, when Schelling talks of limitations in 'limited' wars between nuclear powers, he asserts that the basis of the limits which are self-imposed by the contestants is tradition. As he puts it, 'traditions or conventions are not simply an analogy for limits in war, or a curious aspect of them; tradition or precedent or convention is the essence of the limits'. In other words, it is not the intrinsic nature of nuclear weapons, that is, their destructive capacity, which inhibits their use, but a 'tradition for their non-use'.[22] The weapons themselves are therefore not important but the 'expectations in themselves and not the thing that expectations have attached themselves to'.[23] It is doubtful whether a clear distinction can be made between weapons and an appreciation of their utility or capacity, but if what Schelling is saying is that past behaviour or conceptions which have been derived from past experience govern future situations, then this would seem to be empirically absurd so far as nuclear warfare is concerned. The arms race has produced considerable changes in strategic thought, and defence and foreign policies have been radically changed since the Hiroshima and Nagasaki explosions. It is not a tradition of non-use which inhibits nuclear powers from nuclear war, but the nature of the weapons themselves, and of the nuclear stalemate, as well as a perception of this. However, the weakness of such arguments lies in the attempt to generalise or to assume on the basis of an interpretation of the past, without having an adequate theory which 'explains' past, present and future, in the sense of the kind of scientific explanation discussed at the beginning of this study. The factors which are held constant, such as the notion of gain, or an awareness of the 'rules', the 'rules' themselves, or of the values on which rationality is based, are crucial to this kind of theorising. They are clearly not constants but variables and, as we have seen earlier, extremely difficult to quantify or define. In fact this sort of 'theory' is riddled with assumptions about the behaviour of states and about historical situations, which are used to reinforce the hypothetical argument. The focus is not upon theoretical explanation but upon description. If such policy aids as this kind of bargaining theory seek to explain, then they must fulfil the theoretical criteria for a valid explanation discussed earlier. In practice the type of rationalisation proffered by Schelling is essentially *post facto*.

For example, the point is made that tacit negotiations are possible between opponents, in the sense that both may recognise specific limits to their conflict. As a generalisation it is unexceptionable, if a little vague. But the example cited to support it is the Korean war.[24] Yet this conflict only became limited after the Chinese intervention, and largely as the result of decisions taken in the United States, which concluded that the prosecution of the war meant extending it to other areas. It was not axiomatically limited to the Korean peninsula until these decisions were taken, and they were taken not as the result of a tacit agreement with the Chinese government, or as a consequence of the physical configuration of the terrain, but because of global political considerations, combined with the apparent determination of the Chinese to preserve the People's Republic in North Korea. But if these decisions had not been taken, or if the Chinese People's Republic had not been content with its victory in the north, then the war would have been different. There is something tautological in an emphasis upon the terms of an agreement rather than on the motivations which inspired it.

Another example illustrates this point. Schelling argues that definable frontiers or 'boundaries' constitute limits. Hence, 'The Formosan Straits made it possible to stabilise a line between the Communist and National government forces of China not solely because water favoured the defender and inhibited attack but because an island is an integral unit and water a conspicuous boundary'.[25] But surely the important factor in establishing the two Chinas was not a mutual recognition of a geographical limit, but the military and political facts of powerful American support for the Nationalist government, together with the reasoning on which this support was based. If the United States had abandoned Chiang Kai-shek, then the situation of conflict over Quemoy, Matsu, and Formosa itself, would not have arisen.

In a specific conflict it may be relevant that mutually recognisable positions exist, and that threats and counter-threats may be made, some of which are implicit rather than explicit, but their nature is confined to the circumstances of the conflict and does not permit meaningful generalisations which can be extended to other conflicts. It would appear that this conception of conflict contained in bargaining theory, in which the cause and occasion of the dispute is taken for granted, is both static and limited. In short, it is the 'value' basis itself, and not the strategy which seeks to implement it, which is important in any explanation of international conflict, and which requires examination. A bargaining theory which confines itself to urging an optimal strategy, without considering the policy basis of choice, is a limited technique since the circumstances may so alter as to make the desired objectives themselves change radically, rendering the original strategy irrelevant. Thus in the Korean war the Truman administration first embarked upon a holding operation in order to save the South Korean government, then made the objective the reunification of Korea under an allied regime, and finally, on Chinese intervention, reverted to the original objective. Not only did the conflict itself change its nature, but it cannot be viewed in isolation from its international context, or from American foreign policy as a whole, without great distortion. To treat such a situation as a 'game' or as a static 'conflict situation' is perhaps viable as a limited form of historical interpretation; to use it as a source for generalisations about future 'games' is of very dubious value unless it is supported by a theoretical explanation of conflict behaviour which is capable of verification.

Another theorist who is similarly concerned with the practical problem of using nuclear capacity in conflict situations without actually engaging in nuclear war, or 'losing' the conflict, provides a further indication of the limitations of this kind of argument. Herman Kahn[26] has produced a strategy which he has called escalation, in order to show how conflict may be made both rational and 'winnable'. Escalation consists of the use of threats in order to persuade the opponent to desist from an action by increasing the threat should he persist. The threat may be actually implemented or simply 'escalated'. The opponent is thus confronted with a situation in which his behaviour determines the nature of response, until he reaches a point when the responses contain more disadvantages for him than the maintenance of the original point in dispute. This is a simplification of the course of action in international conflicts where coercion and the use of force or of threats of force, constitute part of the bargaining between states. Again, as with Schelling, the argument does not concern itself with motives or policy but solely with strategy, that is, once having decided on an objective, how best to attain it in the face of opposition. International behaviour is not treated as a form of dialogue between circumstances, attitudes and policies, but as something which can be treated in terms of isolable and static conflicts, or confrontations between states, with a definable notion of success and failure. This is of course a considerable over-simplification of the complexities of political behaviour.

Kahn produces what he calls an escalation ladder[27] of gradually increasing threats or hostile actions, each of which is induced by an opponent refusing to concede the point at issue. He does not consider the qualitative nature of the threats but is concerned only with their effects. Thus the question of what is implied by the threat other than its apparent nature is not considered. For example, in a dispute which does not involve national security, threats may be made which, albeit hostile, do not compromise the opponent's territorial integrity, should they be implemented. However, if these threats should prove ineffective and 'escalation' occurs, that is, the threat is strengthened, then a situation may arise when the enhanced threat becomes a question of national security for both parties. If this is the case, then the original point at issue is irrelevant, for what matters is the credibility of such a threat, and how it may be countered. The conflict is thus transformed into a radically different conflict affecting the most basic of all national interests, that of security. If the ladder, consisting as it does of a transition from 'solemn and formal declarations' to the use of violence on a steadily increasing scale, is designed to indicate a rational course of action in order to win what was originally a relatively minor point, then there seems some irrationality in changing the nature of the conflict so that it then becomes a matter of national survival. Some of the postulated courses of action might be rational in one context but wholly irrational in another. The same problem as in Clausewitz's argument thus appears, that is, the incompatibility of a threat of total war with the notion of war as policy by other means.

For example, the British and French guarantee of the territorial integrity of Poland in 1939 was an implicit threat to Hitler that if he violated it, then he would be faced with a war with the guarantors. But given the nature of the initial dispute, that is, the actual demands made by Hitler on Poland, what was being threatened was a major European war which concerned not simply Poland but the security of the belligerents. Such a war, given the scale of armaments and the organisation for violence in these states, would be a total war. It would appear that Hitler did not consider such a threat as being either rational or capable of being implemented, and that he was prepared to take the risk after ensuring the neutrality of the only state which could give practical aid to Poland, the Soviet Union. The violent conflict which then ensued involved interests and issues vastly more important to the belligerents than the status of Poland. The relation of force or of threats of force to limited political objectives is clearly extremely difficult. It is even more difficult in the nuclear era.

A more recent conflict, that of the Cuban missiles crisis of 1962,[28] affords a further indication of this difficulty. If we examine the course of this crisis stage by stage, the remarkable feature of it in terms of exchanges between the major powers was the absence of any direct threat of nuclear war in the event of the U.S.S.R. maintaining missiles in Cuba. Yet some observers regarded the crisis as bringing about a possibility of nuclear war. Moreover, it has been argued that by posing such a threat of escalation to the nuclear threshold, the United States forced the Soviet Union to withdraw its intermediate-range ballistic missiles (I.R.B.M.s).

Was this really the case? Clearly, if a nuclear exchange had occurred, then the damage would have been the same for both sides, since neither possessed an offensive deterrent capacity. Both states revealed an awareness that a nuclear exchange was irrational, although part of the bargaining aspect of the diplomacy of the crisis was the use of the fear of such an exchange in order to apply psychological pressure. But the United States held the initiative, since it was in a position to take a number of viable courses of action against Cuba, including air strikes, the landing of troops, blockade or even direct nuclear strikes, while holding out at the same time the more limited proposal of dismantlement. The Soviet Union could not oppose any of these possible courses of action, other than by retaliating against American interests in other parts of the world where it possessed the same relative freedom of action which the U.S.A. had in the Caribbean. In such a situation the danger was in an irrational response, that is, a direct nuclear attack, but in this respect it would seem that, to use General Beaufre's phrase, 'the credibility of a determination to commit suicide is not zero but it is very small'.[29] Thus in providing an answer for a Soviet withdrawal, the argument that the U.S.S.R. was afraid of provoking a nuclear war is clearly inadequate, since this was also the case for the United States. The answer must lie in the ability of the U.S.A. to take further measures in the event of non-compliance which would have resulted in the forcible alienation of Cuba from its Soviet relationship.

There are a number of practical objections to this notion of escalation strategy. Firstly, it is designed as a controlled series of actions dependent on the opponent's responses and as a result of the opponent's responses. The assumption here is that each action and response is understood by the participants as being interdependent. Each successive response is rationally derived from the preceding events. This may not follow in practice and an opponent may prove incapable of understanding the intention behind the hostile action. Instead of a gradual and controlled ascent up the escalation ladder, the opponent may hold the gun to the initiating power and force him to make the choice between capitulation on the issue in dispute, or nuclear war. If the ultimate threat is really bluff, then it can be called. The rate of escalation may not be controllable. Secondly, and related to this point, the opponent may not have the capacity to respond in the way desired by the escalating power. The latter state must have an exact knowledge of the technical and material resources of its opponent and also a knowledge of the viable alternatives open to him.

Moreover, commitment to a course of escalation may block any other means of achieving satisfaction, and at the same time its failure may result in more serious consequences than the choice of some other tactic or a withdrawal from the conflict. Its proponents have advocated the strategy as being flexible, in that a large number of responses are open to the escalating power before the nuclear threshold is reached, but as each response or action is an ascending scale it is difficult to run against the direction of the escalator. Since the lower rungs consist mostly of exhortation and a declaration of commitment, it is clear that long before the question of physical force appears, the state engaged in escalation may find that it has lost its freedom of action, since its prestige is at stake.

Perhaps the fundamental practical objection lies in the limitations of its use. Escalation cannot be used in a major confrontation with a nuclear power, since the question of nuclear war immediately becomes involved. In more peripheral areas escalation is related to the freedom of action enjoyed by the escalating power. In other words, the power to intervene at any level is essential for a successful use of this strategy. If this is the case, then it is difficult to see why escalation is necessary, since the national objective can be fulfilled unilaterally. In any case the threat of a nuclear deterrent does not hold good, even if it is disguised in an escalation strategy, unless offensive deterrent capacity is possessed.

The notion of a graduated series of responses increasing in severity appears to be tied to a notion of international conflict almost entirely abstract and unrealistic. The point of this sort of analysis may be that winning with economy is better than an expensive victory, but what is a prerequisite is a clear definition of what victory means in real terms. To give an example, if state A is confronted by state B embarking on a course of action which involves the alienation of state C under conditions of mutual strategic deterrence, it seems absurd for state A to threaten state B with some form of nuclear war in order to deter or make him desist from such inimical action. It is absurd because, firstly, such an alienation, given conditions of nuclear stalemate, does not threaten state A's security but, secondly, the threat of nuclear war *is* a direct threat to the security of state B. The attention of the latter is diverted from his initial actions towards the credibility of such a threat and its consequences for his security. Clearly, a reduced threat of hostile action somewhere else might act as a deterrent without making a qualitative change in the conflict, but the nature of such a threat will depend on a number of empirical circumstances and not upon the abstractions of an escalation ladder.

However, the point is made by Kahn that

> escalation ladders are metaphorical tools that have been found useful in preliminary studies of escalation. No particular ladder should be considered as being a theory of international relations, although it may be a fragment of such a theory. Its utility derives partly from its provision of a convenient list of some of the options available, and partly from its ordering of escalatory activities in a way that facilitates examination and discussion.[30]

From this it would seem that this kind of theorising is evaluative and subjective, in that opinions might differ as to which 'options' were 'open' in any given situation, and as to what might constitute the most desirable outcome of particular conflicts. It is therefore difficult to consider 'escalation' as an *explanation* of decision-making in crisis or conflict situations, and it appears to be another descriptive term belonging properly to historical interpretation and dependent for its meaning on it. As with earlier examples of this type of argument, the problem in evaluating it is that its relationship to the international world it seeks to prescribe for is exceedingly tenuous. Any proposition about the future which purports to be more than prophecy or speculation requires a theoretical explanatory argument to support it. This is not provided in contemporary strategic argument.

There is an additional danger, in using such terms as 'escalation', of substituting for the motivations and the policies of the national participants in international politics a form of rationalisation which cannot be justified in terms of actual behaviour. Prescriptions which are not based upon predictive explanation belong properly to the category of political argument. Our interest in them, as students of international politics, lies in their influence upon policy-makers or in the extent to which they reflect their decisions. In other words, we are concerned with theories of strategy or of negotiation only in so far as they are relevant to an explanation of actual policy or decisions, and not as explanations in their own right. They are neither theoretical in the scientific sense, nor do they constitute historical interpretation. The rationalisations of the policy-maker are more important for our understanding of international politics than those of the external 'objective' observer.

If, then, the arguments of the nuclear strategists are consiuered as being aids for the policy-maker rather than explanations of international politics, or of war, then for our purposes they are neither valid nor invalid. Although they are largely based on general propositions or assumptions derived from the study of past international conflicts, they are almost exclusively concerned with the future and with stating the hypothetical consequences or implications of possible actions related to different capacities for violence. Their utility can therefore be evaluated by the practitioner only in so far as they help him to achieve his objectives with the minimum cost and the maximum efficiency. In our explanation of policy-making and its relationship to motivation, we are concerned with examining the projections made by the policy-maker as an influence upon his decisions. This is particularly true of defence policy, where projections into the future and contingency planning are extremely important.

Large sums of money are spent on a long- rather than a short-term basis, and defence expenditure is one of the biggest and most permanent elements in most national budgets. Hence in examining the relationship between strategy, defence and foreign policy, the use of various techniques devised to establish the cost-effectiveness of weapons and attempts to predict the future become relevant to our analysis. As we have seen, the effect of decisions based upon projection tend to influence what the future will be, but not perhaps in the way initially envisaged or intended. The net effect of the defence planning in the United States and the Soviet Union during the 1950s was the nuclear stalemate of the 1960s, and it is apparent from this unintended consequence that the international repercussions of domestic decisions need to be anticipated if a desired end is to be achieved. The nature of guesses made about the future by defence planners is an important element in any explanation of international politics. In this sense the means chosen to obtain particular ends often prescribe the ends themselves.

It is not possible here to make a detailed examination of the nexus between defence planning, strategic thought, foreign policy and international politics. The main emphasis in this analysis is on the effects of the nuclear arms race described earlier, and the stalemate it has produced, on international politics in general. One point which is important in the context of contemporary strategy is that, as was argued earlier, the advent of mutual strategic deterrence has made possible a clear distinction between the objectives of a foreign policy and those of a defence policy. Prior to the deployment of the I.C.B.M. national strategies were related to the spatial relations of nuclear bomber bases and their targets, and this meant for the United States a reliance on foreign alliances and arrangements. Moreover, the United States was in the position of providing security for Western Europe through its own nuclear superiority and through NATO. However, as we have seen, the I.C.B.M. produced a situation in which defensive deterrence applied only to the national territory of the nuclear power and could be conferred only indirectly to its allies. Thus the distinction between defence and other political objectives is only comparatively recent, dating from the introduction of the I.C.B.M. in the late 1950s, and it is superimposed upon a set of international obligations and commitments which preceded it, and which belong to a totally different strategic situation.

Yet it would appear from strategic arguments, as for example that provided by Kahn, that their purpose is to restore the use of force to greatpower politics and consequently to blur this distinction. In other words, most strategists in the post-I.C.B.M. period are seeking to prescribe on the basis of an offensive deterrent capacity which no longer exists. This is to attempt to make rational a threat of nuclear war as a factor in greatpower diplomacy which is intrinsically irrational, given the conditions of nuclear stalemate.

It is doubtful, however, whether these notions have had much effect on policy-makers, who appear to have been well aware of the significance from the point of view of national security, of the limitations imposed on them by the strategic balance. The period between the Cuban missiles crisis and the present has been one of growing accommodation between the major nuclear powers and a reluctance to indulge in further technological innovations which might resume the arms race. If one of the conditions for nuclear balance is a perception of its rationality on the part of those politicians who are responsible for defence and foreign policy, then so far as the recent past is concerned the historical record provides some evidence of this. This is not to say that rational behaviour within these assumptions of the nature of nuclear war, and the consequent acceptance of restraints by nuclear powers, are immutable or may be made the basis of prognostications about the future.

It was argued at the beginning of this study that the security dilemma led those states which possessed the requisite resources into attempts to control their unstable and dangerous environment. The main conclusion of the power–security hypothesis was that the quest for national security led to the pursuit of power in international politics. This in turn exacerbated the general condition of international anarchy. Yet, as we have seen, the arms race which developed between the ex-allies at the end of the Second World War produced a situation anomalous in international politics, that of mutual strategic deterrence. What effects has this new situation had on the defence and foreign policies of the major powers, their nature as states, and on international politics in general?

The first important question is, has the apparent inhibition on general war, inspired by the certainty of nuclear retaliation in the event of an attack on a nuclear power, had any effect on international instability? It was pointed out that the condition of defensive deterrence provided a guarantee of the security of the state, provided no qualitative change occurred in weapons technology, and provided that statesmen accepted, and acted according to, the rationality of this argument. If this is indeed the case – and the record of successful negotiations between the Soviet Union and the United States and its allies since 1963 appears to support it – then it would appear that security questions can now be distinguished from other issues involving the interests of the major powers.

The basic pattern of contemporary international relations was established over the period 1945 to 1953 and consisted of a major conflict between two groups of states. The origins of this conflict, as was argued in an earlier part of this study, was related to the security interests of the Soviet Union and of Western European states, with the United States adopting an attitude related not to security, but to ideological and other factors. One of its consequences was the *de facto* partition of Europe and another was the rift in relations between communist and other states known as the Cold War. As has been pointed out, an ideological conflict can only be won if the opponent is either exterminated or converted. But clearly, if the opponent is also a nuclear power, then the alternatives are suicide or the abandonment of the contest. Moreover, as we have seen, the existence of mutual strategic defensive deterrence means that security questions cannot be confused with other issues. In the period before this situation appeared, the Soviet Union could claim that control over Eastern Europe and over the areas adjoining its frontiers in Southern Europe and the Far East was essential to its security. Britain and France could similarly claim that NATO and a military presence in Western Germany were not only necessary to their security but were direct consequences of the Soviet position. The United States could also make such a claim for its power in the Pacific.

But the logic of defensive deterrence means that it is unnecessary, on grounds of security, to have a military presence beyond the boundaries of the nation-state.

Having said this, it is clear that the distribution of influence in the modern world was a consequence of pre-nuclear strategies, and that a redeployment of forces to meet changed conditions presents a number of political and economic problems. Disengagement is rarely easy.

Nevertheless, one of the effects of mutual strategic deterrence has been a radical change in the foreign policies of the major nuclear powers. A mutual accommodation has taken place in which the territorial and political changes of the aftermath of the Second World War, described in an earlier chapter, and which were the occasion of the Cold War, have become accepted by both sides. This is not to say that conflict has ceased to be a phenomenon in great-power relations, but that it has changed both its nature and its focus. No power is willing to surrender its influence over other countries if this means a loss of prestige and of tangible advantages. If, for example, the number of countries which adopt Marxist policies increases, then the concomitant of this development would mean an economic distortion disadvantageous to capital-exporting and trading countries. But questions of this nature are peripheral to the central security problem and can be isolated from it.

Thus states can use violence in defence of their non-security interests, without this use extending the conflict into general war. A close relationship can be established between the use of force and the achievement of a specific objective. Any challenge to American economic interests in Latin America, or to Soviet interests in Eastern Europe, can be met by physical intervention, or by limited war, depending upon the circumstances and upon calculations of political expedience. This is no comfort to the non-nuclear powers, who are thus exposed to great-power intervention without enjoying the protection of an alliance.

So far as alliances are concerned, it is clear from what has been said that the only protection which can be proffered by a nuclear ally is indirect, through posing a countering threat to the non-nuclear allies of the nuclear aggressor. For example, a threat from the Soviet Union to Western Germany can be countered not by a direct American threat to the U.S.S.R., but by posing a similar threat to Eastern Germany or some other non-nuclear East European state. Should these threats be implemented, then whatever the consequences for non-nuclear Europe, none of the nuclear powers would be destroyed. But the real protection perhaps lies in the irrationality of such threats, since nothing would be gained by making them. The rationale of the Cold War is removed if both sides accept a détente on security grounds and are prepared to engage in a 'spheres of influence' policy recognising each other's interests. Moreover, the perception of the inefficacy of collective or mutual security under conditions of nuclear stalemate has led those powers which possess resources to develop their own independent deterrents. The alliances have crumbled from within as much as from the removal of an external threat.

If these admittedly speculative and tentative arguments are accepted, then it would appear that, given the conditions for the nuclear stalemate, politics and violence now become compatible in international relations. Wars involving the nuclear powers will be limited and related to specific and definable objectives Political attitudes which are based upon vague and transcendental premises such as 'world revolution', or 'the preservation of the free world', are both irrational and non-viable. While the limited war in Indo-China is the only kind of war which can be fought under conditions of nuclear stalemate, the objective sought by the United States, that is, the preservation of an aligned government in South Vietnam, is meaningless in the context of its global policy. The political relationship which was created before the nuclear détente has an importance after it which is related to prestige only. No question of American security is involved and no tangible economic or political interest is jeopardised by an alienation of the regime in South Vietnam. This is clearly not the case in other parts of the world, and such a limited war would be rational, given the presence of such interests and the existence of more favourable circumstances for intervention. It would appear that American policy-makers have appreciated this point and that a general appraisal of policy objectives and of the capacity to fulfil them is currently being undertaken, not only in the United States,[31] but in other major countries. Defence policy is concerned with maintaining an effective riposte capacity and with providing the specialist forces for interventionary wars. Foreign policy is able to detach itself from defence concerns and to relate directly to the protection of interests abroad.

Thus the only major uncertainty, so far as national security is concerned, lies in the possibility of further technological developments in nuclear or other weapons and in irrational behaviour on the part of nuclear states. This uncertainty cannot be resolved by pursuing an imperialist policy, since this would immediately open the question of nuclear war. A peaceful solution appears to be the only viable alternative and, as was pointed out earlier, the major nuclear powers, with the exceptions of China and France, have gradually formulated a set of rules which impose limitations upon the development of weapons, and which indicate the awareness of their rulers of the need for such accommodation. Concomitant with this attempt at arms control and of self-limiting defence policies has been an acceptance of the political *status quo* and a mutual recognition of interests which originally constituted a *sus belli gelidi*. Such a development is of very recent origin and it is clearly impossible to make prognostications which are anything other than speculative. Nevertheless, it can be said that an avoidance of a nuclear exchange became a major preoccupation in Soviet and American policy in the early 1960s, and this meant essentially, for the latter state, that an accommodation with the former became necessary. The *quid pro quo* for this involved an acceptance in part of Soviet interests and an abandonment of the policy of the global containment of communism.

International politics consists of the activities of sovereign nation-states, and while the states themselves are affected by their relationships in terms of their social, political and economic organisation, such changes in turn affect their environment. We have seen how a change in weapons technology produced an arms race, which created the bizarre situation of nuclear stalemate. What are the consequences of this situation for the nation-state?

Technological innovations have often been ascribed a revolutionary effect both on warfare and on the nature of the state. It is certainly true that new weapons have been given a significance which subsequent events have proved to be undeserved. Nevertheless, the psychological dimension of the expectations aroused in politicians by such innovations is very important in explaining their policies and the type of war which is actually fought. However, perhaps the most important single influence upon the nature of war and the significance of violence in domestic and international politics is that of organisation. By this is meant not simply logistics, that is, the supply and maintenance of armies and navies, etc., and their deployment, but the mobilisation of resources and peoples within the nation-state itself. In the recent history of war, from the French Revolution onwards, it would appear that the major qualitative change in war was the organisation of the state for total war. The new factor was not the innovation of new weapons but the adjustment of the state to a situation in which flexibility of response was necessary in order to provide a safeguard against inimical developments in its international environment. It was the creation of this flexibility in a competitive situation which made new weapons significant, and not vice versa. Hence it was not technology *per se* which imposed the need for planning and organisation upon the state, but the nature of inter-state competition which made its absence dangerous.

In the nuclear era this has meant the concentration, within the state, of control over weapons and external relations. The responsibility for nuclear war rests on the political leaders of the nuclear states. This has, of course, been generally true of the pre-nuclear period, and decisions to go to war or to negotiate a change in political relationships are rarely taken in consultation with the governed, even in countries with a democratic political system. But whereas in the past political divisions over the question of war, and over defence policies, could result in delaying political decision, as for example in Britain over the years 1938 and 1939, any such delay now would be an intolerable handicap to any government. The nuclear powers are bound together in a system which virtually ensures reciprocal strikes in the event of any one state taking a nuclear initiative. Communications between the nuclear powers have been developed in order to preserve some element of choice in a crisis situation. Never have potentially belligerent states been so closely linked in terms of communication.

The point here is that the political element is removed from this area of decision and is insulated from domestic politics. Public opinion and the political process can only have influence on the question of capacity, that is, on expenditure during the initial stages of defence policy. Once a nuclear capacity exists then they become irrelevant. Thus the possibility of nuclear war and the nature of a nuclear strike remove the area of foreign policy and national security more completely from national politics than ever before. Someone must be able to exercise responsibility for the national deterrent at all times, or else the deterrent, regardless of the actual nuclear capacity enjoyed by that state, ceases to exist.

From this we can see that governmental control over technology and science is extremely important. The best example, outside the centrally planned states, is to be found in the United States,[32] where two principal areas illustrate the deliberate insulation of war preparation from politics. These are, firstly, the research and development of rockets and missiles, and secondly, what has been termed the military-industrial complex. In both cases Congressional interference in policy-making has been minimal, even though the expenditure of the administration is particularly exposed to political influence. In the cause of national security billions of dollars have been poured out without much questioning of policy or its premises. It is of course true that many Congressmen have a vested interest in this use of Federal money, since much of it goes into their Congressional districts or states and helps to consolidate or maintain their political position. The eagerness for more Federal investment in local defence installations and production strengthens the insulation of defence expenditure from political influence. The scale of this expenditure is enormous; as of writing, some $80 billion will be spent on defence projects, and this constitutes a tenth of the American G.N.P. Only recently has any political opposition appeared, and this was in connection with the A.B.M. system proposed by President Nixon.

Thus public control over this area of policy-making is minimal, and this is equally true from the other nuclear democracies. A bipartisan policy in Britain has effectively prevented any public debate of parliamentary influence on the policy of the independent deterrent, although it is true that the rising cost of the attempt to develop an independent missile before 1960 provoked considerable political opposition. Yet once Polaris was acquired from the United States, the establishment of a four-submarine defensive deterrent continued through both Conservative and Socialist governments. The "so-called independent, so-called deterrent' has remained the basis of British defence policy ever since Macmillan initiated his 'new and startling defence policy based on the nuclear concept'.[33] Similarly, successive French governments have developed the 'force de dissuasion' since its introduction at the end of the Fourth Republic, without significant political opposition. It can only be surmised that the People's Republic of China has recognised the same strategic arguments in favour of independent national defensive deterrents in developing its own nuclear weapons.

Finally, what effect has the nuclear stalemate had on international politics? Reference has been made previously to the efforts of the two major nuclear powers to find a means of avoiding an arms race without sacrificing national security based on the concept of defensive deterrence. The culmination of the Strategic Arms Limitation Talks (SALT) was the Soviet–American Treaty signed on 26 May 1972. Under the terms of this treaty each country is limited to two A.B.M. systems, one defending the national capital and the other an I.C.B.M. site. An interim agreement limits the number of nuclear weapons to those already in existence or under construction for a period of five years. Furthermore, continuing negotiations on the question of arms control is ensured by the establishment of a standing consultative commission charged with the implementation of the provisions of the treaty and with promoting additional agreements on arms limitations. It would appear from this that the political concomitants of arms control constitute a major revision of foreign policy, amounting to an acceptance of respective spheres of influence on the part of the Soviet Union and the U.S.A. Détente implies both the abandonment of the policy of global containment on the part of the United States and the adoption of a more flexible policy based upon a more precise definition of external national interests.

Thus the second major development in international politics, as was noted earlier, is a radical change in the foreign policies of the nuclear powers. The nuclear inhibition on direct confrontations between these states has produced in recent years a new kind of war, with guerrilla movements and domestic politics becoming peculiarly significant. But while limited war is possible under nuclear conditions, it also becomes unreasonable. The struggle in Vietnam, paradoxically, developed during the attempt over the 1960s to achieve control over the arms race. Yet victory or defeat in South Vietnam is of no significance either to American interests or to American security, nor will victory bring about the fulfilment of the containment policy. If communist countries, which are also nuclear powers, cannot be destroyed or held in check by the threat of violence, and if local conflicts cannot easily be turned to great-power advantages in some meaningful sense, then the whole rationale of maintaining the political *status quo* in the non-communist world disappears. The game of power politics can be played by communist as well as capitalist countries.

Thus while proxy wars and peripheral disputes can take place in the non-nuclear world under present nuclear conditions, such wars cannot be won. The ideological basis of international politics, which has been dominant since 1946 and which has created a twentieth-century war of religion, is in the process of changing, and the main reason for this has been the unintended consequence of a nuclear arms race. The nature of this change is still very uncertain, but one of the most significant developments has been the beginning of an attempt on the part of the nuclear powers to set limits to their use of violence in international politics and to define their interests. The consequences may mean the division of the world into spheres of interest or the breakdown of existing economic and political divisions. It may mean the creation of world unity or simply a 'world of mice ruled over by lions'.[34] It is too early to form any judgement. But it can be said that if existing agreements between the Soviet Union and the United States are kept, while violence will still be a phenomenon in international politics, it will cease to be anarchic in nature. It will be both limited in its effects and related to recognisable interests, not to political mythology.

If we return to the notion of explanation and to the earlier discussion of strategic theory, it will be clear from this exposition of the interaction between war and policy that prescriptive and speculative arguments predominate in this type of analysis. More than perhaps any other political phenomena, preparations for war, or defence policy, and the use of violence as a means of achieving foreign policy objectives, directly involve questions of practical political judgement. The development of any means of violence presupposes contingent situations of conflict which prescribe the development and perhaps its use. As was pointed out earlier, any explanation of defence or foreign policy decisions involves a reconstruction of the thought of the decision-makers. Thus while strategic theory is not a theoretical explanation in the sense used at the beginning of this study, it may (or may not) provide us with some indication as to the motivation behind particular political decisions. For example, it seems apparent that the argument of defensive deterrence is accepted by those responsible for policy in Britain and France, including its political implications, so far as their treaty relationships are concerned. Similarly, the rejection of the argument of offensive deterrence, together with its political concomitants, is apparent in the negotiation of arms-control agreements on the part of the U.S.A. and the Soviet Union. But this is to say that such scenarios or hypothetical descriptions of conflict, governed by assumptions and categories of conditions such as capacity, perfect information, rationality, 'rules', and isolable goals and variables with quantifiable preferences on the part of those pursuing them, are not explanatory. They are relevant to an explanation only in so far as they belong to the strategic thought employed by those actually engaged in taking political decisions.

It should be apparent from this, that such arguments employ the same kind of interpretation as that contained in the analysis of war, policy and international politics in this chapter. In other words, they are based upon a subjective historical examination of politics in which particular facts and phenomena are selected and related in the form of a coherent narrative.

The major difference between strategic 'theory' and historical interpretation does not lie in the systematic abstractions of the former, but in its overtly prescriptive aim. It seeks to project into the future model conflicts derived from past political events and situations, in an attempt to provide advice for political practitioners. In this sense it is a practical political argument and not an explanation. Thus if we reject the theoretical pretensions of the strategic theorists on the ground that their arguments do not satisfy the criteria for theoretical validity discussed earlier in this work, we are left with their evaluation as historical interpretations. If this position is accepted, this means the rejection of the attempt to formulate general propositions about crisis behaviour, or about international negotiation, and of the assumption that such situations share characteristics which support such statements. Thus non-theoretical explanations of situations involving the use of the threat of force in international politics must try to reconstruct the policy basis of choice. Instead of analysing categories of factors or variables asserted to be common to all such situations, such an explanation finds its focus in the perceptions and motivations of the participants, in so far as these can be established on the basis of the available evidence. This is to argue that each conflict situation is unique in one important sense, that is, in the sense that the 'thought' of those engaged in conflict is specific to that conflict. Attempts at generalisation tend to depreciate this factor and are consequently forced to adopt a mechanistic or rationalistic analytic framework. As we have seen, such attempts lack the kind of validity proper to this kind of explanation. So far as historical interpretation of conflict situations is concerned, subjective evaluatory criteria of the kind discussed in an earlier part of this study are appropriate.

It should be clear from this that the preceding analysis of contemporary developments in strategy and politics constitutes an outline rather than a rigorous historical interpretation. As was pointed out earlier, it was not possible, through exigencies of space, to make a detailed examination of the relationships between defence planning, strategic thought and foreign policy, in terms of the perceptions of those engaged in taking political decisions. Nevertheless, such an outline provides the basis for a more viable explanation than that contained in the scenarios, games, metaphors and models of the strategic theorists. While it is possible to establish common grounds for the evaluation of various alternative historical interpretations of this aspect of international politics, it is not possible to establish these for the latter type of argument, unless they are included in the same category of explanation. Clearly, they are not scientific and, as we have seen, historic or other subjective criteria are difficult to establish. They may or may not be useful to political practitioners as guides to action, but they, rather than their proponents, are the judges should this be the case.

REFERENCES

1. Adolf Hitler, *Mein Kampf*, trans. Ralph Manheim, ed. D. C. Watt (London: Radius Books, Hutchinson, 1972) p. 572.
2. Winston S. Churchill, *History of the Second World War*, vol. I: *The Gathering Storm* (London: Reprint Society Edition, Cassell, 1956) p. 307.
3. See E. H. Carr, *The Twenty Years Crisis, 1919–1939* (London: Macmillan, 1946).
4. Talcott Parsons, 'Order and Community in the International Social System' in Rosenau (ed.), *International Politics and Foreign Policy*, pp. 120ff.
5. For a 'political' view of this situation, see Churchill's account in *The Gathering Storm*, p. 192; also Duff Cooper, *Old Men Forget* (London: Hart-Davis, 1953) pp. 189ff.
6. On this point, see G. F. Hudson, 'Collective Security and Military Alliances' in Herbert Butterfield and Martin Wight (eds.), *Diplomatic Investigations* (London: Allen & Unwin, 1966) pp. 176ff; and Arnold Wolfers, *Discord and Collaboration* (Baltimore: Johns Hopkins Univ. Press, 1962).
7. See F. H. Hinsley, *Power and the Pursuit of Peace* (Cambridge Univ. Press, 1967); and Kenneth N. Waltz, *Man, the State and War* (New York: Columbia Univ. Press, 1965).
8. Clausewitz, *On War*, Penguin ed., pp. 402–3.
9. Ibid., p. 405.
10. For example, Herman Kahn, *On Escalation* (New York: Praegar, 1965); see also Robert E. Osgood, 'The Reappraisal of Limited War', in Alastair Buchan (ed.), *Problems of Modern Strategy* (London: Chatto & Windus, for Institute for Strategic Studies, 1970) pp. 92ff.
11. For an account of the nuclear arms race, see Chalmers M. Roberts, *The Nuclear Years* (New York: Praeger, 1970).
12. See David E. Lilienthal, *Change, Hope and the Bomb* (Princeton Univ. Press, 1963) pp. 34–5.
13. See Arthur Schlesinger, Jr., *A Thousand Days* (London: Mayflower-Dell, 1967) pp. 660–8; and Richard Neustadt, *Alliance Politics* (New York: Columbia Univ. Press, 1970) pp. 30–55.
14. See Werth, *De Gaulle*, pp. 329–30.
15. For a statement of McNamara's strategic thought, see Robert S. McNamara, *The Essence of Security* (New York: Harper & Row, 1968).
16. Evidence of Soviet strategic thought is very scant. See H. S. Dinerstein, *War and the Soviet Union* (New York: Praeger, 1962); and V. Sokolovskii (ed.), *Soviet Military Strategy*, trans. RAND Corporation (Englewood Cliffs, N.J.: Prentice-Hall, 1963).
17. McNamara, op. cit.
18. See Thomas C. Schelling, *The Strategy of Conflict* (New York: Galaxy Books, Oxford Univ. Press, 1963) pp. 16, 84–118.
19. Ibid., p. 3.
20. Ibid., p. 4.
21. Ibid., p. 15.
22. Ibid., p. 260.
23. Ibid., p. 261.
24. Ibid., p. 75ff.
25. Ibid., p. 76.
26. Kahn, *On Escalation*.
27. Ibid., p. 39.
28. See ibid., pp. 75–82; also Schlesinger, *A Thousand Days*, pp. 614–48; and André Beaufre, *Deterrence and Strategy* (London: Faber, 1965) pp. 71ff.
29. Ibid., p. 42.
30. Kahn, op. cit., p. 38.

31. See Henry A. Kissinger, *American Foreign Policy* (London: Weidenfeld & Nicolson, 1969) esp. 'An Inquiry into the American National Interest', pp. 91–7.

32. For a discussion of this aspect, see Bruce M. Russett, *What Price Vigilance?* (New Haven and London: Yale Univ. Press, 1970); Alain C. Enthoven and K. Wayne Smith, *How Much is Enough?* (New York: Harper & Row, 1971); Daniel S. Greenberg, *The Politics of American Science* (Harmondsworth: Penguin Books, 1969).

33. See Harold Macmillan, *Riding the Storm* (London: Macmillan, 1971) for an account of the 'new' defence policy.

34. Andrew Boyd, *United Nations: Piety, Myth and Truth,* rev. ed. (Harmondsworth: Penguin Books, 1964) p. 45.

CHAPTER 7

International Economic and Political Relationships

THE relevance of economic factors to international relations has long been recognised by commentators,[1] who have not only drawn attention to their importance in terms of national resources and strength, but have also emphasised their significance as causes of international conflict. It has been argued in other parts of this study that while disputes between nations have sometimes been concerned with such questions as control over external resources and markets, these conflicts are really reflections of political conflicts. The defence or promotion of specific national interests other than security may involve an attempt at creating a political hegemony, or more limited contests with other states, but whatever the apparent cause or motivation, such a contest is over the question of power itself. In short, any attempt to extend control over part of the international environment meets with countervailing responses from other states, and the issue is one which is ultimately decided by force. If national capacity to achieve an object is one which is dependent upon the successful use of violence then this is relative both to resources and to the dispositions of other nation-states. The point is that while a conflict of economic or other interests may be the occasion of an international contest, it is rarely its cause. This last lies rooted in the differential national capacites for violence which exist in international politics at any given time. The separation of the ostensibly non-political from the political becomes a distortion of a complex set of international and domestic political relationships. The capacity to achieve a national objective is the real issue in dispute and the conflict is over this capacity and not the objective. Attempts to reduce international politics to a single causal hypothesis, as we have seen earlier, tend to be narrowly selective and to over-simplify.

Nevertheless, it has been argued that such a power struggle is itself simply the consequence of underlying economic processes. Politics, in this view, can either be explained in relation to these processses or reduced to a peripheral significance in international history as being symptomatic rather than causal in nature. Paradoxically, one such argument, that produced by Hobson[2] and Lenin,[3] provides an explanation which stresses the inevitability of conflict between states, while the other major theoretical approach, that of functionalism,[4] argues the reverse, that is, that economic processes are at work which impose upon nation-states conditions of inter-dependence and co-operation, which inhibit their freedom to engage in conflict. Yet both these broad arguments are linked, in that they share a conception of economic forces, which transcend the temporal political struggle and which either determine its outcome or dictate its nature. They stem from the argument that, towards the end of the last century, a new form of international politics was emerging which was the product of economic changes within the major states themselves.[5]

In the case of the former argument, national governments and politics are subject to the necessities of an international or rather supranational economic system, whereas the latter argument, while accepting this, asserts a distinction between political behaviour on the inter-state level, and a parallel movement towards functional economic integration, which will eventually impose a new political order upon the old. The Leninist argument similarly links this economic determinism with a millennial goal, that of the achievement of world communism. Hobson, while stressing the competitive nature of international politics brought about, in his view, by internal economic processes, was at pains to suggest that there was a latent co-operative international community[6] which could be brought into existence given a change of policy. In this he was certainly less deterministic than Lenin. But both the functionalist argument and what might be called the Hobson–Lenin thesis purport to be explanations of international politics in terms of its empirical phenomena, as an explanation of a process or dynamic, economic in nature, which determines not merely the nature of politics but also prescribes the future. They point to an unrealised state which will be the outcome of the economic process which they describe. In short, they pose a hypothesis about the relationship between economics and political behaviour.

The Hobson–Lenin explanation is thus more than an explanation of the later nineteenth-century phenomenon of imperialism. It is a general or universal explanation of international politics which subsumes this phenomenon. While more reduced in its empirical scope, the functionalist argument is no less universal, since it also asserts the existence of a process in international politics arising out of a new phase in the economies of the advanced industrial countries. In this sense both explanations would concur with Marx's statement in the *Communist Manifesto* of 1848 that

> In place of the old wants, satisfied by the production of the country, we find new wants, requiring for their satisfaction the products of distant lands and climes. In place of the old local and national seclusion and self-sufficiency, we have intercourse in every direction, universal inter-dependence of nations.[7]

It is this interdependence which, on these arguments, changed the nature of international politics.

In some respects the notion that an explanation of politics which depends on the purely political is illusory, is of considerable antiquity. The search for reality in terms of motivation, of interest, of forces – in short, for an explanation which penetrates beneath the surface of things – has produced a number of varying explanations of international conflict. The emphasis upon economic processes, together with their relation to a system or organism, is perhaps the contribution of the nineteenth century to this *genre*. The major proponent of an economic, or material, explanation of political behaviour, Marx, was mainly concerned, in regard to inter-state relations, with the influence of European capitalism upon non-Western societies as a precondition for revolution rather than with any general theory of imperialism. He assumed simply that capitalism expanded as a matter of necessity and he was interested more in the societal effects of this expansion than in its cause or its international consequences.[8] Consequently, although Marx was clearly interested in the relationship between capitalist societies and the non-capitalist world, his interest was not explicitly linked to a theory of capitalist development, which provided an explanation of international politics, or of the phenomenon of imperialist expansion. The territorial expansion of one state, that of Russia, was noted,[9] but was explained not as the effect of some dynamic of capitalist economics, for indeed Russia was an anomaly among European states in this respect, but as an innate or historical characteristic. Russia, in Marx's eyes, was the arch-enemy of revolution and her imperial expansion, unlike that of Britain, was more likely to retard the economic forces leading to a revolutionary situation than to advance them. Nevertheless, in spite of the absence of a specific explanation of imperialism in Marx's writings, we may regard his general approach to an explanation of political and economic behaviour as being the precursor to the various theories of imperialism which appeared after his death.[10]

It was not until the end of the nineteenth century, however, that a coherent theory of political relations between states, based upon economic processes, appeared. This was the thesis advanced by J. A. Hobson in his book, *Imperialism: A Study*, published in 1902. His argument directly related the surge of imperial expansion on the part of the European states after 1870 to economic causes. According to Hobson, a new phenomenon had appeared in the economies of the most advanced industrialised countries towards the latter part of the nineteenth century. This was the appearance of surplus capital arising out of the concentration of production exercised by the formation of trusts and cartels. Since production was restricted as a conscious policy to a fixed level of consumption in the domestic economy, the surplus capital generated by this policy, which could not find sound investment within the country, forced Great Britain, Germany, Holland, France to place larger and larger portions of their economic resources outside the area of their present political domain, and then stimulate a policy of political expansion so as to take in the new areas.[11]

In other words, this theory of under-consumption[12] in the major industrial countries argued that because of the change in their economic structure, an economic dynamic was created which placed great emphasis on foreign investment. In order to promote and to safeguard this investment, an extension of political authority occurred outside the nation-state itself, together with increased production of armaments to meet the inevitable challenge of other countries driven to adopt the same policy, and to provide for the colonial wars concomitant to this policy of imperial expansion. Hence, according to Hobson, his thesis explained both the imperialist expansion of the late nineteenth century and the conflicts which it generated, in conjunction with the related arms races between the major industrial powers.

It is important to stress that Hobson did not regard this economic dynamic as being inevitable, or as some unintended consequence of the conjunction of a number of economic phenomena. In his view an imperialist policy was the product of an economic situation which favoured a particular sectional interest. It was the result of the pressure exercised by a number of interested finance capitalists and their supporters on their respective governments. As he put it:

> In making the capitalist-imperialist forces the pivot of financial policy, I do not mean that other forces, industrial, political, and moral, have no independent aims and influences, but simply that the former group must be regarded as the true determinant in the interpretation of actual policy.[13]

Such a policy, he argued, is reversible, and much of his thesis was designed to point out its evil consequences and to advocate the way in which it should be changed.

This notion of politics is thus based on a conspiratorial thesis which makes certain assumptions about the process of government and of policy-making in a number of different countries. Essentially, all governments are the creatures of the major controllers of investment finance to a greater or lesser degree. In the case of America, Hobson argued, 'It was Messrs Rockefeller, Pierpont Morgan, and their associates who needed Imperialism and who fastened it upon the shoulders of the Great Republic of the West'.[14] An interest group was created by a specific economic situation, which then proceeded to influence the government to protect its foreign investments by making them national responsibilities, and to extend its investment opportunities by expanding the polity.

It is not proposed to make any criticism of this argument at this stage, but to point out that the main difference between this argument and that of Lenin's theory of imperialism, which was largely derived from it,[15] is that the former placed emphasis on individual motivation and interests while the latter regarded this as superficial and placed its emphasis on the economic dynamic. Lenin developed Hobson's argument into an explanation, not simply of the actual territorial expansion of the major European empires, but into a general explanation of international politics. It is not without significance that, as Hobson had been influenced by the Boer war, so Lenin was influenced by the First World War which was still raging when he published his theory in 1916. For him this war was an imperialist war between the capitalist powers, who were anxious for 'the division of the world, for the partition and repartition of colonies, spheres of influence of finance capital, etc.'[16] The real causes of this war, as of most conflicts between these powers, were thus economic, not political.

Lenin's argument has therefore, a wider significance than that of Hobson, since it provides a general explanation of wars and conflicts between the major powers. Although this was implicit in Hobson's work, he was more concerned with the acquisition of territories which, in his view, did not benefit the imperialist country but only a specific vested interest in it.[17] Indeed, Hobson clearly approved of what he termed a 'natural' imperialism which took the form of relations between the 'mother' country and its self-governing colonies, as for example in the case of Britain and Australasia and Canada.[18] The Leninist argument adopted the conclusions drawn by Hobson without going into any detailed examination of his theory of under-consumption and, relating these to other arguments,[19] stressed the significance of the two new phenomena which had appeared in the economies of the capitalist countries. These were the amalgamation of business concerns into monopolies and cartels and an increasing rate of foreign investment.

Thus the cartelisation of industrial production, and the appearance of a finance-capital-dominated economy, created a drive to maximise profits and to utilise surplus capital through foreign investment. As Lenin put it: 'The capitalists divide the world not out of any particular malice, but because the degree of concentration which has been reached forces them to adopt this method in order to get profits.'[20] The national economy thus expands internationally and this expansion leads to an expansion of political control over other countries and territories. Such control is necessary, according to this argument, firstly, to protect and promote investments, and secondly, to prevent other competitors from doing the same. Hence international conflict is endemic in this competition between monopolies for ever-larger markets and investment opportunities. This he expressed, citing Hobson, as:

The new imperialism differs from the older, first in substituting for the ambition of a single growing empire the theory and practice of competing empires each motivated by similar lusts of political aggrandisement and commercial gain, secondly the dominance of financial or investing over mercantile interests.[21]

The process is described as beginning with the concentration of national capital into national monopolies, with bank capital merging with industrial capital to become 'finance capital'.[22] Concomitant with this is the creation of a new financial oligarchy. From this national economic base the monopolies expand into international cartels which then divide the world into spheres of 'economic territory'. This is then translated into the actual territorial division of the world between the greatest capitalist powers. Finally, because the economic dynamic is not appeased by this division, these powers seek to redistribute the world and eventually turn to conflict and war in order to achieve a complete monopoly. Wars can therefore be explained by the attempts of capitalists in the final development of capitalism, i.e. imperialism, to redistribute the economic territories of the world. These economic territories are not simply colonies, for, as Lenin argued:

> The division of the world into two main groups of countries – colony-owning countries on the one hand and colonies on the other – is not the only typical feature of this period; there is also a variety of forms of dependent countries; countries which officially are politically independent, but which are in fact enmeshed in the net of financial and diplomatic dependence.[23]

The nature of this dependence, as will be seen, is really the crucial issue in this analysis of the significance of economic factors in international political relations.

Some writers[24] have criticised this argument on the grounds that it is empirically unsound as an explanation of colonial expansion in the late nineteenth century. They point out that while foreign investment was indeed significant in this period, its direction was between the major capitalist powers and not between the capitalist' and the non-capitalist countries.[25] In short, colonial expansion cannot be explained on this argument because the colonies did not receive the bulk of capitalist investment during this period. Such criticisms, although valid for Hobson, are misconceived so far as Lenin is concerned, since the crux of his theory is the domination of the economically developed countries by finance capital and, from this, the domination of the rest of the world by finance capitalists. It is true that he conceived of 'backward' countries[26] as receiving such investment but these were nominally sovereign states, not colonies, and the whole point of his argument is that the economically advanced states competed for control and monopoly over the less advanced countries. The consequent imperial hegemony was an 'invisible' one.

Thus the acquisition of colonies was not only designed to secure investment outlets, markets, or even sources of raw materials, although these were undeniably motives in specific cases, but, more significantly, to deny these to the other capitalists. Imperial expansion is therefore only one facet of inter-state and inter-capitalist competition. The denial of a potential investment opportunity or of raw material exploitation[27] to a competitor was, in Lenin's view, the main motivation. It is not therefore the actual direction of capital investment which is important in this respect, but rather its volume, its increased significance in the capitalist economies, and its relationship to foreign policy and international politics.

While external economic interests had always been important in international politics, as Lenin recognised, the point was that a new situation had developed in which capital turned from the exploitation of national to that of international resources. The political concomitant of this development was a form of imperialism in which the whole world outside the countries which had achieved this stage in their economies became 'economic territory'.[28] Not only were colonies acquired as a consequence of this new situation, but a whole network of states, politically and economically dependent upon the capitalist countries, was created. The increasing significance of foreign investment in capitalist economies, the dependent relations which it creates, and the ensuing conflicts between the capitalist states for economic territory, is the burden of Lenin's argument. The territorial gains of the late nineteenth century were peripheral to the pattern of relationships created by this development, although they reflected it. This was to assert the primacy of economic factors over all other influences on international relations.

The difficulty with this type of hypothetical argument is that the most important aspects of a political situation are not explained. It is a sketch, not an explanation. Thus while it may have been empirically true that the relative economic significance of foreign, as opposed to domestic, investment changed over this period, and that finance capital was organised under monopoly conditions, this provides no more than a rationalisation for both the acquisition of colonies and the kind of political relations and conflicts which culminated in the First World War. It has been pointed out that the colonies were neither the major recipients of such investment, nor were they acquired at the time when this new economic dynamic may be said to have been the major motive for their acquisition. If the economic motive is accepted, the vital link which needs to be established beyond cavil is that between the finance capitalists and national governments. Lenin, like Hobson, assumes without offering any empirical evidence that the alleged financial oligarchy, with its interests and motivations, is in control of the nation-state, or exercises a pivotal role in policy-making. Such an oligarchy is assumed to constitute a perfect monopoly with no conflicting interests.

In this sort of hypothesis there is no distinction between 'capitalist' govern-ments and capitalists. This is a highly dubious assumption, both on empirical and on theoretical grounds, and one which grossly over-simplifies the political processes which actually existed during the period under discussion in the various countries concerned. Even if it could be shown that governments did not actually infringe the interests of capitalist interest groups, or in certain cases sought to promote them, it is a considerable step to assume that all external political activity was their promotion.

It could be argued that there is more agreement between foreign investors organised into monopolies than disagreement, and that one feature of a monopoly is its organisation of a market and its regulation of competition. In other words, there is more utility in dividing markets than in a fight to the death to monopolise them. A resort to violence, and to the disruptions of war, in pursuit of a world monopoly would appear to be irrational in theory and difficult to establish in practice. Moreover, the reciprocity of economic relationships, and the connection between investment and trade, are ignored in this hypothesis. In certain cases the distinction between debtor and creditor nation can be maintained, but the main areas of economic exchange were in relations between the advanced industrial countries. The pattern of investment and of trade is thus really multilateral and not bilateral, except in relatively few cases. In a sense it could be argued that capital investment had become supra- or extra-national and co-operative rather than national and competitive. Certainly, the growth of economic relationships between states, as will be seen subsequently in this study, has created both interdependence and co-operation as well as conflict. Since Lenin was interested in an economic theory as a fundamental explanation for human behaviour, he emphasised those aspects of economic activity which in his view were responsible for major political conflicts between capitalist states. Political activity is thus considered as being subordinated to economics.[29]

A political explanation of the phenomena which Lenin was seeking to explain, that is, of the growth of international economic relations, imperial expansion and wars, is avoided, since such an explanation would not be compatible with a materialist explanation of history. Thus the central weakness in this form of explanation is the lack of any detailed political analysis. In his attempt to make his argument consistent at the general level, Lenin skirts evidence, which is either ambivalent or conflicting, and resorts to assertions that his view is objective since it subsumes 'subjective' phenomena. Thus the First World War is explained by asserting that its 'real' cause was not the diplomatic and political manoeuvrings which preceded it, but 'the *objective* positions of the ruling classes in all belligerent countries'.[30] These ruling classes, driven by an economic force which demanded ever-increasing profits from investment, sought to gain complete control over the world, and thus began a general war in order to settle the issue. Nowhere in his argument does Lenin consider the actual policies and decisions taken by the belligerent governments. These he considered to be peripheral to the true cause of the war. Factors such as values, beliefs, domestic politics and public opinion are similarly ignored, as are factors which were either adventitious or specific to this conflict situation. The conception that the war was not fought over, or caused by, economic factors, but over the problem of security, or as a consequence of the ideas and reasoning of the participant politicians, is dismissed, in the case of Hobson, in favour of a conspiratorial myth, in which the finance capitalists manipulated their governments for their own ends and, in the case of Lenin, for an economic force which drove these capitalists willy-nilly to foment wars and promote imperialism. Reduced to this level, the argument appears a simple-minded one.

Of course, economic factors are relevant in an explanation of this particular international conflict. The conduct of Britain and France after the defeat of Germany, Turkey and Austria indicates this. The colonies of the defeated powers were divided among the victors, and certain of the financial and economic clauses of the Versailles Treaty[31] were clearly designed to remove Germany as a commercial competitor to Britain. Commercial rivalries as well as power politics were involved in the struggle. As a general explanation of relations between the major powers, which not only explains this conflict in particular, but all relations in general, Lenin's theory appears to be a rationalisation of economic interests allegedly pursued by governments. Such interests may exist, but the essential part of any explanation or hypothesis is in establishing their precise relevance to the level of political action. To indicate that a specific interest may exist is not to prove that a mode of behaviour is caused by its existence. The argument that armaments manufacturers make increased profits in times of war does not prove that wars are caused by armaments manufacturers. Such a proposition confounds consequences with causes unless empirical evidence is advanced to support it. On this level of argument, Hobson's explanation is preferable to that of Lenin, since he stresses the importance of human volition and motivation as relevant factors,[32] without stipulating that these are determined by forces beyond human control. It may or may not be true that a Pierpont Morgan had an interest on specific economic grounds in promoting imperialist expansion, or in fomenting wars, but at least it is possible empirically to examine his relationship to the political process, and to discover what influence he actually had on American external policy. We need not assume that he was merely an agent of an economic process which he did not control. Thus Hobson's argument is really a form of historical interpretation in which one kind of motivation and interest within the political process is asserted as being peculiarly significant in explaining a particular political phenomenon, that of imperial expansion. Since it is not a general hypothesis but an explanation of particular events, it may be criticised on historical grounds.

Lenin, however, goes much further than this, and argues that there is an economic dynamic which underlies motivation, and which alone affords an explanation of political behaviour. It explains not only colonial expansion in the late nineteenth century, and the occurrence of great conflicts such as the First World War, but all relations between states,[33] and is an extension of the general materialist theory of human behaviour propounded by Marx. How can such a hypothesis be evaluated? On empirical grounds it is possible to make a number of criticisms. The major assumptions relating to the economic process may also be criticised on these grounds. For example, the cartelisation of industry was much more highly developed in Germany than in Britain or France, yet the latter countries enjoyed a much greater colonial expansion than the former state. Certain of the imperialist countries, notably Russia and the United States, were themselves major recipients of capital investment. Moreover, although sources of raw materials certainly existed in colonies, and were thus monopolised by their metropolitan rulers, it can be shown that the capitalist countries were themselves major exporters of raw materials and of food. So far as markets were concerned, trade between the capitalist countries was far more significant than between these states and the non-capitalist world. In short, the economic world itself, and its pattern of relationships, was vastly more complex than Lenin appreciated. While cartels certainly existed and while foreign investment increased over the period, these facts by themselves do not support the Leninist hypothesis and its conclusions.

On the hypothetical level itself the argument is weak. Although Lenin adopted Hobson's conclusions, which were based on a theory of underconsumption explaining the appearance of surplus capital, and abstracted from Hilferding the notion of finance capital, his argument is curiously lacking in theoretical rigour. It is really a set of assertions rather than a theory. Even if the growth of international cartels is accepted as a historical fact, it is not axiomatic that they retain their national basis or that they are innately competitive, to the extent that international violence is a normal extension of their activities. Nor is it axiomatic that an economic interest of this kind is either realised by financiers and industrialists, or directs a government's foreign policy. So far as the first point is concerned, it is assumed that capitalists behave according to the rationality of such an interest, whether they recognise its existence or not.

It is, however, the link between political decision- and policy-making, that is, the political level, and the alleged economic interest, which is important to students of international politics. Are governments agents of their domestic capitalists? Empirical proof is necessary to support such a proposition. Lenin does not go into any details as to the influence of vested financial interests in national politics, nor does he describe the interactions between governments which, according to his argument, are the outcome of the activities of these interests. It is assumed simply that political behaviour corresponds to the rationality of an internal economic force and thus acts out on the level of politics, in perfect conformity, its logic. The discovery of new weapons, international rivalry in armaments, developments in communication and transport, nationalism and other ideologies, social and political organisation, the understanding and misunderstanding of diplomats, and the personal idiosyncrasies of rulers and politicians, etc., are all factors which are dismissed as either irrelevant or as being merely symptoms of the underlying economic process. Such an argument is convincing only when the real world is ignored, and its success in influencing subsequent explanations of international politics can be attributed to its simplicity. It appears to go back to first causes in explaining complex political behaviour and thus renders a bewildering variety of phenomena intelligible. But its intelligibility is purely internal, and when the argument is applied to actual historical situations its inadequacy as an explanation becomes immediately apparent.

It was pointed out at the beginning of this examination of the relationship between economic factors and international politics that such factors have always been present in international history. There are many examples in the past of conflicts occurring between states, in which trading or investment interests and economic resources have been relevant, either in causing a conflict or in resolving it. While the growth of industrial economies may be regarded as being significantly new in world history, we must distinguish between the argument which asserts that this growth introduced a qualitative change in international politics, as Lenin has it, and the problem of evaluating its effect. If the general hypothesis is rejected, there remains a problem of historical interpretation. The question might then be rephrased as, to what extent do economic interests and relationships impinge on foreign policy and on international politics? It is possible that a viable hypothesis might emerge from such a enquiry, but it would have to be more rigorous than extant hypotheses and susceptible to some means of validation. In short, it would have to be a theory in the sense used in the first part of this analysis.

If we turn away from the period before the First World War towards contemporary international politics, we find a revised version of Lenin's theory of imperialism known as neo-colonialism.[34] It is perhaps ironic that the period in which the great colonial empires collapsed should also be a period in which an 'informal' empire governed by the capitalist powers has been asserted. The abdication of direct political suzerainty by the major colonial powers has been considered by some commentators to be a device which maintains both political and economic dependence without incurring social and other responsibilities. Thus the Final Document of the Second Conference of Non-Aligned Countries held in 1964 roundly declared: 'Imperialism uses many devices to impose its will on independent nations. Economic pressure and domination, interference, racial discrimination, subversion, intervention and the threat of force are neo-colonialist devices against which the newly independent nations have to defend themselves.' One can imagine Lenin heartily agreeing with this formulation.

Such a view does not explain why the imperial powers gave up their empires with such celerity. What was the special advantage to be gained in substituting indirect for direct rule? Was such a transfer the result of the excessive expenses of colonial administration, the declining economic importance of the empires, or of the political problems caused by the appearance of independence movements within the colonial territories? It would appear that wars of intervention, and the maintenance of a military posture to support such wars, are at least as costly as colonial wars in the past, and that the risks and uncertainties of indirect rule would appear to be greater than the maintenance of colonial dominion. In short, while the neo-colonialist argument tries to take into account the new phenomenon of colonial dismantlement, it neither explains why this phenomenon occurred, nor does it provide a satisfactory answer as to why imperialism took the new form which it asserts. If indeed the major colonial powers were forced to give up their empires, then clearly the thesis of their domination over the non-capitalist world is weakened. If they gave up their empires of their own volition, then this policy is left unexplained in the neo-colonialist argument. It may be generally true that parts of the empire were liabilities and parts were assets, in economic and political terms, and that colonial policy sought, in the latter case, to preserve advantages for the metropolitan state on granting independence, but the whole movement towards colonial independence cannot be explained as a new form of imperialism. Once independence occurred, then the new government was free to interpret its relationships, both to the ex-metropolitan state and to the world at large, and while there was an inducement to maintain the former, many chose to widen the pattern of their external relations. Certainly, it cannot be said that the ex-metropolitan state remained in control over the new situation.

However, the neo-colonialist argument tends to concentrate on relations between the developed and the underdeveloped countries, and not specifically on those between the former colonial rulers and the ex-colonies.[35] The emphasis is on relations between capitalism and the non-capitalist or peripheral world, excluding of course the communist states. This is a revision of Lenin's original thesis, which argued that, although imperialism implied the acquisition of imperial authority, direct and indirect, it stemmed from contradictions within the capitalist system itself, and led to conflicts between the capitalist states. But the neo-colonialist argument conceives of the capitalist world as being united in exploiting the non-capitalist countries, rather than in fighting over the spoils. More precisely, while imperialist relations are alleged as existing between the ex-metropolitan states and their former colonies, the major imperialist power is conceived of as being the United States. World hegemony, no less, is considered to be the objective of this state. Although this argument is a version of the Hobson–Leninist thesis, it does not afford an explanation of relations between the major capitalist countries, in terms of the competition between international cartels for economic territory, which leads to large-scale international violence.

Thus the neo-colonialist thesis seeks to explain relations between the capitalist and the underdeveloped countries in terms of an imperialist hypothesis. The capitalist powers seek to find investment opportunities, to control sources of raw materials and to expoit markets, but do not take their competition to the point of fighting wars over economic territory. No explanation of the Second World War has been forthcoming on the basis of economic causation, and few commentators have argued that wars between capitalist powers are the necessary concomitant of this new form of imperialism. Certainly, the conflict between the Western European states and the United States, and the communist countries, has been represented by some commentators[36] as being imperialistic, in the sense that the former countries are governed by the desire to protect their socio-economic system, and to extend it, by destroying the communist states and suppressing revolution in the underdeveloped countries. In this sense national security, or apparently 'political' policies, are glosses on what is primarily economic motivation directing external relationships.

The main point of the neo-colonialist thesis is not that there is some utility in promoting economic interests on the part of capitalist countries, or that aspects of foreign policy have an economic motivation, but that political relationships are *primarily* motivated by economic factors directly related to capitalism. In other words, like the argument of Lenin and Hobson considered earlier in this analysis, it is an attempt to explain international politics in economic terms. As one commentator puts it, 'The most important branch of the theory of neo-colonialism is . . . the theory of economic imperialism', which he defines as 'the economic domination of one region, or country, over another'.[37] Two questions will be considered in this examination: firstly, can a generalisation or hypothetical proposition be made about 'the economic domination' of developed countries over the underdeveloped world? and secondly, what relationship has this phenomenon, assuming it to exist, to political domination?

Before seeking answers to these questions, some examination of the notion of dependency should be made. Often the use of the expression 'dependent' in describing economic relations between countries assumes some norm or model against which degrees of dependency can be measured. Yet no state, however powerful it is, or has been, is independent, in the sense that it enjoys complete autarky, is immune from external influences, or is capable of controlling its external environment. As we have seen in earlier parts of this study, much of international politics consists of efforts made by states, either to counteract the effects of their environment, or in seeking to widen the area of their activities in order to protect themselves and their interests. All states are, to a greater or lesser degree, interdependent, and therefore subject to the effects of events and circumstances which they control only very loosely. International politics consists, in terms of its empirical phenomena, of actions, reactions and interactions between states and lacks normative institutional means of regulation. Clearly, there are differences, in this respect at least, between states, and those which appear to have been most successful in influencing their external environment commonly enjoy the appellation of 'great powers'. The point is that an unqualified use of the term 'dependent' presupposes a 'pure' or ideal state of political or economic independence in international relations. More specifically, it often contains assumptions of equity or morality relating to political behaviour.

In short, while in political usage the term 'power' is useful in describing inter-state relations, without introducing ethical or other value connotations, the use of the term 'economic dependence' tends to be more moralistic. A power struggle between states can be discussed without involvement in value judgements, although of course, as we have seen, other theorising assumptions might be implicit in such an examination; but a conflict between states in the economic sphere becomes exploitation, or domination, with the inference that the successful state is in some way immoral. Yet an equitable economic world does not exist any more than an equitable political world does. It might be urged that economic and political transactions between states or individuals should be based upon ethical principles, but this is a different kind of argument from that which asserts that all political behaviour is determined by economic interest. The former is a moral argument while the latter is an explanation of the causes of behaviour itself. We must be careful in distinguishing between the two in explaining the relation between economic factors or forces and international politics.

This implicit moral bias is especially true of discussions of the question of economic development and its related social and welfare problems. On the one hand, the major industrial powers are urged to promote development in the economically backward countries on altruistic grounds, and on the other are castigated for their self-interested policies. It may or may not be valid to assert a fundamental conflict of interest between developed and underdeveloped countries on economic questions, but it is certainly inappropriate to include ethical questions in an examination of their economic and political relationships. This stricture also applies to those Marxist or neo-Marxist commentators[38] who relate their enquiries to an implicit model based upon an ideological argument. The concern in this analysis of aid programmes and trade and other economic relations between the developed and the underdeveloped countries is with their political

significance, and not with their effects on the progress of economic development in the latter countries. Does a close economic relationship imply a
close political relationship, and is the latter determined by the former? Is
the 'imperialist' power impelled into creating political hegemony by
domestic economic forces, and does such a hegemony in fact exist in the
underdeveloped world?

An aid policy is one which may be regarded as having primarily political
objectives, while a trade policy has the objective of providing economic
advantages to the trading country. Clearly, there must be reciprocal
advantages accruing to both partners, otherwise such relationships between
donor and recipient countries, and between trading states, would not be
viable or undertaken. There is no principle governing such relationships,
however, which stipulates that the advantages should be equally distributed.
If an underdeveloped country is content to abstain from undertaking
certain relationships with developed countries, as is the case with Burma's
attitude towards aid, or is unprepared to align itself economically and
politically with one power, as was the case for Egypt and India, then it is
in some respects 'independent'. It is not exposed to the threat of a
suspension of aid or trade, nor is it forced to undertake certain political
obligations as a condition of an economic transaction. In this sense at least,
underdeveloped countries are free to accept inhibitions upon their nominal
independence or to reject them. Indeed, this is generally true for all states,
developed and underdeveloped. In order to get around this element of free
choice in international relations, some commentators argue that imperialism
is a relationship between puppet or subservient regimes and the major
capitalist powers, in which, in exchange for economic parasitism, the
regime is supported in power by the foreign government. It thus acquiesces
both in the economic exploitation of its national patrimony and in the
political concomitants of its relationship with an imperialist power. Indirect
rule is thus exercised by the latter state through its control over a local
government.

There are a number of objections to this simple model, but the most
important is that while an affinity of interests can be traced in a number
of such relationships, especially in the case of underdeveloped countries
which have been independent for a relatively long time, as for example the
Latin American countries, 'indirect rule' cannot be inferred without concrete evidence. Even if such evidence is forthcoming, or it can be shown
that an 'imperialist' power seeks such a relationship, some evidence as to
economic motivation must be provided in addition, in order to substantiate
the neo-colonialist argument. It is clearly very difficult to distinguish
between a self-imposed inhibition which prevents a government from undertaking one of a number of hypothetically 'independent' courses of action,
from an inhibition directly imposed on it by a foreign power. Mutual
interest and reciprocity can explain a close relationship between states, but

then so can the fear of sanctions if it is broken by the 'dependent' power. Again, recourse must be made to empirical examination in order to test the general proposition advanced by the neo-colonial theorists, that is, that the major capitalist powers in general, and the United States in particular, impelled by the logic of an internal economic dynamic, seek to create an international political hegemony in order to fulfill economic interests. Their foreign policies and their external political relationships are thus explicable in terms of the advancement of these interests. It should be stressed that this is a general proposition which applies to international politics and which subordinates all other motivation and behaviour to this fundamental thesis. It is not enough to show that in particular instances an economic motive or interest prevailed, or that a particular external relationship had an economic significance, to validate such an explanation. Conversely it can be invalidated by showing that in a number of instances the primary motivation for a political action or decision, or for the negotiation of an external relationship, was not economic, although of course it may have economic significance.

If, then, we return to the notion of economic dependence, we may perhaps define it in two ways   firstly, as the dependence of one country upon another for its major source of foreign exchange, derived either from capital investment, aid or exports, and secondly, as the dependence of a country on international trade or aid in terms of its G.N.P. This last can be narrowed even further to a dependence upon the export earnings derived from the export of a particular primary commodity. The two main points in determining the degree to which a country is economically dependent are, firstly, how significant external economic transactions are to its economy; and, more important for our purposes, to what extent it is dependent upon a single trading partner or aid donor. It is important to emphasise that while many neo-colonial theorists tend to confuse their arguments by references to capitalism, the point we are seeking to establish here is not the dependence of trading countries on a world capitalist 'system', however this may be defined, but their dependence upon other states. A distinction should be made between 'capitalism' and a 'capitalist' state.

These are evaluative, not rigid, criteria and, when applied to the under-developed countries, reveal a wide variety of different forms of economic dependence. Thus both India and Pakistan are not trade-dependent in the second sense, since they derive less than 5 per cent of their G.N.P. from trade. Nevertheless, in the first sense they also receive aid and in the case of India food aid is an important contribution to her economy. Further qualifications need to be made in that India is a recipient of aid from a variety of sources including communist states, while Pakistan for the most part receives aid from one major donor, the United States. Moreover, while external trade tends to be heterogeneous for the former state, Pakistan is dependent on one major commodity, that of jute, for her export earnings.[39] It is difficult, therefore, to make a generalisation concerning economic dependence regarding these two countries, although it can be said in general that, since both are concerned with programmes of economic development, the question of foreign exchange and imports is important to their economies. If we relate this to political relationships, then the paradox emerges that while India was for a long time one of the major 'unaligned' nations, her government has become more and more dependent on the United States and has pursued in recent years a 'quietist' policy, while Pakistan, a member of two western alliances, SEATO and CENTO, has become more and more critical of western policies and has opened up relations with the People's Republic of China. How can this paradox be explained? Part of the explanation lies in the mutual hostility of these countries over Kashmir, and part lies in the successive crop failures which occurred in India, the consequent dependence upon American surplus wheat, and the insistence on the part of the United States on a strict neutrality towards its activities in Vietnam. In spite of these factors, the recent involvement of India in supporting the secessionist movement in Bangladesh, against the wishes of the United States, provides an illustration of the indeterminate nature of political influence exercised through economic relationships.

Another example of the complexity of economic and political relations, and the difficulty of making generalisations about economic dependence, can be seen in the Middle East. Egypt has been a major aid recipient and dependent on the production and export of cotton for its export earnings. Before Suez its trade was overwhelmingly dominated by Britain, but this did not prevent the nationalisation of the Suez Canal, any more than the cessation of aid on the part of Britain and the United States for the Aswan Dam induced the Egyptian government to sever its newly established connections with communist states. Although trade between Britain and Egypt never recovered its former level, Egypt received aid from the United States and from the Soviet Union, with the latter state absorbing much of its cotton crop. Moreover, the appropriation of the Suez Canal was successful, with both the United States and the Soviet Union intervening to prevent the British and French attempt at invasion. There is no clear generalisation which can be made here about the close connection of economic and political relations, and an explanation of the course of Middle Eastern politics since 1956 hinges on the relationship between the Arab states and Israel. The latter state has been very heavily dependent on aid and loans from the major western states, much of which has taken the form of private investment motivated by Zionist and religious sentiment. It has also received reparations from the Federal Republic of Germany. Yet it would be difficult to assert that Israeli foreign and defence policy has been dictated by the United States. The conflict between Egypt and her allies and Israel is inexplicable on economic grounds, and the involvement of the major powers reveals a helplessness in influencing events which does not support the neo-colonialist hypothesis.

Thus although economic dependence may be established in relations between developed and underdeveloped countries, these two examples indicate the difficulty of assuming that the necessary concomitant is political subservience, or that political behaviour is the direct product of the workings of economic forces. The American interest in India and in Pakistan is clearly related to her global policies, in the same way as her interests in the Middle East. In the case of the latter area there is the additional factor of investment in oil, although this does not apply specifically to Egypt, Israel and the Levant. The complexities of such situations and their anomalies are usually glossed over by some neo-colonial theorists, by asserting that the fundamental objective of the United States is the preservation of its economic system and that its involvement in world politics is directed to this end. Such a transcendental view is facile and begs a number of questions. Certainly, the United States did not create either the Kashmir or the Palestinian dispute, but its involvement in these conflicts is related to policy objectives which are political rather than economic in nature.

One form of economic dependence which is asserted by neo-colonial theorists is that which stems from foreign investment.[40] For example, some underdeveloped countries are dependent upon earnings from investment concentrated in one extractive industry, as in the following cases: the United Fruit Company in the Central American states, Union Minière in Zaïre, Firestone Rubber in Liberia, Unilever in the West African states, Bookers in Guyana, Alcoa in Jamaica, etc. We are not concerned with the argument that the activities of these companies have a deleterious effect on the economies of their host countries, but with the questions as to what extent this private investment is motivated by foreign governments as a conscious imperialist policy, and what are its political consequences. Such an investment might constitute an external economic interest which requires protection as a national asset, but does this necessarily mean that foreign governments exercise indirect rule in these countries?

The case of Guatemala has often been cited as a typical example of economic imperialism.[41] The involvement of the United States in domestic politics in 1954 was prompted by the threat of the expropriation of land belonging to the United Fruit Company, and it resulted in the maintenance of the *status quo* and of a friendly government. Perhaps a better example is the earlier Iranian oil crisis, during which the British government used diplomatic pressure, the threat of force and a boycott of Iranian oil in order to return the Anglo-Iranian Oil Company to private ownership.[42] The consequent economic crisis within Iran helped to bring about the downfall of the Mossadegh government and a compromise. There are many other examples, including the major intervention of the British and the

French Suez expedition, of the close involvement in the domestic politics of other countries on the part of the major powers. Nevertheless, a number of underdeveloped countries have been able to nationalise, appropriate or force concessions from foreign companies, without incurring such intervention. Argentina, Cuba, Chile, Peru, Egypt, Libya, Indonesia, Sri Lanka and Iran all succeeded in nationalising foreign property, in some cases without the payment of compensation, and avoided direct intervention. Clearly, there were factors present in these cases which inhibited the major capitalist states, in spite of the alleged control which is asserted to exist where such investment occurs. These factors are not economic in nature, but political.

There is obviously an external interest on the part of a capital-exporting country in providing safeguards for its investment, but it is a gross exaggeration both to infer that the main interest of a government is the promotion of this investment and, from this, in the extension of political control in the area in which investment takes place. A government, like all Western governments, is under pressure to safeguard the interests of its citizens abroad, and sanctions have been created through legislation such as the Hickenlooper amendment,[43] designed to restrict governmental freedom in this respect. Yet on occasions governments have shown themselves to be politic in their attitude towards the appropriation of national assets abroad, and to ignore the claims of their citizens. No generalisation about the exertion of indirect political control by major Western governments in underdeveloped countries where substantial investment has taken place is possible on empirical grounds. A distinction should be made between the kind of rationalisation which asserts that every prudent man wishes to safeguard his investment, and the assumption that this is what he, or his government, actually does or tries to do. Certainly, investing companies have shown a readiness to call in the secular arm, as was noted above, in order to protect their interests, but this is not the same as saying that there is no difference between the investor and his home government. In certain cases a government has intervened in order to protect its citizens' interests, but in other cases, while adopting a sorrowful attitude, has refrained from doing so.

Not all countries default on their commercial obligations, and it might perhaps be argued that one of the reasons for their restraint is the possibility of economic reprisals. There are, it would appear, enough sanctions which can be applied by international investors without the necessity, even when it might be obtained, of political intervention by a government. If a foreign government defaults on its loans as a matter of course, then either the source of loans dries up, or the interest rates on new loans become prohibitive. More direct sanctions can be taken, as for example, in the case of Cuba, the suspension of the sugar quota, or a total boycott on trade. There is, in investment as in trade tariffs, an element of reciprocity which permits manoeuvre but not an outright breach of the conventions governing the transaction. The case of investment is somewhat different where the exploitation of raw materials or public utilities is concerned, and where these may have a strategic or political significance both for the investor's government and for the host country. The point is that the assumption that a close dependent relationship of the kind discussed here means political subordination to a capitalist state requires empirical evidence. It can be argued that such a relationship is not without its political significance, but any attempt to formulate generalisations about invisible empires and political dependence becomes tendentious without such evidence.

It can be shown, moreover, that the underdeveloped countries are not the main recipients of investment from the major capital-exporting states. Although, in this respect, the United States is predominant, these states invest in each other's economies. As we shall see when their political and economic interrelationships are discussed later on, the neocolonialist thesis breaks down completely when it is applied to relations between capitalist countries. Some attempt has been made to modify the significance of the fact that the main direction of capital has been to the developed rather than to the underdeveloped area, by asserting that the rate of profit is higher in the latter than the former, and that this area of investment has a pivotal significance in the capitalist economies.[14] Whatever the merits of these arguments, they do not support the contention that the main drive of the capitalist countries has been towards investment in the underdeveloped countries, nor its political concomitants.

Thus while in certain cases intervention in the domestic politics of another country in defence of an economic interest can be shown to have taken place, such interventions of themselves do not substantiate the neocolonial argument. Moreover it could be argued, especially in cases where foreign investment is in extractive industries, that nationalisation would not only deter an inflow of capital but would also jeopardise existing markets, unless an alternative and non-discriminatory market was available. Consequently most states which act as hosts to concentrated foreign investment have been content with various arrangements which give them an increasing share of profits and some measure of influence over the activities of the foreign company.[45] There are, obviously, limits which exist on how much profits and control can be enjoyed by governments in this situation. The point is that while there is a conflict of interest between such a business activity and the country in which investment is made, in the sense that the former is concerned with maximising profits while the latter is concerned with obtaining as great a share of these as possible, as well as with the social and economic repercussions stemming from the presence of such capital, such a conflict is not so absolute as the neocolonial argument would suggest. The situation is essentially a political one, and accommodation rather than expropriation is the more normal means of resolution.

Thus unless an autarkic policy is urged, with the absorption of mineral or other production within the national economy, and the industrialisation which this implies, or alternatively a total withdrawal from the world economy, it is hard to see how a policy of nationalisation is possible, except under very favourable circumstances, without alienating the provision of external capital or existing markets. It is as difficult for an underdeveloped country, as it is for a developed state, to break out of its network of economic interchange, and to achieve a complete 'independence' in economic and political terms, without risking considerable internal disruption. Within such a network, however, there is a considerable variety of relationships and dependences, consisting of a series of bargaining situations rather than the condition of transcendental conflict postulated by the neo-colonial hypothesis. The example of Indonesia illustrates this. During the Sukarno regime the economy was supported by loans and grants derived from a number of sources including western and communist countries. The pursuit of an aggressive policy towards Malaysia resulted in a 'confrontation' with Britain. This policy eventually brought about almost complete political and economic isolation except for a growing relationship with the People's Republic of China. So far as the western countries were concerned, the withdrawal of Indonesia from the United Nations made her isolation total. For some time before this break in political relations the Indonesian economy had been in great difficulties, and indebtedness exceeded receipts of capital. When the government nationalised all foreign assets, as well as those of the ex-metropolitan power, it was not surprising that aid and economic support from the capital-exporting countries dried up completely. The quest for independence on political and economic fronts brought Indonesia into conflict with the western powers and produced a growing dependence on communist countries. However, internal opposition to this policy, together with a highly confused domestic political situation, which has never been satisfactorily explained, brought about a change of government and a change of policy. Almost immediately the western governments offered loans and assistance to enable Indonesia to pay compensation for nationalised assets, and organised a means of loan amortisation.

This example indicates the complexities of economic and political factors and relationships and the difficulty of formulating a generalisation which corresponds to the neo-colonial thesis. There is a price to be paid in economic terms for the severance of relations with major markets and sources of capital, but this price may be paid, and it is difficult to assert that the existence of such relations constitutes a form of indirect rule.

We come now to the question of international commodity trade, which has been asserted as creating another form of dependence for underdeveloped countries. Monopoly conditions, in the form of agreements on markets and prices which exist for certain manufacturers and minerals, do not exist for primary commodities, and a strong element of competition prevails between producers. This competition can be offset by the negotiation of quotas and preference arrangements with major consumers. In general, this is the case for commodity trade between ex-colonies and their ex-metropolitan rulers. Similarly, the United States had such an arrangement with the Philippines, and with Cuba until 1960, in respect of sugar. But the price paid for the security which preferential arrangements confer is an enhanced dependence upon specific markets. Moreover, the problem of over-production and of consequent price fluctuation, inherent in commodity trade, makes the producer even more vulnerable, since he is unable to control the conditions which cause this instability. He is forced to depend even more on the guaranteed market provided by a bilateral trading agreement.

Thus the two main features of primary commodity trade – the dependence on a major consumer for a market, and the fluctuations in price as a factor of production and of competition – produce a form of economic dependence, especially in cases where primary commodity trade produces most of a country's foreign exchange. For example, Brazil derives most of its exchange from the sale of coffee, primarily to the United States. A threat of a reduction either in price or in quota would have serious consequences to the Brazilian economy, unless it could be offset either by finding another market or a subsidy. The spread of coffee production, especially in African countries, and the production of 'instant' coffee which utilises inferior grades of coffee beans, increases the force of such bilateral agreements and also exacerbates a situation in which over-production and falling prices are endemic. Of course, this situation is highly favourable to the consumer and, as was seen in the case of foreign investment, a conflict of interests between buyer and seller can be postulated.

Yet there are other considerations which ameliorate this situation. The primary commodity producers sought for a long time, both in the United Nations and out of it, to obtain some means of regulating commodity trade and stabilising prices. The failure of the Commission on International Commodity Trade, set up in the face of western opposition and a United States and British boycott of its operations, led to increased pressures from the underdeveloped countries. The western states eventually acceded to these pressures and agreed to the convening of the first United Nations Conference on Trade and Development (UNCTAD) in 1964. Political factors such as the support given to this movement by communist countries, and the intervention of the Soviet Union in commodity markets through the purchase of Egyptian cotton and Cuban sugar, indicated that an alternative market existed in the event of a breakdown of relations between western consumers and the primary commodity producers. Consequently the United States modified its attitude towards the regulation of this trade and negotiated the Coffee Agreement in 1965. This agreement, as with the earlier Sugar and Tin Agreements, did little to diminish the dependence of the producers, although in the former case it stabilised the price of coffee temporarily. In effect this agreement pegged the price of coffee above the national 'free market' price and thus constituted a form of subsidy conferred by the consumer on the producer. This price was paid by the United States largely for political reasons.

Unless a radical change in this kind of economic system is postulated – and indeed, such a change is both unlikely and hard to define – such economic relationships will continue to be unequal and to contain an element of conflict. If a major change in consumption takes place, or if synthetic substitutes are preferred, then primary commodity producers would be as adversely affected as they are when a low-cost competitor appears, or an innovation in production methods occurs. Their problem is one of relative inflexibility in their economic structures and their inability to diversify, combined with a dependence on primary commodity production. However, it is not possible to examine the complexities of this economic situation here. The argument that the major developed countries should help the primary commodity producers to diversify their economies, and to accept the measure of subsidy involved in price stabilisation, has an ethical rather than a political or economic basis. A definition of a just or equitable price or mechanism for fixing prices is fraught with difficulties and in practice depends upon what bargaining power exists in a given situation.

The point here is that while this kind of unequal relationship, and its consequent problems for the economies of the underdeveloped countries, place the latter in a vulnerable and dependent position, in so far as their economies rely on export earnings, the political significance of this is consequential rather than causal. Clearly, the dominant partner, the consumer, would like to perpetuate such a dependence on economic grounds, but, as was seen in the case of Brazil, there are limits to the political utility of such a policy. Political alienation may occur, as in the case of Cuba, and within this situation there is room for bargaining and accommodation of conflicting interests, especially when political factors are relevent. For example, the bargaining position of the South American states in relation to the United States over economic transactions was much enhanced after the Cuban alignment with the Soviet Union. It cannot be argued with validity that the basis of American foreign policy is the creation of such relations, although their maintenance as well as their amelioration may constitute an external political interest.

One of the problems in assessing the nature of economic dependence, through a study of trade relationships, is that of making a clear distinction between trade and aid. Aid has been defined as

> a transfer of real resources or immediate claims on resources (for
> example foreign exchange) from one country to another, which would
> not have taken place as a consequence of the operation of market forces
> or in the absence of specific official action designed to promote the
> transfer by the donor country.[46]

This definition is difficult to apply in practice. It is far from clear, for
example, whether barter transactions between communist states and underdeveloped countries constitute aid, or where commodities are purchased
at a price higher than the hypothetical 'free market level'. Thus apart from
direct grants and 'soft' loans, which in any case are usually tied to the
purchase of the donor country's goods, compensation for balance-of-
payments deficits or commodity price fluctuations, the sale of commodities,
such as wheat, for local currencies, the importation of commodities at
higher prices than the free market price, or on the basis of a guaranteed
price over a long period of time, a guarantee of a share of the market, and
the provisions of long-term credits for the purchase of goods from the
creditor, would all constitute a form of 'aid' and an interference with 'free'
market conditions. Economic relations between the underdeveloped
countries and the developed states are full of such agreements and arrangements. The pattern of trade is thus largely determined by a series of
bilateral arrangements between these countries.

However, we are not concerned in this analysis with the question
whether a transfer of 'real' resources has taken place, or with the effects
of these aid transactions upon economic development, but with their
political significance. The conferring of aid, unlike other economic interchanges, is essentially a political act undertaken by governments and may
be regarded as part of foreign policy. We may define aid as an economic
transaction which is primarily motivated by political considerations and
which, but for these considerations, would not have taken place. This
would include the provision of technical assistance as well as military aid.
The assumption contained in this notion of aid, that is, that aid is politically
motivated, requires some empirical evidence to support it. This is found
in the statements made by policy-makers in support of an aid policy, in
the political relationships between donor and recipient countries, and in
the various fluctuations in the pattern of aid related to political events.
The neo-colonialist argument has it that, although apparently related to
political objectives, aid is designed to further economic ends and is part
of the process of creating an invisible empire.

So far as official explanations of motivation are concerned, it would
appear from the statement made of the purposes of the Mutual Security
Act of 1951[47] that political objectives were paramount in American aid

policy. This policy was intended to discourage aggression, protect states from subversion, strengthen the will of the peoples of the Near East and Africa to resist aggression, encourage them in their efforts to achieve stability and progress and to remove sources of dissidence and unrest. In this statement references were made to the need to preserve external sources of strategic minerals and to deny these to the USSR. These objectives were strongly influenced by the Korean war, which was not only interpreted as presaging a new communist offensive in the underdeveloped area, but also indicated American unpreparedness in the provision of war material. The areas referred to in this document were devoid of any American military presence, although a number of America's European allies maintained military bases and authority. Placing this new aid policy in its political context, it marked the beginning of an extension of American influence outside Europe in areas which had hitherto been remote from American interests.

The concern of the American government at this time with the problem of the supply of strategic minerals has often been cited by advocates of the neo-colonial argument as evidence of an economic interest.[48] There is a circularity in an argument which says that the need to guarantee external sources of material essential to American security was really to preserve a particular socio-economic system. The preservation of American capitalist society, according to this argument, was the real motivation behind its external interests. The tautological element in this view can be revealed by arguing that the interest of the Soviet Union in Eastern Europe, after the end of the Second World War, was motivated by its desire to protect a particular socio-economic system and that its security needs were merely a disguise for this. It is clearly difficult to separate the concept of national security, that is, the preservation of the state from external or internal threats, from the preservation of its institutions and its way of life. The point is that this policy statement linked aid both to political and economic objectives.

Of course, we should not take these official arguments at their face value, since an aid policy has been in the main unpopular in Congress. Some politicians have been sceptical as to the concrete gains derived from such a policy, while most have been united in their reluctance to allow the administration a free hand in disbursing aid appropriations without some political surveillance.[49] Others have sought, sometimes successfully, to secure to American business concerns some advantages in the aid programme and to ensure that it did not compete with private investment. Certainly, prolonged wrangling between the administration and Congress over aid appropriations does not suggest the cohesion between capitalist interests and governments which is one of the main postulates of the neo-colonialist argument. Thus the administration is continually forced not only to advance convincing arguments in favour of a generally unpopular policy, but also to palliate it by including measures designed to placate business opinion and interests.

When the political advantages obtained by an aid policy designed to maintain the *status quo* appeared to be more intangible than usual, the policy was defended on economic grounds. Thus preference to domestic manufacturers, non-competitiveness of public aid with private investment, the disposal of food surpluses, aid tied to the purchase of American goods, the opening of new markets, and the provision of an economic infra-structure for private investment, were all advanced as arguments in defence of successive aid programmes. It was clearly difficult for the administration to provide convincing evidence for its Congressional critics of the success of its aid programme, without politically embarrassing the recipients. The policy became even more difficult to defend when the phenomenon of non-alignment and Soviet aid competition appeared and certain states, such as India, Afghanistan, Egypt and Indonesia, showed a willingness to accept aid from both sides.

Nevertheless, the record of American aid disbursement over the post-war period indicates that the majority of aid, both economic and military, has gone either to states closely allied to the United States, such as Taiwan, South Korea, South Vietnam, the Philippines, Greece and Turkey, or to states which have a pivotal position in international politics such as Yugo-slavia and Israel. For certain other countries American aid has been of considerable economic significance; for example, one-third of the Bolivian budget in 1960 consisted of aid from the United States.[50] Although Latin American states were recipients of aid, it is noteworthy that Yugoslavia received more aid from the United States over the period 1945 to 1960[51] than the whole of Latin America. In short, the flow of aid from the U.S.A. has been closely associated with political objectives. It is hard to see what economic advantages the American government derives from its support of Taiwan, Yugoslavia, Israel, or South Korea and South Vietnam.

The value of aid as a political weapon is, moreover, rather dubious in the light of past experience. Aid to Yugoslavia, for example, has waxed and waned as relations between this state and the U.S.S.R. have improved or deteriorated, but without having an apparent effect on Yugoslav policy. Similarly, although the United States has been a major donor of loans and assistance to Israel, the Israeli government has not shown itself to be dominated by the American government in respect of its dealings with the Arab world. Even in the case of South Korea and South Vietnam, the American commitment has meant that unless a radical change in policy occurred, local governments enjoyed considerable freedom. In a sense the inflexibility of the commitment inhibited American ability to influence the course of internal politics, rather than extended 'indirect' rule.

To return to the general argument, we can see that the foregoing dis-cussion revealed a variety of economic relationships between the developed and the underdeveloped countries, and that many of them were based on unequal terms. The point is, firstly, do these relationships constitute a conscious policy of imperial expansion in the sense used by neo-colonial theorists, that is, with economic motivation determining political behaviour? and secondly, does a close dependent economic relationship between countries mean the political domination of the superior partner? A further gloss on this argument has been added by some commentators,[52] who assert that with the appearance of socialist states as participants in international politics, the capitalist states are forced on the defensive. Thus capitalism, instead of expanding, now seeks to prevent the contraction of its economic territory. In this view the United States is seen as the organiser and leader of the capitalist attempt to prevent assets, sources of raw materials and markets from diminishing. This suggests, *per contra* to Lenin, that the capitalist states constitute a political and economic unity, that competition between them is no longer of significance, and that the main area of their political and economic interest is in the underdeveloped world.

The first part of this argument can be disproved by reference to the policies and behaviour of the major powers in the post-war world. Certain aspects of this, notably the conflict between the United States and her allies with the communist countries, and the premises of American foreign policy, have been touched on elsewhere. So far as the former is concerned, this conflict has had two broad aspects, neither of them connected, except peripherally, with economic motives or causes. The first is that of security, and the conflict has been marked by the development on both sides of war capacities and alliance systems, and most significantly by a nuclear arms race which has had an important and unexpected effort on the conflict itself. The second aspect is that this struggle has an ideological content, since the burden of the opposition of the United States, if not of her allies, to the Soviet Union was that communism presented a threat to the West, not because of its superior military strength, but because of the nature of the Soviet system and its ideological foundations. Both these aspects are considered in other parts of this study, but the important point here is that the protagonist, the United States, at the beginning of the Cold War, had both a nuclear monopoly and possessed an economy which was virtually autarkic and the strongest in the world. The United States, whatever the fears of her policy-makers for the future, had nothing to fear from any other state in security terms at the end of the Second World War. This is of course in itself a rationalisation, for American policy was conducted on the premise that the Soviet Union was indeed a threat. But the nature of the threat and its perception have always been ambivalent in policy-making. The neo-colonialist explanation of American policy is also a rationalisation and, as was seen earlier, there are alternative and conflicting explanations of the origins of the Cold War and of the continuing

conflict between the United States and the communist countries. The truth
lies in the influence of circumstances and events, in the participants' perceptions of these, and in the network of international commitments and
relations which prevailed at the time, rather than in the over-simplifications
of a dilute Leninism. American policy responses to political changes were
influences on succeeding changes, and this is seen most clearly in the field
of military technology. It is strange that the supporters of the neo-colonialist
argument, themselves proponents of a deterministic system, should have
ignored the effects of arms races on political behaviour. Not only have the
assumptions made by politicians about the world been significant in shaping
it, but the unintended effects of their actions, particularly in the development
of weapons and technology, have also had considerable influence.

It can thus be argued that the major conflict between the West and the
East, which has dominated international politics since the end of the Second
World War, was the consequence of political and not economic factors,
although these last have been relevant. Paradoxically, the importance of
the underdeveloped countries has not been the consequence of their role as
suppliers of raw materials, as investment opportunities or as markets, but
as a result of the East–West conflict itself. It has been their significance as
allies, or perhaps the deprivation of their allegiance to the enemy, which has
influenced great-power attitudes towards them. This is not merely true of
American, but also of Soviet and Chinese policy towards the underdeveloped countries. The stalemate of the nuclear arms race has perhaps
also provided an additional significance, since these small non-nuclear states
constitute the only area in which great-power politics and its concomitant
violence can take place without incurring the risk of destroying the major
powers themselves. The inhibition upon war between nuclear powers has
given the only remaining area of political fluidity in international politics
an enhanced importance. Yet this importance is itself a consequence of the
nuclear stalemate and of the dominant influence of great-power policies.
If a growing détente between the major powers as a consequence of the
nuclear stalemate is postulated, then the underdeveloped world will cease
to have this peculiar significance in international politics. The corresponding
loss of interest in them on the part of the developed states will consign
them to the same sort of relative oblivion as that of Latin American states
in the nineteenth century. Certain interests in particular underdeveloped
countries will persist, and perhaps their basis will be economic, but this
will hardly amount to the pursuit of world empire in the sense used in the
neo-colonial argument.

None of this is to say that economic factors are irrelevant in international
politics or in foreign policy-making. It is, however, a denial that economic
factors and motivation constitute a determinant for political commitments
and relationships. There are relationships which are almost entirely determined by economic considerations, as for example in the relationship

between the United Kingdom and the Republic of South Africa, but these are exceptional in international politics. The argument that the struggle between the United States and the Soviet Union is based upon an economic dynamic in the former country is impossible to validate on empirical grounds and depends upon the vague assertion that 'capitalism' or 'imperialism' has innate expansionist tendencies. More specifically, the assertion that the United States has pursued an imperialist policy in the post-war world because of its finance-capital-dominated domestic economy is neither borne out by the facts of her external economic interests and the part which these play in her economy, nor by its political behaviour. American economic strength and its influence on the economies of other states have certainly been exercised, in some cases to obtain an advantage which favours its economy but in others to support the main objectives of its foreign policy in the conflict with the Soviet Union and the People's Republic of China. In short, if the term, 'neo-colonialism' is given a reduced meaning signifying attempts to use an economic relationship, or to create one, in order to obtain a political advantage, then this is true not merely of the United States but of all states which are able to do so. It certainly was not Lenin or his followers who invented the *quid pro quo* in political and economic relations. If, alternatively, it is given a meaning similar to that in Lenin and Hobson's theory of imperialism, then it suffers from the same lack of precision and from the absence of empirical verification.

This brings us to the second part of the argument, that of interpreting the political significance of dependent economic relations between nations. This is largely a matter of interpretation within the confines of the major political conflicts between nations. On the strictly economic level, such economic relationships are conducted on business principles between private citizens, with governmental intervention constituting a more or less permanent factor. So far as the developed countries are concerned, as will be seen subsequently, the existence of multilateral economic relations appears either to be irrelevant to political affiliations or interests, or to reinforce them. The notion that the European countries became political satraps of the United States after the receipt of Marshall Aid or as a consequence of American investment is obviously nonsensical if their policies and attitudes are examined in any detail. The difficulty is that there is always some truth in a rationalisation, or in this case that close economic relations have political significance. Of course they may do, but their relevance is always one which depends upon circumstances and upon politics. For example, the United States was able to urge Britain towards the creation of the state of Israel as a condition of the major loan which was granted at the end of the war.[53] Similarly, economic pressure was used against Britain in order to bring about a withdrawal from Suez.[54] Yet the United States was not able to align Britain in supporting political intervention in Asia, or to make the British government abandon its policy of creating an independent nuclear deterrent. In spite of a major economic crisis in which the British government was very much dependent upon financial backing from the United States, the latter was not able to obtain more than diplomatic support for its intervention in South Vietnam.

Thus as in the parallel case of Comecon and the co-operative economic and financial arrangements of the eastern states, in which one state assumes a predominant role, the political relationships are the parameters for the economic and not vice versa. It was in spite of common economic ties that the Hungarian government in 1956 and the Czech government in 1968 sought a form of political independence of the Soviet Union. It was not through economic pressure that the Soviet Union re-established its hegemony over these countries, but by the use of the factor which created this hegemony in the first place. In other words, intervention through the use of force occurred. The Red Army, and the establishment of a government politically dependent upon the Soviet Union, determined the issue in both cases. Nor can it be argued that the Soviet Union needed these countries as political allies for economic reasons. These two examples of intervention parallel those made by the United States in order to reinforce friendly governments or to prevent political alienation. For all the economic domination of Cuba through military aid to the Batista government, the presence of American investment and the preferential sugar quota, the American government was unable to prevent either the nationalisation of American assets or the subsequent defection of Cuba to the Soviet camp.

What has been termed 'polycentrism' in alliances,[55] that is, the weakening of the influence of the dominant ally, is more characteristic of international politics than the kind of dominion advanced by the neocolonial argument. Even before the nuclear stalemate, divisions in the western alliances were apparent, particularly on issues outside Europe itself. The attempt made by the United States in 1949 to achieve a collective embargo on trade with communist countries failed largely because of the refusal of her major allies to support it.[56] More recently, in 1964, the United States cut off 'military assistance' to the United Kingdom,[57] France and Yugoslavia because these countries continued to trade with Cuba, without having an effect on their policies. Moreover, as will be seen in other parts of this study, there were serious divisions between the allies on the question of strategy and the military infrastructure of NATO, on control over nuclear weapons and on the very purpose of the treaty itself. Outside Europe, differences existed between the European allies and the United States over the conduct of the Korean war, the neutralisation of Indo-China in 1954 and, as was noted, over the Suez expedition in 1956. The United States sought to wield its economic and political strength in order to obtain conformity to its policies, and while it was successful in some instances, it failed notably in others. This hardly suggests the sort of dominion contained in the notion of imperialism, or indeed the kind of fundamental conflict between the capitalist powers, which in spite of their disagreements have remained united in an alliance system since 1949.

If the divisions within the western and the eastern camps reflect the relative independence of allied countries, then the phenomena of neutralism and non-alignment also reflect this in the underdeveloped world. And of course, as was noted earlier, the alleged phenomenon of neo-colonialism is found not in relations between the capitalist powers themselves, or between the communist states, but between these countries and the under-developed world. More particularly, it is argued, the United States has in effect usurped the European empires, and has embarked upon a policy of political dominion through control over the economies of the under-developed states.[58] The main motivation for this policy is asserted to be economic. As was noted earlier, that part of Lenin's theory which explained politics and wars between the capitalist countries as the consequence of a new form of capitalism, with its drive to expand into economic territory, has conveniently been dropped. Instead the argument has concentrated upon the extension of dependent relations between the capitalist world and the non-communist underdeveloped nations. The communist states them-selves, although economically and politically related to some of these states, are left in a kind of theoretical limbo. But socialist states cannot also be capitalist, even though their efforts at political dominion seem indistin-guishable from those of the western powers. In short, there is much which is left unexplained by the neo-colonialist argument, and a good deal of the phenomena in international politics would appear flatly to contradict it. It is plausible only at the very general level. Of course, the assertions of circumstances, of the influence of personalities and the multiple effects of complex interactions specific to certain political situations are countered by supporters of this argument, who admit their relevance but assert that they are subsumed within the general hypothesis of economic motivation. We are back to the generalisations about history, its driving force and so on which characterise historicist explanation.

It was said earlier that the imperialist and neo-colonialist arguments, while pointing out the element of interdependence in modern international economic and political relationships, nevertheless ignored, or minimised, the factor of mutual advantage and reciprocity in these relationships. We come now to the opposite view, expressed in the functionalist hypothesis, that is, that co-operation and not conflict between states is the product of new economic forces which exert an influence upon politics between nations. Like the arguments discussed earlier, they posit an international economic system which imposes limits on national sovereignty. There are, as was noted, traces of this view in Hobson's argument,[59] which implied that sectional interests dictated a policy of imperialism against the interests of the state as a whole. Such a policy could be changed on the adoption of a democratic and socialist political system, thus allowing the genuine co-operative and integrative forces, which already existed in the world, fulfilment.

Such a liberal view is the forerunner of President Wilson's approach to the problem of international peace, and exists in a number of other interpretations, notably that of Norman Angell in his influential book *The Great Illusion.*

The functionalist explanation of international politics should not be confused with the kind of structural-functional theory discussed in the earlier part of this study, although they share a number of concepts.[60] Both place emphasis on the contribution made by a functional component to the maintenance of some entity. The ideas of feedback and of systemic relationships, characteristic of systems theory, also exists in functionalism. However, as will be seen, the functionalist argument is partly hypothetical and partly interpretative, and lacks the rigour of structural-functional theory. The major assumption of what will from now on be called functionalism is that the modern industrialised state is incapable of sustaining economic growth, or of maintaining its existing economic structure, through its own efforts. It is therefore forced into a number of interdependent relations with other countries. This set of relationships exists beyond the control of individual states, and a new corporate authority, capable of regulating and controlling them, comes into existence. The appearance of international organisations in international politics is thus explained as a consequence of a nation's inability to control its own political and economic destiny. Co-operating states are impelled into an international co-operation, initially operating on a diplomatic level, but which succeeds to a new kind of regulative authority. National sovereignty is transferred through the functioning of these modes of authority to a new supranational entity.

Hence the emergence of international co-operative agencies in the nineteenth century, such as the U.P.U. and the I.T.U., is conceived of as a consequence of the necessity for some regulation of international communications. There is, according to the functionalist, a process at work in international relations which is caused by the needs of complex industrial economies and which gradually erodes the independence of sovereign nation-states.[61] This is linked to a prescriptive value, that is, if all states were industrially advanced, then the area of international integration would be extended and the ensuing state of interdependence would inhibit conflict and international violence. The economic development of underdeveloped countries, and the welfare function of international organisations, are thus related to the functionalist argument. This aspect is considered elsewhere in this study; the main application of this argument has been to relations between countries with more or less parity in their economic and social development. In a sense it represents a turning away from the universalist organisation, such as the League of Nations and the United Nations, as the main locus for international integration, with its emphasis on conscious political means of attaining this end, to the regional organisation and indirect means based on economic processes. But the prescriptive end remains the same, that is, the creation of a world community which enjoys the same harmony and relative peace as that enjoyed in the western democratic states. Functionalism in this sense is another way of achieving world peace.[62] Nevertheless, its proponents claim that it is not merely another statement of values in the Wilsonian manner, that is, an assertion of the desirable, but that it is an explanation of reality.

What is the nature of the evolutionary process at work reducing the autonomy of nation-states and which forces them to integrate in a new political entity? The functionalists argue that from an initial reliance on interdependent relations maintained by diplomacy and negotiation, the technical and economic aspects of these relationships will expand into the competitive political area.[63] The nation-state can no longer fulfil its functional needs and so it must turn to agencies which gradually assume more and more of the functions of the state. It is argued that the implications of economic and technical co-operation are such that the political area is directly involved. In other words, once co-operation on this level begins, then the co-operative agency assumes an independence and encroaches upon responsibilities and powers formerly within the province of national governments. The freedom and authority of governments are thus reduced and eventually transferred entirely to a new political authority. Although this is called a process or dynamic, it is essentially the projection of the new phenomenon in international politics, that of the international technical agency, and it is based on the argument that these bodies act as growth points for the new authority. The vehicle for such a transformation is not an international agency, but one which is non-national, controlled by bureaucrats and technical experts who have no national allegiance. The technical agencies, therefore, rather than the diplomatic bodies, form the prototypes for future agencies with greater ranges of responsibilities and functions. The expert, the technocrat and the administrator are the community-builders and the heirs to national authority.

There are, of course, secondary assumptions here regarding the apolitical nature of the expert and of the non-national agency. They are considered to be insulated from national competition and from the intervention of political interests, and to represent a conception of the common good free from international conflict. It is precisely from this freedom from partisan conflict that, it is argued, their utility to the co-operating nation-states is derived. The participating state transfers its functions to such a body, not only because it cannot fulfil them in any other way, but also because such a body is conceived to be politically neutral. The purely international body composed of national representatives is prone to dissension and to useless or impracticable compromises and is incapable of constructive action. Consequently the impartiality of the non-governmental agency is a guarantee both of effective regulation and of a non-involvement in explicitly political conflicts. The delegation of responsibility is not a willing but an unconscious surrender of authority, since the state is concerned for a practical solution to the problems caused by the complexity of its economic relationships. This process is reinforced by the conscious dissemination of values by the new agencies and their promoters, which stress the normative values of co-operation and the notion of community over and above competing national interests. Thus the process eventually culminates in a form of integration in which a new political nexus appears and the nation-state itself disappears. The nature of this new political aggregate is not defined in the functional argument, apart from the assumption that it will exercise political authority and replace the nation-state. Whether it will take a federal or unitary form is in some measure dependent upon whether the participant nations at some point in the process consciously accept federal or confederal union, or whether the evolution of institutions imposes its own logic and influence upon the new political structure. If the former is accepted as a possibility, then it suggests that the governments concerned can accelerate or arrest the process of integration, and this weakens the force of an argument which asserts a dynamic beyond the control of the nation-state. There is, in this, the difficulty of separating a rationalist argument from a hypothesis, and the resultant confusion produces an ambivalence between the notion of an irresistible economic process, based upon theoretical analysis, and the prognostic element in a political forecast, based upon a historical inter-pretation.

The central problem then in evaluating this type of argument, as we have seen earlier in the case of the conflict hypothesis of interdependent relations between states, is that much of it is hypothetical, related to models of economic growth, and much of it is speculative and interpretative and derived from historical referents and empirical argument. There is a predictive element in the argument in that it asserts that the outcome of a historical process will produce in the indeterminate future an integrated international community. Now unless the hypothesis includes a statement of the process in terms of laws, then this is prophecy rather than prediction. We must distinguish between historical interpretation, which includes some speculative statements, and a theory which explains past, present and future according to its own laws, and with some means of empirical verification. Thus while we might agree that there is a relatively high degree of international co-operation in recent history compared with the more remote past, this generalisation cannot be projected into the future without a supporting explanation which is non-historical. In other words, the dynamic asserted by the functionalists, if it is to be more than a rationalisation of a belief in world order, or of the most effective way of achieving economic and social goals, must form part of an explanation which enables predictive statement. The functionalists do not provide such an argument. In its place they substitute the hypothesis that if certain factors and conditions remain constant, then a particular consequence will ensue. If a nation-state is unable to provide for itself, then this provision must be found elsewhere, and the consequence of this is that it then loses its political sovereignty to the agency which fulfils its needs. This is a very general argument, since it does not satisfactorily explain existing phenomena but asserts some form of functional necessity without being able to show how and why a particular phenomenon will result from its fulfilment.

One of the major assumptions of this argument is that interdependent relations between states are the product of a necessary co-operation between developed industrialised states. In another part of this study the nature of international interdependence has been examined and the conclusion reached was that this term really means the dependence of some states upon others. In other words, a hierarchy of states emerges in international politics rather than a collective. Interdependence may mean a loss of independence, but this is not equally true for all states, since some will have an accretion while others a diminution of power. In both cases an individual state is free to break its contractual obligations to other states or to reinterpret them in the light of changed circumstances. The point here is that no real or permanent transfer of sovereignty takes place unless the element of coercion or force enters the relationship. There may be utility in maintaining a commitment and accepting the inhibition on independence which this entails, but this is largely a matter of national interpretation. The argument produced by the functionalists that sovereignty is lost in an inter-dependent relationship is true only if there is no means of retrieving freedom of choice and reverting to independence or to other relationships. It should be remarked in this context that, like the imperialist notion of dependence, this implies a hypothetical notion of 'independence' which applies to all states alike. The loss of national freedom of choice in the past has been due to the absorption of states into a new political structure, or into an empire, and this has rarely been achieved peacefully. Yet the functional notion of interdependence is non-political and consists of economic and technical relationships which impose limits on the exercise of national sovereignty and which cannot be evaded by a reversion to unilateral action. The concept is thus not one of imperial or political hegemony, but of a new kind of political order in which a supranational authority appears. The arrival of this authority occurs when the boundaries of separate national responsi-bilities to their subjects are weakened by, firstly, a sharing in, and finally, an assumption of them, by the new political locus. This would constitute a new phenomenon in international politics.

Changing power ratios and inequalities of resources have long been influences in international politics, and their consequences have been a multiplicity of different associations between states. Different degrees of dependence and of self-sufficiency have existed in the past, but these have entailed a sacrifice not of sovereignty but of independence, and that for relatively short periods. Few sovereign states have disappeared over the last two hundred years and many new states have come into existence. In pursuing its national interests, however these may be defined, the nation-state enters into various commitments, treaties, conventions and other contractual obligations. Its freedom to act, and the formulation of objectives in its defence and foreign policies, may all be influenced by the complex of international relationships at any given time. However, whatever restrictions there may be on a nation's capacity to achieve its objectives, or on the choices open to it, the fact remains that the state is the only autonomous political unit involved in international politics and that non-governmental and international organisations have, in this sense, no independence of their own. Their activities are different, but not distinct, from those of international politics.

The functionalists make a distinction between this kind of international political activity and that which is associated with the administrative functions of non-governmental agencies. The former, it is argued, consists mainly of conflict and the latter of co-operation. While the latter impinges upon the former, it is not conceded that the reverse may happen. It could of course be maintained that this form of co-operation was itself the product of an international political harmony and that its conditions and motivations were thus overtly political. Such conditions are subject to change and are in any case related to local rather than to universal groupings of states. As will be seen subsequently, within such areas of co-operation economic affiliations have been used to strengthen national positions and represent an extension of international conflict. In other words, the kind of economic association actually existing in the con-temporary world, rather than the projection envisaged by the functional hypothesis, is simply another aspect of international politics. It represents a form of discrimination against other states which parallels, and perhaps reinforces, the distinctions made by political associations.

In an attempt to transcend the limitations placed on integration by this predominence of political relationships, the functionalists emphasise the role of the technical body and of the expert. As was noted earlier, their activities are conceived of as being both apolitical in one sense and politically creative in another. Insulated from international politics, they are involved in the creation of a new polity. However, again there is little empirical evidence to support the contention that non-national agencies are so insulated as to be independent of their political context. Technical questions are related to problems of priority and therefore of choice, and any consensus formed in technical agencies is produced by a political process. Experts can disagree over objectives as much as the representatives of national governments. But this point aside, the basis of the functionalist claim is that, however these bodies decide their policies and programmes, this process is independent of national influence and yet itself influences national behaviour. They are thus independent of international politics as such, although they are involved in activities which will eventually transform international politics.

Although there are a number of international and regional co-operative agencies, there are only two which have a political locus. These are the European Economic Community and the Comecon. While the major western developed states are linked in a number of different economic, financial and technical organisations, which are functional in the sense of this hypothesis, there is little empirical evidence to suggest that a new polity is in the process of emerging from them. In the case of the Comecon too little is known of the political concomitants of this economic co-operation to be able to formulate a functionalist argument.[64] It is in the E.E.C. that functionalist commentators see the working-out of their hypothesis.

So far as the E.E.C. is concerned there are two broad interpretations of its political significance. The reasoning which is implicit in the Rome Treaty was based on the common advantages to the signatories involved in the creation of a customs union and market. To this extent the Community can be conceived of as a limited *mariage de convenance* which was created by, and is subject to, the activities and policies of the participants. Sometimes the lack of a withdrawal clause in the treaty is stressed as being significant, but there have been 'perpetual' alliances in the past which proved no more immutable than any other less grandiose association. It is not on legal clauses that the functionalists base their theory of political integration. The other view asserts a political independence in the non-national sector of the Community's activities and projects the development of a polity on the lines indicated earlier.

Before examining these two interpretations, a brief description of the constitution and institutions of the Community would seem appropriate. The main conclusion of the functionalist argument is that a new political locus will emerge from the interdependent area. If we examine the bodies of the E.E.C. on this basis, we should expect to see evidence both of the expansion of the integrative sector and of the appearance of a new authority with extra-national attributes.

Like most declarations of principle in the preambles to international treaties and conventions, that contained in the Rome Treaty is no exception to the rule that a lofty tone and an ambiguous content is *de rigueur*.[65] Perhaps the most pervasive, and illusive, concept in the treaty is that expressed in the terms 'common' and 'community'. The participants are enjoined to inaugurate not only a common customs union but also a common commercial policy, a common agricultural policy and common transport policy, a common Social Fund and a common Investment Bank.

A useful distinction has been made by some commentators between positive and negative integration.[66] By this is meant a distinction between the creation of a form of integration over and above the participating nation-states, and that which merely avoids discriminatory practices between these states. Common policies may thus mean policies which are decided by a common authority, or simply the harmonisation of separate national policies in order to avoid conflict or discrimination. It is the former conception, that of positive integration, which forms the basis of the functionalist argument. The latter may involve the reduction of national independence, but does not reduce or compromise national integrity. It seems apparent from the provisions of the Rome Treaty that it is this conception of 'common' which prevails. The emphasis in the institutional and procedural provisions is upon means, not ends, and this is reflected in the virtual absence of any definition of the substantive content of the policies to be adopted. In other words it is left to the participating states themselves to interpret, and to negotiate, what their conception of 'common' policies will be.

Thus it is to the institutions and to their activities that we must turn for any evidence of functional or positive integration. The national or representative organ in the E.E.C. system is the Council of Ministers, which is composed of nine ministers, one from each of the member governments. These representatives may be the foreign or economic ministers of the nine participant states, depending on the agenda of the Council and on the nature of the proposals submitted to it by the Commission. Decisions taken by this body are made on the basis of weighted voting which is so devised as to give the major powers more votes than the smaller countries. Thus France, the Federal Republic of Germany, Italy and Britain have ten votes each, Belgium and the Netherlands each have 5, Ireland and Denmark have three and Luxembourg only two. Forty-one votes out of the total of fifty-eight are needed to compose a majority provided that at least six states vote. But more important questions, such as applications for membership or a reversal of the Executive Commission's proposals require unanimity, so that, in effect, each state has a veto. In theory apart from these questions, the Council of Ministers can take decisions on a majority basis and impose its will on a dissenting minority. However, although this is the supreme political organ of the Community and is responsible for all decisions taken it can only decide on proposals made by another organ. It does not possess the power to initiate proposals of its own.

This capacity exists in the European Executive Commission, which was described by General de Gaulle as 'an areopagus of technocrats without a country and responsible to no one'.[67] It is certainly true that the fourteen members of this organ lack a country, but their responsibility is to the E.E.C. itself. In effect its main function is the initiation of proposals which, on the approval of the Council of Ministers, then become E.E.C. legislation binding on member governments. In theory it also has independence of the Council in administering the treaty provisions and in planning and administration. If the functional prophecy is to be fulfilled, it is this body which will become the supreme authority in the E.E.C. and the Council of Ministers, together with the governments it represents, will gradually wither away.[68]

There are two other institutions which are non-national in composition; these are the European Parliament and the Court of Justice. The former body has some 142 members, 36 each for France, Italy and the F.R.G., 14 for Belgium and the Netherlands and 6 for Luxembourg. The number of representatives is thus weighted in favour of the larger countries. These members are in effect appointed from the respective national parliaments, but not exclusively from the governing parties. The Parliament observes parliamentary procedures, including the exercise of the right to ask questions of the Executive Commission. It also has the power to dismiss the Commission on a two-thirds majority vote. It has no other powers apart from that of acting in a consultative capacity and clearly does not reflect any broad European party-political consensus. There exist proposals for direct election and for an expansion of its powers, but these are at present in abeyance. The Court of Justice exercises the function of judicial review of the Rome Treaty and the implementation of its provisions, and it has the power to reverse unconstitutional provisions of the Commission and the Council of Ministers.

To restate the functionalist argument, the movement towards international integration is one which involves increased co-operation between states, of which the E.E.C. is one example. From this it is argued that the final goal of political integration is achieved, not by governments agreeing on a formal treaty relationship with each other, but by a process which involves the gradual usurpation of political and economic functions by non-governmental organisations and by technicians and experts concerned with specific areas of co-operation. Modern technology and industrialised economic structures have created the need for this form of co-operation. To relate this to the Common Market, the growth of a bureaucracy and the existence of an important non-governmental organisation, the Executive Commission, means that political integration will stem from their activities. Thus given the integration of areas of social and welfare concern, and of areas of revenue and fiscal control, as a consequence of the earlier economic integration, the process of administration, planning and control carried on largely by experts and bureaucrats will gradually take over the political area as well. From assuming responsibility for areas of policy- and decision-making formerly belonging to national governments, these agencies will eventually take over their political responsibilities.

If this hypothesis is valid we should expect the Executive Commission to have had an expanding role during the more than fifteen years of its existence. Yet if the actual development of this body and its activities is examined, there is little sign of this process. It has not developed into the major authority of the E.E.C., nor has it been much more than a bureaucratic agency exercising delegated powers. The functionalist dynamic has not manifested itself. Why has this not been the case? The crisis of 1965 perhaps affords an answer. In June 1965 the French government began a seven-month boycott of the Council of Ministers. In January 1966 the boycott ended but without the issue being formally settled. This was the question as to whether any agency of the E.E.C., including the Council of Ministers itself, could overrule a member country and impose a decision without its consent. The immediate issue was the establishment of a common agricultural policy, but this was really only the occasion of the conflict and not its cause. The French government insisted that national consent was necessary on questions which directly involved national interests. This was to assert national over Community interests. Decisions could be concluded on common grounds, but where a conflict between states was implicit or actual in the proposals under discussion, then the proposal should be dropped.

At the same time as this conflict involving the authority of majority votes in the Council of Ministers, the French government attacked the Executive Commission on the grounds that it had been making proposals which were not acceptable to the French representatives on the Council. According to the French, the Commission was behaving as if it were independent of governments and was exceeding its mandate. The Commission, the French argued, should consult governments before making radical proposals and should obtain some measure of approval from governments before submitting proposals to the Council. Thus the French government, in insisting on the need for the Commission to consult governments before it exercised its functions, and on the principle of unanimity in the Council, was in effect trying to establish a national veto on any important decision or action of the E.E.C. All the emphasis in the French interpretation of the Rome Treaty was placed on the multilateral nature of the Community rather than on its supranational character. Control over every stage of the Community's activities was to be maintained by governments, any sign of independence on the part of its non-governmental components should be checked, and national interests should be in harmony with any proposed new stage in the development of the Community.

Such a position is clearly incompatible with the development of any supranational authority in the E.E.C. and many commentators have argued as if it were this attitude alone which has frustrated any such development. The French have been stigmatised for their nationalist and conservative attitudes. However, it is doubtful if the other members of the E.E.C. are really so complaisant about Community development as they are made out to be. Perhaps it may be true that the smaller members, such as the Benelux countries, have little to lose by their fusion into a new political entity, although it should be stressed that even for these countries, with their high degree of mutual co-operation and interdependence, this question is still academic. The religious and language questions alone would make a union between Belgium and the Netherlands fraught with difficulties. But in any case the constitutional questions raised by the French were perhaps premature, since as yet few decisions have been taken by majority vote which have left one of its members in a minority position on an issue involving its national interests. In other words, no state has been forced to accept proposals prejudicial, in its judgement, to its policies and interests. Thus the French argument was in a sense academic, since it was really concerned with the question of what might happen in the future if the Commission was allowed to possess independence and if the majority rule was to prevail in the Council of Ministers.

Indeed, it has been suggested by one commentator[69] that the Commission itself has taken a restricted view of its functions and has in any case sought to obtain some measure of preliminary agreement before submitting proposals to the Council. If this is the case, then it reduces the force of the argument that the Commission conceives of itself as having an integrity outside national control. It is the substance of the decisions actually made, and the consequences of these for the Community, which are important for the functionalist argument, not the way in which they are taken. The emphasis on the negotiating activities of the Commission and its contribution to the ethos of a European Community is misplaced if the limits set to this activity by the need to obtain governmental consent are ignored. In other words, the Community advances only as far as the respective member governments want it to, and not how far the Commission would hypothetically like. If there has been no crucial test of authority and competence between the Commission and the member governments, it is because the former body has been circumspect in its attitude. The attitudes of the nation-states thus set the limits for the Commission's activities rather than the other way round. A gradualist approach towards the reduction of these limits would appear to be unproductive in that no real transfer of authority has yet been achieved, and such an approach, in practice, appears to be related more to survival than to growth.

It is often argued that it is the next stage in the development of the Community which is important from the functionalist point of view. But so far the E.E.C. has not moved in the direction of a transfer of national responsibilities in the fields of energy, social welfare, taxation or transport. Only when the Community has a common social welfare system, common taxation, integrated transport and communications systems and so on, capped by a common legislative body, will the sovereignty of the member states be seriously eroded. There is little sign of this happening, and even less indication that the Executive Commission is assuming the mantle of sovereign responsibility.

In their emphasis on the mechanics of economic and technical co-operation, the functionalists tend to minimise the political context of the E.E.C. Apart from utopian dreams of creating a Third Force in international politics through the federation of Europe, there has been relatively less concentration on the political significance of the E.E.C. or on the nature of the political union envisaged as the culmination of the functional dynamic. The preconditions for political union are conceived of as a transfer of allegiance from existing national authorities to the new political locus. Whether this new locus will be the existing European Parliament or some other, perhaps federal, institution is left vague, as is the process of transfer itself. Clearly, there must be some means of transferring the loyalties of peoples at present confined to existing national entities, as well as the transfer of power itself. Specific proposals on this subject have been avoided either through fear of offending national susceptibilities and thus hindering the process, or because of the vagueness of the notion of political integration.

Yet there are two main factors – the domestic political situations in the member countries, and their external relationships – which are relevant to any interpretation of the E.E.C. The argument that these, although temporarily dominant, are nevertheless irrelevant in the long run, is an assertion which has no theoretical justification and which on general historical grounds appears very dubious. It is possible to regard the E.E.C. itself as being both created by, and as external to, external international relationships. So far as the domestic factor is concerned, there is no evidence that the electorate of each member state, as opposed to specific national interest groups, have shifted their allegiance to an external authority. The argument that this is what actually will happen, once it is perceived that there is an external authority, is obviously speculative. To assume that, given the new institutions, they will inevitably do so, is either to deprive them of choice or to ignore the consequences of political controversy on this issue within the member states. All that can be said at present is that it is not a relevant political issue, but that should it become one, the outcome is indeterminate. It has been pointed out by some commentators that some 25 per cent of the electorate of France and Italy, those who vote for communist candidates, have been deprived of representation in the European Parliament.[70] So far as the French electoral system is concerned, this is also true on the national level, given the number of seats obtained by the communist party in recent elections, related to the number of votes cast for their candidates. Whether this sort of political distortion can be maintained in new European parliamentary institutions is a matter of considerable doubt. The functionalist argument in this respect tends either to an overt mechanical conception of politics in democratic countries, or to assume that the conditions for political harmony are already met, even when they are not made explicit. This is to assume what should be established, and to engage in the kind of tautological reasoning which takes refuge in terms such as 'integration', without either closely defining it or rigorously examining all the conditions for its fulfilment.

However, the main contention here is that the E.E.C. is more profoundly influenced by international and domestic politics than acting as an influence upon them, in the way indicated in the functionalist argument. The rebuttal of this assertion lies in ignoring the political world and posing an integrative dynamic which exists outside politics. If the speculative and hypothetical aspects of this approach are deleted, it must be admitted that there is little empirical evidence to support this argument. Yet the E.E.C. exists and it is not lacking in political significance, although this last may be far from what is desired by the functionalists. If the Community is related to the developing pattern of international relationships since the early 1950's, that is, to its political context, then it becomes both explicable and significant. It came into being not only as a purely European response to certain economic problems, but also in response to a profound change in the international political situation. It is in this wider context that the difference in policies and attitudes of the member states falls into perspective. It is perhaps surprising, although explicable in terms of their rejection of politics, that the functionalists have ignored an argument which stresses the rationality of European co-operation. This is the argument of strategic nuclear deterrence which stems from the nuclear balance which emerged at the same time as the genesis of the E.E.C. Of course, to stress the rationality of a particular argument is not to establish either that it is accepted by politicians, or that the reasoning remains valid over a period of time.

This particular argument has been examined elsewhere in this study, but the main point here is that the nuclear stalemate between the Soviet Union and the United States resulted in the disintegration of their respective alliance systems. It was the realisation that the nuclear umbrella held over Western Europe by the United States was no longer effective which led both Britain and France to develop their own nuclear deterrents. The French, after seeking to persuade the United States into a renegotiation of NATO, then withdrew from the material, if not the contractual, parts of the treaty. Britain was not so openly hostile to NATO, but all substantive decisions taken in the defence and foreign policy fields in effect amounted to a recognition and acceptance of the same reasoning which motivated the French. Briefly, this argued that a deterrent is essentially defensive, given the existence of retaliatory capacity after a nuclear attack. A limited war with another nuclear power becomes possible only on non-nuclear territory, and in theory this inhibits any aggression on non-nuclear allies. But clearly, a non-nuclear ally remains a hostage to the intentions not only of a potential enemy, but also to those of its nuclear ally. In other words, if Britain and France's only protection against a Soviet nuclear attack was an American response in the form of an attack on the non-nuclear allies of the Soviet Union, then this was not only a risky security, but it also reduced their political independence considerably.

The defence policies of these two European powers are thus based upon the possession of sufficient retaliatory capacity to inflict intolerable damage on a nuclear aggressor. The problem, however, is that these policies are formulated within the parameters set by the major nuclear powers. The current state of nuclear strategy is one of mutual defensive deterrence which inhibits direct war between nuclear powers, and which, as we have seen, is dependent upon the two conditions of invulnerable retaliatory capacity and vulnerable territory. The implications of this for international politics have been considered elsewhere, but the point is that if these conditions are broken by further technological development, or by an arms race in nuclear weapons systems, then the European powers will have to respond to this change in order to preserve the rationality of their defence policies. At present Britain depends upon the implementation of the Nassau agreement with the United States for the supply of the Polaris missile. The French are developing their own missile system. Both countries produce their own nuclear warheads. Thus both programmes are dependent upon external factors which brought them into being and which are susceptible to changes which the European powers do not control or influence.

It is this situation which makes European co-operation in the nuclear and defensive spheres both rational and politically desirable. For example, if the Soviet Union and the United States seek to change the conditions of nuclear balance through an arms race, in which each attempts to make its territory invulnerable through the development of an anti-ballistic missile system, then the consequence for European security will be disastrous. The cost of such a system is beyond the capacity of any single European state, and in any case the technological limitations of existing prototype A.B.M. systems, with their early warning requirement, limit their use for Western Europe if a Soviet threat is postulated. The solution, given this hypothetical development, would therefore seem to be a European collaboration in a joint nuclear programme and a defensive system which would be European and not nationally based. Such a development would have profound political consequences and, it is suggested, would lead to a European integration far more swiftly than any functionalist programme of gradual integration through non-political co-operation.

This is, of course, speculation, but the point is that political integration, if defined as the aggregation of authority, is more likely to occur through political rather than non-political means. In any case, the rationality of the argument outlined above is as rational as the functional necessity of economic and technical co-operation and is as likely to be accepted by governments. The E.E.C. at the moment represents a minimal level of co-operation between governments, on the basis of non-discrimination, which is regulated and controlled by them and not by any non-governmental agency. If there is to be similar co-operation in the areas of defence and foreign policy, then this will be equally under governmental control. However, since this will be linked to crisis situations and to the very question of national survival, a new kind of political alliance and of authority will have to be envisaged. This raises the question of collective security but in a new guise, since the exigencies of deterrent strategy and of crisis reactions under nuclear conditions impose a new discipline upon political behaviour.

It will be apparent from this analysis of two broad contrasting explanations of international politics based upon economic processes, that the major objection has taken the form of advancing political and historical interpretations of the same phenomena. In a sense both arguments may be regarded as hypothesis and counter-hypothesis, and indeed their genesis occurred at the same time at the turn of the century. But neither the imperialist nor the functional hypothesis is a theoretical explanation in the sense that it proffers general propositions or laws of political behaviour. On theoretical grounds they may be criticised not only for their imprecision but also for the absence of any means of validation. In short, they are really forms of historical interpretation which seek to explain in general terms the phenomenon of international interdependence which was conceived of as being new in international history. They differ in that the former argument interprets it in terms of violence arising out of a new economic condition, while the latter, to some extent accepting the economic argument, asserts the political significance of co-operation and economic integration in creating a new world order.

One may conclude this discussion by saying that, apart from the detailed criticisms contained in the analysis of these arguments, contrary explanations of the same phenomena should make us wary of accepting either of them as a valid explanation.

REFERENCES

1. See, for example, Pierre Renouvin and Jean-Baptiste Duroselle, *Introduction to the History of International Relations* (London: Pall Mall Press, 1968); Raymond

Aron, *The Century of Total War* (New York: Doubleday, 1954); Elie Kedourie (ed.), Introduction to *Nationalism in Asia and Africa* (London: Weidenfeld & Nicolson, 1970).

2. J. A. Hobson, *Imperialism: A Study* (London: Allen & Unwin, 1968), first published in 1902.

3. V. I. Lenin, *Imperialism: The Highest Stage of Capitalism* (New York: International Publishers, 1939), first published in 1916.

4. See D. Mitrany, *A Working Peace System: An Argument for the Functional Development of International Organisation* (London: Royal Institute of International Affairs, 1943); Ernst B. Haas, *Beyond the Nation-State* (Stanford Univ. Press, 1964) pt. I, pp. 3–126; James P. Sewell *Functionalism and World Politics: A Study Based on United Nations Programs Financing Economic Development* (Princeton Univ. Press, 1966).

5. See Norman Angell, *The Great Illusion* (London: Heinemann, 1910).

6. Hobson, op. cit., pp. 10, 167.

7. Karl Marx and Friedrich Engels, *The Communist Manifesto* (1948) *in Selected Writings,* vol. I (Moscow, 1962) pp. 37–8.

8. See Avineri (ed.), *Karl Marx on Colonialism and Modernisation,* pp. 2 ,59 ,70.

9. Ibid., p. 63.

10. On this point, see Avineri, *The Social and Political Thought of Karl Marx,* p. 171.

11. Hobson, op. cit., p. 80.

12. Ibid., pp. 81–93.

13. Ibid., p. 96.

14. Ibid., 6. 77.

15. Lenin acknowledged his debt to Hobson in op. cit., Preface to the Russian Edition, p. 7.

16. Lenin, op. cit., p. 9 of the Preface to the French and German editions.

17. Hobson, op. cit., pp. 46, 106.

18. Ibid., pp. 6–7.

19. For example, Lenin, op. cit., refers to Rudolf Hilferding, *Finance Capital,* p. 15; to Hermann Levy, *Monopolies, Cartels and Trusts,* p. 19; and Fritz Kestner, *Compulsory Organisation,* pp. 25–7.

20. Lenin, op. cit., p. 75.

21. Ibid., p. 92.

22. Ibid., pp. 47–61.

23. Ibid., p. 85.

24. See D. K. Fieldhouse, 'The New Imperialism: The Hobson–Lenin Thesis Revised', in George H. Nadel and Perry Curtis, *Imperialism and Colonialism* (London: Macmillan, 1964) p. 78, and idem., *The Theory of Capitalist Imperialism* (London: Longmans, 1967) Introduction, p. xv.

25. See A. K. Cairncross, *Home and Foreign Investment 1870–1913* (Cambridge Univ. Press, 1953); and A. R. Hall (ed.),*The Export of Capital from Britain 1870–1914* (London: Methuen, 1968).

26. Lenin, op. cit., p. 63.

27. Ibid., p. 83.

28. Ibid, pp. 75, 81.

29. Ibid, pp. 7, 15; see also his attack on Kautsky, ibid., pp. 112–22.

30. Ibid, p. 9 of Preface to French and German editions.

31. See *Treaty of Peace between the Allied and Associated Powers and Germany, Versailles, June 28th 1919* (London: H.M.S.O., 1923) pts. VIII, IX and X, Reparations, Financial and Economic Clauses.

32. Hobson, op. cit., p. 196.

33. Lenin, op. cit., p. 8.

34. For example, see Michael Barratt-Brown, *After Imperialism,* rev. ed. (London: Heinemann, 1970); Magdoff, *The Age of Imperialism;* Kwame Nkrumah,

Neo-Colonialism (London: Nelson, 1965).

35. See Magdoff, op. cit.; Pierre Jalée, *The Pillage of the Third World* (New York: Modern Reader Paperbacks, 1968); Charles P. Kindleberger, *Power and Money* (London: Macmillan, 1970) pp. 77–82; George Lichtheim, *Imperialism* (London: Allen Lane, The Penguin Press, 1971) pp. 101ff; and Tom Kemp, *Theories of Imperialism* (London: Dobson, 1967) pp. 165–74.

36. For example, Isaac Deutscher, 'Myths of the Cold War', in David Horowitz (ed.), *Containment and Revolution* (London: Blond, 1967) pp. 13ff.

37. R. I. Rhodes (ed.), *Imperialism and Underdevelopment: A Reader* (New York and London: Monthly Review Press, 1970); see J. O'Connor, 'The Meaning of Economic Imperialism', pp. 101ff.

38. For example, see Kemp, op. cit., pp. 1–7.

39. That is, until the loss of East Pakistan in 1972.

40. See Magdoff, op. cit., pp. 55–62.

41. For a standard neo-Marxist explanation, see Horowitz, *From Yalta to Vietnam*, pp. 160–81.

42. For an account of this crisis, see Knapp, *A History of War and Peace 1939–1965*, pp. 376–81.

43. The Hickenlooper amendment to foreign aid legislation in the United States requires the administration to suspend aid in the event of a recipient appropriating or nationalising the property of an American company.

44. See Magdoff, op. cit., pp. 177–201.

45. For example, the negotiations in 1972 between petroleum-exporting countries in the Middle East and the major importers moved in this direction.

46. Raymond F. Mikesell, *The Economics of Foreign Aid* (London: Weidenfeld & Nicolson, 1968) p. 194.

47. Joint Report of Committee on Foreign Relations and Committee on Armed Forces of U.S. Senate, Report No. 703, 27 Aug. 1951.

48. For example, see Magdoff, op. cit., pp. 50–4.

49. On this point, see P. J. Eldridge, *The Politics of Foreign Aid In India* (London: Weidenfeld & Nicolson, 1969) p. 38; and J. D. Montgomery, *The Politics of Foreign Aid* (New York: Praeger, 1962) pp. 197ff.

50. See Schlesinger, *A Thousand Days*, p. 158.

51. Ibid., p. 150.

52. See Deutscher, 'Myths of the Cold War', p. 13; and Michael Barratt-Brown, *Essays on Imperialism* (Nottingham: Spokesman Books, 1972) p. 40.

53. Forrestal, *Diaries*, p. 182.

54. See the account of Suez in Macmillan, *Riding the Storm*.

55. See Max Beloff, 'Polycentrism in the West', in Evan Luard (ed.), *The Cold War* (London: Thames & Hudson, 1964) pp. 263ff; and Neustadt, *Alliance Politics*.

56. See Gunnar Alder-Karlsson, *Western Economic Warfare 1947–1967* (Stockholm: Almquist & Wiksell, 1968) pp. 37–49.

57. J. W. Fulbright, *Old Myths and New Realities* (London: Cape, 1964) p. 29.

58. Magdoff, op. cit., p. 21.

59. See also Norman Angell, *The Great Illusion: 1933* (London: Heinemann, 1933) p. 358.

60. See Haas, op. cit., p. 5.

61. Ibid., pp. 86ff.

62. See, for example, Inis L. Claude, Jr., 'Economic Development Aid and International Political Stability', and Harold Karan Jacobson, 'New States and Functional International Organisations', in Robert W. Cox (ed.), *International Organisation: World Politics* (London: Macmillan, 1969).

63. See Sewell, op. cit., pp. 3–28, 245–252.

64. For further information, see Michael Kaser. *Comecon: Integration Problems of the Planned Economies* (New York: Oxford Univ. Press, 1965).

65. For the text of the Rome Treaty, see Ruth C. Lawson (ed.), *International*

Regional Organisation (New York: Praeger, 1963) pp. 109ff; and for a commentary on its provisions, see D. W. Bowett, *The Law of International Institutions* (London: Methuen University Paperbacks. 1963).

66. David Coombes, *Politics and Bureaucracy in the European Community* (London: Allen & Unwin, for P.E.P., 1970) p. 54.

67. See ibid., pp. 72–5, for a discussion of the French attitude.

68. For a discussion of the political role of the Commission, see ibid., pp. 234ff; Leon N. Lindberg and Stuart A. Scheingold, *Europe's Would-be Polity* (Englewood Cliffe, N.J.: Prentice-Hall, 1970), pp. 92ff.

69. Coombes, op. cit., p. 272.

70. Ibid., p. 45.

CHAPTER 8

International Organisation and International Politics

ONE of the most unusual features of recent international history is the appearance of the universalist organisation charged with general welfare functions and with the maintenance of world peace. Its antecedents came in the early nineteenth century with the creation of private international agencies concerned with problems which had a humanitarian aspect, as for example the abolition of slavery or the alleviation of human suffering arising out of wars or natural disasters. The growth of political and ideological movements and of commercial and economic co-operation similarly produced a variety of international bodies.[1] One major reason for this development was that by forming extra-national combinations, influence could be brought to bear more effectively upon a number of governments engaged in, or related to, particular practices. Hence the private international agency acted as a kind of pressure group within a number of national polities, representing some specialised interest or concern which became international in character.

The increase in the number of these organs prompted some attempt at control and definition and status. Control was related both to the apparent need for co-ordination and to the achievement of some measure of recognition from governments. Thus in 1910, a year in which no fewer than 985 separate meetings of private and public international organisations occurred, a Union of International Associations was set up. This body defined an international organsation as a body which had some degree of permanence in the form of a standing representative agency, concerned with international questions and having a universal membership. These broad qualifications require closer attention later in this study. The next important development came with the establishment of the public administrative bureau. This phenomenon was the result of the assumption by governments of the responsibilities of private agencies. A number of negotiations produced international conventions and the international technical agency came into existence. This process of transformation suggests that governments responded to some practical or functional need rather than from a concern for the conscious promotion of internationalism. Of course, not all the private international bodies were absorbed in this way, and non-governmental agencies existed side by side with public bodies. Moreover, additional functions became the province of the newly created public administrative bureaux, and these represented a form of international co-operation brought about by technological innovations and the need for co-ordination. For example, the Danube Commission was created in 1856, the International Postal Bureau in 1863 and the International Telegraphic Bureau in 1865. Most of these bodies fell into two categories; their concern was either for an international waterway, or for the regulations of international communications.

The procedures and functioning of some of these organs anticipated developments in the later universal political organisation. Thus the Universal Postal Union was founded in 1874 and provided for a quinquennial congress of plenipotentiaries, a conference of delegates from national postal administrations, and a permanent international bureau. The conference was empowered to alter the founding international convention, and the practice of majority voting was adopted, instead of the insistence on unanimity characteristic of normal international negotiations. On technical matters relating to the international transit of mail, dissenting countries were forced to adhere to the arrangements adopted by the majority, or to accept impediments to their postal communications as a consequence of refusal.

By 1914 there existed a large number of public and private international organisations which together represented a growing national concern with problems which defied national solution. This concern found continuing expression in the creation of increasing numbers of such bodies, culminating in the establishment of the League of Nations itself. The essential feature of such organs was that of a permanent executive agency, with its own staff, possessing an international competence. Their discretionary powers varied. Some agencies were directly controlled by frequent conferences of national delegates, while others had a considerable amount of freedom to take decisions which then became binding on the national members of the international body. For the most part their institutional arrangements were flexible and closely related to limited and practical functions. Questions of procedure and formal decision-making processes were relatively unimportant and there was no need for complex organisation. The agreement between governments which had brought them into being continued throughout their activities and political conflicts were rare. This reflected both the relatively small number of states which existed at this time and the very limited nature of the activities of these bodies.

It has been argued by some commentators[2] that the success of these international organisations was due to the *ad hoc* nature of their growth and to the clearly perceived need for technical co-operation on the part of the participating governments. Political rivalries were thus irrelevant to their activities and a minimal consensus was present at all times. While this may have been true in the early period of their existence, it would be inaccurate to consider them as being entirely apolitical, since the nature of technological development, and its relationships to defence and foreign policy, make a clear distinction between technical and political questions very difficult. As will be seen later in this study, few international agencies, whatever their nominal functions, have been free from political conflict. Far from acting as an influence in creating an international community, as some commentators have argued, international organisations rather mirror international politics and reflect the controversies which exist in the international system, albeit that this reflection has its own peculiarities.

The next stage in the development of international organisation came with the creation of universalist bodies primarily concerned with the solution of major international problems, such as war and economic and social inequalities, considered to be causes of international conflict. These were extensions of the multilateral or bilateral international conference which up to 1919 had been the more characteristic means of resolving inter-state differences. The creation of what was, in effect, a standing diplomatic conference charged with the avoidance of war was designed to avoid the weaknesses of *ad hoc* conferences convened during crisis situations. A long-term solution to the dangers of general war arising out of crises was sought in the form of a permanent agency composed of all states. The unwieldiness of the *ad hoc* conference, which required some minimal agreement on its terms of reference before it could be convened, was an argument in favour of a new type of international organisation.

Again, as with the technical agencies, the nation-states which participated in creating the new international peacekeeping agency were not seeking to implement an idealistic scheme for world government, but were concerned to repair a deficiency in extant diplomatic practice and to prevent a breakdown in relations which might lead to unavoidable or accidental war. The experience of the diplomacy immediately preceding the First World War contributed to this attitude. The *ad hoc* international conference, and the normal procedures of diplomacy, were not therefore superseded by the new machinery but supplemented by it. There were, it is true, departures from diplomatic practice in the new universalist institutions, and the establishment of organisation and procedures presented new problems, not the least of which was achieving minimal agreement between participating, yet dissenting, states without destroying the institution or prejudicing its future activities. Decisions taken by international conferences are usually achieved through the unanimous agreement of the states engaged in the negotiation. A dissenting state, however, is under no compulsion to ratify or accept the Final Act, and in any case such a conference may not reach a successful conclusion. The fact that some measure of preliminary agreement is necessary before the conference is convened generally provides some guarantee that negotiation will prove fruitful, but the point here is that the participating nation-state remains a free agent and is under no obligation, other than that of political expedience, to compromise its own interests in order to achieve an agreement.

A *standing* diplomatic conference with broad membership and competence is both a forum for negotiation and also a political body. By this is meant that participation in its involves wider obligations than those incurred in *ad hoc* negotiations, and some involuntary restriction of national independence is imposed, by virtue of its organisational form and its procedures. An organisational or quasi-parliamentary form of political activity is the consequence, and political differences between states on substantive issues become translated into a covert struggle to retain or gain control over the institution. In short, the creation of universalist international organisations with broad competence produces a new kind of political activity distinct from that found in the international political context in which these bodies exist. This study is concerned with the examination of the nature of this form of politics. Such an exercise is unusual since it involves the appraisal of a political phenomenon which, in form at least, has institutional characteristics. As was noted earlier, the major distinction between national and international politics is that the latter possesses no polity and is lacking in governmental or political institutions. It is an anarchy in the strict sense of the word. Thus in analysing the universalist international organisation, care should be taken to avoid any comparison with institutions within the nation-state which appear to be similar in nature. Such a comparison is at best analogous, and an emphasis on similarities between, for example, the parliamentary form of debate in the General Assembly of the United Nations, and that of congressional or parliamentary institutions in states, tends to ignore the distinctiveness of the political processes of international bodies. It will be argued in this study that the institutional nature of these organs is more apparent than real and that their distinctiveness lies in a particular kind of political activity peculiar to them.

However, in studying these bodies we find a problem additional to those related to the various forms of explanation discussed earlier. This lies in making an evaluation of the value or ideological element implicit in them. Whatever emphasis is placed on their practice, on their significance as political agents in international politics, or on their organisational relationships, some consideration of their promotional and prescriptive aspects is necessary to make an interpretation complete. The universalist international organisation is charged with objectives which are formally idealistic in principle and which are directly related to the achievement of a new kind of political order. Thus it is necessary to examine not only their political antecedents and contexts, but also the ideas which influenced their constitutions, and which are embodied in them.

Yet in doing this it is difficult to avoid accepting, albeit unconsciously, the values expressed in their foundations, and using them as the criteria for critical analysis. We may or may not conceive of world peace, however this is defined, as a desirable or attainable object, but any study of these universalist institutions cannot avoid its consideration and its definition. If the idea of world peace is left imprecise, or if its formulation in the provisions of the Covenant or the Charter is accepted uncritically,[3] then any evaluation of the League of Nations or the United Nations will be value-loaded. Similarly, any study which ignores the value and prescriptive aspects of these bodies will contain an implicit bias. In one sense all that is done by these organs has a significance on a value level, yet on the behavioural level most of their activities and decisions are essentially political and are related to international conflict and co-operation. They are composed of representatives of states, charged with promoting and defending national interests, yet their constitutions and their formal functions are related to common beliefs and common values. At the same time, the provisions for collective action in support of these values, and the premises on which these provisions are based, reveal an understanding of the political exigencies of the time in which they were formulated. It is therefore something of a problem to disentangle the idealistic from the practical, in evaluating the political significance of these universalist bodies. This is not only a problem of different levels of analysis, but one of choosing an appropriate focus for an enquiry without prejudicing it through dubious or invalid assumptions.

First of all, what are these ideological or value elements, implicitly and explicitly embodied in these institutions? In many respects it is possible to regard the Charter of the United Nations as a continuation of the Covenant of the League, not so much in its political and constitutional provisions, but as an expression of beliefs in the nature of peace and the way in which it should be preserved. Consequently the two constitutions can be considered together in the following discussion, in spite of the very different political contexts in which they were negotiated. As with most kinds of ideological argument, there is a strong prescriptive content in these two documents. Some of the assumptions on which certain provisions are based[4] are derived from past experience and the current political situation, but some of them[5] relate to the attainment of a desirable goal. Of course, all interpretations of political behaviour which are historical in nature depend upon observation and experience: the assumptions of the *Real*-politician no less. The distinction between idealistic and other approaches towards international politics and world peace is that, in the former, peace is regarded both as something which exists and as something which is to be attained. Perhaps this can be explained by the fact that the Covenant and the Charter were formulated after two major wars, that is, when wars to end war had been fought, apparently successfully, and the cause of war, naturally enough, was attributed to the criminal conduct of the defeated powers. Peace was both the victory of the forces of good over the forces of darkness, conceived of as a temporal struggle and as something which was millennial. The Covenant and the Charter were therefore concerned with establishing a mode of conduct for states which maintained peace in the sense of preserving a particular political *status quo,* but were also concerned with the achievement of peace, and this possessed a revolutionary rather than conservative aspect.

As will be seen subsequently, there is an inherent ambivalence in universalist international organisations, in that peace, based upon a particular international polity, is assumed to exist, but the conditions for a permanent peace have yet to be established. The political and welfare provisions in the constitutions of these bodies thus contradict each other in terms of their assumptions about the nature of peace. The argument that the universalist organisation is a formal recognition of an underlying harmony between states, albeit subject to periodic disturbances, was first brought into political practice in 1919 with the negotiation of the Covenant of the League of Nations. This conception owed a great deal to President Wilson's interpretation of the preconditions for world order, although this argument was not confined to the United States and it has had a considerable history.[6] Nor was President Wilson entirely idealistic in his approach to international politics, for his conduct of American foreign policy, as opposed to his more detached view of European political problems, was based upon as 'realistic' a view of national interests as those of his allies. To put it in another way, his conceptions of world peace did not conflict with American interests, and it is even possible to regard them as a rationalisation of a policy which had been followed consistently by the United States since 1812. Thus the view held by some commentators[7] that his idealism was corrupted by the politicians of the Old World is more a testimony to their idealism than to his. Nevertheless, those provisions in the Covenant which relate to peace and world order owe more to the American proposals at the Paris Peace Conference than to any other source.

The American draft proposals[8] began with the statement that international civilisation had failed to produce a fabric of law in the same way as the nation-states themselves had created systems of national law, to which their peoples responded with 'obedience and deference'. But beyond the nation-state 'unmoral' acts were sanctioned by public opinion. It is not clear in this context whether Wilson and his advisers were referring to the overwhelming support given to the Kaiser by all parties, except for a small fraction of the socialist opposition, but this statement was linked to the view that republican democracy was an essential foundation for international harmony, since this type of politics permitted the people to express their genuine views. Thus underlying the extant political systems of the world was a 'common set of ideals' and standards of honour and ethics, etc. This conception of the common man found expression in the Charter of the United Nations where the Preamble begins 'We the peoples of the United Nations', rather than, as in the Covenant itself, 'The High Contracting Parties', the traditional language of diplomacy. Perhaps the Charter goes further than the Covenant in this respect by stressing the rights of the individual: ' . . . to reaffirm faith in fundamental human rights, in the dignity and worth of the human person, in the equal rights of men and women and of nations large and small'. In this statement is found the apogee of Wilson's ideas. Equality in international law is the same as equality in national law; the rights of the individual and of the state are synonymous.

International society is thus seen as an extension of national society, and this last, in turn, is conceived of as democratic pluralist western society with common values, common rights and common law. The great emphasis placed on human rights in the Charter can be explained not only by the value placed on welfare and political rights by the major negotiants within their own societies, but by the moral revulsion caused by Nazi policies towards minorities within the Third Reich. Genocide became an international crime. So great was this revulsion that the sole surviving fascist state, Spain, was debarred from membership of the United Nations because of its political system.[9]

President Wilson thus assumed that there was a world community in embryo, and that all that was needed to realise it was the spread of self-determination and democracy. Yet with the refusal of the American Senate to ratify American participation in the League, and with the rise of Marxism and fascism, neither of them liberal democratic ideologies, the inter-war period was an inauspicious time for the application of this view. Self-determination, as Nazi diplomacy revealed, could serve the purposes of non-democratic regimes, and even in those newly created states freed from autocratic rule, democracy was but a feeble plant.[10] The end of the war saw the collapse of fascism but with the most powerful states divided in their political ideologies. Nevertheless, while the problem of political heterogeneity was avoided in the negotiation of the Charter, with the exception of Spain, there was an assertion of common obligations and values. While, as Alfred Zimmern pointed out,[11] the League assumed the existence of a world community but disregarded the means of establishing its pre-eminence, the United Nations went further. Both organs were concerned with establishing interstate obligations, but it was the United Nations which placed greater emphasis on the need for the preconditions for peace being realised. These were conceived of as economic and social in substance rather than political. Yet they could be realised only within the framework of great-power co-operation, although, as we shall see, the organisations themselves sought through institutional growth to break away from the confines imposed by the international political situation.

In the short term, peace was to be maintained by the great powers enforcing it on the rest of the world. But clearly it was not the small powers who were excessively fond of warfare. If the major powers fell into conflict, how then was world peace to be maintained? On this problem both the Covenant and the Charter were silent. Without great-power co-operation there could be no peace. Both these organisations sought to evade the difficulty by taking the view that world peace was endangered by the irrational behaviour of certain states, and assuming that most states desired peace. A means of restraining aggression should therefore be provided. But the implications of this argument meant that, in effect, every new war would be a contest in which the organisation ceased to be universalist and became partisan. In the event of a major power resorting to war, the universalist organisation ceased to exist. Peace, then, in the short term, consisted of great-power harmony. In the long run the harmonisation of the world was to be achieved by removing all social and economic inequalities between individuals and states and thus removing the fundamental causes of war. Here again the provisions of the Charter went further than those of the Covenant.

Thus while President Wilson argued in his Fourteen Points[12] in favour of the removal of all trade barriers and of the equality of trade conditions for all nations, these were not given prominence in the Covenant. Article 23 prescribed principles which should be observed by nations in their external economic relations. Member states were enjoined to take steps to prevent and control diseases, while the League itself was to exercise general supervision over trade in drugs and arms and to assume responsibility for the prevention of traffic in women and children. The majority of these provisions echoed the previous concern shown by private international organisations for international humanitarian questions. While many of these continued to function as independent bodies, the League acted as a general clearing-house for their activities. But the much more complex and politically sensitive questions relating to international economic exchanges were ignored in the Covenant. No mention was made of trade, of monetary co-operation or of economic development. It is true that the League did subsequently develop a number of co-operative ventures in the general field of economic relations, but these were largely nullified by the breakdown of international trade following the Wall Street crash in 1929. In any case there was no explicit connection between economic and social equality and world peace in the provisions of the Covenant, or in the activities of the League.

It was the Charter of the United Nations which made this connection explicit, for while one of its major functions was the maintenance of international peace, it also had two other functions which were equally important. These were the removal of economic, social and cultural inequalities and the promotion of respect for human rights and fundamental freedom. Chapter IX of the Charter states: 'With a view to the creation of conditions of stability and well-being which are necessary for peaceful and friendly relations among nations . . . the U.N. shall promote higher standards of living, full employment, and conditions of economic and social progress and development.' In this statement we have the full expression of the belief, introduced into international politics by President Wilson, that international harmony was founded on the material welfare of all peoples, and that wars were caused by international political, economic and social inequalities. This is almost a Marxist conception, and it is easy to see how it was possible for at least some minimal agreement to exist on such provisions among the heterogeneous states which negotiated the Charter.

The paradox is that although these ideas permeate universalist organisations, the realist view, that is, the recognition of the primacy of power politics, and the necessity for great-power co-operation as a condition of peace, dominates the political provisions of the Charter; while the idealist view, that is, that peace is dependent upon the creation of harmony through the promotion of the general welfare, is most developed in the economic, social and human rights provisions. Yet the latter are almost totally dependent for their fulfilment on the former. If world peace, in the temporal political sense, is dependent upon the co-operation of the major powers, it is the organisation only which assumes responsibility for the promotion of the general welfare. A division thus exists between the two conceptions, firstly, of the preservation of the power *status quo* as reflected in the extant major power relationship, and secondly, the creation of a new world order, which transcends the former, and which is achieved through the promotional activities of the organisation proper. Clearly, the co-operation of the most powerful states in economic and political terms is necessary for the achievement of the latter, but this implies a surrender of national interests and the abandonment of the great-power balance which preserves the short-term peace. The reconciliation of these two opposed interests, those of the major powers and those of the organisation, presents serious difficulties.

In the Covenant all the states are equal in the decision-making process, but while this provision in theory permitted a small-power veto on League action, more significantly it allowed a major-power veto as well. The Charter of the United Nations was more explicit and made all enforcement dependent upon great-power unanimity. Thus this latter organ based the notion of peace-keeping on great-power co-operation and accepted the notion of inequality in international relations. If a major power breaks the peace, then the organisation is helpless and its role is either that of passive spectator or partisan. An essential preliminary for successful peace-keeping is great-power harmony. This is to say that a universalist organisation is effective only in terms of the conditions which permit it to be effective; in this case when the great powers find themselves in agreement, or in other words when a condition of world peace already prevails.

Of course, if it is assumed that the major powers really desire peace, but that because of misunderstanding, or accident, they may be propelled into war, then there is a case for providing additional machinery to supplement the existing diplomatic repertoire. This, as we have seen earlier, was part of the reasoning underlying the creation of the League of Nations. If, however, this is not the case, and a major power is prepared to risk war in pursuit of its interests, then a power struggle, and not peace-keeping machinery, decides the outcome of the issue in dispute. This so-called realistic principle was tacitly accepted in the League, where enforcement was left entirely to its members, and explicitly in the United Nations, where, as we have seen, enforcement was made entirely dependent on great-power agreement.

If the argument is accepted that international peace-keeping agencies are ineffective if there is a major war or conflict between the great powers, then they can be regarded as being extensions of international politics. In studying them we can see the interplay of temporal political forces and regard them as mirrors for contemporary struggles between states. But it is also possible, in this view, to regard them as providing another dimension to international conflict. From being ostensibly a means of resolving disputes between nations, they become themselves an additional source or locus of conflict. Their complex organisations, their quasi-parliamentary procedures and the nature of their functions and activities constitute a framework within which participating nation-states seek to gain control and to exert influence in pursuit of their several conflicting national interests. To the extent that each member state is forced to accept the peculiarities of this environment in order to achieve some measure of success for its position, there exists a distinctive political process. Thus political activity within these bodies becomes more than simply an extension of external international politics, or of national foreign policies, although these are essential to its interpretation. Over and above the *ad ·hoc* agreements, controversies, factional groupings and bargaining there is an organisational dimension which has its own distinctive processes and its own identity.

This is not to assert that international organisations are political agents in their own right, or that they are supranational agents capable of influencing nation-states, but rather to argue that an explanation which confines itself to a study of national policies within them is incomplete. In other words, these universalist organisations constitute more than the consensus of the day on a particular issue. and they represent a form of political activity peculiar to themselves. The problem lies in evaluating this political identity. Perhaps two main questions can be posed: in what ways do international organs participate in and influence international relations? and in what sense is there a distinctive political process within them? Various answers to these questions have been related to a variety of different approaches, ranging from explicitly prescriptive argument, historical interpretation, and the type of hypothesis discussed in the first part of this work. We can distinguish between a value-prescriptive interpretation, which consciously promotes the involvement of international organisations in the creation of a particular type of normative order; systems and functional theories which seek to explain on a scientific basis the relationship between the political processes of these organs and the international political system; and various methods and techniques which seek to offer partial explanations of some of the political phenomena within the organisations themselves.

It was said earlier that one of the difficulties in evaluating the political significance of international organisations was that of making a clear distinction between the values implicit in their constitutions and nominal functions, and their nature as political phenomena. It is possible to examine them in value terms not only in the sense of their effectiveness in promoting 'United Nations' principles, but also in terms of their relationship to the promotion of a particular kind of political system, or the propagation of particular political and social ideas. For example, some commentators[13] have been concerned with the question as to how 'effective' the United Nations has been in promoting world peace, or in inducing nations to settle their differences by peaceful means, in inculcating the observation of human rights, in preventing racial and other forms of discrimination, and in removing economic inequalities. Enquiries of this kind are fraught with difficulties, not the least being the definition of concepts such as 'freedom', 'aggression', 'equality', 'development' and 'peace' which are essential to any evaluation which is related to normative principles.

The absence of general agreement on such concepts is indicated not only in the literature, but also in the United Nations itself. Thus the prolonged debate over the adoption of two covenants on human rights revealed fundamental disagreement on specific questions. The Commission on Human Rights succeeded in drafting two international covenants in 1954, but for the next ten years the General Assembly engaged in protracted wrangling over the substantive articles.[14] Although agreement on the main parts of these covenants was reached by 1965, there remained considerable disagreement upon the most important clauses relating to implementation. Similarly, the attempt to define 'agression' undertaken by a special committee[15] set up in 1953 ran into major difficulties occasioned by differing national positions on what constituted aggression. Adjournment followed adjournment and the question was allowed to lapse into desuetude. The permanent officials of the United Nations, who might perhaps be expected to take the lead in defining, or at least promoting, a United Nations position on such questions, have generally chosen to take the path of accommodation in seeking to avoid controversies between member states.

However, this study is concerned with explanations of international organisations as political phenomena rather than with prescriptive interpretations, and the main question to be considered at this point is the nature of theoretical and hypothetical approaches to the study of these organs. There are perhaps two general hypotheses which either provide a specific explanation of international organisations, or which subsume them within a wider explanation of international and national politics. The first, that of systems theory, has been discussed at length earlier in this study, while the second, that of functional theory or functionalism, will be considered later on. Without going over the ground covered at the beginning of this work, it will be apparent that international organisations, like any other political phenomenon, are susceptible to a general systems approach. If we refer back to M. A. Kaplan's analysis of international systems we can see that one of them at least, the universalist international system,[16] corresponds very closely to a political system in which a universalist international organisation such as the United Nations has assumed political functions and responsibilities which directly influence national behaviour.

As he puts it: 'The Universal international system conceivably could develop as a consequence of the extension of the functions of a universal actor in a loose bipolar system.'[17] The United Nations is conceived of, in this respect, as a 'universal actor'. Such a system is characterised as being 'integrated and solidary', possessing decision-making bodies which 'will operate formally and for some important functions at least, will constitute the ultimate authority'.[18] It also possesses administrative officers who, although appointed by the participating nation-states, owe their allegiance directly to the system. Significantly, one of the conditions for the existence of such a system is the acceptance by the nation-states of rules which inhibit their recourse to violence.[19] Thus a state of world peace is a prerequisite for the universal system. It is a necessary condition for its existence that states accommodate the pursuit of their interests to the maintenance of the basic rules of the system, and the consequence of this is a feedback between the values and decisions of the universal actors and the behaviour of the states themselves, which further reinforces the integration of the system.

Moreover, according to Kaplan, such a system, consisting as it does of universal actors with nation-states acting as sub-systems, may be transformed into a hierarchical international system which loosely corresponds to the notion of a world state. In other words, an international system, in which there is a duality between nation-states and universal actors, with the latter acting as the locus of the process of integration, may evolve into a system in which the nation-states disappear as 'independent political systems'.[20]

What relevance has this type of theorising[21] to an explanation of international organisations as political phenomena? It was noted earlier that models of this kind tend to ignore the process or political dynamic which creates or maintains the system. The universalist system is one in which organs such as the United Nations exercise an influence upon nation-states, these last accepting a form of self-restraint upon their actions and policies in order not to disturb the 'system'. It is clear that such an analysis concentrates upon elucidating rules which are considered to be optimal for the existence of the system, rather than on establishing hypothetical generalisations about behaviour itself. We are not told why, for example, nation-states accept limitations on their sovereignty or on their independent action. It is simply asserted that in order for a universal international system to exist, such limitations are necessary preconditions. This is to describe rather than to explain. As we shall see subsequently, while it is perfectly possible to describe in systematic terms the activities of international organisations, such a description does not provide an explanation. In this more limited sense of 'system', the relationships between the various organs of the U.N. complex and their decisions and activities may be traced, but unless the United Nations as a whole is described as a 'political' system in the sense used by Easton, such an examination has no theoretical grounds. If indeed the latter meaning is used, then such an enquiry is open to the same objections which were raised in the early part of this work, namely the vagueness of the organising concept of 'polity', and the absence of any general propositions governing the relationships between the asserted variables which can be used to provide empirically testable statements about behaviour. On empirical grounds it is difficult to conceive of the United Nations as possessing 'authorities' which 'allocate values'. Thus the use of systems analysis for the internal workings of the U.N. 'system' really means the use of a new kind of terminology dependent upon historical interpretations and generalisations, or else provides an extended analogy derived from the natural sciences.

But in any case, as Kaplan himself points out,[22] there is no direct correspondence between his model of a universal international system and empirical reality. The model is therefore not an explanation of the United Nations as an extant political phenomenon in international politics. It is clear from the model which Kaplan actually applies to international politics, that of the loose bipolar system,[23] that the United Nations is not a 'universal actor', nor is it possible to ascribe to it any significant role in this particular international system. Thus the United Nations would appear to be anomalous in any system approach either applied to its external or to its internal relationships.

If we turn to the other general hypothetical approach, that of functionalism, we can see that although it is related to systems analysis in adopting some of its concepts, notably that of feedback and integration, it differs in that it is concerned far more with processes than with structure. As was pointed out, Kaplan did not concern himself to any great extent with the process by which his model system came into existence, other than by stating what he considered to be the optimal terms for its survival. While he envisaged the universal actor as providing 'authority' and 'allocating' norms and values to national actors, and thus possessing some of the functions and attributes more usually attributed to governments, he is not concerned with the process of the erosion of sovereignty central to the functionalist hypothesis. Such a transfer of authority is presumed to have taken place in order for the universal international system to have come into existence.

The functionalist hypothesis[24] asserts that international organisations have emerged in response to the 'needs' of modern industrialised states. It points to the growing interdependence of states and the consequent need for some form of international regulation of their relationships. No state is in a position to pursue a policy of political and economic autarky in the modern world; hence the proliferation of international organisations following the transformation of economies by the industrial and technological revolutions in the nineteenth century. Such an interpretation thus asserts a gradual erosion of national independence, produced by the ever-increasing need for industrial societies to co-operate, in order to maintain their rate of economic growth and to maximise their industrial capacities. This argument is linked to a prescriptive value, closely related to that found in universalist organisations and referred to earlier. This is the argument that if all states were to advance industrially, then international co-operation through a recognition of the interdependence of industrial economies would prevail over temporal political conflict, and a genuine and lasting international community would appear. Thus one aspect of the activities and functions of international organisations – the welfare function – is specifically linked to the hypothesis of functional development. More generally, all specialised agencies concerned in various aspects of international co-operation help to promote a growing interdependence and fulfil functions which cannot be fulfilled effectively by bilateral or unilateral national agreements and actions.

This view has been examined elsewhere. Its proponents take a reduced view of the significance of universalist organisations in this respect, on the grounds that they are dominated by the contemporary political struggle, and hence are unable to exercise an integrating influence upon inter-state relations. The United Nations is considered to be a source of conflict rather than a means of resolving it through functional integration. The functionalist argument as we have seen earlier, is directly related to a wider theory of international economic and political relations.

If these two hypothetical 'explanations' are rejected as providing a general approach to the study of the political significance of universalist international organisations, how can they be evaluated? What can be said, in what terms and on what grounds, about their nature as political organs and their relationship to international politics? Any alternative explanation which is not explicitly ideological or value-based will be historical in nature, and will take the form of selection and interpretation from the record of the activities and decisions of these bodies. To return to the two questions asked earlier, we are concerned with evaluating the political significance of these organisations in terms of the way in which they participate in, and influence, international politics, and with whether there is a distinctive political process within them. Without begging these questions by adopting narrow assumptions, we can begin by examining the way in which these bodies have exercised their responsibilities as laid down in their constitutions, and the consequences for their institutional and political development and for international politics in general.

How has the United Nations exercised its peace-keeping function? It was said earlier that the essential condition for the involvement of the United Nations in a political conflict is that of great-power unanimity expressed in the Security Council. It is important to realise that while the competence of the Security Council, according to the Charter, was virtually unlimited once it was seised of a dispute or of a situation affecting the peace, it was not anticipated that it would be involved automatically in every international dispute. Thus Article 33 states that the parties to a dispute shall '*first of all* seek a solution by negotiation, enquiry, mediation, conciliation, arbitration, judicial settlement, resort to regional agencies, or arrangements or other peaceful means of their own choice'. In this sense the United Nations was the last rather than the first resort for states seeking a peaceful solution for their conflicts. If they could resolve them without violence outside the organisation, then this by no means denigrated it. So far as the peaceful settlement of disputes is concerned, the United Nations was an additional facility which could be used or not, according to the desires of the disputing states. In this context it should be pointed out that the World Court has no powers of compulsory jurisdiction in any international dispute. It can adjudicate only by the consent of the disputing parties.

The difficulties arise with conflicts which either involve the major powers, or where the disputants are unwilling to submit their quarrels to external arbitration. If peace-keeping and the prevention of war by the settlement of disputes are dependent upon great-power unanimity, then this is as true outside the United Nations as inside it. The assumption behind this conception of the role of the organisation is that of the great-power concert. But should they be in dispute, then the same powers who find themselves in discord outside the United Nations are in effect being asked to settle in it what cannot be settled outside it. It was recognised by the framers of the Charter, and for this particular provision these were the major powers themselves,[25] that no United Nations decision involving peace-keeping could be made binding upon a great power without its consent. Hence this meant the provision for a veto in the decision-making procedures of the Security Council. The United Nations can be used, or not, to settle disputes, but if the condition for their resolution is great-power unanimity and this actually exists, then this means in effect that there is no dispute, and if recourse is made to the United Nations this merely ratifies a pre-existing agreement. If, alternatively, there is an irresoluble great-power conflict, then the United Nations is helpless, unless the Security Council and its veto provision are circumvented. The only conflicts which can therefore involve the Security Council are those between small powers. This is the constitutional position, in spite of the ambiguity in the Charter provisions relating to peace-keeping.

However, the major powers who created the United Nations failed to maintain their war-time co-operation and consequently the Security Council has not emerged as the dominant organ, nor has it undertaken much in the way of either peaceful settlement or enforcement. In effect a *de facto* change has occurred in the division of responsibilities between the Security Council and the General Assembly. This has been due to the attempt of the United States and its allies, in the early years of the United Nations existence, to use it as a partisan in their conflicts with the communist countries, and to the subsequent predominance in the United Nations of the small unaligned nations. Even before the Uniting for Peace Resolution of 1950,[26] the General Assembly had been used in order to exert political influence in situations which involved great-power confrontations. As Inis Claude[27] points out, it was the General Assembly which assumed responsibility for the Spanish and Greek problems in 1946 and 1947, and it was concerned also in the Palestinian dispute. The South Korean elections of 1947 and the recognition of the legitimacy of the 'Republic of Korea' were similarly the subject of General Assembly resolutions.[28] It was the Korean war itself which saw the United Nations actually engaged as a participant in what was conceived of at the time as a confrontation between the western states and communist aggression. The return of the Soviet Union and its allies to the Security Council and the other U.N. organs, after their abortive boycott on behalf of the representation of the People's Republic of China, resulted in the transfer of the Korean question to the Assembly and to the adoption of the Uniting for Peace Resolution. This gave the General Assembly direct responsibility for peace-keeping in the event of the absence of unanimity in the Security Council.

The shifting of major responsibility for peace-keeping from an organ which operated on the principle of unanimity, to one which took decisions on the basis of a two-thirds majority, amounted to a *de facto* revision of the Charter principle which stated that great-power agreement was necessary for the resolution of international conflicts. The division of responsibility between the major organs of the United Nations, although ambiguous in the letter, was clear in spirit. Thus while Article 10 empowered the Assembly to discuss any matter, provided that it was not at the same time being discussed in the Council, and Article 11 permitted it to consider questions related to peace and security, it was clear that decisions which involved action or enforcement were solely the prerogative of the Security Council. It was this body, with its Military Staff Committee, which had the primary responsibility for political action, while the Assembly had only residual and general competence, and in any case could only make recommendations. Of course, reference to the 'spirit' of the Charter is open to any disgruntled state anxious to interpret provisions in the light of its own interests, but in this instance it is difficult to see what justification there was in the Charter for an infringement of the unanimity principle.

It would seem that the framers of the Charter expected the Assembly to be concerned with economic, social, cultural and human rights questions, since they gave primary responsibility for policy and decisions in this area to this body. All the other organs of the United Nations concerned with these questions were subordinated to the Assembly and not to the Security Council. Since the issues arising out of the consideration of these general topics affected the general welfare not simply of the participating states but of mankind as a whole, and recommendations concerning them were conceived of as being neither political nor enforceable, majority voting appeared to be reasonable. In welfare terms all states were equal. The confusion of responsibility between the two major U.N. organs is thus also a confusion of function and of procedure. Whether any inter-state conflict, whatever its substance, is resoluble by majority voting is doubtful, as is the distinction made between political and non-political questions, but the transference of questions directly related to great-power interests to a majoritarian organ was a very dubious action and one which was promoted by partisan considerations.

This confusion of function has helped to obscure the real issues which confront the United Nations and to make any evaluation of its activities difficult. Essentially, the General Assembly, with its quasi-parliamentary procedures, and its general competence over all the other organs of the United Nations, with the exception of the Security Council and the World Court, assumed responsibility for all the promotional activities of the United Nations. It was primarily concerned with creating, through recommendation and technical assistance, the preconditions for peace. Such a task was distinct from the temporal problem of resolving conflicts between states, since these last were conditional upon either the states themselves being willing to settle their differences peacefully, or through the use of force, in which case the stronger powers decided the issue. The former task could not be fulfilled without the support and participation of the nation-states, but, in theory at least, it was considered to be independent of their political struggles. Unfortunately the involvement of the General Assembly in the political differences between the major powers resulted in the spread of the conflict into the so-called non-political areas of the United Nations' activities. Whether this could have been averted through the separation of peace-keeping, as opposed to peace-creating, activities, is open to question.

However, while the General Assembly has maintained its position as the dominant organ of the United Nations, the nature of its activities has changed. It has not become less political, but the issues with which it is concerned have ceased to be closely linked to the conflicts between the major powers. It has become a small-power organ and represents small-power interests. The political implications of the Uniting for Peace Resolution have not been realised, and in the main the General Assembly has not been enlisted as a partisan by one or other of the major powers. As will be seen, the major questions with which it has been concerned, for example colonial independence, economic development and human rights, involve conflicts between the small states and the major powers rather than between the latter. To some extent the communist states have identified themselves with the small powers and have thus helped to strengthen their position. So far as the western powers are concerned, their original enthusiasm for transferring competence from the Security Council to the General Assembly has waned at the same rate as their control over the latter body. The Assembly has not been able to return to its Charter role of promoting the general welfare in order to achieve a lasting peace, mainly because this activity has been conceived of by the small underdeveloped countries as being the promotion of their interests, and these have been in conflict with those of the western developed countries. In other words, a new conflict has arisen within the United Nations which, although related, is distinct from the major conflict between the great powers which dominated international politics since its foundation. The main point here is that the United Nations is not primarily concerned with peace-keeping, in spite of the attempt made by the western powers to make it a partisan in their struggle against the communist states. The voice which the General Assembly can have on issues involving world peace is necessarily limited, and this would be generally true whatever procedural or organisational changes were instituted. Its vitality in this respect is derived from the policies and influence of one or more of the major powers. If these powers were unanimous, then clearly this would be true whether the United Nations existed or not. Similarly, if they are divided, then the United Nations either becomes a partisan or remains irrelevant to the conflict.

Some commentators have argued[29] that while this may be true for great-power conflicts, nevertheless the United Nations and the General Assembly have a viable peace-keeping role. They point to the precedents set by the operation of United Nations forces UNEF, ONUC and UNFICYP. It is conceded that the course of the Korean war would have been much the same if the United Nations had not existed and that the responsibility for both the fighting and the peace-making fell upon the American government and not on the 'majority' of the General Assembly. At the same time, it is argued, there are some situations involving breaches of the peace in the world which do not directly involve the major powers but which are irresolvable by any means short of United Nations intervention. The flaw in this argument is that the United Nations has not in the cases cited above involved itself in peace-keeping, nor can they be taken as precedents for a continuing United Nations function. The tendency in such arguments is the reverse of that which asserts the failure of the United Nations as the result of the disagreement of its members. In other words, credit for the 'settlement' of these crisis situations, if this term may be used, has been given to the U.N. force itself, rather than to the states which agreed to create it, or to the circumstances which imposed constraints upon unilateral intervention or the use of force. The assumption in such arguments is that a U.N. force, whether permanent or *ad hoc*, can act as some kind of panacea applicable to situations akin to that of the Middle East in 1956 or the Congo crisis of 1960. In reality, the limitations of these forces, and the very restricted circumstances in which they can be used, makes each such United Nations operation unique.

A brief examination of these situations[30] will give some general indication as to the nature and scope of a United Nations peace-keeping operation. With the exception of the Korean intervention, the use of a United Nations force has been on the basis of great-power agreement, either tacit or explicit, rather than on majority approval as expressed in the General Assembly – although this must be qualified by saying that the latter has been relevant in certain cases. However, the point is that the necessity to obtain a consensus in the Security Council, or to obtain agreement informally outside it, was the essential element in the cases of U.N. intervention in Suez, in the Congo and in Cyprus. Clearly, the circumstances in which this agreement is forthcoming will have very narrow limits. The balance of gain or loss in using the United Nations in this way must be conceived of as being favourable for all the major powers. Once this consensus has been achieved and a United Nations force created, or a presence established, then the problem still remains of determining the scope and direction of its activities. This is the major problem, because it is here that the permanent members of the Security Council have greatest opportunity for disagreement, and for manipulating the force to serve national objectives.

No major power is in favour of relinquishing this task to the Secretary-General, and his independence is in any case limited by the logistical and other material problems of peace-keeping operations. The international and politically neutral character of the force is in jeopardy, once it commences operations and becomes subject to changing circumstances and to the attempts made by various states either to use it to serve their interests, or to prevent other states from doing so. All the problems which have beset

United Nations forces in the past – their command, financing, composition and mandate – stem from the reluctance of the members of the United Nations to surrender control and influence over their activities after bringing them into existence.

The Secretary-General, who is the nominal commander of such a force, is in the difficult position of being dependent on political support in the United Nations, while at the same time exposed to attack from dissenting states. The mandate on which he acts is also ambiguous because of the very fine limits of the agreement which created it and the compromise on which it is based. Under such conditions, since he is unable to be independent, he is forced to choose his dependence in the interests of the organisation which he serves and of the success of the operation. This has meant in the past a reliance on the material and political support of the United States, and the consequence of this has been a close identification of peace-keeping operations with American foreign policy. This naturally reduces even further the confidence of those states opposed to United States policy, and lessens the possibility of such a force acting as a precedent for future United Nations operations.

It is when the function of the peace-keeping force is considered that we can see how very limited its role really is. It has no place in the settlement of disputes between major powers. It has been used in situations which were either insoluble by other means, or which involved greater risks in the event of a unilateral intervention than through U.N. action, or where nominal agreement existed on resolution, but where the need for face-saving occurred. Thus the case of Suez was one in which strong American pressure had persuaded Britain to withdraw and the United Nations was used as a device for enabling the withdrawal to occur,[31] with the minimum of political instability and embarrassment to an ally. The dominant influence in this crisis situation was undoubtedly American. The United States was concerned with the multiple problem of extricating Britain, France and Israel from their difficulties without either antagonising the Arab states, damaging Israel or allowing the Soviet Union to intervene. Once the cease-fire had been accepted by the parties concerned, then the United Nations was used as a means of reducing the tension and restoring the *status quo*.

The Congo situation was of a different order, since it was not the actuality of international conflict but its possibility which was the problem both for the United Nations and for the major powers. It is true that the Congolese government had appealed to the United Nations for help in restoring internal order, but it was not axiomatic that the United Nations should necessarily respond to this request. Governments and factions have appealed to the United Nations before and have been ignored. In this case there was a strong possibility that a civil war might result in which the Soviet Union and the United States found themselves supporting rival factions. Thus the situation was unusual in that the major powers, including the Soviet Union, formally agreed to send a United Nations force to the Congo on the basis of a Security Council resolution.[32] This apparent harmony did not last very long, and the continued involvement of the United Nations force depended upon the support given to it by the United States and the majority of the smaller powers. At various stages the Soviet Union, France, Britain, Belgium and a number of African countries expressed their dissatisfaction with the conduct of operations. The continued political and material support given to ONUC by the United States may be explained by the desire of the American government to insulate the Congo from external intervention and to prevent the Soviet Union from acquiring political influence in Africa.

Finally, the involvement of the United Nations in Cyprus had unusual features, since two nominal allies proposed to make a violent intervention in the territory of an independent state, in defence of their respective ethnic affiliations. The government of Cyprus appealed to the Security Council on the grounds that an invasion by Turkey was imminent. Although France, the Soviet Union and Czechoslovakia demurred on certain provisions, the Security resolution appointing a mediator and establishing a peace-keeping force was adopted unanimously.[33] As in the earlier cases, the United States was anxious to avoid a direct conflict between her two Eastern Mediterranean allies and to prevent any consequent opportunity for Soviet influence in this area. United Nations action was thus consonant with these objectives of American foreign policy. The communist states objected to their exclusion from any influence or control over the proposed force, but their position was not very strong in a conflict which involved two states both committed to anti-communist alliances.

Such crisis situations may well recur given the prevalence of United States policy and influence, and the consequent interest in political stability and the containment of communism. This is one, at least, of the parameters which has governed the use of United Nations peace-keeping forces. It may be that the indeterminacy of unilateral intervention in pursuit of national objectives will encourage the use of the United Nations as some kind of political insulator in areas where great-power interests are not pre-eminent. But the factor which operates in such cases is the inability of a major power to separate conflicting policy objectives, combined with the general inhibition on war between the major powers imposed by conditions of nuclear balance. This aspect has been considered elsewhere in this study. The point here is that these are factors conditional upon the policies pursued by the major powers. The use of the United Nations in this respect is related to an attempt to make it work for the national interest, but in order to do so, some form of compromise, and possibly loss of control, is necessary to persuade other states to agree to its use. On balance there have been relatively few occasions on which the United Nations has exercised its peace-keeping function, and in the cases cited above it has been the United States which has been most influential in the conduct of operations.

The accretion of influence expected by communist countries through participation in these peace-keeping activities has not been forthcoming, and their attempt to exert control over the Secretary-General through the 'troika' proposal failed to obtain support.[34] Consequently their attitude towards future activities of this sort cannot be regarded as favourable. However, without speculation, it can be said that United Nations peace-keeping is an *ad hoc* activity and is closely related to the general international environment. Its scope and nature are thus dependent upon, and intimately related to, international politics rather than creating a new kind of political accord.

This is not to denigrate the activities or the functions of the United Nations, for, as was pointed out earlier, universalist organisations reflect political realities so far as their peace-keeping or political role is concerned. When they do not, as was the case for the League of Nations during the 1930s, then they are ignored. Although their role in this respect is peripheral, the utility of a standing diplomatic conference in which the representatives of all states, including those of disputants, are in permanent contact, has certain advantages. The first suggestion that the Soviet Union was prepared to negotiate over the Berlin blockade came from a Soviet diplomat in the United Nations,[35] and more recently both the United States and the Soviet Union used the United Nations as a forum for the discussion of their respective positions during the Cuban missiles crisis of 1962.[36] In this sense the United Nations is never wholly irrelevant to international political situations which involve great-power conflict.

Its use in this way is entirely dependent upon the will of the potential or actual belligerents. The claim of those states not directly involved in such disputes to be concerned in their settlement is a weak one. The former Secretary-General, U Thant, has argued that the major powers should be prepared to submit to the judgement of the majority of the members of the General Assembly. As he put it, 'we must eventually arrive, in the affairs of the world, at a state of political maturity in which it will be considered statesmanlike rather than weak, for even a great country to alter its course . . . in deference to the will of the majority'. Yet if the small powers have had any influence in this respect, it is because of their utility as allies in the contests of the great. Such a utility is a product of the foreign policies of the major powers, and should these change, then the political significance of the small powers may well diminish. Without too much speculation, the restraint on the great powers imposed by the strategic nuclear deadlock may give the United Nations an enhanced political significance in conflicts which involve small states. Its unique nature as a permanent organ for international co-operation is of importance in a world in which general war has become irrational for the first time in human history. But even if this is indeed the case, it is unlikely that majority decisions of the General Assembly which exclude the most highly developed states will have much influence on international politics or upon the policies of these countries. Moreover, it can be argued that one of the effects of this changed strategic situation is the diminished importance of the small unaligned countries in great-power policies and a consequent reduction of their influence within the United Nations.

At the same time the weakness of the United Nations in the event of a great-power conflict within the organ itself is exemplified by the so-called 'dues issue' during the 19th session of the General Assembly.[37] The crisis which followed the American attempt in October 1964 to implement Article 19 against twelve countries, including the Soviet Union and France, both permanent members of the Security Council, resulted in the virtual suspension of the activities of the General Assembly. This deadlock, in which the Soviet Union and France were faced with the possibility of losing their votes, was eventually broken in August 1965 by the United States dropping its attempt to force them into paying their share of the expenses of UNEF and ONUC. While it is true that these countries had exposed themselves to this sort of attack, it appeared inconceivable to them, and indeed to observers at the time, that the United States and a majority of the members would indeed force them to make a choice between paying dues, which they conceived of as being illegally imposed, since they were based on a General Assembly rather than a Security Council resolution, or losing their votes.

On the face of it, this crisis seemed to be of a constitutional nature, related to the continuing problem of the deficit in the United Nations budget but also related to the question of strengthening the western position by forcing the Soviet Union and France to accept the financial consequences of peace-keeping operations established by majority voting. Yet this construction does not explain the sudden withdrawal of the proposal by the United States, nor the obvious reluctance to force it to a vote. Had a majority vote been achieved on this question, then, effectively, it meant that the Soviet Union and France would leave the United Nations. There is no evidence that this is what the United States and Britain wanted in making their proposal. A more plausible explanation can be found in terms of the pursuit by the American administration of a more limited objective, closely related to their policy towards South Vietnam.

In the context of the decision taken in 1964 to make a large-scale military intervention in South Vietnam and to make heavy air raids on North Vietnam early in 1965, American diplomacy was concerned throughout the late summer and autumn of 1964 with removing political opposition, at home and abroad, to the implementation of this policy. The point, so far as the United Nations is concerned, is that this consideration on the part of President Johnson and his advisers prompted the most serious crisis in its existence. It was clear from the failure to obtain a Security Council resolution condemning North Vietnam for its alleged attack on American warships in Tonkin Bay in August 1965 that strong opposition to American policy existed, not only, as might be expected, on the part of the communist members of the United Nations, but was also revealed by ostensible allies, notably France. The question of the non-payment of dues by two chief opponents of American policy was thus invoked in order to neutralise the General Assembly during the critical period when the engagement of American forces in Vietnam became a matter of public knowledge. The compromise formula which permitted the General Assembly to meet, but not to vote, effectively prevented a majority hostile to American policy from emerging in the United Nations and finding concrete expression in the form of a condemnatory resolution, during the period December 1964 to the following August 1965. It ensured that the United Nations was too preoccupied with its own internal troubles to concern itself with the developing Vietnamese situation. When the need for this enforced quiescence lapsed, the dues issue was dropped by the United States and the financial derelictions of the Soviet Union, of France and of ten other countries were quietly forgotten.

The importance of this crisis cannot be underestimated in any evaluation of the political significance of the United Nations, for it testified both to the importance of the United States as an influence within it and to the vulnerability of the organisation to an attack of this kind. In a sense it is a form of non-participation, akin to the boycott of the communist countries in 1950, but with the difference that the chief saboteur in this instance was the biggest contributor to the United Nations' finances. Clearly, the ease with which this state can neutralise the United Nations emphasises its peripheral position in international politics. So far as international conflicts are concerned it is irrelevant, unless the most influential major power and its supporters make it relevant. Perhaps the main point is that influence in this sense relates not to the capacity to enlist the United Nations as an agent of national policy, but to the ability to prevent any development within the U.N. system which appears to be inimical to national interests. It may be that the future distribution of influence within the U.N. will reflect changes in international politics, but whatever these may be, it will be no more independent, and no less political, in exercising its peace-keeping function.

If the political significance of the United Nations role of peace-keeping has been the main focus of attention during its existence, then this is the fault both of its propagandists and of its critics. It was maintained in the previous discussion that the universalist organisation is peripheral to the major conflicts of international politics and that this is reflected in its constitution and in its activities. Yet a clear distinction between economic, social and political questions is not easy to make. This is not only because of the international implications of the so-called 'non-political' functions of the United Nations, and their connection with competing national interests, but also because of the decision-making process peculiar to international organisations. All questions, whether procedural or substantive in nature, are decided by a process of negotiation and mutual accommodation between national representatives, with the secretariat sometimes assuming a mediating role, which is formally ratified by an open vote. As will be seen, each national participant, even where the issues are marginal to the interests of his country, is concerned with maintaining influence in the organisation and with improving a bargaining position which might prove important on other issues more directly related to national interests. Few issues are isolable from this process, from other issues or from national interests. The structures and procedures of the organs in the United Nations system, together with their relationships, constitute a political environment in which compromise is the most characteristic political mode. Thus while the second major function of the United Nations, that of the promotion of the general welfare, might appear to be apolitical, in practice all the activities in this field are closely related both to international politics and national policies and to the political process within the organisation.

There are three main aspects of the economic and social activities of international organisations relevant to this study. The first is concerned with the relationship between the promotion of the general welfare and international conflict. The question here is how far the efforts of these bodies in this area have contributed to the removal of economic and social inequalities between individuals and between states, and thus contributed to world peace according to the prescriptive arguments considered earlier. Although this is related to the second aspect, that of the economic development of underdeveloped countries, it is in the main concerned with the general question of economic co-operation between states, and the contribution made by United Nations organs towards creating a condition of political and economic interdependence in international relations.

The second aspect is concerned with the conflicts between states in the context of the United Nations and their relationship to external politics. Although the Cold War dominated both the United Nations and international politics over the post-war period, this gave way within the former body to a different conflict which has remained pre-eminent. This is the prolonged contest between the developed western states and the underdeveloped countries over the questions of economic development and colonial independence. In many respects this has been the most significant political division in the United Nations, especially since it is in this institution, rather than in bilateral relationships, that its main focus is to be found. It has not only dominated nearly every United Nations organ, regardless of its nominal functions, but it has also been the biggest single factor in promoting the organisational growth characteristic of the United Nations since the early 1950s.

Finally, the third aspect is one which has already been touched on briefly, and that is the relation of the economic and social activities of United Nations organs to functional interdependence between developed countries. This is considered in detail elsewhere in this study.

It was noted earlier that in the constitutions of both the League of Nations and the United Nations there existed the idea that, in some undefined way, world peace could be created by the promotion of economic co-operation between states and by reducing economic and social inequalities. This belief did not find concrete expression in the form of institutions, nor did it find much response in terms of national behaviour over the inter-war period, but nevertheless it persisted and found its apogee in the constitution, structure and functions of the United Nations. Such a view asserted that economic co-operation was both an important reinforcement to international harmony, and a precondition for a permanent world peace. There were, broadly, two major approaches to defining the connection between economic and political relationships. Firstly, the growth of an international economy was regarded as creating a situation of mutual interdependence which made political conflicts less likely, by providing an inhibition on the propensity of a state to use violence as a means of attaining its objectives. Thus the growth of inter-dependent economies, involved in complex trade relationships which were open to disruption through international violence, provided a disincentive to war. This is, of course, a rationalisation which urges the folly of war because of the waste of material and the economic loss involved. But this argument implies that all states share the same rational assumptions and that they are equally vulnerable in this respect. If it is accepted that some states may see an advantage in attempting political suzerainty over others, then the use of a particular pattern of economic relationships as the basis for rationalisation becomes invalid. Change may be sought and expressed in political terms, but the pursuit of power in international politics may be rational, in the material sense, for some states, regardless of the con-sequent disruption of a particular pattern of economic relationships. Short-term sacrifices on the economic level may be made in order to achieve future political and economic gains. Nevertheless, while accepting the fact that unequal relationships might rationalise the use of violence for some states, this reinforces the parallel argument that the removal of such inequalities will also reduce the rationality of war, by making the outcome of such a contest more doubtful, and making the losses con-sequent on war equal for all states.

This leads to the second approach, which asserts trade and economic relationships as cross-cutting political and purely national interests. In this view, trade is an activity which is conducted by institutions and individuals acting outside the direct control of nation-states. Because this activity takes place outside national boundaries, it acts as an integrating force between states. In this sense it constitutes an international interest. When President Wilson urged economic co-operation between states he was asserting something which was neither controversial nor unacceptable to the major powers. But, like other forms of international co-operation, the problem was that if this activity occurred outside the state, there was no collective identity which could preserve a common interest. Thus when elements of instability in national economies appeared, as a consequence of international transactions or of changes within the state, appeal could not be made to an international regulative authority. The only recourse was to unilateral action, and very frequently this intensified the initial instability which prompted it.

While trade constituted a general and international interest, in which the greatest utility came with co-operation between states and an avoidance of political disputes which disrupted it, its economic significance varied for different states. Although individuals or corporative institutions concerned in trade might be said to have a common interest in stability, this is not generally true for all states or indeed for all traders and investors. Nevertheless, the experiences of the 1930s revealed that when trading countries imposed high protective tariffs as a response to economic instability, then the net general effect is a restraint upon world trade and a global shrinkage of markets, thus exacerbating national problems. In a multilateral trading situation, while one state might find a temporary advantage or relief in unilateral restrictions on imports and in a protectionist policy, the other trading partners are forced to follow suit and the net result is adverse for all trading nations. In some respects the sequence of action and response is similar to that found in arms races, and indeed it has sometimes been described as economic warfare.

The alternative to unilateral action was an attempt at establishing some form of international regulation, either through negotiated agreements, or through the establishment of institutions. The problem is that whatever machinery is created, it is essentially co-operative, given the continued existence of the nation-state and its concern for its own interests. In other words, while co-operation appears rational from an international point of view, or in terms of individual trading interests, national reactions can, and do, take an opposite view. A high value on co-operative methods of regulating economic relationships may exist, but this presupposes a continuing interest in co-operation on the part of the participating states. If such a community of interest prevails, then it does so only because there is a common element in national conceptions of their interests. Otherwise, instead of co-operation, national competition asserts itself. Given variable factors of economic change and development, and the heterogeneity of national economies, such a coincidence is *ad hoc* rather than permanent, and economic co-operation is as susceptible to instability and change as political alliances are in the sphere of political relationships. In the 1930s, for example, some states, notably France, rejected moves to reduce tariffs, largely because the French economy was not so dependent on trade as those of other countries. It can be argued that the very slow recovery of French industrial production after the world economic crisis was due to the overall shrinking of world trade, and that French policy was short-sighted in not accepting short-term losses in order to revive it. But where questions of relative advantage occur in international relations, then disparate national responses to changing conditions may be expected. The world economy as such is never in deficit, but nations often are. Moreover, domestic political interests and factors should not be ignored as an influence upon national trade and economic policies. In certain situations governments may be helpless, since a choice of a rational external economic policy may result in political suicide. The emphasis placed upon international regulative institutions as a new form of international economic co-operation should be qualified by reference to the national basis of these organs.

While the League of Nations promoted economic co-operation through *ad hoc* conferences, it did not institute formal functional or technical machinery in this field. Indeed, as its political significance waned, so its economic and social activities flourished, but these took the form of promoting international conferences and meetings between government representatives and officials. There was a conscious avoidance of institutional development, and the view expressed by the Economic Committee and the Secretariat of the League was that international co-operation in the economic sphere could only be grounded on national agreement.[38] It was the function of the League, therefore, to provide a means of communication and to act as a catalyst for co-operation, rather than as its main vehicle. This was in line with the argument that a political consensus was necessary before either peace-keeping or economic co-operation could take place. In other words, the League provided technical facilities and information, but refused to act as an agent. Decisions could not be made binding on states, whatever their substance or nature, unless they both negotiated and ratified them. Such a conception of the role of the international organisation in this respect is reflected in the cautious approach which prevailed in the I.L.O. Even the encouragement of international conferences was dropped towards the end of the League's existence, for a report published in 1942 concluded that 'When applied to complex questions which affected different countries in different ways, and to varying degrees, and to problems affecting the central issues of national economic policies, the method of general diplomatic conference and convention revealed serious limitations'.[39] This was a criticism of the numerous conferences which had been convened over the inter-war period under League auspices, in order to remove restrictions on world trade. All had failed. What was required, according to the Economic Committee,[40] were smaller meetings between interested parties. In other words, a regional approach was being advocated. The political element involved in larger and more heterogeneous meetings militated against genuine agreement.

This conclusion reflected the view that economic co-operation depended on the prior settlement of political disputes. According to this argument:

> That chronic lack of confidence in permanent peace in Europe was really of fundamental importance. It was fundamental because European governments inevitably tended to approach the problem of commercial policy primarily from the angle of national defence and national power; if they endeavoured to enhance the economic welfare of their peoples, to find solutions for economic and social problems. they sought, to combine these ends with the overriding political end and to refrain from policies incompatible with the latter; inevitably their commercial relationships with other countries, and more especially those directly feared, were imbued with the spirit of conflict rather than co-operation.[41]

Thus what was necessary as 'the first essential for the achievement of commercial policies designed to promote trade is the establishment of a mechanism for the preservation of peace so adequate and sure as to create confidence despite antipathies or mistrust'.[42] This view flatly contradicts the Wilsonian argument, for it asserts that economic co-operation, rather than providing the preconditions for world order, can only be achieved through political harmony itself.

The post-war period saw two main developments in international economic co-operation, one reflecting the cautious pragmatic regional approach recommended by this League report, and the other the broad universalist approach. As was noted earlier, the second of these two approaches found its greatest expression in the Charter and organisation of the United Nations. This consisted of an increasing ramification of organs, set up for the most part under U.N. auspices, all with heterogeneous national membership, and concerned with a number of multifarious and overlapping economic, social, cultural and technical functions. But while the United Nations went much further than the League of Nations in this respect, in creating an elaborate structure of bodies[43] concerned with the promotion of the general welfare, parallel to this development were a number of regional groupings composed of nation-states with common interests. Thus international co-operation in this field consisted of the universalist United Nations system on the one hand, and a number of regional or particularist economic associations on the other, of which the western system was the largest and most dominant. Any assessment of the

United Nations system, and its contribution to international economic and social co-operation, must take into account the fact that most regulative and co-operative activities have taken place outside it. Yet the United Nations bears formal responsibility for the creation of conditions for world peace through the promotion of the general welfare and is alone in exercising this function.

It was not anticipated, when the Charter provisions on economic and social co-operation were being negotiated, that the world would break up into a number of fragmented attempts at international co-operation. This development was, in any case, intimately related to the emergence of conflict between the western states and the Soviet Union, and while there were clearly strong economic ties between the former states, it would be a distortion to present them as being independent of the political alliance which was being formed at the same time as these ties found institutional and practical expression. Western economic co-operation, like communist economic co-operation, was closely related to political cohesion, to common security problems and to the Cold War conflict. Only in the United Nations did these opposed groups of states find themselves linked in activities and organs devoted to world economic co-operation. Thus although the economic and social provisions of the United Nations Charter were far more sweeping in spirit than those of the League, it was clear that the primary interests of the major developed countries in the area of economic co-operation lay, firstly, in the reconstruction of their war-devastated economies, and secondly, in supporting a defensive alliance system, rather than in any more altruistic programme of world economic development or in creating economic conditions for world peace.

Nevertheless, the belief that certain economic activities, notably in trade and monetary exchanges, were best regulated through some international agency, persisted. Hence the two Specialised Agencies, the I.M.F. and the I.B.R.D., although part of the United Nations structure, were firmly under the control of the major western states, who were the major subscribers, and the former organ, in particular, exercised a continuing function in controlling exchange rates and resolving the balance-of-payments difficulties of these countries. An attempt was made to establish an organ for the regulation of international trade, but differences between the western and the communist states resulted in the collapse of the Havana Charter, with its provision for an international trade organisation, in 1948. Shortly afterwards the United States organised a strategic embargo on trade with communist countries and prospects of any general agreement on world trade disappeared altogether. Until the United Nations Trade and Development Conference of 1964 was convened, the Havana negotiations were the last to be held between the western countries and the communist states under the auspices of the United Nations. Thereafter regional and bilateral arrangements in the economic field paralleled those in the political field, and the idea of world co-operation lapsed. So far as the western developed countries were concerned, the General Agreement on Tariffs and Trade (GATT) took the place of a universal trade convention, together with the later series of Kennedy Round agreements on mutual tariff reductions. The Coal and Steel Community and the O.E.E.C. (later O.E.C.D.) were created as Western European co-operative ventures, and the E.E.C. and EFTA emerged as regional economic organisations concerned with trade co-operation. The communist countries similarly combined in Comecon, and the non-communist underdeveloped world related to these two economic groupings as best as it could, or sought its own form of economic co-operation.

It is not proposed to go into detail here, either on the more limited forms of regional co-operation, or on the development of the United Nations system of agencies. The former is considered elsewhere in this study, while there is only space for a few points about the latter. United Nations economic and social organs can be categorised into agencies which are closely connected to, and controlled by, the major developed countries, those which are concerned with various aspects of aid and technical assistance for economic development, and finally, those bodies which, although universalist, are concerned with specific and limited technical functions. None of these categories is exclusive, and the general tendency in the United Nations structure has been an overlapping and an extension of activities beyond nominal functional limits, especially in the area of economic development. On the basis of this classification, one might include in the first category the International Monetary Fund, which, as was noted, is concerned with the regulation of currency exchange rates and with problems of monetary stabilisation within the western economic area. Although a number of underdeveloped countries subscribe to this body, the communist countries do not. Similarly, the International Atomic Agency is concerned with the peaceful uses of atomic energy and, naturally enough, is closely connected to the limited number of states which possess nuclear capacity. The Inter-Governmental Maritime Consultative Organisation and the International Civil Aviation Organisation, both concerned with aspects of sea and air communications, are dominated by those states with a preponderance of civil airlines and with large merchant navies. In the main these organs both serve the interests of the major developed countries and are largely controlled by them.

The second category includes a number of Specialised Agencies which were formerly unconnected with the problem of economic development, but which have since become closely associated with it. The oldest of these is the International Labour Organisation, which was founded in 1919 and whose main formal concern, until comparatively recently, has been the improvement of labour conditions in the developed countries. Similarly, the World Health Organisation, the Food and Agriculture Organisation and the United Nations Educational, Scientific and Cultural Organisation were formally charged with functions which were related to the interests of the developed countries, but, as the membership of the United Nations expanded, these bodies became dominated by the underdeveloped countries and their activities were diverted to serve their interest in the problems of development. In this category might be included the International Bank for Reconstruction and Development, which originally was concerned with reconstruction in the Western European countries, but which became more closely involved in financing economic development. Although this body is controlled by the major subscribers, and has pursued a fairly conservative loan policy, it has responded to pressure from the underdeveloped members of the United Nations to the extent of expanding its activities and creating two affiliates, the International Finance Corporation and the International Development Association, which finance pre-investment projects in underdeveloped countries.

Finally, the third category of Specialised Agencies is that of organs concerned with international regulation in some technical field. These are the Universal Postal Union, the International Telecommunications Union and the World Meteorological Organisation. Even in these cases they are concerned in the field of economic development to the extent of providing technical assistance to underdeveloped countries. They are, however, perhaps the most directly functional of all the international organisations, and consequently the least political, both in terms of their policy and decisional processes, and in terms of their significance in international politics.

Unlike the rest of the United Nations system of subsidiary organs concerned with economic and other non-political questions, these agencies enjoy almost complete autonomy. While much of their revenue comes from the United Nations regular budget, and from the voluntary financed appropriations for technical assistance, they are virtually free from control. It is not proposed here, for lack of space, to examine the complex network of control and influence within the United Nations system, but the point is that this freedom from direct control by a central United Nations body was originally insisted on by the major western powers in order to maintain their own position and interests in them. Nominal supervision over their activities was vested in the Economic and Social Council (ECOSOC),[44] a body with restricted membership and, until comparatively recently, dominated by the major powers, rather than by the General Assembly with its universal membership. While the communist countries maintained a boycott of these agencies and United Nations membership remained small, the western states were able to control their activities. However, with the ending of the communist refusal to participate, and with the influx of newly independent states into the United Nations, the major western states lost their predominant position in all the Specialised Agencies, except for the

I.B.R.D. and the I.M.F. This development was echoed in the Economic and Social Council, and a process of devolution of powers and responsibilities began in the economic and social area which favoured the small underdeveloped countries and was encouraged by them. The consequence has been a protracted struggle for control between the major western states on the one hand and the underdeveloped countries supported by the communist states on the other. This has resulted in the transformation of most of these functional bodies into miniature General Assemblies and the exacerbation of competition between them.

However, the main point is that, regardless of the diversity of the United Nations structure of organs concerned with non-political questions, a preoccupation with the problem of economic development and with the interests of the small underdeveloped countries pervaded all agencies. The period of struggle for control over the 1950s was resolved in favour of these states, and while this left the United Nations in a state of organisational chaos, nevertheless a form of coherence existed in a broad concern for economic development. The defeat of the major western powers, however, was more apparent than real, and divisions between the small states themselves appeared after their victory. But in effect, most of the elaborate structure of economic and social organs is concerned less and less with economic solutions to the problem of world peace, and more and more with the local problems of the small underdeveloped countries.

It was noted earlier that the problem of economic development has been linked to the larger problem of creating conditions for a lasting peace.[45] But most wars in the past have been between belligerents of relatively equal economic capacities, and the small states have either been fortunate enough to have their neutrality respected, or have become partisans or victims in great-power contests. Wars in a general sense are conflicts over the question of which state shall dominate the international environment. If this argument is accepted, then it is not easy to see how world peace is achieved through increasing the number of states with economic capacities to fight major wars. This question has been considered elsewhere, but the point here is that the relative economic and social backwardness of undeveloped countries may make them vulnerable to external intervention, but war itself is a product of great-power conflicts, and the source of these lies in their capacity to compete. The small states might constitute the object of their competition, but it is not their weakness which constitutes its cause. A distinction can thus be made between economic co-operation, conceived of as a condition of interdependent relationships between equally developed countries, and economic development. This last, in terms of the activities of the United Nations, and of relations between developed and underdeveloped countries, consists of a kind of tutelage exercised by the former over the latter. So far as the emphasis placed on economic development by United Nations organs is concerned, it is hard to see how its activities are related to linking the promotion of the general welfare to world peace. It would appear that in this sphere, as in the political sphere, the United Nations exercises a peripheral role. But as in the previous consideration of its peace-keeping function, this does not mean that its activities are irrelevant to international economic relationships.

So far as the small powers are concerned, the United Nations represents the only means, outside their own bilateral representations, of applying pressure on the developed countries in the pursuit of their interests.[46] They have thus tried to use the United Nations system to increase the amount of aid and technical assistance, to accelerate the process of self-determination in the empires, to promote human rights in order to eliminate racial discrimination in certain countries, and to improve the terms of trade for countries economically dependent upon the production and export of primary commodities. In the main these states have been uninterested in major power conflicts or in the wider question of international political and economic co-operation and world peace. These have been regarded as the province of the major powers themselves.

Two groups have thus emerged in mutual opposition within the United Nations on issues connected with the promotion of the general welfare. These are the underdeveloped states, supported by the communist countries, and the western developed states. There are of course member states in both categories whose attitude on economic and social questions is either equivocal, or sympathetic to the 'other side'. For example, the Netherlands, although a major developed country, has adopted a position of support for the underdeveloped countries on a number of issues in which the latter states were opposed by Britain, France and the United States. Similarly, Nationalist China, certain Latin American states and members of alliances such as Portugal, Greece, Turkey and Iran have frequently aligned themselves with the major developed states on controversies concerning development issues. Nevertheless, even a cursory study of the progress of these questions, from their initial appearance in a United Nations organ to their embodiment in the form of resolutions, or in the creation of new machinery, indicates that the most characteristic controversy is that between the developed states, led by the United States, and the underdeveloped countries.

The former group of states have found themselves in a minority position on nearly every question related to economic development, human rights and colonial emancipation, especially after the great expansion of United Nations membership in the late 1950s and early 1960s. Moreover, most of these conflicts occurred on initiatives either proposed or taken by the underdeveloped states. In short, western attitudes have been in the main responsive and defensive. Indeed, the only major western initiative was the Point Four proposal[47] made by the United States to create an extended programme for technical assistance (E.P.T.A.). The programme which was set up by the United Nations in 1950 left control over the disbursement of funds, largely provided by the western states, in the hands of Specialised Agencies and the Secretariat, giving the major political body, the Economic and Social Council, only a nominal supervisory role over technical assistance activities. The creation of the E.P.T.A. was an attempt on the part of the western states to placate the growing demands from the underdeveloped for United Nations involvement in economic development. This demand expressed itself in a proposal made by India for a United Nations Economic Development Agency.[48] While the United States was prepared to provide additional funds for mutilateral aid, it was most unwilling to relinquish control over their disbursement to organs which had communist membership, and which could not be trusted to align themselves with American policy on certain issues.

The creation of the E.P.T.A. was to constitute the only major initiative taken by a developed state in the field of economic development, and from 1949 onwards the western states sought, through a number of procedural and diplomatic devices, to delay and obstruct decision on a wide variety of proposals made by the under-developed countries. The proposal for a Special United Nations Fund for Economic Development (SUNFED) met with steady opposition,[49] combined with attempts at conciliation through the extension of the development-financing activities of the I.B.R.D., and the creation of the International Finance Corporation and the International Development Authority. A Special Fund was created as an adjunct to the E.P.T.A. in 1958. But although this conflict over financing development continued throughout the whole period of the United Nations' existence, and the point was actually reached in 1962 when statutes for a Capital Development Fund were drafted, the western powers, although in a minority on this issue, were never pushed into a formal defeat. It was clear that their consent, as major exporters of capital and donors of aid, was essential to the success of this Fund, and that this consent was not forthcoming. This controversy had lasted for twelve years and, while the western powers made various concessions, at no point did they surrender their control over the disbursement of their contributions to the United Nations aid and technical assistance programmes, or made any significant diversion of their financial resources to a multilateral agency. Both the I.F.C. which was created in 1955 and the I.D.A. in 1959 were affiliates of the I.B.R.D. and therefore free from United Nations control, and the Special Fund had its own independent organisational structure.

This prolonged conflict between the western countries and the underdeveloped countries existed on a number of other economic and social questions. On the subject of food aid, for example, the western powers led by the United States were unwilling to establish a world food programme under the aegis of the F.A.O. or the United Nations, and retained control over the provision of wheat as bilateral aid.[50] In the field of international trade the western powers objected to the proposal made for a United Nations commission on international commodity trade. When the commission was formally established in 1954, the United States and Britain refused to participate in its activities. Steady opposition also existed to the convening of an international conference on trade and development problems, although this refusal was dropped in 1962, allowing the establishment of UNCTAD. Again, in the field of industrial development the western powers rejected the notion that rapid industrialisation was the solution to many of the problems of the underdeveloped countries. In spite of a directive from the General Assembly to the Economic and Social Council to establish a commission on industrial development, the western powers were able to use their influence in the Council and succeeded in obtaining a compromise by establishing a committee with reduced powers and functions instead of the major body requested by the Assembly.

The role of the communist countries was important in this conflict between the developed and the underdeveloped countries. At first, in the early years, the communist states adopted an attitude of indifference to proposals made by the underdeveloped countries and made their own doctrinaire contribution to debates. Their virtual abstention strengthened the western position and enabled them to resist the demands of the underdeveloped states. However, Soviet policy began to change in the early fifties, and the decision of the U.S.S.R. to participate in the E.P.T.A.,[51] which came shortly after Stalin's death, marked the beginning of continuous communist support for measures advocated by the small powers. Although the communist states continued to press proposals related to their conflict with the United States and its allies, they tended on the whole to support the initiative of the underdeveloped countries, rather than make their own proposals on development questions. This both strengthened the position of the underdeveloped countries, especially in the period before the major expansion of United Nations membership, and further isolated the western developed countries. Although the Soviet Union made occasional attempts to turn these initiatives into support for Soviet policy, these were resisted by the small powers who were by no means anxious to involve themselves in great-power conflicts. For example, the Soviets had been anxious since the beginning of the strategic embargo policy of the United States to use the United Nations to condemn trade discrimination. Consequently, when the underdeveloped countries were urging the creation of machinery for the supervision of trade between the developed and the underdeveloped countries, the Soviet Union and its allies tried to expand the proposals related to this concern into a general proposal for a survey of world trade which would include discriminatory practices. The small powers evaded this, and the Soviet Union was forced to follow more limited initiatives which the western powers found no less inimical to their interests.

With the expansion in U.N. membership which occurred in the early 1960s,[52] the underdeveloped countries found themselves in a commanding position. They had been able to force concessions from the western powers over the 1950s, and from 1960 onwards they were able to control almost every major U.N. organ, with the exceptions of the Security Council and the I.B.R.D. and I.M.F. But although these countries gained control over the economic and social machinery of the United Nations, all they had succeeded in doing was to institutionalise their problems. It became relatively easy to outvote the western developed countries, but not so easy to persuade them to modify their attitudes on the subject of stabilising primary commodity prices, or to increase their aid contributions through multilateral agencies. It is true that limited successes were made, and the western powers were forced to make concessions in order to buy time, or to stave off more radical proposals. But no concession was made on a question of substance. The consequence of small power pre-eminence in the United Nations has been to expand its organisational structure through the creation of a large number of organs charged with economic and social functions related to economic development and to racial and other social problems. The days in which the major powers were able to abolish organs whose activities were inimical to their policies, as for example in the case for the subcommission on the Prevention of Discrimination and the Protection of Minorities in 1951, were over long before the influx of new members. Even in this case just cited, the General Assembly with its universal membership overruled the decision of the eighteen-member ECOSOC.[53] The creation of new organs has been one characteristic of developments in the United Nations. The other has been the increasing number of exhortatory resolutions which reflect the attitudes of the underdeveloped countries. Both these trends have been substitutes for action.

It was said earlier in this study that, while the United Nations reflects the political realities of its international context, nevertheless it has its own mode of politics and identity. By this is meant that its organisation, procedures and composition constitute a political environment, which acts as an influence upon the national participants. National representatives must take into account the peculiarities of the United Nations political process in order to win success for a national position or to frustrate other states. It can be said that the most characteristic action on the part of the organs of the United Nations is the avoidance of decision. This is a reflection of continued great-power opposition on most substantive proposals made by the small powers, and the composition of the organs in which these proposals were made. The device of referral to another agency, or *ad hoc* committee, was used as a compromise between those seeking a substantive decision and those rejecting it. The controversial issue was thus not advanced, but neither was it rejected. As a French representative put it: 'The procedures of postponement or reference were used by most public bodies simply as a means of obviating the necessity of stating plainly that some proposal was not desired.' In this context it was a means of keeping an issue alive, without going to the length of forcing the major western powers into a minority position.

Thus over the early period of the United Nations' existence the small underdeveloped countries were willing to accept compromises which in effect transferred controversial questions to other permanent United Nations organs, to *ad hoc* committees specially created for the purpose, or to the ultimate limbo, the Secretariat, for study and report. This last was very popular with the western powers, who could rely on the Secretariat to avoid controversy and thus refrain from making substantive recommendations in its report. Hence the whole process of referral could start again and frequently did so.

Less advantageous to an opposition was the referral of an issue to an *ad hoc* body. In the early years the western states revealed a predilection for the expert committee, as an alternative to a body composed of governmental representatives. The problem was that the conclusions of the former body were apt to be unpredictable and, once created, it was difficult to get rid of without coming to some decision on its recommendations. This was especially true of the various committees formed specifically to discuss the SUNFED proposal. The creation of such bodies implied some recognition of the issue itself, making the tactic of referral more difficult to apply. The main advantage of such a tactic was that delay on a decision of substance was achieved and controversy within the political organs avoided. But enthusiasm for this procedure waned when a series of expert committees made recommendations which supported the proposals of the underdeveloped countries. Thus the western states came to regard a decision which established such committees as adverse.

Similarly, referral to other United Nations bodies, particularly the Specialised Agencies, was a favourite device of the western opposition. But as these organs became dominated by the underdeveloped countries themselves, this tactic ceased to be useful. By the end of the 1950s the General Assembly began to apply pressure on those bodies in which the western states had most influence, notably the ECOSOC, and delaying manoeuvres ceased to be important. The final resort of the western powers was an appeal to the opinions of member governments, with the clear implication that no substantive decision should be taken without the consent of the major powers.[54] This was to apply the veto principle to the 'non-political' area of the United Nations' activities. If, after all this, an adverse decision was taken, then, as in the case of the Commission on International Commodity Trade and the Capital Development Fund, the western powers were able to refuse to participate or to acknowledge the implications of the decision. Not only could they resist being led to the water, but having been forced there they could still refuse to drink.

Although, as was noted, the United Nations has involved itself in expanding its organisation and in adopting a large number of resolutions on a wide variety of economic and social topics, which largely reflect the attitudes of the small underdeveloped countries, in general the western powers have been very successful in delaying decisions and in achieving compromises. This success is, of course, not simply due to the diplomatic skill of western representatives in using organisational diversity and procedures to their advantage, but is also due to their political and economic significance in international politics. This has been somewhat qualified in the United Nations, especially in the non-political area, mainly because of the remarkable cohesion of the small states in making their case, and because of the importance for the United States, in particular, of gaining their support in the Cold War conflict. Hence an outwardly hostile attitude towards underdeveloped countries' proposals has been avoided in preference to the devices referred to above, which, although negative in their effects, nevertheless include some measure of conciliation and compromise. For example, in the area of human rights and colonial questions the United States has sought to temper the wind to her imperial allies, but not at the expense of alienating the small anti-colonial powers. Here as in the economic field there have been limited successes gained by these countries, notably the arms embargo against South Africa and the adoption of sanctions against the government of Southern Rhodesia.[55] These measures were adopted in the face of western opposition but with the United States pursuing a mediatory role, which considerably modified this opposition and produced a compromise which rejected more extreme measures.

There have been two major emphases in the study of the United Nations and other universalist organs. One has been the concentration on national policies within them, in an attempt to evaluate national influence and to relate these bodies to foreign policy.[56] The other has been the analysis of political behaviour in them. This last has produced a number of studies on voting and decision-making and on group cohesion.[57] Clearly, some elements of national foreign policy will be present in any attitude adopted by national representatives in these organs. Diplomats are concerned with representing national interests and in promoting or defending them. Enough has been said earlier, for example, to indicate the basis of the interest of the United States in the peace-keeping function of the United Nations. Similarly, the conflict between the underdeveloped countries and the western developed states is based on a clash of interests both economic and political in nature. But it is rare for such conflicts to find explicit expression in the form of an intransigent position adopted by a state. United Nations agencies are essentially bodies in which a process of negotiation and accommodation takes place, resulting in the adoption of compromise resolutions which represent, more or less, a balance of opinion.

The main differences between this type of diplomatic activity and that which takes place outside the United Nations is that the subject of negotiation is prescribed for the negotiants, rather than chosen by them, and that it takes place in a number of organs, which differ in composition and procedures, but which generally take their decisions by vote. This variation in membership, which is true for all organs with the exception of the General Assembly, combined with the lack of any authoritative direction from within the United Nations system, provides an opportunity for nation-states to manoeuvre in order to block or support proposals. The point is that this organisational complexity constitutes a dimension to political activity in the United Nations which is lacking in other forms of negotiation.

The study of national attitudes on specific questions or in terms of national foreign policy tends to ignore this dimension, and most studies concentrate upon political behaviour in one selected organ. Where an examination extends across a long period of time and is concerned with an organ with universal membership such as the General Assembly, then some degree of continuity in national attitudes may be detected and used as evidence for the exposition of national policies. But even in this case the other major factor, that of the internal context, is apt to be minimised in such an approach. National positions adopted on most issues are usually, though not always, intended to achieve some measure of success. Since this depends on the positions adopted by other members of the organ in which an issue is discussed, then obviously it was often as much a reflection of the balance of opinion as a simple extension of national policy. This explains, together with the organisational variations referred to above, the widely observed phenomenon of variant national attitudes on the same issue in different United Nations bodies.

Thus although national policy objectives or interests will be present in any attitude, there are relatively few occasions when member states adopted a position in the initial debate on an issue and refused to alter it in the succeeding negotiation. It can be said that, apart from 'kite-flying' proposals, comparatively few states adopted any position except as part of an elaborate manoeuvre. Member states were reluctant to prejudice success by revealing their position in advance or without 'informal consultations'. In cases where polemical or radical proposals were made, the introduction of such a proposal may be explained by the need to test opinion in the organ and to establish a clear position against which the attitudes of other states may be brought out into the open. This kind of gambit was typical of minority groups, which had little prospect of success for their position and therefore had no interest in seeking a compromise which would invariably reflect the attitudes of their political opponents. This was especially true of the communist members of the United Nations in its early years. Generally, however, accommodation and compromise were the typical political modes in U.N. organs, and national attitudes as such reflected the composition of the organ and the attitudes of other states. Hence few proposals are made in the United Nations without prior consultation with other states, and many draft resolutions are sponsored by a number of countries. There is therefore some measure of compromise involved in joint draft proposals before these are publicly submitted to the body for debate and decision.

Thus if national attitudes are seen as being derivative from positions adopted in debate, then this is open to objection unless other evidence is available from outside the context of the debate, or unless the state in question consistently maintained a position over a period of time in various organs on the same issue. Separate 'nation' studies should therefore examine national behaviour in terms of its context, and so far as the major organs of the United Nations are concerned, this means the study of decision-making and the interrelationship between national positions. Since all member states require support, there is high value on prior agreement and on continuing assistance throughout the debate. Such 'informal' agreements are frequent and they present a further difficulty in the assessment of national attitudes on the basis of behaviour in U.N. organs. This phenomenon is also of importance in establishing caucusing or group behaviour as a political phenomenon.

However, whatever the provenance of the issues considered by U.N. organs, the interchanges in debate, the amendments proposed and the final vote afford indications of national attitudes and policies. There is some difficulty in interpretation where positions are adopted for tactical reasons. An extreme or radical position, radical that is within the terms of the debate, may be adopted in order to acquire bargaining strength, in order to exact concessions, or to advance as a concession a modified version of the proposal. Thus the context of the debate is important for the evaluation of such manoeuvres.

Some commentators have eschewed the detailed examination of the Byzantine complexity of U.N. debates in favour of the analysis of votes[58] as a concrete expression of national attitudes. Such analysis is usually confined to the examination of roll-call votes in the General Assembly. A roll-call vote is a procedure by which states publicly declare their positions on the proposition. It can be used on the request of any member and, while it might encourage a higher number of abstentions than other less public means of voting, it provides a clear indication of a national attitude on an issue. Roll-call voting usually occurred when sharp divisions existed on an issue and when one of the contending member states wanted some public demonstration of position. This zest for publicity may have been connected to the belief that it might have a coercive effect on certain states. Otherwise the obscurity of simple voting was preferred by national representatives, who were acting in what was essentially a diplomatic context. Consequently the use of roll-call votes as a means of studying national attitudes tends to exaggerate the amount of controversy in the United Nations and to suggest an excessive preoccupation with political questions, since most such votes occurred on political issues.

But the use of roll-call votes or of voting behaviour generally as an indicator of national attitudes, and as a means of establishing group or caucus-based politics in United Nations organs, is open to objection. It has been argued by some commentators that the analysis of votes provides an objective basis for judgement in that it is non-impressionistic.[59] The exclusive use of data of this kind, however, tends to ignore the process of negotiation towards a consensus which normally precedes the actual vote. A roll-call vote has the effect of reducing public negotiation, since the real contest has been fought out in the preliminary 'informal' discussions in committees and in U.N. lobbies. Thus the various draft proposals and amendments are usually negotiated in advance of the formal debate leading to a roll-call vote. It is this process which is important to an understanding of political behaviour, since it contains both the original proposals made by participating states, together with their various shifts and accommodations made in order to obtain the necessary majority support. The vote itself, in short, is an indication of the compromise (or otherwise) reached and of national attitudes towards it, and gives no indication as to the changes in national positions which preceded it. The examination of this process and the achievement of a consensus is necessarily impressionistic and evaluative.

The fact that a two-thirds majority is necessary for the adoption of a resolution on an 'important question' places a high premium on political techniques designed to achieve a consensus, but an emphasis on the vote tends to concentrate on the tail-end of the political process rather than on its workings. Such an analysis needs to take into account the nature of the decision within the context of its discussion, rather than by the assertion of external categories relating to political alignments. More cases of unanimity occurred in the referral of controversial questions for further study, or for non-committal resolutions, and the most characteristic decision taken by United Nations organs is, as was noted earlier, the avoidance of a decision.

It is not surprising therefore that studies of roll-call voting, in an effort to establish group behaviour within the United Nations, tend to be inconclusive. There are broad correlations between states and the way they cast their votes on issues, but it is not possible, with the exception of the allies of the Soviet Union, to assert a high degree of cohesiveness for particular groups of states. Broad categories such as the Afro-Asian group, the old Europeans, the White Commonwealth, the Latin Americans, the underdeveloped states or the western countries are terms of convenience rather than precise distinctions. In short, the issues really determine the groups rather than vice versa, and the issues are the consequence of a process of bargaining centring around various initiatives and counter-proposals made by various states. Such groups are therefore at best *ad hoc* alliances brought about by this process for the purpose of adopting or rejecting a compromise proposal. In some cases, as for example on the question of the Arab–Israeli dispute, it is not surprising to find the Arab states closely organised and acting in collusion over a long period of time. Other questions, such as those relating to racial practices in South Africa, similarly find a corresponding cohesion among African states. But an emphasis on these major political issues, and on the public confrontations which occur in the General Assembly on them, tends to exagerate their significance within the context of political behaviour within the United Nations system.

Perhaps an example might clarify some of the points made in this discussion. The questions of regulating primary commodity trade and stabilising prices, together with trade aspects of economic development, have been major issues involving a number of United Nations organs. Although not so dramatic or so directly related to international politics as the problems of *apartheid* or of colonialism, nevertheless the discussion of these questions reveals a fundamental clash of interests between the western developed countries and primary commodity producers, and involves both roll-call votes and protracted negotiations. The lead in urging United Nations action on stabilising commodity prices was taken by a number of Latin American states who proposed in 1951 that the United Nations should ask for expert study of the problem. The existing machinery at this time, apart from the general concern of both the ECOSOC and the General Assembly for economic problems of this kind, was a body which had been set up in 1947. This was the Interim Co-ordinating Committee for International Commodity Arrangements (I.C.C.I.C.A.), and its main function was convening inter-governmental study groups and making recommendations to the Secretary-General for convening international commodity conferences. The Secretary-General himself was empowered to convene such conferences and a number of these had met, although no agreement had been successfully negotiated at this early period. Clearly, this method of calling large conferences of states concerned in primary commodity trade as consumers or producers was both unwieldy and dependent on the co-operation and participation of the countries involved. The small underdeveloped states, led by the four Latin American members of ECOSOC, Chile, Mexico, Peru and Uruguay, were dissatisfied with this arrangement and wanted closer supervision over commodity trade.

The result of this initiative was a resolution[60] which empowered an *ad hoc* expert committee to consider and report on this problem. While this committee advocated in its report long-term commodity agreements, it made no proposal for additional international machinery. The western members of the ECOSOC argued that new machinery was unnecessary, in view of the existence of the I.C.C.I.C.A. and of GATT, and the resolution finally adopted[61] simply urged governments to consider the effects of their policies on other countries, and asked the I.B.R.D. and the I.M.F. to adopt more flexible attitudes in time of recession. This should be seen against the background of considerable fluctuations in commodity prices as a consequence of the Korean war and American procurement policies. Although it was clear from discussions in the Council that the majority of underdeveloped countries were anxious for U.N. action on this issue, this resolution reflected the conservative attitude of the major developed countries and the indifference of the communist countries.

However, the General Assembly took a different attitude, and after eight roll-call votes adopted a resolution[62] which established an *ad hoc* committee to report on practical measures for controlling fluctuations in primary commodity prices. Almost as an afterthought it was instructed to make its report to the ECOSOC. The Secretary-General was also directed to prepare a report on commodity trade. The voting on this issue indicated that the main objections to United Nations involvement came from the western developed countries, including Canada, Australia, China and South Africa. The communist states abstained, but the great majority of small underdeveloped countries supported the resolution. Although, naturally, the findings of the expert committee could not be anticipated, nevertheless its institution and its terms of reference constituted a major defeat for the western developed powers. While these states had been able to prevent the ECOSOC from taking an initiative in this direction, it was clear that the General Assembly with its larger membership was determined to force the Council to take action.

1953 marked a hiatus in the consideration of this issue, since the expert committee was not to present its report until 1954. Some clearing of the decks began, however, in the Council, with the increase in membership of the I.C.C.I.C.A. to four[63] thus giving it a greater appearance of solidity. The western developed countries, which had formerly objected to the use of this body as a regulatory device for international commodity trade, now manoeuvred in readiness to support this relatively weak non-political organ against proposals for new machinery. The 17th session of the Council received the report of the *ad hoc* committee which made an unequivocal recommendation for the establishment of an international trade-stabilisation commission.[64] For the first time in the consideration of a controversial economic question, the western developed countries received no support from the other members of the ECOSOC, and they were roundly defeated on a roll-call vote.[65] All the western members of the Council, the U.K., the U.S.A., France, Belgium and Norway, voted against the draft resolution establishing a permanent advisory commission on international commodity trade, and the remaining developed country, Australia, abstained. The rest of the Council, including all the three communist countries, China and Turkey, voted in favour.

The debate, both in the Economic Committee of the Council and in the

Council itself, resolved itself into a contest between the western powers, who were supported in their attempt to delay decision by India, Pakistan, Egypt and Yugoslavia, and the other underdeveloped countries, notably Cuba, Argentina, Ecuador, Venezuela, Turkey, the Soviet Union and Czechoslovakia. The central issue was over the western attempt to delay, rather than over the question of the establishment of this body, although it was clear that these powers were hoping to achieve an indefinite postponement through this procedure. The communist countries, after seeking to change the proposed terms of reference of the commission in order to include the general question of East–West trade, and finding little support, came down strongly on the side of the proposal. It was this support which was critical for the underdeveloped countries, for without it their attempt to establish the C.I.C.T. would have failed through lack of a clear majority.

Although the western powers succeeded in delaying the adoption of the organisation and terms of reference of the new body until the following Council session, they were unable to prevent the Council from approving, in principle, the creation of the C.I.C.T. Nor were they able to use the delay to any effect, for the Council completed its work by ratifying the proposals contained in the draft resolution proposed by Argentina and electing members to the new body. Those states which had vacillated, such as Egypt and Yugoslavia, or had supported the western manoeuvre to delay the issue, such as India, Pakistan and China, all moved to support the position of the underdeveloped proponents of the new machinery. But the western powers, in spite of the failure of their attempts to prevent the creation of this commission, were still able to reject the substance of the decision by refusing to participate in the organ. Since the great world consumers of primary commodities boycotted the machinery created by a major United Nations organ to proffer advice on and to make studies of international commodity problems, it was hardly surprising that the underdeveloped countries soon realised the inefficacy of resolutions which, although supported by the majority, were nevertheless opposed by the few major developed powers. It was this realisation, perhaps, which prevented the underdeveloped states from using their dominant position to outvote the western states on issues which required their practical co-operation, such as the SUNFED proposal.

When the full effects of the British and American boycott were felt, the other members of the Economic and Social Council decided in 1958 to conciliate them by reconstituting the C.I.C.T.[65] and making its terms of reference more palatable to the position of the major developed consumers of primary commodities. This reconstitution represented a concession to the western view that the main function of such a body was the *study* of international commodity problems. However, a revival of militancy on this and on other economic issues affecting the interests of the underdeveloped countries occurred with the influx of new members into the United Nations. It was expressed in the form of a number of General Assembly initiatives which sought to urge the ECOSOC into some form of action. While the major developed countries still retained their predominance in the latter organ, the membership of the United Nations had changed radically and the General Assembly became increasingly dominated by the small under-developed countries. In 1959 the Assembly established the principle of compensatory financing for losses incurred by primary producers in market fluctuations.[66] The C.I.C.T. was asked to consider the question of providing temporary assistance to victims of sharp drops in commodity prices, and the regional economic agencies and the Specialised Agencies were urged to give 'special attention' to problems of one-export countries.

From this point onwards pressure mounted on the Council, and the western powers were faced with a flood of proposals emanating from the Assembly, and from the underdeveloped countries, which were both inimical to their interests and which could not be delayed as in earlier years, partly because of their loss of control over certain U.N. organs, and partly because of the magnitude of these demands for U.N. action. The Council was given little discretion in interpreting Assembly resolutions, and although it took note, made requests for further study and deferred decision, it proved impossible to evade the effects of the growing pressure.

By this time the question of international commodity trade had become merged with a wider series of proposals concerned with the regulation of international trade as a whole. These were the proposals leading to the convening of the United Nations Conference on Trade and Development. The communist countries for a long time had been asking for a general conference on international trade on the lines of the abortive Havana Conference. But as was seen in the C.I.C.T. proposal earlier, the under-developed countries were very reluctant to involve their own economic problems with questions relating to East–West relations. Although these states were anxious to extend United Nations influence in international trade, as a counter to the protectionism of GATT and the newly created European Economic Community, they avoided linking these to proposals which were sufficiently general as to enable the communist countries to exploit them for political advantages. Nevertheless, the underdeveloped countries were gradually coming to the point when a general conference on their trade problems was considered to be the most efficacious way of draw-ing attention to their difficulties.

Thus in 1961 the General Assembly adopted a resolution[67] which asked the Secretary-General to report on the advisability of convening an inter-national conference on international trade problems. Member governments were asked for their views and the whole issue, including the report, was to be considered by the ECOSOC. The Council was not, however, left to its own devices and the Assembly made certain, by prescribing the membership of the preparatory committee, by stipulating its terms of reference, by stating the agenda of the proposed conference and by fixing a date 'no later than early 1964', that the Council would have little opportunity for delaying tactics. But clearly, the consent of the major developed powers was necessary and this dictated the terms on which such a conference could be convened. For their part the western powers had resisted every proposal for international involvement in their trade relations, either openly or indirectly through procedural devices. But their attitude was difficult to sustain in the face of the overwhelming support given to the UNCTAD proposal, and they gradually accepted it once they had been reassured that the communist states would have little influence in formulating its agenda.

As might be anticipated, western agreement to convene UNCTAD in 1964 did not indicate any substantive change in their attitude towards trade relations with the underdeveloped countries, or in giving the United Nations a regulatory or supervisory function in this field. The conference succeeded in creating new machinery and in merging the C.I.C.T. and the I.C.C.I.C.A., but this represented no more than a guarantee that trade issues would continue to be discussed under U.N. auspicies. No International Trade Organisation was created at this conference, although a Trade and Development Board was established and authorised to meet twice a year.

It will be seen from the development of this issue that economic questions are no less controversial than the major political disputes within the United Nations, and the consequence has been an impasse no less significant than that which exists in the concern of the United Nations for maintaining peace. As was noted earlier, the notión of economic co-operation as a major condition for peace has been abandoned in favour of a secular conflict between the underdeveloped countries and the western powers. Whatever the ethical implications of this conflict, its relevance to the problem of world peace as envisaged by the creators of the Charter of the United Nations is peripheral. The major powers have shown their reluctance to use the United Nations as a major vehicle for their economic co-operation, and whatever co-operation exists in their economic relationships occurs elsewhere. Certainly, compromises have appeared which have been reflected in United Nations action in the field of technical assistance, in the same way as limited peace-keeping operations have been undertaken on the basis of compromises between the major powers. But the pursuit of co-operation through the United Nations ended in the late 1960s when the General Assembly virtually abandoned its attempt to establish principles governing international economic relationships. The problems of reconciling the world's heterogeneous economic systems and of the rival claims of the developed and the underdeveloped countries were insoluble.

Perhaps the major effect of this deadlock has been, paradoxically, the expansion of the organisation of the United Nations. In the absence of any substantive agreement between the developed minority and the underdeveloped majority, the illusion of action on the problems of the latter countries has been maintained by the proliferation of U.N. agencies. As was seen earlier, although UNCTAD failed to give any concrete satisfaction to the primary commodity producers, nevertheless it became established as a permanent part of the United Nations. The fifty-five-member Trade and Development Board has four main subsidiary organs: the Committee on Commodities, the Committee on Manufactures, the Committee on Invisibles and Financing related to Trade and the Committee on Shipping. An Advisory Committee was also set up to advise the Board, the Secretary-General and the Committee on Commodities. This elaborate machinery was placed under the nominal supervision of the ECOSOC and reported through this body to the General Assembly. Thus the machinery of the United Nations has been expanded, together with the opportunities for political manoeuvre, as the prospects of substantive agreements on the major controversial questions in the economic and social fields became ever more remote. So long as the major developed countries are concerned with avoiding hostile, if impotent, declarations by U.N. bodies on aspects of their foreign or domestic policies, they are compelled to participate in the political process. But while the underdeveloped countries have almost pre-empted the decision-making process in the United Nations, and reduced the capacity of an opposition to procrastinate and to obtain compromises, the sterility of decisions which exclude the major developed countries is apparent. A more moderate attitude on the part of the underdeveloped countries thus permits negotiation and gives some semblance of reality to United Nations debates. This qualifies the point that the very success of the underdeveloped countries in achieving control over U.N. bodies has reduced the area of compromise because the major powers no longer have anything to gain from accommodation.

If the United Nations has developed its own distinctive political system in the sense of an organised form of politics, in what way is this related to external international politics? It was noted earlier that international political and economic relationships developed independently of the United Nations, and that these have exerted an influence upon this universalist organisation. This influence is diffused and distorted by its internal politics, and consequently the United Nations cannot be interpreted in terms of its organisation and activities solely by an examination of great-power politics and their conflicts. But can the United Nations be regarded as an international 'actor' exerting its own influence upon its external political environment?

It must be admitted that it has a peripheral role in this respect. Although the small underdeveloped and unaligned powers have treated the United Nations as an important locus for the representation of their interests, the major powers have been only marginally involved in its activities. As we have seen, they have been concerned with defending their own position rather than with extending the activities of the organisation. The United Nations thus serves as a forum for the discontented, as a means of exerting pressure upon the major developed countries, as a field for polemic and propaganda, and as the repository for statements of principle and reports on a wide variety of political, economic, social and cultural topics. Its utility in the field of peace-keeping is conditional on a number of political factors, all of them extraneous to the organisation and dependent upon great-power policies. In the field of economic co-operation the United Nations has virtually abandoned its role of creating harmony between the developed countries in favour of the promotion of the economic development of the underdeveloped countries. Even in this field its limited technical assistance programmes and multilateral financing facilities prevent it from emerging as the major instrument for development, and the underdeveloped countries are forced to rely on bilateral programmes of aid with their political concomitants. Nor can it be maintained that the trusteeship system of the United Nations and the provisions of the Charter relating to non-self-governing territories, together with the numerous resolutions on colonial independence and self-determination, have had a significant effect in accelerating the dissolution of the European empires. The United Nations is a political organisation and it reflects both world politics and its own variety of politics, without having any discernible effect on its international environment.

Yet political realities are closely bound up with the perceptions of political practitioners, and these in turn with idealistic as well as with practical considerations. Perhaps the question can be put in the terms used by Dag Hammarskjöld when he argued that two contrasting concepts dominated any interpretation of the international role of the United Nations:

> The first concept can refer to history and to the traditions of national policies of the past. The second can point to the needs of the present and of the future in a world of ever-closer international interdependence where nations have at their disposal armaments of hitherto unknown destructive strength. The first one is firmly anchored in the time-honoured philosophy of sovereign national states in armed competition of which the most that may be expected in the international field is that they achieve a peaceful coexistence. The second one envisages possibilities of inter-governmental action overriding such a philosophy and opens the road toward more developed and increasingly effective forms of constructive co-operation.[68]

This is of course to urge the utility of such co-operation rather than to assert it as a value and, as we have seen, while states have in fact sought to co-operate, especially in the economic area of their interests, they have done so largely outside the United Nations. Nevertheless, the United Nations might be important more in terms of the values it represents than as a practical vehicle for world integration. But any evaluation of its significance in this sense is extremely difficult.

Yet some commentators have argued that the United Nations and its associated agencies have made a contribution to the establishment of some form of normative order in international politics. Talcott Parsons, for example, has asserted that an embryonic international community exists[69] which is not intrinsically different from the type of order found within national societies. He argues that in both cases order is maintained by what he terms 'normative components' which operate either as norms or as values. These last he defines as 'generalised formulations – more or less explicit – of expectations of proper action, by differentiated units in relatively specific situations'.[70] In other words, there are strong regulative factors in society consisting largely of 'expectations of proper action' which serve to maintain order. These factors may be explicitly recognised as such, for example in the functioning of a body of law and methods of law enforcement, but they also exist in the form of values, that is, in a general and prevalent belief in law and order. One perhaps would not quarrel over-much with this generalisation that members of a community, whatever their interests or organisation, have at least a minimal interest in order, and that over a period of time conventions and institutions tend to reinforce and maintain this interest. But Parsons goes further and extends this argument to inter-state relations and asserts that the same types of norms exist.

These, he argues, cross-cut the national interest and international competition as they cross-cut the temporal conflicts within the state, and they provide a general conception of community and a minimal order which acts as a context for international political activity. The evidence for this assertion is found not only in the form of religion and ideologies, in international trade and economic relationships, in cultural movements and in tourism, but in international organisations acting as embryonic social institutions. All these kinds of relationships and phenomena operate beyond the control of individual nation-states and exercise a restraining influence on independent national behaviour. They provide, in his words, a 'nexus of solidary relationships which cross-cut the divisions on the basis of "national" interest'.[71] Such an interpretation depends upon a hypothesis derived from and related to the study of national societies. It assumes the existence of some institutionalised structure capable of exercising authority, albeit moral, and of responding to external events. The difficulty with this sort of argument, as we have seen with Kaplan, is that if such empirical assumptions are not made, then the problem arises of defining some normative principle to which actual behaviour is related. This usually takes the form of some generalisation derived from a historical interpretation of behaviour itself. In this case concepts related to a hypothesis about the workings of society are applied to a field which lacks the kind of empirical evidence to support them. The United Nations is not a political institution in the same sense as a national political institution.

Thus the problem with the view that the United Nations makes a contribution to the establishment of order in international politics is that the notion of order itself is cloudy and undefined. It may represent a value in which co-operation and conciliation appear to be more desirable than the use of violence in the pursuit of national interests, but the significance of this value in actual political decisions taken by nation-states, or as an influence on international relations, is very difficult to evaluate. In any case, such an evaluation is bound up with speculative and prescriptive argument which belongs to political practice rather than to historical interpretation.

It will be seen from this lengthy discussion of the political significance of the United Nations that, like the other phenomena of international politics considered in this study, it is not susceptible to the kind of reductionist explanation or theoretical argument examined earlier. The major problem with an explanation of this organisation lies not so much in its structural complexity as in its amorphousness as a political institution. Essentially, its procedures and activities are *ad hoc* rather than creating through practice and precedent a stable political process and institutional growth. It is far more a standing diplomatic conference of representatives with limited competence, than a parliamentary body establishing conventions which produce, albeit in embryonic form, a form of world order, a body of international law or a coherent political practice. In other words, in spite of its apparent permanence, its elaborate organisational structure and its bureaucracy, the United Nations is an institution in form only, and although its multifarious activities and its organs may be described, there is no continuity of practice or institutional coherence which may serve as a focus for analysis. If constant change is the chief characteristic of international relations, then this is doubly true for this organisation, reflecting as it does its political environment.

Yet if the United Nations is inherently unstable as a political institution, it possesses, as was argued earlier in this discussion, a distinctive political process which is capable of explanation. In this sense it is a political phenomenon in its own right and with its own identity. Such an explanation, however, is historical in nature and any interpretation of its significance is open to criticism on the grounds of the evalutory criteria proper to this kind of argument.

REFERENCES

1. For an account of the development of international organisations before 1918, see F. P. Walters, *A History of the League of Nations* (London: Oxford Univ. Press, 1967) pp. 8ff; and Inis L. Claude, Jr., *Swords into Plowshares*, rev. ed. (Univ. of

London Press, 1964) pp. 17–35.

2. See the functionalist argument discussed in the preceding chapter.

3. For the texts of the Covenant of the League of Nations and of the Charter of the United Nations, see Claude, op. cit., Appendix I, pp. 409ff, and Appendix II, pp. 418ff.

4. For example, Article 12 of the Covenant, which stipulates a cooling-off period of three months in the event of a dispute, clearly relates to the diplomatic crisis immediately preceding the First World War. Similarly, Articles 39–51 of the Charter, which provide the United Nations with a means of using force against an aggressor, were formulated with the alleged inadequacies of the League in this respect in mind.

5. For example, those provisions of the Covenant, notably Article 8, which concern themselves with peace and disarmament. Almost all the Charter provisions relating to human rights and welfare are of this character.

6. See Hedley Bull, 'The Grotian Conception of International Society', in Butterfield Wight (eds.), *Diplomatic Investigations,* pp. 51ff.

7. For example, see Harold Nicolson, *Peacemaking 1919* (London: Methuen, 1964); and John Maynard Keynes, *The Economic Consequences of the Peace* (London: Labour Research Department, 1920) pp. 44–50.

8. For an account of the negotiations of the Covenant, see Walters, op. cit., pp. 15ff; and Alfred Zimmern, *The League of Nations and the Rule of Law* (London: Macmillan, 1936) pp. 137ff.

9. This decision was rescinded largely on an American initiative and Spain was admitted as a full member of the United Nations in 1955.

10. Of the succession states, Yugoslavia, Poland, Romania, Hungary, Austria and Czechoslovakia, only the latter country can be said to have had a democratic government by 1938.

11. Zimmern, op. cit., p. 285.

12. These were points 2 and 3. For a summary, see Nicolson, op. cit., pp. 39–41.

13. See Philip E. Jacob and Alexine L. Atherton, *The Dynamics of International Organisation* (Homewood, Ill.: Dorsey Press, 1965) pp. 1965) pp. 10ff; and Leland M. Goodrich, *The United Nations* (London: Stevens, 1960) pp. 164ff.

14. The Economic and Social Council refused to get involved in the substantive discussion of human rights questions largely because of their controversial nature and transferred the draft proposals of its daughter commission to the General Assembly. Resolution 545 (XVIII).

15. See *Everyman's United Nations,* vol. XX (New York: United Nations, 1968) pp. 453–5.

16. Kaplan, *System and Process in International Politics,* pp. 45–8.

17. Ibid., p. 45.

18. Ibid., p. 46.

19. Ibid., p. 47.

20. Ibid., p. 48.

21. For an attempt at applying systems analysis to the study of international organisations, see Jacob and Atherton, op. cit., pp. 2–9.

22. Kaplan, op. cit., p. 21.

23. Ibid., pp. 36–43.

24. See Haas, *Beyond the Nation-State,* pp. 450–1.

25. The United States, Britain and the U.S.S.R. For an account of the veto negotiations, see Dwight E. Lee, 'The Genesis of the Veto', *International Organisation,* vol. I, no. 1 (Feb. 1947) pp. 33–42.

26. This resolution was adopted by the General Assembly on 3 November, 1950. It states that, in the event of a disagreement in the Security Council on a question relating to the maintenance of peace, the General Assembly is empowered to deliberate the question and to take enforcement action. For the full text of Resolution 377.A(V), see *Charter Review Documents,* pp. 557–61.

27. Claude, op. cit., pp. 144, 161.

28. See Leon Gordenker, *The United Nations and the Peaceful Unification of Korea* (The Hague: Nijhoff, 1959).

29. For example, Gabriella Rosner, *The United Nations Emergency Force* (New

York: Columbia Univ. Press, 1963); and Arthur L. Burns and Nina Heathcote, *Peace-Keeping by U.N. Forces* (New York: Praeger, 1962).

30. For a discussion of preventive diplomacy, see Claude, op. cit., pp. 285–302.

31. The General Assembly passed a number of resolutions relating to the Suez crisis, the most important calling for the withdrawal of troops by France, Britain and Israel. Resolution ESI 1602 (IX), 7 November, 1956, and Resolution 1122 (XI), 26 November, 1956, which established UNEF.

32. Security Council Resolution 4387, taken on 14 July 1960.

33. Security Council Resolution of 4 March 1964, 186(1964), S/5575.

34. For an account of the 'troika' proposal, see Alvin Z. Rubinstein, *The Soviets in International Organisations* (Princeton Univ. Press, 1964) pp. 256–61.

35. See Knapp, *A History of War and Peace 1939–1965*, p. 133.

36. See Schlesinger, *A Thousand Days*, pp. 627–42.

37. For an account of this crisis, see Herbert G. Nicholas, 'The United Nations in Crisis', in David A. Kay (ed.), *The United Nations Political System* (New York: John Wiley, 1967) pp. 390–9.

38. For a statement of this view, see A. Loveday, *Reflections on International Administration* (Oxford: Clarendon Press, 1956).

39. See *Commercial Policy in the Inter-War Period: International Proposals and National Policies* (*Geneva:* League of Nations, 1942), p. 162.

40. The Economic and Financial Committees of the League of Nations. See *Report to Council on the Work of the Joint Session, London, 27th April–1st May* (Princeton, N.J.: League of Nations, 1942).

41. Ibid., p. 134.

42. Ibid., p. 157.

43. For a detailed description of these bodies, see Robert E. Asher *et al*, *The United Nations and the Promotion of the General Welfare* (Washington: Brookings Institution, 1957); and F. J. Tickner, *Technical Co-operation* (London: Hutchinson University Library, 1965).

44. For an account of this organ, see Walter Sharp, *The United Nations Economic and Social Council* (New York: Columbia Univ. Press, 1969).

45. See Inis L. Claude, Jr, 'Economic Development Aid and International Political Stability', in Cox (ed.), *International Organisation: World Politics*, pp. 49–58.

46. This must be qualified by reference to recent developments, such as the growing bargaining power of the Organisation of Petroleum Exporting Countries (OPEC) which operates outside the United Nations system.

47. So-called from President Truman's inaugural speech of 20 January 1949, in which his fourth point urged a 'bold new programme for making the benefits of our scientific and industrial progress available for the improvement and growth of under-developed areas'. See 'Harry S. Truman: Point Four', in Robert A. Goldwin and Harry M. Clor (eds.), *Readings in American Foreign Policy* (New York: Oxford Univ. Press, 1970) pp. 553ff.

48. This was made by R. V. Rao in the 3rd session of the sub-commission on economic development, a subsidiary body of the Economic and Social Council, in 1949. E/CNI/65.

49. For an account of the progress of this issue through the United Nations, see Sewell, *Functionalism and World Politics*, pp. 75ff.

50. This was provided as 'food aid' under Public Law 480.

51. This decision was announced by the Soviet delegate to the Economic and Social Council ,A. A. Arutiunian, on 15 July 1953. *Official Records* for 16th Session, p. 142.

52. Between 1955 and 1965 the membership of the United Nations rose from 60 to 115 states.

53. General Assembly Resolution 532.B(VI).

54. The French representative pointed out in 1955 that 'It was, of course, always possible for a majority to take a formal stand against a minority, but a decision by a majority which did not include those members of the United Nations which had the leading parts to play in the scheme (SUNFED) might turn out to be nugatory and even stand in the way of a development which was not only feasible but generally

desired.' Economic and Social Council, *Official Records,* 20th Session, p. 176.

55.   See J. E. Spence, *Republic under Pressure: A Study of South African Foreign Policy* (London: Oxford Univ. Press, for Royal Institute of International Affairs, 1965); and R. B. Sutcliffe, *Sanctions against Rhodesia: The Economic Background* (London: Africa Bureau, 1966).

56.   For example, Lincoln P. Bloomfield, *The U.N. and U.S. Foreign Policy* (Univ. of London Press, 1967); Geoffrey L. Goodwin, *Britain and the U.N.* (London: Oxford Univ. Press, 1957); and Alexander Dallin, *The Soviet Union and the United Nations* (New York: Praeger, 1962).

57.   For example, Thomas Hovet, Jr, *Bloc Politics in the United Nations* (Cambridge, Mass.: Harvard Univ. Press, 1960); Robert Riggs, *Politics in the United Nations* (Urbana: Univ. of Illinois Press, 1958); Hayward R. Alker, Jr, and Bruce M. Russett, *World Politics in the General Assembly* (New Haven: Yale Univ. Press, 1965).

58.   See Alker and Russett, op. cit., pp. 19ff; and Hayward R. Alker, 'Dimensions of Conflict in the General Assembly', in Kay, op. cit., pp. 161ff.

59.   Alker and Russett, op. cit., p. 2.

60.   Economic and Social Council Resolution 341(XII) and also 367A(XIII).

61.   Economic and Social Council Resolution 427(XIV).

62.   General Assembly Resolution 623(VII).

63.   Economic and Social Council Resolution 462.A(XV).

64.   E/2156, *Measures for International Economic Stability.*

65.   This was done in 1958 by Economic and Social Council Resolution 691(XXVI).

66.   The General Assembly asked the Secretary-General to appoint an expert committee to examine machinery to assist in offsetting fluctuations in commodity prices and balance of payments. Resolutions 1422 and 1423(XIV).

67.   General Assembly Resolution 1707(XVI).

68.   Dag Hammarskjöld, 'Two Differing Concepts of United Nations Assayed', in Kay, op. cit., pp. 110ff.

69.   Talcott Parsons, 'Polarisation of the World and International Order', in *Sociological Theory and Modern Society,* pp. 466–89, and 'Order and Community in the International Social System' in Rosenau (ed.), *International Politics and Foreign Policy,* pp. 120–9.

70.   Ibid., p. 120.

71.   Ibid., p. 124.

CHAPTER 9

Theory and Explanation in International Politics

THE notion of explanation has been the central theme of this study. A variety of arguments have been extensively criticised as explanations of human activities in general, and of international politics in particular. We come now to an attempt to seek common ground for an evaluation of enquiries into the nature of international politics. This entails placing it in the context of a mode of enquiry which has its own explanatory autonomy, its own structure of argument and logic, and its own evaluatory criteria. In seeking to do this, it is possible that we may discover that the very substance of 'international politics' turns out to be illusory or amorphous since, following an earlier argument, the phenomena in empirical enquiry are established by the explanation, rather than the explanation by the data. In other words, each mode of enquiry which has explanatory autonomy confers its own meaning and identity upon empirical phenomena. Alternatively, there may be a number of different and equally valid ways of understanding, or 'explaining', what we loosely call international politics. Consequently, we turn to these rather than to the facts of relations between states.

But in so doing, we are immediately involved in two questions: what is explanation, and what kind of explanation is appropriate to this area of enquiry? It should be clear from what has been said in earlier discussions that the nature of explanation poses an unavoidable problem and involves fundamental philosophical questions. Hence, in trying to explain what we do when we proffer an explanation of some human action or event, we face questions which are not confined to the immediate area of the particular explanation; they ultimately lead to a systematic attempt at elucidating a philosophy of explanation. This is clearly beyond the scope of this work. But the problems it raises must at least be considered if we are to make good any claim that the study of international politics leads to explanations which are both viable and autonomous in nature.

Explanations, according to some commentators,[1] can be categorised on the basis of their logical structure and on the logical implications of their arguments. But although we can distinguish between arguments in terms of their premises and assumptions, and the nature of the reasoning from which conclusions are derived, this leaves unresolved epistemological questions

319

relating to knowledge and to validity. A typology of explanatory arguments based upon their logical structure does not therefore take us very far. It is, of course, important to make such distinctions, especially in view of the claims or statements of intentions made by those proffering explanations, which on logical analysis prove misconceived. But after establishing that a particular explanation, to use Nagel's categories,[2] is of a deductive, probabilistic, functional, teleological or genetic type, we are still faced with the questions: does it explain, and in what way does it explain? A deductive argument which is consistent in its logic and whose conclusions follow from its premises may yet be false or wholly trivial. It may also be irrefutable, that is, axiomatically true. Teleological arguments, to take another example, can be classified but not refuted or proven. An argument which contains presuppositions, or logically extensible terms of a causal or genetic nature, might be incomplete as a causal explanation but, judged on grounds other than its internal logical or the entailments of its conceptual content, it may be none the less a satisfactory explanation.

Hence our search for an explanation in international politics must recognise the logical implications of particular arguments and theoretical claims; but it must also concern itself with establishing criteria other than that of logical structure to determine their nature and their validity. It may be, as we have seen, that some proffered explanations are confused in their internal logic. Because of the vagueness, inconsistency and indeterminacy of their terms it is not easy to make any further judgement. In this sense, they are not explanatory arguments. Alternatively, some arguments are *a priori* in nature and proceed by making a set of *ad hoc* definitions which are then linked together in an abstract system or conceptual scheme. Since we are concerned with *empirical* explanation, unless we can relate such systems of reasoning to the phenomena of international politics in some meaningful sense, we are forced to dismiss them as irrelevant. However, this does not preclude them from being some form of explanation.

On this argument, we can accept that the implications of premises and the propositions derived from them are important to any evaluation, but what is of particular significance in determining the nature of argument is the notion of truth to which it is related. An explanation must 'explain' in the sense that it renders the thing explained in some meaningful and communicable way. Yet, as was noted earlier, it is not enough for an explanation *simply* to confer meaning upon its subject, since this may be incommunicable and the notion of truth contained in it wholly idiosyncratic. It is therefore impossible to evaluate such arguments unless common grounds are established for criticism, and this involves some notion of validity other than stating, in value terms, approbation or disapprobation. A distinction can thus be made between explanation and meaning. But making such a distinction precise presents a number of difficulties. As we have seen, explanations do confer significance and meaning on the phenomena which they seek to explain, and this constitutes both a trans-formation and a recognition of objects which are asserted as having an independent empirical existence. Consequently, it is difficult to make a clear separation between knowledge and meaning. Nagel points out, in criticising the view that scientific 'objects' such as molecules, genes, electrons, neutrons, etc., possess physical reality, that 'molecular theory would still continue to formulate the traits of molecules in *relational* terms – in terms of relations of molecules to other molecules and to other things – not in terms of any of their qualities that might be directly apprehended through our organs of sense'.[3]

This argument indicates that explanations not only use terms, the meaning of which is established independently, either by common usage or by other explanations, but also create their own particular meaning for their concepts and theoretical terms. But this raises the difficulty that, if the notion of truth is conceived of as a relationship between empirical 'reality', i.e., an external and independently meaningful world of objects, and explanatory conclusions, as a correspondence between fact and theory, how can this apply to arguments in which the 'facts' are determined by the theory? In other words, if the phenomenon to which we relate our know-ledge for judgement is itself created by our knowledge, how do we know what we know, and how can our knowledge grow or progress? Such a notion of truth can only apply to explanations for which it is possible to attest through independent means the existence of the phenomena it seeks to explain. This would suggest that explanations which explain relations between non-observable objects, or which depend upon definitions and meanings established solely through their internal argument, should be judged on different grounds from those which posit a relationship between its own argument and an external empirical reality. Whether the former type of argument is an *empirical* explanation is difficult to assert.

The argument which has been stressed throughout this study is that truth does not constitute a certainty which can be substantiated on the basis of an objective criterion, to which all explanation and knowledge can be related, but rather that it is essentially a convention, which will vary between different forms of explanation, and which is the chief means of distin-guishing between them. Such a convention must be both communicable and recognisable. Thus the 'objectivity' of an argument consists simply in its relationship to a means of evaluation which is independent of it. This provides grounds considered reasonable for the evaluation of arguments in a particular field of enquiry, and will establish also the distinctiveness of that enquiry and its subject-matter. It confers meaning and enables demar-cation. But this is not to say that it is conventional in the sense that the mere factor of agreement is the crucial factor in its delineation, for further conditions for acceptability are that it should not entail logical or analytic absurdities, and that it should be capable of definition. For example, the

Flat Earth Society are convinced that the world is flat – as indeed were most people a relatively short time ago – and in so far as this belief posits an in-principle observable physical phenomenon, any explanation based upon it which accepts empirical confirmation as its evaluatory criterion can be refuted. In so far as it posits a belief with no such reference, then it belongs to a different category of argument subject to different evaluatory criteria or, alternatively, it falls outside our general notion of explanation altogether.

Thus the meaning which is attached to statements of any kind depends on the nature of the explanation to which they are related, and this in turn depends on the notion of validity which constitutes its main critical or evaluatory criterion. Such an assertion that the earth is flat cannot be simply refuted by the application of one particular such convention, since the possibility exists that it may be true in another sense. Before it is possible to make any evaluation at all, it is necessary to formulate and to agree on appropriate criteria, as well as to examine their logical implications. Clearly, there will be as many kinds of explanations and enquiries as there are recognisable and communicable evaluatory conventions. These will not only vary from field to field but will also change from generation to generation and are thus relativistic in nature. Only if a universal conception of understanding and knowledge is asserted, subsuming diverse branches of human activities and experience, either in the form of a theoretical system or of a universally valid explanation, would the problems of relevance and of criticism disappear. In the absence of such a theory of knowledge, with its absolute or objective notion of truth, the problem as to which convention fits which particular explanation is both difficult and debatable, and it is here that questions of intention or purpose, of internal consistency, and of the nature of the reasoning employed, become significant. But it is important to stress that, before these can become relevant, it is first necessary to examine the notion of truth and the related evaluatory criteria appropriate to it.

If, then, we turn back to the beginning of this study and re-examine the nature of scientific explanation, we find that it is a distinctive mode of enquiry which possesses theoretical autonomy. It explains, that is, confers meaning and establishes knowledge, in a distinctive way. A scientific theory defines phenomena and their relations through a set of propositions organised in a deductive logical form, from which are deduced general statements which assert that, given specific conditions and relationships, specific conclusions will ensue. Such an argument is based on assumptions *a priori* or inductive in nature, and upon the recognition and measurement of factors and variables. While the validity of the theory depends on a confirmation between its conclusions and the phenomena it seeks to explain, this only establishes that it is not false rather than that it is true. If it is not falsified, then such a theory will permit both prediction and retrodiction. But the distinctiveness of scientific explanation arises not out of its logical structure, or its techniques of observation and experiment, or out of the peculiarities of its subject-matter, but from the convention of empirical testability central to it.

Before examining this argument the opposite view should be considered: namely, that explanation and meaning in science are established through a logically consistent theoretical system, which alone provides the criteria for demarking and validating argument. Such a system is universal, since to demarcate on its basis means establishing the grounds on which a particular argument is *not* as well as what it is. In short, it creats categories which enable us to distinguish between types of argument and which are not based upon logical form or structure. But all such categories are related to the idea of a unity of knowledge of which they form merely parts. Hence, before we can proceed to make judgements about purported explanations, we need to establish an explanation of explanations in which particular assertions of knowledge are validated and subsumed within a theory of knowledge having universal application. This cannot be derived from extant explanations, since this would be to accept the terms on which they purport to explain; rather they must be considered in terms of a universal theory which is imposed upon them and is derived from external grounds.

Thus the critique made by Oakeshott of the notion of an empirical reality which science explains, and through which scientific explanations are validated, asserts the true nature of science as a 'world of absolutely stable experience'.[4] It is a world of 'quantitative concepts'[5] and its general propositions are 'analytic generalisations derived from the analysis of the structural concepts of the world of scientific knowledge, and they express the relations between these concepts which are inherent in the concepts themselves'.[6] Through speculative hypotheses, derived from this conceptual framework, a world of ideas is created, and innovation proceeds through continued hypothetical reasoning which seeks to render consistent all postulated relationships in quantitative terms. Scientific knowledge expands, or grows, through this process and not by enlarging a knowledge of an external reality, for there is no external reality which can be known outside the conceptual frame work which creates it. As he puts it: 'Science does not explain the character of those things which are outside us; it explains the world in so far as it can be explained when conceived under the category of quantity.'[7]

The truth of hypotheses, and of general propositions derived from them, is not obtained through a correlation between theoretical conclusions and empirical observation, for there are no objects external to the theory, 'No experiment or observation whatever in science can be held to be a process of verification',[8] and a 'single observation is never of significance in science and nature; the matter in scientific experience is not a world of percepts but a world of pure quantitative ideas'.[9] Thus general propositions in science are not universally applicable empirical laws verified through experience, but they are experience in the sense that they are statistical generalisations which establish consistent relations between a system of concepts. They do not explain reality, for they *are* reality.

Now this argument has many implications, some of which were considered earlier in this study, but the concern here is with the relationship of this notion to that of the conventional standard which was asserted as the criterion central to an explanation. According to Oakeshott there is only one valid test which is independent of particular explanations, and this is not empirical verification or falsification, but coherence.[10] He is not concerned with the question whether scientists or other claimants to explanatory validity and autonomy accept this criterion, but with the argument that it is the only criterion which is appropriate to their arguments. As we have seen, this involves the rejection of conflicting claims. Thus, unless scientific practitioners accept the notion of their experience as constituting a world of quantitative concepts, and coherence as the test of its validity, they cannot make valid judgements about their arguments, although they can make judgements. Whatever they think they explain, they can only explain in this particular way.

But what is coherence? '. . . it requires neither modification nor supplement and it is operative always and everywhere – it is alone and complete in itself.'[11] We saw what this meant for the notion of historical explanation; what does it entail for that of science? The world of science, in this view, is incomplete because it is an 'abstract and homegeneous' world which of its nature precludes any explanation of the real totality of experience. It can only be concerned with its own reality and this excludes any other. Hence it is an arrest of experience, since it is incoherent in absolute terms.

While the notion of coherence provides a rule for the demarcation of arguments which purport to be explanations, it does not enable us to apply it to any particular aspect of enquiry within a category. Either the asserted argument falls within the systematic category, in which case it is knowledge of a sort, or else it does not, in which case it either falls into the catch-all of the world of practice, or remains in some sort of epistemological limbo. But even if we can accept this notion of science as a quantitative conceptual scheme, albeit only partially coherent or complete, we are faced with the twin problem of resolving controversies between proponents of diverse or conflicting and partial explanations, and of determining equally consistent worlds of ideas which satisfy the theoretical criteria of a particular mode. On what grounds do we make our choice? Can any world of ideas, albeit incomplete and incoherent, qualify, provided it is internally consistent? It would appear that, using this criterion, we can classify but not criticise or evaluate. Yet if all that is observed by scientists is determined by a predisposition to perceive in a particular way, it is difficult to see how any communication can take place, or how a body of scientific knowledge could change or develop, A multiplicity of conceptual schemes fundamentally incompatible one with the other would result. But such predispositions, if they exist, are provisional and the observations and experiments themselves induce change. Coherence is thus a criterion which stands or falls by the theoretical system to which it is central, but of itself cannot be given any more precise meaning. If there is a total world of experience or reality which enables us to judge attempts at explaining it, and if this is defined as an absolutely coherent world, then it enables us to make the judgement that they are incomplete, but it must be on other criteria that we can establish the particular distinctiveness of science, history, art, etc. On other criteria, since the notion of coherence itself is abstract and analytic and any attempt to apply it to what is actually done must depend upon what is claimed by those engaged in arguments and enquiries, and on what these arguments actually say. Hence, part of this conceptual scheme must rest upon selected assertions about the actual practice – selected in order to make it compatible with the theory of experience which is being advanced.

In short, it is argued here that the notion of an external objective physical reality constituting both the basis and the test of scientific knowledge, which is criticised by Oakeshott, is certainly open to analytic and critical examination, but the step from this to the assertion of the coherent theory of truth does not axiomatically follow. The core of Oakeshott's critique of science is that an empirical reality does not exist independent of the argument which asserts it, and hence, whatever means we adopt for asserting scientific knowledge, this cannot be through the testing of general propositions derived from hypotheses against empirical observation. It is thus denied that science concerns itself with 'observed' facts, and the assertion is made that it is solely concerned with quantitative relations between concepts. Although this may be true of some arguments in science, it is not true of all of them. Speculative hypotheses are formulated positing general propositions *about* things, which are then matched to experiment and observation. Anomalies or events which do not conform to the theoretical conclusions refute the attempted explanation. But an unrefuted explanation does not constitute truth because there is no means of establishing the assumption of the uniformity of nature necessary to the assertion of the continual or infinite validity of its conclusions. As many commentators besides Oakeshott have recognised, 'no rule can ever guarantee that a generalisation inferred from true observations however often repeated is true'.[12] In this sense, all such generalisations are probability statements and are inductively obtained. But it does not follow from this that they are either purely analytic statements or statistical in nature. Untestable hypotheses, symbolic or conceptual arguments, such as mathematical models or calculi, do not constitute empirical explanations. They may indeed be closely related to such explanations, in that they provide the hypotheses or the variables or definitions from which propositions capable of an empirical test are derived, but, as Nagel points out, if this level of abstraction is to be useful 'as an instrument of explanation and prediction it must somehow be linked with observable materials'.[13] It is true that the nature of this link presents some formidable analytic difficulties relating to the status of the general propositions of the theory, to the precise connection between the level of abstraction and its empirical derivatives, and to the inductive or deductive nature of the argument; but the point here is that, given the notion of an empirical test, we have a means of making evaluative judgements between particular arguments in science other than that of asserting their simple logical consistency or absolute coherence. Such a notion is conventional since, as Popper argues,[14] while it can enable us conclusively to reject purported explanations at the time the test is made, it cannot enable us to assert certain knowledge. Indeed, the progression of scientific knowledge has been through the rejection or the supersession of explanations which were temporarily irrefuted, or were irrefutable under their temporal circumstances. This progression is only possible if there is some notion of a commonly acceptable test. It can be argued, although there is no evidence for this, that refuted explanations may be put on their legs again by means of the same test, given more precise observations, or better i.e. more comprehensive, theories. On this argument, what is 'known' is relative to the acceptance of such a conventional standard, and the effects of its application will be temporal and temporary. The 'truth' of an explanation is neither universal nor certain. As Urmson argues:

> There is a difference between the cases of mathematical knowledge and knowledge of immediate experience on the one hand and our knowledge of empirical fact on the other. Types of error are logically possible in the case of empirical knowledge which are not logically possible in the case of the two other types of knowledge. For example, it always makes sense in the case of empirical knowledge to say 'Maybe facts will turn up which will make us abandon this' but this is not so in the other cases.[15]

If this argument is accepted, the notion of science as a system of quantitative relations which is logically consistent must be rejected, since there can be no refutation of its arguments other than through purely logical criteria, that is, logically necessary contingent relations.

But to accept this argument is not to accept the notion of an outside world which is gradually unfolded and made clear by better and better explanations. If this is what Oakeshott is attacking, then he is far from being alone in his criticisms. We may regard the notion of experience or reality in science as being not that of an independently experienced concrete object but as a conditional agreement as to the nature of the object which is related to the proffered explanation. In this sense, reality is indeed created, in that it cannot be separated from the argument without the 'it' changing its nature through becoming part of another experience or explanation. But the special relation between reality, that is, as a thing which has significance conferred on it by an explanation, and the explanation, is such as to make the former identifiable and not as tautologically or analytically present in the explanation. In a logical sense, the 'it' is independent of the explanation but not in a concrete existential sense. As Popper puts it, the basic statements which assert an observed event are 'accepted as the result of a decision or argument, and to that extent they are conventions. The decisions are reached in accordance with a procedure governed by rules'.[16] Thus, recognition of the in-principle observable event is necessary before any communicable explanation can be evaluated, and this recognition depends upon the prior acceptance of some criterion. Such criteria are objective in the sense that they are independent of the particular observer, and of the particular explanation, but they are relative, in that the 'knowledge' of the event-in-explanation will change as the explanations and so the events change. In short, there is nothing universal or permanent about the objects or their explanation in arguments governed by this notion of evaluation. But the notion of an in-principle observable event must be part of such an explanation.

Now while it is true that systems of quantitative relations between concepts exist in science and that what have been called higher-level propositions cannot have any empirical, i.e. experiential, referent, these systems seek to relate propositions which do have such a referent. As Braithwaite says, 'theoretical concepts are only a particularly elaborate way of making these connexions and theoretical terms only a particularly striking case of contextual meaning'.[17] They are neither isolated from the empirical argument nor are they a substitute for it. If this last were the case, then each system could be judged only in terms of logical consistency and their ultimate justification would rest on some quasi-metaphysical principle or idealist system. Thus the sense in which the world of science is a world of ideas does not exclude the sense in which it is concerned with empirical explanations. But a disconformity between the level of observation and the empirical explanation will weaken the theoretical argument which posits universal propositions; this is involved in the application of an empirical test. The world of ideas or the universal theoretical system is exposed to the possibility, on the observational level, of singular contradictions and is therefore susceptible to constant changes or modifications. In this sense, the activity of scientific theorising consists of attempting to make coherent through universal theories sets of empirical propositions which themselves are subject to empirical tests. A singular event can contradict a universal proposition but a universal proposition cannot empirically validate a singular event.

The notion of validity in this argument is relativistic and does not imply the *verification* of empirical propositions through the coincidence between hypothetical conclusions and behavioural reality. It is true that the capacity to predict is taken as a criterion for the acceptance or rejection of explanatory conclusions, but prediction does not mean more than a statement that if the laws governing sequences of relationships are known, then future states in that set of relationships may be deduced from them. If this can be established through an observational or experimental test, the proffered explanation is acceptable. This does not mean that the general proposition is either true or universal, or that it has the sole claim to acceptability. Acceptance is no more than a temporal judgement, since alternative hypotheses may produce the same conclusions or contradictory conclusions which are not falsified, or a 'larger' theory may supersede the accepted explanation. Nevertheless, accepting the argument that propositions which are susceptible to such a test are incomplete, tentative, and only probable, and that their truth cannot be established as a certainty, given the impossibility of establishing the inductive principle on which they are based, it is clear that a convention exists which is generally recognised by scientists and which enables them to agree and to disagree about the nature and the acceptability of their explanations. Such a convention is external to both their proffered explanations and to their subjective feelings or predilections. Using it, distinctions can be made between arguments which are analytic and abstract or merely symbolic, and arguments which are explanations in a meaningful sense. These distinctions are neither purely logical, based on the formal structure of the argument, nor are they based on external idealistic criteria, but are, in this view, essentially conventional.

The pursuit of scientific enquiry, historically, has produced a great variety of arguments and theories, some of which are confined to a very narrow focus, and some of which constitute a theoretical framework for others. But while the *label* 'science' covers in fact a multiplicity of varying pursuits, the notion of a scientific *explanation* has a more precise definition. It would appear in principle that there is nothing which would preclude its application to the field of human activities. It is sometimes argued that human cognition would either falsify or change the terms of any casual explanation which sought to predict actual behaviour. This is to say that an adequate scientific explanation would have to take into account this possibility and subsume it within the terms of its argument. The error in this 'objection, therefore, is applying the form or structure – not the content – of such an explanation to our present non-scientific knowledge of human experience and activities. If we accept the argument that the explanation establishes the nature of our knowledge, it would seem that a scientific explanation of human phenomena would define and explain it in a radically different way from our extant non-scientific explanations. Thus the sceptical position of asserting that a scientific explanation of human affairs is not possible cannot be sustained on the grounds of the intractability of the material alleged to be its subject-matter. The content of an explanation of this type would constitute a different knowledge from that which we already know. Having said this, however, it is clear that none of the attempts to produce a scientific explanation in the social sciences has been successful. In certain cases this is not surprising, in view of the attempt to cram non-scientific *knowledge*, i.e. things known in a non-scientific sense, into a scientific mould. As we have seen, empirical generalisations, variables and factors derived from non-scientific explanations have been incorporated into arguments which assume the forms of science. The definition and meaning of such transcripts are thus derived from outside the kind of argument to which they are transformed.

If we return to the discussion of structural-functional theory and systems analysis in the early part of this study, it will be recalled that, apart from internal criticisms of the inconsistencies and ambiguities of their argument, the substance of the criticism was that the various hypotheses and theoretical models considered could not be subjected to any empirical test. It was argued that the logical implications of such theories required the satisfaction of the same requirements as deductive or causal arguments in science which seek to explain empirical phenomena. In the case of structural-functional theory the assertion of necessary relationships between phenomena posits an organising or normative principle, which in turn requires a general causal proposition to which the functional values of its component parts and the process of regulation can be related. In other words, the answers to the questions as to which and why certain conditions are necessary to the existence (or maintenance) of what, posit the theoretical requirements of a scientific explanation. The same kind of argument is implicit in systems analysis, although, as we saw, the organising concept was even more vague than in the case of the former theory. The major criticisms of this type of theorising might be listed as being: first, that no structural norm or organic entity has any empirical existence; second, that empirical referents contained in the argument are historical generalisations or based on interpretations taken out of context; third, that the perception and motivation of the agents whose actions form the subject of explanation are virtually ignored; fourth, that no general proposition is deducible from the argument; fifth, that the variables said to be in relationship are neither recognisable nor quantifiable; and sixth, that, as was noted, the argument is incapable of any empirical tests. Hence, on these grounds, it was concluded that the nature of this type of theory is non-scientific.

But, as was also noted, there are three other possibilities relating to their nature which require examination. The first is that, although these arguments do not correspond to those of a valid scientific theory, nevertheless they are a means of achieving such a theory. In other words, the *method* employed is scientific. In the absence of concrete achievement, such a claim is both easy to make and difficult to refute, since a confutation would require a theory of the provenance (and non-provenance) of theories. It cannot be axiomatically or dogmatically stated that all such endeavours are bound to be fruitless, although we may use explanatory and theoretical requirements as a guide to criticism. But while we may avoid arrogance and take into account the possibility of serendipity or a chance discovery, extant attempts at applying scientific method to human affairs can be criticised as being either explanations in their own right, albeit of a non-scientific nature, forms of political argument and prescription, or scientific metaphors or analogies with no explanatory content. If the previous argument is accepted, namely that theory precedes observation, then it is difficult to regard any attempt at organising empirical material or applying various techniques of analysis as being anything other than hypothetical formulations of varying degrees of rigour. In other words, methods *are* explanations and a mode of enquiry cannot be separated from the hypothesis to which it properly belongs. Facts are selected (and rejected) on the basis of theorising assumptions, and the enquiry proceeds by making a number of presuppositions about its subject. It is not surprising that often as a result the conclusions simply reiterate the assumptions so that the whole argument is axiomatically true or a tautology.

Moreover, certain of these 'strategies for research' can be regarded as being disguised normative or prescriptive arguments. It is sometimes urged that social science should be useful. Its sole interest in the past, in this view, is in the extrapolation of hypotheses which can be related to the present and the future in an effort to guide political decision. We have traces of this bias in the various attempts to explain war, crises, conflicts and bargaining, and decision-making examined in this study. Once a valid theoretical explanation of these phenomena is found, then the predictive capacity of such a theory can be used for prescription. Cures can be found for social and political ills or, alternatively, effective advice can be given, enabling a policy or a party to emerge victorious from political struggle. Where such arguments have a theoretical structure we can apply the same criteria as was applied to systems analysis, that is, they can be considered as norms of explanation. But where this is lacking, as in game theory and bargaining and conflict theories, these arguments can be considered simply as aspects of political argument or practical politics, in the same sense as opinion polls or election studies.

As we have seen in the analysis of various strategic theories and their relationship to policy, the assumptions of complete information, rational behaviour, mutual recognition by contestants of the rules governing political and military behaviour, of isolable and measurable goals or objectives, and of optimal capacity to engage in specified courses of action, are all implicit in the argument. Such assumptions are not critically examined, and the rationalisations of the 'theory' proceed without any attempt to formulate testable hypotheses or theoretical justification. Each 'scenario' or hypothetical conflict situation is really a form of historical argument, based upon interpretations of the past, but with the difference that it is made to apply to future contingencies and is thus speculative in nature.

The second possibility is that extant theorising in the social sciences, in spite of its ostensible goal of establishing a valid scientific explanation, really constitutes a radically different kind of explanation. If this was the case, it would have its own evaluatory criteria and theoretical autonomy. Thus we might reject the claim that conceptual schemes provide a theoretical framework for empirical research, without excluding the possibility that they are explanations in their own right. The general theory of action, Marxist and other explanations of historical processes, structural-functional theory and perhaps systems analysis can be considered as systems of concepts which are logically related and which seek to explain a wide variety of human phenomena. They are universalist theoretical explanations. But, as was argued earlier, the empirical content of such theoretical systems is both selective and peripheral: selective in the sense that historical events and interpretations are utilised to support *a priori* definitions and terms, and peripheral in that the argument itself is non-empirical in nature. Both meaning and explanation are confined to the internal terms of the argument and there is no means of validating its propositions through an empirical test. Consequently, we are forced to regard it simply as a system of concepts which is either logically consistent or coherent but which, in an empirical sense, is irrefutable. It cannot 'explain' in the same way as a scientific explanation because there is nothing empirical which it can be related to, or tested against.

We might agree with Reichenbach that 'logical necessity and emptiness go together and make up the analytic or tautological nature of logic'.[18] Our judgement is therefore confined to the internal logical structure of such conceptual schemes and, on these grounds, those examined earlier were found to be lacking. But the main point here is that they are not *empirical* explanations and therefore have no relevance to empirical enquiries into political and social activity. They do not help us in achieving an explanation of international politics, if we conceive of this as concerned with phenomena which are in principle observable and, in a sense, external to our explanation. As we have seen, while the nature of an empirical reality is difficult to determine, nevertheless it is posited in science that it is 'not something that we have – in any meaning of the word – invented ourselves'. If we accept that a conceptual scheme is simply a 'world of ideas', then outside its own internal coherence we have no means of evaluating its truth. Any critical judgement which seeks to evaluate a variety of these schemes is forced to depend on such subjective factors as taste or belief. And it is apparent that this excludes the common ground for agreement or disagreement necessary for communication. We may be able to agree on a definition of such a world but we can proceed no further.

We now come to the third possibility, namely that much of the theorising in the social sciences is really a form of historical argument. This is not to accept, as a number of social scientists have recently urged, the necessity for 'greater historical depth' on the part of the social sciences, for this begs questions as to both the nature of their enquiries and the relevance of their view of history. It will be recalled that the claim has been made in this study that there is no fundamental difference between explanation in this field and that of history. Before seeking to substantiate this assertion, it would be helpful to review the arguments discussed earlier concerning the nature of historical explanation. The argument that historical writing is really a form of scientific explanation is based upon the logical implications of the presuppositions contained in any attempt to explain a phenomenon in terms of its antecedents. From this, it is asserted that in spite of the historian's ostensible concern for the unique or the particular in the past, his argument posits general propositions which transcend his selected focus. As we saw earlier, the position that historical explanation of its nature is concerned with causes in the same way as genetic explanation in science is also fundamental to historicist arguments which seek to explain processes in history. The Marxist and neo-Marxist hypotheses of economic processes, which impose conditions upon human action and which develop from one stage to another, are in this sense 'scientific'.

Thus, as Hempel puts it: 'Historical explanation too, aims at showing that the event in question was not a "matter of chance" but was to be expected in view of certain antecedents or simultaneous conditions.'[19] In explaining an event, the historian posits necessary and sufficient conditions without which the event could not have taken place. A complete historical argument, therefore, would be able to assert a set of statements establishing the occurrence of the event which is the subject of explanation, a universal hypothesis containing a law-like statement, and the logical deduction of the event from these terms. In principle, such a theoretical explanation should be capable of empirical validation, or falsification, since its conclusions are applicable anywhere and everywhere. The event explained becomes one of a class of events and the exclusive concern of the historian for a unique and unrepeatable past is thus untenable. Indeed, 'history' ceases to have any purely temporal meaning. If this argument is accepted, it removes any distinction between the social sciences and history and, indeed, this has been the contention of a number of social scientists. But these are not the grounds for asserting in this study that the form of explanation characteristic of history is also characteristic of that found in the social sciences.

We may accept that historical interpretation contains assumptions which have theoretical implications. Any attempt to explain why a particular event or action took place implies a concern with causes. As we have seen, even the narrowest selection of data, historical or sociological, implies a criterion of selectivity and some organising or referential principle, however implicit these may be. These features are present in any attempt to employ reason-giving statements about the past or about aspects of human experience. The conceptual content of such arguments and the logical implications of their assumptions can be extended to posit the kind of hypothesis proper to a covering-law explanation. For example, the phenomenon of a daily milk delivery calls for such an explanation, with a statement of conditions, necessary and sufficient, to explain why a bottle of milk arrives on our doorstep every day. But we are able to explain and confer meaning on this phenomenon in a communicable way without making such an extension. Such explanation makes assumptions about the world and posits knowledge outside its categories without finding it necessary either to make these explicit or to pursue their logical implications. In short, if it is asserted that the theoretical requirements for a covering-law explanation, including that of empirical validation, must be satisfied before we have an explanation of human phenomena, then it must be admitted that, to date, we are unable to explain. Yet this is to confine the notion of explanation to one particular form, that of genetic explanation in science, and to assert its logic as the sole basis for evaluation.

Now while we may accept that, in principle, such an explanation of human affairs is at least possible – although if it were achieved it would not be historical or sociological – and that any attempt to explain solely in terms of causes implies a hypothesis which contains a general law, this does not mean that other forms of explanation of equal validity cannot exist. Nor does it mean that the logical implications of presuppositions and assumptions constitute the only grounds for asserting explanatory forms. Before looking at this argument, the claim that historical explanation is distinctive because of its subject-matter should be examined. 'Events' in the past are neither concrete nor 'observable', and they are not, as we have seen, susceptible to quantitative techniques. Although in science observation is sometimes indirect and in some cases not possible, nevertheless the subject-matter of a scientific explanation is quantifiable. There is some difficulty in defining the notion of an observable external reality to which theoretical conclusions may be related, but, in principle at least, this is essential to the notion of a scientific explanation. The historian, however, is concerned with the evaluation and selection of the perception, motivation and experiences of historical agents. In order to explain why particular actions were undertaken, he seeks to establish the nature of the understanding of those undertaking them. In eliciting this understanding, the historian makes the actions intelligible without asserting that it is a sufficient condition for their occurrence. Each such 'understanding' is unique to each such action or event.

Hence he is concerned with the particular, but in a sense which does not, and indeed cannot, exclude general presuppositions which are present in any explanatory argument. Yet although, as will be argued subsequently, there is something which is distinctive in the focus of the historian, it is clear that this does not provide the main grounds for characterising historical argument, any more than the nature of material phenomena confers distinction upon scientific argument. In this particular case it is difficult to separate the view that a past 'thought' explains a past 'action', from the argument that, given a specific mental condition, a specific action must follow. In other words, this too can form the subject-matter of a scientific explanation. An insistence on the peculiarities of the phenomena it seeks to explain is therefore not tenable as the criterion of an explanation. We should look for distinctiveness in the way we understand rather than in what we understand, since the latter is created by the former rather than vice versa. If the historical focus is distinctive, it is not because of the nature of the phenomena it seeks to explain, but because of the nature of the mode of explanation which establishes this peculiarity. On this argument, historical knowledge is intrinsically different from scientific knowledge, although the actual process of reasoning may share common characteristics.

It was argued earlier that explanations involve some notion of truth related to the communication of knowledge. This suggests that a means of validating explanation is a prerequisite of explanation. We have seen what this entails for scientific explanation. Such criteria are inapplicable to any argument which establishes a concern *solely* with the notion of the past. They can, of course, be applied to arguments which *inter alia*, subsume the past, and which therefore are not temporal in nature. What, then, is the criterion of validation appropriate to historical argument, if this is to be established as distinctive from that of science? In what sense is there historical knowledge and how can we recognise it? It will be recalled that some historians have asserted an objective criterion independent of particular historical argument. Thus the idea of the total past enables an assessment of a particular representation in relation to it, and permits historical knowledge to progress as more and more of the past is discovered. The idea of the past is both a guide to historical research and an evaluatory criterion. In this view, there is only one past and this has a reality external to representations of it.

But the problem with this notion of a means of validating particular arguments and of establishing historical knowledge is that it assumes this knowledge rather than defines its nature. In other words, unless we can know the totality of the past, we cannot evaluate what is asserted to be a part of it, nor can we regard any historical argument as a progressive step towards this knowledge. The main objection to the position is that the past, in this sense, is an unknowable. Even if it were not, it must have an empirical existence if it is to be used as an objective criterion. As we argued earlier, phenomena are dependent upon the explanation to which they are related for their significance and meaning. In the case of historical evidence and facts, the historian is dependent upon materials which exist in his present. He cannot relate these to the 'past' since this is the only evidence that he has of the past. Such evidence is incomplete in a way which cannot be known. Hence, reliance on an objective criterion, namely a past independent of these materials, cannot be substantiated as a means of evaluating claims to historical knowledge.

The claim of historical argument to be an empirical explanation is based upon survivals which are taken as evidence for the existence of a past. Such evidence is selected and interpreted by the historian. In other words, a past fact does not become a historical fact until it is incorporated into a historical argument. Hence a correspondence between facts and the evidence – documents, artefacts, historical accounts and chronicles, etc. – which attests to these facts is not a criterion for objective truth. The reasons for this are, firstly, that there is no means of observing past facts as an external reality and thus attesting to the truth of the evidence itself, and secondly, that historical interpretation is not solely concerned with establishing facts as being true. It is concerned with interpreting them by incorporating them in an explanation. The truth of the fact is a matter of evidence, that is, a relationship between the alleged fact and some grounds for believing it to be true; but the truth of a historical explanation is not simply a matter of attesting the truth of its factual content. Of course, we can criticise the criterion of relevance employed by a historian, by applying it to facts and discovering inconsistencies in its application, but the criterion itself cannot be attacked on the grounds of the criterion of objectivity considered above. Moreover, while existing evidence may establish a fact, we cannot know to what that particular fact is related in a causal or any other sense, where there is no evidence. The historian can make inferences, but this poses problems relating to rationalisations and to the kind of implicitly posited psychological or reductionist hypothesis referred to earlier. Yet the contextual relationships of facts are important to historical argument, and when 'new facts' or 'new evidence' are discovered, this frequently means the rewriting of history.

If, then, we accept that historical argument cannot be assessed on the basis of a past external reality, this means that we are forced to seek evaluatory criteria from within rather than outside the explanation. This leads on to the argument that history is a world of ideas created by the historian. As we have seen, both the assertion that history is a mode of experience and the assertion that a historical argument is a re-experiencing of the thought of the historical agent in terms of the historian's own experience result in incommunicable explanations. A coherent world of ideas, as was argued for the conceptual schemes discussed earlier, can only be judged on the grounds of its internal logical consistency, since the external criterion of the coherent unity of knowledge – to which such a mode is alleged to be related – is inherently non-empirical and metaphysical in nature. Similarly, the idea of history as being the historian's own experiences raises the difficulty of establishing criteria for the comparison and evaluation of such experiences. If, as was argued earlier, such criteria are lacking as part of the proffered argument, then the resultant explanation is incommunicable. Thus, on the basis of the criticism of historical objectivity, we might accept the argument that history is created by the historian and that it is innately subjective in nature. But if we do so, we must establish criteria which enable us to evaluate such creations before we can say that they constitute an explanation.

This brings us back to the problem of agreeing on the criteria proper to historical knowledge and explanation. It has been asserted that historical argument should be value-free and *per contra* that it should consist of values. Thus the discounting or the assertion of particular elements have been considered to be the basis for the evaluation of historical writings. The problem associated with these criteria is that we cannot know in any precise way the extent to which values enter into historical argument. If the discounting of specific values or beliefs is acceptable to a particular histori-cal school this constitutes a convention which permits at least a distinction between observance and non-observance. Alternatively, if explicit values are asserted as being the basis for a historical argument, this also permits the operation of a conventional judgement. But the operation of these conven-tions does not enable us to make evaluations between arguments which are alleged to be historical and which either posit differing sets of values, or claim to be value-free. Nor within the framework of such conventions is it possible to make further evaluation, unless additional criteria are adduced. Nevertheless, such conventions appear to be the only alternative to the assertion of an external objective criterion, or of purely internal logical grounds, for the evaluation of historical argument.

However, before examining this possibility, the argument that historical knowledge is innately subjective and relative requires further consideration. It is sometimes asserted that relativism consists of the view 'that no his-torical work grasps the nature of the past (or present) immediately, that whatever "truth" an historical work contains is relative to the conditioning processes under which it arose and can only be understood with reference to those processes'.[20] In other words, this argument maintains that all historical work has an implicit bias relating to the psychological, social, political, economic, cultural, religious, etc., conditions under which the historian writes. He is conditioned by his environment to write a particular form of history. This interpretation of historical relativism is misconceived, since the point of the relativist argument is not that historical judgement is biased by the conditions under which it is made, but that the nature of its bias cannot be established. If we cannot know the way in which a historical explanation distorts 'reality', then we cannot evaluate any such explanation in terms of its objective truth. It is, in this sense, a negative argument arising out of the difficulties of determining criteria external to, and independent of, historical argument which are 'objective' in nature. But relativism is not scepticism, in that it does not deny the possibility of an objectively based historical knowledge, for it only asserts that we cannot distinguish between proffered explanations by presuming the existence of such a knowledge. As this commentator recognised, 'unless we go back to the usual view of objectivity and say that historical objectivity resides in the historian's ability to portray the *real* character and relations of historical events, we shall find no escape from relativism'.[21]

Thus the relativist is not asserting the particular nature of bias in historical argument, for his is the position of denying that there is at present a means of establishing objective truth on the basis of criteria independent of the argument to which it is applied. If it was simply a matter of establishing which particular environmental conditions formed which particular historical school, then we should have a theoretical explanation of the phenomenon of historical literature, if not of history. But this is not a relativist argument, even if it were actually possible to undertake such an exercise. The reason why every generation rewrites its own history is not because it is forced to do so by changing cultural conditions, but because of the innately subjective nature of historical argument. There are sufficiently diverse views within generations as to the nature and value of specific historical interpretations which attest to this. We might also regard changing cultural conditions, however these are conceived, as a product of historical and other contributions, rather than as their cause.

In other words, in asserting that there is no valid or viable external objective criterion on which historical explanation can be judged, the relativist is not abandoning the notion of historical explanation as a meaningful exercise. While this particular criterion might not exist, it is nevertheless possible to establish other standards. These standards will be relative and not universal or absolute in any sense. We may regard them as consisting of conventions agreed on by historians for the evaluation of particular historical arguments. A satisfactory, but not a true, historical argument will be one which satisfies a number, but not necessarily all, of these critical criteria. While such standards will be concerned with questions of internal logic, with consistency in argument, with the relationship between hypothesis and argument, with the type of assumptions and presuppositions used, with the relationship between evidence, facts and inferences and their interpretation and with the kind of data, statistical or testimonial, no one of these categories is sufficient to enable definitive criticism. Indeed, one might say that the current fashion in historical interpretation is to avoid arguments which turn on a reductionist argument, whether psychological or dispositional, or on a single-factor causal hypothesis such as economic or power theories. Prescriptive argument, which is based on ethical or ideological premises, and argument which is linked to speculation about contingent situations in the future, are also conceived of as 'non-historical'. But even if these sorts of explanations are considered to be outside the historical repertoire, this still permits a wide variety of argument which may lead to conflicting and equally acceptable interpretations of the same factual or material content.

In summary, if we accept this argument, historical explanation consists of a way of making selected present evidence of the past intelligible through the construction of a narrative argument. Such a construction, although using assumptions derived from other fields and other explanations, and although depending upon a logical process of reasoning, cannot be judged solely on the grounds of its theoretical presuppositions or on its logical structure. Nor can it be judged on the basis of the relationship between its conclusions and empirical reality. Its factual content must have a relationship to evidence; but this alone is not a sufficient critical criterion. Neither is historical argument incommunicable or idiosyncratic, since it is evaluated on the basis of standards which, although conventional in nature, nevertheless exists. On these grounds, it is possible to distinguish between good and bad history and non-history, in the same way as it is possible, using grounds equally conventional in nature, to distinguish between science and non-science, between an argument which can be falsified and one which cannot.

Before attempting to relate this conception of history to the various interpretations contained in this study, perhaps the contention can now be examined that sociological explanation, and indeed much of explanation in the social sciences, is no different in nature from that of historical interpretation. It will be recalled that the claim to scientific knowledge found in both historical argument and in social science was found to lack substance. This is to say that, if knowledge is grounded in explanation, then in the absence of this kind of explanation we have no science of human affairs. We can distinguish between arguments which take the *form* of a scientific explanation and those which do not, but this is a formal distinction. Again, as we have seen, much of social science is concerned with the past – the same past as that which concerns the historian, namely present survivals of the past – only in so far as past facts or historical material can be used to substantiate arguments which have relevance for the future through their predictive capacity. Such a concern is essentially non-historical. Nevertheless, it is dependent upon the kind of historical interpretation, either indirectly from its borrowings or directly through its own creations, which we have considered here. As was argued in the case of historical explanation, such evidence is very important as a critical criterion for the evaluation of an argument, although it is not the sole criterion for establishing its nature. This is no less true of explanations in the social sciences, for they stand in the same relationship to facts and data as historical explanation. Those arguments which depend upon historical interpretations as their main source of empirical referents can be criticised on the same grounds as those used by Collingwood in his condemnation of 'scissors and paste' history.[22] If the view is taken that the attestation of evidence and the dependence of an explanation on such criteria constitute evaluatory criteria for historical argument, then this is equally true for social science. But an argument which claims to be scientific must satisfy theoretical requirements properly belonging to that form of explanation. If it does not, it remains an untestable hypothesis, a conceptual scheme, or a political or social prescription. It hangs in an explanatory limbo, being incapable of any judgement other than that related to its internal logical consistency.

The question is: can the arguments found in social science be conceived of as historical in nature? Do they constitute a form of knowledge of past human affairs which is relative and which is established on the basis of innately subjective criteria, conceived of as evaluatory conventions? If this is the case, then, while the actual content of the various explanations, their assumptions, criteria of relevance and selectivity and materials, offered in the social sciences and in history will vary, the nature of the grounds on which such arguments can be evaluated is essentially the same. The point is not one of finding an appropriate label, for it does not matter if we use the terms 'social science', 'history' or even 'geography' to describe various academic activities. The label 'science', as we have seen, is sufficiently vague as to cover a wide variety of different intellectual activities. Rather, our concern is with the nature of the arguments offered as explanations, and if current arguments in various 'fields' appear to share certain characteristics and to be susceptible to the same judgement, the question is one of elucidating the grounds for this assertion.

It can be argued that explanation, in history and in the social sciences, is concerned with the problem of human volition in giving reasons for human actions and their consequences. A distinction can be made between a reason-giving explanation and a theoretical explanation. Thus a historian seeks to explain in terms of the historical agent; this involves not the imposition of presently held notions of the context of action, but an attempt to relate the agent to *his* perception. It is *his* sense of the past, *his* knowledge and *his* perceptions which the historian seeks to create on the basis of surviving evidence. There is no objective or external reality to which the historian can appeal in order to substantiate an explanation of motivation and action. He is not concerned to say that the historical agent was right or wrong, or to explain why he thought in that particular way, but to establish what he thought as an explanation of what he did. And such a concern is not with a dispositional, rationalist or psychological theory, which asserts the inevitability of human action or its necessity, but with making human actions explicable in a way which emphasises the individual basis of action and not the forces, processes or contextual circumstances sometimes alleged to be the mainsprings of history. The criterion of relevance for the historical narrative lies in establishing the perceptions or awareness of individual historical agents.

Now, according to the preceding argument, we cannot actually *know* these in any empathetic sense or indeed in any way other than through our own formulations based on a use of historical materials. We cannot relate the historical agent to *his* past other than through evidence of his awareness of it. The assertion of the contemporaneity of events as an explanatory basis is a reflection of the historian's own past, not of that of the individual's whose actions he is seeking to explain. Hence it is the relationship which is asserted between these materials and the historian's own construction which constitutes a 'historical' explanation. Thus if a theoretical explanation, which subsumes such individual perceptions in a general, genetic or causal argument, is eschewed, this problem would seem to be central to both historian and social scientist. The process of establishing a construction of perception and motivation is different in nature from that of formulating a general hypothesis which explains human action. As we have seen in the earlier discussion of the general theory of action, of systems analysis and of decision-making theories, the emphasis moved away from individualist conceptions of motivation to that of *typical* action, role-behaviour, role-functioning, acting, and of systemic or functional behaviour. Clearly, such an extension is necessary in order to posit comparisons between social and political acts and situations, to enable generalisation, and to formulate the terms of a theoretical explanation which transcends the particular and the past and which permits predictive statement. But such theoretical extensions derive some, at least, of their presuppositions from the same kind of interpretation as that found in historical argument.

As we see, an attempt is made to derive concepts, categories and variables from a subjective understanding of particular human events and situations. It is largely because of this extrapolation that historians have criticised such exercises as being 'un-historical', and conversely, because of the refusal of most historians to establish grounds for generalisation and comparison, their histories have been condemned by social scientists as being 'theoretically unstructured'. But having established a distinction between two forms of argument on the basis of theoretical intent, we can see that such controversies arise out of an inability to establish common grounds for agreement and disagreement. If, as an alternative, such common ground is found in the innately subjective basis of the interpretations of past human activities which belong to both types of argument, it is possible to establish evaluatory criteria. It has been contended throughout this study that these criteria, although equally conventional, are distinctive from those appropriate to scientific argument.

In conclusion, it would seem appropriate to a critical exercise of this kind to attempt a critique of its own interpretations. A wide variety of arguments have been considered and an attempt has been made to state the grounds on which a critical analysis may properly be made. At the same time a number of interpretations of contemporary international politics have been advanced whose purpose is not simply to illustrate various theoretical or critical points, but to provide some kind of plausible alternative. In particular, a specific approach towards historical explanation has been suggested as a more viable alternative to those which depend for their validation on an internal coherence and consistency, or on some notion of an external empirical reality. Although none of these constitutes more than a sketch of a historical explanation, it might be appropriate to indicate the major kinds of criticism which can be made of them, and the requirements which they should meet before they can be considered adequate as explanations. There are four general interpretations in this work: the first consisting of a study of the origins of the Cold War; the second, of the development of a nuclear arms race and its political consequences; the third, of the influence of economic factors on foreign policy and international politics; and the fourth, of the political significance of universalist international organisations.

These interpretations can be criticised on a number of grounds, including, of course, those rejected in this study. But it should be borne in mind that when evaluation proceeds on the basis of an alternative mode of explanation, such an explanation, together with its own critical criteria, must first be established as more appropriate than that which is the subject of criticism. The rejection of various claims to knowledge and explanation in the field of human activities in general, and in international politics in particular, was based upon the nature of such claims and not on the assertion of a more appropriate explanation. Nevertheless, as we have seen, such a rejection left this question open and an attempt was made to provide an answer to it. Thus, in approaching a criticism of these general interpretations of aspects of international politics, the criteria considered to be relevant stem from the notion of historical explanation outlined above. If we accept this, our central concern is whether they are good or bad *historical* interpretations. They owe nothing to the systematic search for a scientific explanation of human behaviour, nor are idealist or rationalist criteria appropriate to their evaluation.

It will be recalled that after the rejection of a number of reductionist or single-factor hypotheses which sought to explain the origins of the Cold War, the most plausible interpretation offered was one which explained this phenomenon in terms of the thoughts and motivations of President Truman and his consequent actions and decisions. According to this argument, Truman pursued a policy of 'firmness' in negotiating with the U.S.S.R. in order to offset a relatively weak bargaining position on questions involving Eastern and Southern Europe. Agreements on other issues, which had been accepted in substance or in principle by his predecessor and his allies, were made dependent on an acceptance by the Russians of the American position on the Polish and German settlements. Such a policy led to hostile Soviet responses, to mutual misunderstanding, to the pursuit of objectives on a unilateral basis, and to the complete breakdown of relationships known as the Cold War. Although the nature of Soviet responses and demands, the attitudes of Britain, France and Italy, the domestic political circumstances in the liberated countries, and other factors, were considered relevant, the main determinant of the developing international situation after the war was considered to be Truman's policy. How can such a selection and the interpretation to which it is related be justified?

Firstly, we must consider the question of the relation between facts and their interpretation, that is, between what survives *now* as evidence of what the participants believed *then,* and a historical construction based on this material. It must be admitted that such 'evidence' is partial and incomplete in a way which cannot be known. An emphasis on American foreign policy as the chief determinant of this political situation may simply be a reflection of the relative abundance of material which is American in origin. Virtually nothing is known on the Soviet side. But any explanation would have to contend with this problem. Accepting this, the interpretation of diaries, memoirs, letters, state papers, speeches and official publications, sometimes written during the events to which they relate and sometimes very much later, presents a number of difficulties. There can be no very precise criterion on which this 'evidence' can be evaluated. A good interpretation should not only be internally consistent but should be compatible with other inter-pretations. In other words, the best argument is one which makes this material coherent and takes into account objections which might be raised on the basis of conflicting meaning or significance of particular sources. For example, in the case of Truman's personal account of his policy, his constant assertion that the Soviet Union was bent on world conquest, and the value-loaded terms in which he describes its socio-economic system, cannot simply be ignored or dismissed as irrelevant to an explanation of his actions. Rhetoric must be shown to be rhetoric. Thus we might qualify these statements by reference to other passages in which Truman reveals his awareness that negotiation and the inhibiting factor of superior American military capacity could produce stable political agreements. Bearing in mind that this account is essentially *post facto,* it could be argued that the 'value' content relates to the period after 1947 when the attempt to negotiate had been abandoned, and the 'political' content to the period when 'firmness' appeared to be a viable policy. Alternatively, it could be argued that there was nothing contradictory in believing that the Soviets would not keep agreements, while at the same time attempting to conclude agreements with them. Inconsistency is, after all, a characteristic human failing. The view could also be taken that although Truman believed Soviet policy was expansionist, nevertheless he thought that American power could provide both a check to this expansion and a basis for lasting political settlements once its implications had been appreciated by Stalin.

Closely related to this ambivalence in interpreting evidence and establish-ing historical 'facts' is the problem of motivation. A number of different constructions can be placed on Truman's own explanation of his actions; but in what sense do they explain his motives? The way in which a historical agent explains his world may be inconsistent with his 'real' understanding. Not only may his explanation be deceptive in this respect, but it is difficult to distinguish between political argument which is designed for a particular audience and intended to elicit support or to command respect, and that which reflects genuine beliefs about the external world. The apparent and often-declared motive stated by Truman as the basis of his policy was the need to succour 'free' states from communist tyranny, as a means of upholding democratic values. But was this idealistic standpoint a motive? Here again, we have both to explain its expression and to evaluate its political significance. In order to do so, both inference and reference to contextual factors have to be employed to supplement such statements. The fact is that, if motivation is construed as the innermost beliefs of politicians, firstly, we have no means of knowing these, and secondly, even if we did, we have no means of relating them to their actions and decisions. All that can be done is to try to place whatever evidence of reasoning is available in a framework of interpretation which is as consistent as possible. Such a framework must take into account both the idiosyncratic and the unforeseen in explaining the development of a political situation.

For example, it was asserted that one of the motives for Truman's policy of firmness was his desire to be seen as a 'strong' President. The consequences of this attitude were the breakdown of negotiations with the U.S.S.R. and the political alienation of Eastern and most of Southern Europe. Now we can regard these consequences as being either intended or unintended. If the former, then it would appear that the containment policy was decided on shortly after the defeat of Germany. If, however, the latter view is adopted, not only was Truman's policy unsuccessful, that is, if he intended to come to some agreement with the Soviets, but the policy of containment itself stemmed from this lack of success. There is obviously scope for controversy over these two possibilities. The latter was adopted in this interpretation of the Cold War. Truman's belief in the efficacy of a diplomatic tactic produced hostile reactions from the U.S.S.R., which in turn induced increased 'firmness' from the United States and so on. Because of his relatively weak domestic political position, Truman could not afford to admit failure in his foreign policy, and in any case was forced to respond to the changed circumstances produced by Soviet reactions to it.

But it could also be argued on very much the same evidence that Truman's delay in implementing his containment policy and the apparent drift in attitudes over the period 1945 to 1947 were due to factors which he could not control, and to the need to prepare his country for the major commitment of a long-term involvement in European politics. Whichever view is taken, however, the problem of motivation arises and this cannot be resolved by an inference from the course of events which, as we have seen, permits different interpretation. One motive which is often advanced is that of Truman's concern with the promotion of economic interests, stemming from the need to expand, characteristic of the particular stage of development which the American economy had reached. Another view, partly reflecting this, is one touched on previously, namely that his ideological commitment constituted a motive. Yet another turns on the necessity to fill the power vacuum created by the defeats of Germany and Japan. As we have seen, these are not motives, but reasons which belong to various kinds of hypotheses, more or less deterministic, which transcend the understanding of the individual politician. The 'evidence' supporting them and their theoretical presuppositions is thus external and derived from a context which is alleged to be 'objective' in nature. Enough has been said earlier about these arguments, but they indicate the difficulties of establishing the nature of the context for policy- and decision-making.

The argument that the chief architect of the Cold War was President Truman requires further explanation as to the factors relevant to his under-standing and his policy. By these are meant those factors immanent in the decisional context which were external to the participants, but not to their perception. For example, the development of the atomic bomb and the defeat of Germany, together with the war-time agreements which had been concluded between the allies, were the products of Truman's predecessors. If a purely causal argument were being advanced to explain the Cold War conflict, then the problem of infinite regress arises of the 'for want of a nail the battle was lost' variety. As was argued earlier, an argument of this kind belongs to a different kind of explanation, and we are not concerned here with the derivation of theoretical propositions related to a genetic or causal hypothesis. The point is that a historical explanation selects out of the context of events those factors, precedent or contemporaneous, which are considered to be germane to the phenomenon explained. But the criterion of relevance in this case is asserted to be the perception and reasoning of a historical agent. Thus the factors actually selected in this particular inter-pretation – the influence of advisers, the possession of a nuclear monopoly, the pressure of the United Kingdom, the security concerns of the Soviet Union, the presence of communist parties in Western European countries and the weakness of their economies and so on – are not presented as an objective external context to which the actions of the participants are related, but as factors which were relevant in *their* eyes.

While events or factors of this kind are, in some sense, external to the actual understanding of the historical agents, that is, they exist as past facts so far as there are grounds for asserting them as facts, our concern with them is with their relationship to the situation we are seeking to explain. Their significance as historical facts depends upon their relevance to the policy-maker. It is in this sense that the historical world is not simply a world of events but a world of thought. It will be recalled that one of the problems associated with the diplomatic significance of the newly-found nuclear monopoly of the United States was whether President Truman conceived of it as adding to his political strength during his negotiations with the Soviets. Whatever the interpretation adopted, this is at least a question proper to historical argument. It is not enough to assert retrospectively that such a monopoly conferred strength on the United States through the mere fact of its existence. Similarly, assertions as to the inhibitory or determining influences of the domestic political context, of economic and financial resources, of external alliances and obligations, etc., must be supported, in this view, by evidence that these alleged factors entered into the decision-making process, and are not grounded upon external rationalising criteria.

Yet even when this has been done, there is still a problem of evaluating their relative significance, so far as the historical agent is concerned. There may be evidence that such factors were considered, but in the absence of any indication as to their priority or importance, inferential or contextual judgments become necessary. As we have seen, such judgements may produce a number of differing interpretations. In evaluating them, recourse must be made to evaluatory criteria concerned with the scope and consistency of the way in which an argument deals with the available evidence. Inferences can be made, but the degree to which an argument is inferential or speculative will afford one indication as to whether it is an adequate historical explanation.

If we turn to the second interpretation. that of the development of the nuclear arms race and its influence on policy and international relations, we can see that this poses different problems from the one considered above. While the interpretation of the origins of the Cold War concentrated upon a number of decisions and negotiations undertaken by a few policy-makers over a relatively short period of time, that of the post-war arms race presupposes a characteristic pattern of events over a very much longer period. Moreover, it contains speculative or hypothetical arguments relating to strategy and defence which posit a number of unrealised contingencies. Rather than seeking to understand the past of the historical agents, or their immediate present, we are concerned here to understand what they conceive to be their future and the effect of this conception on their policy decisions. Such conceptions are prone to change, both as a consequence of these decisions and as the reciprocal effects of technological innovations are felt. Hence we are concerned with constant revisions and reappraisals of policy and strategy and with making an evaluation of these.

The thesis of this interpretation was that the interplay between national conceptions of security and foreign policy produced unforseen consequences which resulted in an unintended major change in the latter. As with the earlier argument, if this is to be more than speculation or external rationalisation, then it must be grounded in the perceptions and motivations of the participants. But the problem here is that the assertion of a historical period characterised by a particular mode of behaviour implies a sequence of events which possesses an autonomy independent of those participating in them. This is not to argue that an arms race possesses a dynamic which determines the course of events regardless of the perceptions of politicians. The mathematical theory of an arms race posited by L. F. Richardson was rejected largely on the grounds that it either ignored these, or treated them as a set of quantifiable factors. Yet an explanation of an arms race asserts a continuum in time, in which a particular trend of political activity occurs, and this posits a historical judgement other than that solely based upon the construction of specific motives and perceptions. What is the justification for the presentation of a 'history' of an arms race as a historical interpretation?

It will be recalled that the analysis began with an idealised argument describing the security dilemma which, it was alleged, confronted all nations. Two notions were presented as being mutually contradictory: firstly, that any attempt to create a condition of security for the state resulted in increased insecurity for other states, thus perpetuating the dilemma; secondly, that most policy-makers believe in the efficacy of violence in order to achieve non-security objectives. The notion of war as 'policy by other means' is inherently irrational, since the use of violence results in the transformation of a conflict into a struggle directly involving the security of the contestants. Only under very favourable circumstances can war be limited, and therefore rational. But this argument, as it stands, is a rationalisation rather than a historical interpretation. In this sense that it contains a historical generalisation derived from past conflicts and their consequences, it is descriptive, but not very useful in explaining particular situations. However, the situation which developed from 1945 contained a new element, in that the effects of nuclear weapons could be precisely measured in terms of their destructive capacity. These weapons introduced a qualitative change in the nature of warfare, making it immensely more destructive and dangerous to the state than any previous innovation in weapons technology. The problem of relating violence to policy became particularly acute.

It was argued that the first response to the American monopoly of nuclear weapons, on the part of allies and opponents alike, was the parallel development of programmes designed to produce such weapons. It shows that one aspect of the significance of this innovation was appreciated, namely its security implications, given a one-nation monopoly. Initially, the pattern of alliances and international relations developed under the shadow of this monopoly and, in a sense, was independent of it. But the consequences of the spread of nuclear weapons, apart from an intensification in technological innovation, were the eventual weakening of alliances and the gradual erosion of the policy of global containment. Thus the exigencies of security requirements and defence policies produced a situation in which they predominated over foreign policy objectives. The unforeseen consequence of the nuclear arms race was the end of the Cold War and of the policies associated with it. Such a result was neither premeditated nor appeared a possibility during the three administrations which created post-war American defence policy. It is true that politicians were preoccupied with the problem of relating superior military capacity to the attainment of political objectives throughout this period, but the notion that these objectives would prove unattainable largely through the development of this capacity was not realised until the early 1960s.

Thus the arms race is advanced as an explanation for the situation of mutual defensive deterrence and its political concomitants. Acting on one set of assumptions, politicians created conditions which caused them and their successors to formulate quite new assumptions on which they based policy and action. The link can be established *post facto,* and this is essentially a historical exercise. Yet it rests upon a construction of political thought and not on a set of rationalisations derived from 'objective' criteria relating to the capacity of nuclear powers and the hypothetically contingent situations in which it may be utilised. Strategic theories, it will be recalled from earlier discussion, were relevant to explanation only in so far as there is evidence that they exerted an influence upon political decision, or existed as a political phenomenon in their own right.

But having outlined the argument, together with these reservations, it is clear that the connection between perception and strategic hypotheses in a political locus is extremely difficult to establish. It is subject to all the problems relating to motivation and evidence referred to in the earlier discussion of President Truman's foreign policy. Direct evidence is even more difficult to obtain, given the secrecy surrounding defence programmes and the premises on which they are founded. There is almost a total absence of evidence relating to Soviet and Chinese policies. Hence the argument rests a great deal on inference based on the tangible evidence of the weapons themselves and the content of various negotiated agreements concerning arms limitations. For example, successive British governments have, with the aid of the United States, developed a Polaris missile force. How can this be explained in terms of the reasoning underlying this programme? These governments have repeatedly stressed the continuing significance of NATO and the American relationship, yet at the same time have been extremely ambiguous in defining the precise relationship of this force to the alliance. France, equally determined to maintain an independent deterrent, has made no secret of its attitude towards NATO and its rejection of its defensive strategy. On the face of it, the assertion that mutual strategic deterrence has resulted in a weakening of alliances appears to be true for France but not for Britain. Yet both countries have adopted identical defence policies based on invulnerable I.C.B.M.s

This apparent anomaly can be explained in terms of Britain's non-strategic interest in maintaining influence in European politics, and in a close relationship with the United States. Public statements which stress the continuing importance of NATO can be regarded as political argument rather than as evidence of strategic throught. The Defence White Paper of 1957 can be considered as setting the framework for the long-term development of British security policy and was formulated in the light of the innovation of the long-range missile. From this time onwards, successive British governments sought to create an independent nuclear force and took a number of decisions reflecting their reliance on a deterrent basis for security. These included the abolition of conscription, the reduction of the Territorial Army reserve, cuts in naval and air forces and the running down of a large number of foreign bases. In spite of American pressure, during the 1961 Berlin crisis Britain refused either to mobilise reserves or to introduce a modified form of conscription. When the attempt to develop a British missile broke down in 1960, considerable weight was brought to bear on the Kennedy administration in order to obtain the Polaris missile. In short, there is a consistency in attitudes and actions over a period of time, from which can be inferred the acceptance of a particular strategic argument, that of defensive deterrence, and the concomitant inability of a defensive alliance based on American nuclear capacity to deter.

Of course, there are alternative explanations of these events and of the associated reasoning. The abolition of conscription was a popular decision and could be explained on political and economic grounds. Similarly, the succession of defence cuts and the gradual running down of armed forces and foreign bases can be explained as economies forced upon governments which suffered from continuing balance-of-payments problems. In an age of colonial dismantlement, foreign bases were not only expensive to run, but were political anachronisms. While these factors were certainly relevant – and an attempt was certainly made to provide political justification for this policy which could create advantages for the government in power – they stemmed from radical changes which mutual strategic deterrence had created in national security policies. It was not only Britain which sought to possess its own defensive deterrence, but also France and China. To say that these countries wanted nuclear weapons for reasons of prestige does not appear very convincing.

Although interpretations of the relationship between defence and foreign policy and strategic thought tend to be based on inference, this is partly a reflection of the speculative basis of defence planning and of the ambiguity with which governments explain their policies. All preparation for war is concerned with a problematical and hypothetical future and, as was argued, the terms and assumptions which are made with regard to possible contingencies are peculiarly liable to change. The historian has the task of constructing the thought of one point in time and relating it, and its consequences, to that of subsequent thought. He is concerned with establishing its significance in terms of these consequences, foreseen and unforseen. But it must be admitted that direct evidence is difficult to obtain. For example, the installation of an A.B.M. system by the Soviet Union was treated as an important event by the United States. Yet the reasoning behind this step is completely open to speculation. The fact that it prompted a serious attempt to reach an accommodation on the question of arms limitations may or may not have been an intended consequence. An earlier example, that of the introduction of the hydrogen bomb by the United States, is also a matter for conjecture. There was no obvious strategic justification for this move, and indeed it was cancelled out very quickly by the Soviet development of the bomb. Thus while it is possible to attribute significance to events of this kind, it is impossible to do more than make a number of speculative inferences as to the motivations and perceptions which underlie them.

It should be clear by now that the discussion of an arms race, contained in an earlier chapter, is of the same order as that of the negotiations between the allies at the end of the Second World War: it is descriptive rather than explanatory. Although it has an organising principle and contains various assumptions, it is not an adequate explanation because it lacks an adequate analysis of the understanding of the participants. The point here is that the use of terms such as 'arms race', 'action–reaction phenomenon', or even that of 'the Cold War' itself, is a form of descriptive shorthand which glosses over the complex political relationships they label. An arms race cannot be treated as independent of the activities it describes and consequently cannot have a 'history'. Nor can one such phenomenon be compared with another in order to sustain general propositions. Any generalisation which attributes characteristics to a particular period of time must be derived from the reasoning of the historical agents. Of course, unforeseen consequences and the continuing effects of political actions form part of a historical analysis, but these have relevance only in so far as they are perceived by those acting in a political context. While the nuclear stalemate of the early 1960s was not envisaged by those responsible for the earlier decisions which brought it about, the nature of the stalemate itself was well understood by those responsible for policy subsequent to it. The argument of the logic of events is no more appropriate to a historical argument than that of their purely fortuitous nature.

Thus references to trends, development, processes, origins and turning-points, to name but a few of the terms sometimes used to make a narrative coherent, lead to postulating a form of continuity which is a reflection of the narrator's own past rather than that of the historical agents whose actions he seeks to explain. Moreover, such an argument comes dangerously close to the assertion of a pattern in the past, even though this may be more implicit than explicit, and it thus ceases to be a historical explanation in the sense used in this study. An explanation of the course of events known as an arms race, in making purely retrospective judgements and in asserting its autonomy as a political phenomenon, tends to move away from the level of understanding which is asserted to be the proper historical focus.

Nevertheless, an interpretation must seek to resolve inconsistencies in the available evidence and to achieve a coherent narrative, and the extent to which it is necessary to base this on inference and speculative argument is an indication of its strength or weakness as a historical explanation. In this respect, this particular interpretation can be considered to be the least satisfactory of those presented in this study as historical interpretations.

Turning to the third major interpretation in this study, that of the economic factor in international politics, it was argued that an attempt to establish the significance of economic considerations in political decisions and policies can be distinguished from reductionist explanations which turn on a single-factor causal hypothesis. Such an attempt should not be confused with the type of argument which seeks to make generalisations extending across time, and concerned with particular past situations only in so far as they are typical of a class of such situations or illustrate a historical dynamic. Neither a reductionist nor a historicist argument constitutes a *historical* explanation. Hence the historian, in seeking to determine the significance of economic factors, does so in relation to other factors considered to be relevant to his construction and to their appreciation by the historical agent.

There were two broad aspects of economic influences in international politics considered, the first relating to the pursuit of foreign policy objectives by capitalist states and the second to the economic factor in contemporary international politics in general. Neither were developed as historical interpretations, since the primary purpose of the analysis was critical and concerned mainly with illustrating the shortcomings of economic hypotheses as historical explanations. Nevertheless, the assertion was made that American foreign policy in the post-Second World War period could be understood as being influenced more by ideological and political factors than by economic or materialist motives. This is to reject one hypothesis by proffering a counter-hypothesis and, as we have seen, the only justification for this is to assert the latter as an intrinsically different kind of explanation. The latter argument is not really a hypothesis at all, but is grounded in an examination of the policy-making process, historical in nature, which establishes significance in terms of the evidence for the understanding of the policy-maker. It should be clear that, whatever the outcome of such an examination, the result is unlikely to be the vindication of arguments which depend upon economic determinism, transcendental idealism, power–security competition, or simply accident, as the explanatory focus. Such explanations are irrefutable and equally valid and are concerned with political events only in so far as they afford illustrations of the hypothetical process.

Yet a historical explanation will, perforce, contain some elements of these particular approaches, firstly because political argument is often couched in such terms and therefore becomes part of the phenomena which is its subject, and secondly because any attribution of influence or cause assumes that such factors can be isolated and categorised. Hence the terms 'political', 'ideological', 'economic', etc., contain postulates which can be extended into reductionist argument. The purpose of historical interpretation is neither to produce systematic abstractions nor to indulge in a kind of academic Mrs Beetonism, in which different receipts for different situations are concocted out of such elements.

This brings us back to the problem of the relationship between a generalisation or abstraction and historical interpretation. As was noted earlier, most, if not all, historical narratives contain presuppositions which imply generalisation of one sort or another. This is a characteristic of empirical and practical explanations, including those of science. But the historian is not concerned with pursuing their theoretical implications, or with the systematic formulation of a conceptual scheme which makes them, logically at least, coherent or consistent. If he does so, then he is led into a form of idealist and non-empirical argument or into the kind of theory characteristic of science, possessing theoretical requirements which he is unable to fulfil. Some would argue that this is indeed what he should attempt. However, enough has been said to indicate that such attempts have either proved notably unsuccessful or have resulted in an explanatory dead-end. This is not to say that arguments of this type are somehow illegitimate or unattainable in principle, but that they are irrelevant to the historian. If the question central to a historical enquiry is answerable only in general hypothetical terms, then it is the wrong question.

In this instance, if it enquires into the 'economic' causes of political events, then the answer is almost inevitably forced into a form which postulates a general explanatory hypothesis which explains not the particular but the general. The historian finds his focus in particular contextual relationships as reflected in individual awareness at the time. The question must therefore be rephrased to consider the distinctiveness of past situations in terms of this awareness, rather than a level of generalisation which properly belongs to other types of explanation. It should be clear from this that any controversy between those who advocate reductionist theories, such as Marxism, and those who criticise them because they ignore historical facts or reality, is based on false grounds. Neither type of explanation can pre-empt the other, nor can they be compared or related.

Thus 'economic' considerations enter into historical explanation only where they are conceived of by the historical agents as relevant to their decisions and activities. For example, it was Macmillan's realisation of the dangers to sterling caused by American oppositions to the Suez expedition which persuaded him to abandon his support for Eden's policy. A historical interpretation of the Suez crisis would have to evaluate such economic factors as balance-of-payments problems, the position of sterling as an international currency, the necessity of a guaranteed supply of oil and the importance of trade routes, but only in so far as they existed in the perceptions of the participants. There is no 'economic' explanation of British foreign policy decisions which is independent of the reasoning and understanding of those engaged in making them.

The final example of historical analysis in this study was the examination of the politics of universalist international organisations and their relationship to international politics. This involves a problem different in nature from those considered above, since it posits the existence of an institution possessing a historical identity. In common-sense language we know what the 'United Nations' is, just as we know what the terms 'Parliament' or 'Congress' mean, but a historical interpretation of their origin, their institutional growth and their political significance assumes some kind of pattern or genetic development over a period of time and within a political context. In other words, they are alleged to have a history, as for example the medieval English Parliament is asserted to have some kind of connection with later parliamentary forms. Now while, perhaps, this may be justified for national institutions, especially where there is a direct connection with a body of interpretative constitutional law, to which precedents and change can be related and legitimised on a normative basis, this approach is less obviously justifiable for international institutions.

The central difficulty in treating the United Nations as an institution with a 'history' is that of finding a focus which can be conceived of as a meaningful historical question. This was found not in its complex organisational structure, nor in its 'constitution', nor even in its decisions or activities, but in the behaviour of its members. Hence it was asserted in the analysis that the United Nations had a characteristic political process which provided a means of interpreting the organisation and a subject for explanation. But such a process was as typical of the early years of the United Nations' existence as of the present. In short, it was argued that although major changes have occurred in the organisational structure of U.N. organs, in the substantive content of its deliberations and in its activities, the underlying politics to which these changes can be attributed remains essentially the same. This is to say that no decision is made which constitutes a precedent for later decisions, and no organic changes occur which represent a development from prior organisational developments. The United Nations, in this sense, is in perpetual flux and the only constant consists of the peculiar nature of its politics. Thus both an institutional and a constitutional approach were rejected in this analysis.

Yet while accepting the argument that the U.N. is no more than the sum of its members at any given time, a concern with behaviourism was eschewed in favour of the kind of subjective, and perhaps impressionistic, argument which has been characterised in this study as historical explanation. It was argued that counting votes and the use of elaborate techniques to detect group behaviour in committees and other gatherings produced little in the way of historical argument or scientific hypothesis. They did no more than refine upon assumptions, impressionistic or historical in nature. Having said this, however, it should be clear from what has been said earlier that the assertion of a particular form of political activity in a historical interpretation should be closely related to the perceptions and understanding of those engaged in it. Diplomats, no more than politicians in office, are not given to making frank expositions of their briefs or of the political stratagems devised to protect or promote their country's position on a particular issue. Consequently, any explanation of their vote or of their attitudes must be based on inferences derived from the activities of particular national representatives in a variety of U.N. organs, over a period of time, in connection with identifiable issues. This is in default of evidence from national archives or U.N. Secretariat files.

Like the other problems considered in this study of international politics, this involves us in the difficult question of establishing motivation. For example, up to 1951 the Soviet Union and the other communist members of the United Nations adopted a cold and uncompromising attitude towards the issue of the economic development of underdeveloped countries. They advocated the severance of economic links with capitalist countries and the adoption of a socialist planned economic system. Shortly after Stalin's death, however, this attitude changed into a warm espousal of most of the initiatives proposed on this issue by the underdeveloped countries. Although the significance of this change in terms of the internal politics of the U.N. can be established, the reasons for it cannot. It can be inferred that the Soviet Union wished to obtain support for its policies and to strengthen its minority position, but there is no direct evidence for this, nor is there any indication that this is what actually happened. Similar changes in the attitudes of other countries lend themselves to this kind of inferential judgement, but direct evidence is lacking. Nevertheless, it appears that one major factor in determining the positions adopted on particular questions is the organisational complexity of the United Nations and the ambiguities in defining the competence and powers of various U.N. organs. Depending on the composition and procedures of an organ, a national representative adopts a position on an issue which is calculated to achieve the maximum success possible within the context of other national attitudes. It is this admixture of organisational and procedural factors and national attitudes and diplomacy which produces a process of decision-, or more correctly non-decision-making, characteristic of the United Nations. But in the absence of any direct evidence for motivation other than the assertion of the influence of environmental factors within the U.N., it must be admitted that the analysis is more descriptive than explanatory.

To conclude this discussion and indeed the work as a whole, such attempts at interpreting recent international politics are suspect and open to criticism on a number of grounds. But the main point so far as their status as explanations is concerned is that these grounds are derived from common criteria. A reconstruction of past human activities or events is concerned not with an empathetic or systematic approach but with a coherent and consistent argument which relates events or factors to evidence of their perception on the part of those engaged in them. Inferences may be made if direct evidence is lacking, but the degree to which a historical interpretation is inferential or speculative will reduce its force as a historical explanation. All such arguments will in any case be partial and incomplete to an extent which cannot be known, but this is inevitable for they have an intellectual context which does not permit complete detachment and which constantly changes. This is, of course, not confined to historical argument but is generally true of all forms of explanation. But in the former case it is possible to have different interpretations of the same historical materials without vitiating the notion of explanation or disallowing genuine agreement and disagreement. Yet, admitting the innate subjectivity and relativity of historical interpretation, it is possible to establish criteria on which communication and the evaluation proper to an explanation can proceed. Such criteria are conventional in nature and consist of the sort of relative judgements and grounds discussed earlier which, in this view, are peculiar to historical argument and confer distinctiveness upon it. It is the thesis of this work that these are more appropriate to the interpretation of international politics than the proffered alternatives.

REFERENCES

1. See, for example, Carl G. Hempel, 'Studies in the Logic of Explanation', in *Aspects of Scientific Explanation* (New York: Free Press, 1965) pp. 245–96.
2. Ernst Nagel, *The Structure of Science* (London: Routledge & Kegan Paul, 1968) pp. 20–6.
3. Ibid., p. 146.
4. Michael Oakeshott, *Experience and its Modes* (Cambridge Univ. Press, 1933; reprinted 1966) p. 170.
5. Ibid., p. 172.
6. Ibid., p. 182.
7. Ibid., p. 195.
8. Ibid., p. 200.
9. Ibid., p. 201.
10. Ibid., pp. 57–81.
11. Ibid., p. 37.
12. Karl R. Popper, *Conjectures and Refutations* (London: Routledge & Kegan Paul, 1963; rev. ed. 1969) p. 53.
13. Nagel, *The Structure of Science*, p. 21.

14. Popper, *Conjectures and Refutations,* p. 41.
15. J. O. Urmson, *Philosophical Analysis* (Oxford Univ. Press, 1967) p. 178.
16. Karl R. Popper, *The Logic of Scientific Discovery* (London: Hutchinson, 1959) p. 106.
17. R. B. Braithwaite, *Scientific Explanation* (Cambridge Univ. Press, 1968) p. 82.
18. Hans Reichenbach, *The Rise of Scientific Philosophy* (Berkeley and Los Angeles: Univ. of California Press, 1968) p. 223.
19. Carl G. Hempel, 'The Function of General Laws in History', in Patrick Gardiner (ed.), *Theories of History* (New York: Free Press, 1959) p. 348.
20. Maurice Mandelbaum, *The Problem of Historical Knowledge* (New York: Harper & Row Torchbooks, 1967) p. 19.
21. Ibid., p. 174.
22. R. G. Collingwood, *The Idea of History* (New York: Galaxy Books, Oxford Univ. Press, 1956) pp. 257–61.

Select Bibliography

HISTORIES AND SURVEYS

Raymond Aron, *The Century of Total War* (Garden City, N.Y.: Doubleday, 1954).
Herbert Butterfield and Martin Wight (eds.), *Diplomatic Investigations* (London: Allen and Unwin, 1966).
P. Calvocoressi, *World Politics since 1945* (London: Longmans, 1968).
D. F. Fleming, *The Cold War and its Origins, 1917–1960*, 2 vols. (Garden City, N.Y.: Doubleday, 1961).
John Herz, *International Politics in the Atomic Age* (New York: Columbia Univ. Press, 1962).
W. Knapp, *A History of War and Peace, 1939–1965* (London: Oxford Univ. Press, for Royal Institute of International Affairs, 1967).
P. Renouvin and J. P. Duroselle, *Introduction to the History of International Relations*, trans. Mary Ilford (London: Pall Mall Press, 1968).
C. L. Robertson, *International Politics since World War II* (New York: Wiley, 1966).
Hugh Seton-Watson, *Neither War nor Peace: The Struggle for Power in the Post-War World* (New York: Praeger, 1960).

INTERNATIONAL INTEGRATION

Bela Balassa, *Theory of Economic Integration* (Homewood, Ill.: Irwin, 1961).
Miriam Camps, *Britain and the European Community, 1955–1963* (Princeton Univ. Press, 1964).
W. Hartley Clark, *The Politics of the Common Market* (Englewood Cliffs, N.J.: Prentice-Hall, 1967).
J. F. Deniau, *The Common Market,* 4th ed. (London: Barrie & Rockliff, 1967).
Werner Feld, *The European Common Market and the World* (Englewood Cliffs, N.J.: Prentice-Hall, 1967).
Ernst R. Haas, *The Uniting of Europe* (Stanford Univ. Press, 1958).
Stephen Holt, *The Common Market: The Conflict of Theory and Practice* (London: Hamish Hamilton, 1967).
L. M. Lindberg, *The Political Dynamics of European Economic Integration* (Stanford Univ. Press, 1965).
E. Plishke (ed.), *Systems of Integrating the International Community* (Princeton, N.J.: Van Nostrand, 1964).
A. J. Zurcher, *The Struggle to United Europe, 1940–58* (New York Univ. Press, 1958).

INTERNATIONAL ORGANISATION

M. Barkun and R. W. Gregg, *The U.N. System* (Princeton, N.J.: Van Nostrand, 1968).
James Boyd, *United Nations Peace-Keeping Operations: A Military and Political Appraisal* (New York: Praeger, 1971).
Andrew W. Cordier and Wilder Foote (eds.), *The Quest for Peace* (New York: Columbia Univ. Press, 1965).
S. S. Goodspeed, *The Nature and Functions of International Organisation* (Oxford University Press, 1967).
C. W. Jenks, *The World Beyond the Charter* (London: Allen & Unwin, 1969).
D. A. Kay, *The New Nations in the United Nations* (New York: Columbia Univ.

357

Press, 1970).
—— (ed.), *The United Nations' Political System* (New York: Wiley, 1967).
H. G. Nicholas, *The United Nations as a Political Institution,* 4th ed. (Oxford Univ. Press, 1971).
N. J. Padelford and L. M. Goodrich, *The United Nations in the Balance: Accomplishment and Prospects* (London: Pall Mall Press, 1965).
J. G. Stoessinger, *The U.N. and the Super-Powers: U.S.–Soviet Interaction at the U.N.* (New York: Random House, 1966).

IMPERIALISM

M. Barratt Brown, *After Imperialism* (London: Heinemann, 1963; rev. ed., Merlin Press, 1970).
Andre Gunder Frank, *Capitalism and Underdevelopment in Latin America,* rev. ed. (London and New York: Monthly Review Press, 1969).
E. Kedourie (ed.), *Nationalism in Asia and Africa* (London: Weidenfeld & Nicolson, 1970).
A. G. Kenwood and A. L. Lougheed, *The Growth of the International Economy, 1820–1960* (London: Allen & Unwin, 1971).
Charles P. Kindleberger, *Power and Money* (London: Mcmillan, 1970).
R. Koebner and H. Schmidt, *Imperialism: The Story and Significance of a Political Word, 1840–1960* (Cambridge Univ. Press, 1964).
G. Lichtheim, *Imperialism* (London: Allen Lane, The Penguin Press, 1971).
Roger Owen and Bob Sutcliffe, *Studies in the Theory of Imperialism* (London: Longman, 1972).
Robert I. Rhodes (ed.), *Imperialism and Underdevelopment: A Reader* (New York and London: Monthly Review Press, 1970).
Paul M. Sweezy and Harry Magdoff, *The Dynamics of U.S. Capitalism* (New York and London: Monthly Review Press, 1972).
A. P. Thornton, *Doctrines of Imperialism* (New York: Wiley, 1965).

PHILOSOPHY OF SCIENCE

P. G. Frank (ed.), *The Validation of Scientific Theories* (New York: Collier Books, 1961).
Nelson Goodman, *Fact, Fiction and Forecast* (Indianapolis and New York: Bobbs-Merrill, 1965).
Norwood Russell Hanson, *Observation and Explanation* (London: Allen & Unwin, 1972).
——, *Patterns of Discovery* (Cambridge Univ. Press, 1958).
Werner Heisenberg, *Physics and Philosophy* (London: Allen & Uwin, 1959).
S. Korner, *Experience and Theory: An Essay in the Philosophy of Science* (London: Routledge & Kegan Paul, 1966).
Imre Lakatos and Alan Musgrave (eds.), *Criticism and the Growth of Knowledge* (Cambridge Univ. Press, 1970).
P. H. Nidditch (ed.), *The Philosophy of Science* (Oxford Univ. Press, 1968).
C. Taylor, *The Explanation of Behaviour* (London: Routledge & Kegan Paul, 1964).
Stephen Toulmin, *The Philosophy of Science* (London: Hutchinson Univ. Library, 1967).

PHILOSOPHY OF SOCIAL SCIENCE

Kenneth J. Arrow, Samuel Karlin and Patrick Suppes (eds.), *Mathematical Methods in the Social Sciences* (Stanford Univ. Press, 1960).
Max Black, *Models and Metaphors* (Ithaca, N.Y.: Cornell Univ. Press, 1962).
Robert Brown, *Explanation in Social Science* (Chicago: Aldine, 1963).
Edmund Husserl, *Phenomenology and the Crisis of Philosophy,* trans. Quentin Lauer (New York: Harper & Row, 1965).
A. R. Louch, *Explanation and Human Action* (Oxford: Basil Blackwell, 1966).
Richard S. Rudner, *The Philosophy of Social Science* (Englewood Cliffs, N.J.: Prentice-Hall, 1966).

W. G. Runciman, *Sociology in its Place and Other Essays* (Cambridge Univ. Press, 1970).
Alan Ryan, *The Philosophy of the Social Sciences* (London: Macmillan, 1970).
Alfred Schutz, *The Phenomenology of the Social World*, trans. George Walsh and Frederick Lehnert (Evanston, Ill.: Northwestern Univ. Press, 1967).
Vernon Van Dyke, *Political Science: A Philosophical Analysis* (Stanford Univ. Press, 1960).
Peter Winch, *The Idea of a Social Science and its Relation to Philosophy* (London: Routledge & Kegan Paul, 1970).

PHILOSOPHY OF HISTORY

H. S. Commager, *The Nature and Study of History* (Columbus, Ohio: Merrill, 1965).
Alan Donagan and Barbara Donagan (eds.), *Philosophy of History* (New York: Macmillan, 1965).
William H. Dray, *Laws and Explanation in History* (Oxford Univ. Press, 1957).
W. B. Gallie, *Philosophy and the Historical Understanding* (London: Chatto & Windus, 1964).
Sidney Hook (ed.), *Philosophy and History* (New York Univ. Press, 1963).
H. Stuart Hughes, *History as Art and Science* (New York: Harper & Row, 1964).
Arthur Marwick, *The Nature of History* (London: Macmillan, 1970).
Hans Meyerhoff (ed.), *The Philosophy of History in Our Time* (Garden City, N.Y.: Anchor Books, Doubleday, 1959).
Karl R. Popper, *The Poverty of Historicism* (London, Routledge & Kegan Paul, 1963).
Morton White, *Foundations of Historical Knowledge* (New York: Harper & Row, 1965).

HISTORICAL INTERPRETATION

Geoffrey Barraclough, *An Introduction to Contemporary History* (London: C. A. Watts, 1964).
E. H. Carr, *The Twenty Years Crisis* (London: Macmillan, 1946).
G. R. Elton, *The Practice of History* (London: Collins, Fontana Library, 1969).
H. P. R. Finberger (ed.), *Approaches to History* (London: Routledge & Kegan Paul, 1965).
Pieter Geyl, *Encounters in History* (London: Collins, Fontana Library, 1967).
James L. Henderson (ed.), *Since 1945: Aspects of Contemporary World History* (London: Methuen, 1966).
David Rees, *The Age of Containment* (London: Macmillan, 1967).
A. J. P. Taylor, *The Origins of the Second World War* (Harmondsworth: Penguin Books, 1964).
David Thompson, *World History, 1914–1968* (Oxford Univ. Press, 1969).
D. W. Urwin, *Western Europe Since 1945*, 2nd ed. (London: Longman, 1972).

INTERNATIONAL THEORY

R. Aron, *Peace and War: A Theory of International Relations*, trans. R. Howard and Annette Baker Fox (Garden City, N.Y.: Doubleday, 1966).
A. L. Burns, *Of Powers and their Politics* (Englewoood Cliffs, N.J.: Prentice-Hall, 1969).
J. W. Burton, *Systems, States, Diplomacy and Rules* (Cambridge Univ. Press, 1968).
W. D. Coplin, *Introduction to International Politics: A Theoretical Overview* (Chicago: Markham, 1971).
Karl W. Deutsch, *The Analysis of International Relations* (Englewood Cliffs, N.J: Prentice-Hall, 1968).
N. Forward, *The Field of Nations* (London: Macmillan, 1971).
Stanley H. Hoffmann, *Contemporary Theory in International Relations* (Englewood Cliffs, N.J.: Prentice-Hall, 1960).
Herbert C. Kelman (ed.), *International Behavior: A Social-Psychological Analysis* (New York: Holt, Rinehart & Winston, 1965).

Louis Kriesberg, *Social Processes in International Relations: A Reader* (New York: Wiley, 1968).
C. A. McClelland, *Theory and the International System* (London: Macmillan, 1966).
George Modelski, *A Theory of Foreign Policy* (New York: Praeger, 1962).
P. A. Reynolds, *An Introduction to International Relations* (London: Longman, 1971).
Bruce M. Russett, *Economic Theories of International Relations* (Chicago: Markham, 1968).

WAR, DEFENCE AND STRATEGY

Andre Beaufre, *Introduction to Strategy* (London: Faber, 1965).
Kenneth E. Boulding, *Conflict and Defense: A General Theory* (New York: Harper & Row, Torchbooks, 1963).
Bernard Brodie, *From Crossbow to H-Bomb* (New York: Dell, 1962).
Alastair Buchan, *War in Modern Society* (London: Collins, Fontana Library, 1968).
Michael Howard (ed.), *The Theory and Practice of War* (London, Cassell, 1965).
Henry A. Kissinger, *Nuclear Weapons and Foreign Policy* (New York: Harper & Bros., 1957).
K. Knorr, *On the Uses of Military Power in the Nuclear Age* (Princeton Univ. Press, 1967).
D. G. Pruitt and R. C. Snyder (eds.), *Theory and Research on the Causes of War* (Englewood Cliffs, N.J.: Prentice-Hall, 1969).
B. M. Russett, *What Price Vigilance?* (New Haven: Yale Univ. Press, 1970).
Thomas C. Schelling, *Arms and Influence* (New Haven: Yale Univ. Press, 1960).
K. Waltz, *Man, the State and War* (New York and London: Columbia Univ. Press, 1965).
Quincy Wright, *Study of War,* 2nd ed. (Univ. of Chicago Press, 1965).

NATIONAL FOREIGN POLICIES

Elisabeth Barker, *Britain in a Divided Europe, 1945–1970* (London: Weidenfeld & Nicolson, 1971).
Miriam Camps, *Britain and the European Community, 1955–1963* (Princeton Univ. Press, 1964).
Alfred Grosser, *La Politique Extérieure de la 4ième République* (Paris: Librairie Armand Colin, 1963).
——, *La Politique Extérieure de la 5ième République* (Paris: Editions du Seuil, 1963).
M. Donald Hancock and Dankwart A. Rustow, *American Foreign Policy in International Perspective* (Englewood Cliffs, N.J.: Prentice-Hall, 1971).
Stanley Hoffman, *Gulliver's Troubles, or The Setting of American Foreign Policy* (New York: McGraw-Hill, 1968).
P. H. Jouiler and H. W. Morton, *Soviet Policy-Making* (New York: Praeger, 1967).
Ernest Lefever, *Ethics and United States Foreign Policy* (New York: Meridian Books, 1957).
Roy C. Macridis, *De Gaulle: Implacable Ally* (New York: Harper & Row, 1966).
F. S. Northedge, *British Foreign Policy* (New York: Praeger, 1962).
Robert E. Osgood *et al., America and the World* (Baltimore and London: John Hopkins Univ. Press, 1970).
A. M. Schlesinger, *A Thousand Days* (New York: Mayflower-Dell, 1965).
William P. Snyder, *The Politics of British Defense Policy, 1945–62* (Columbus: Ohio State Univ. Press, 1965).
John W. Spanier, *American Foreign Policy since World War II* (London: Pall Mall Press, 1962).
J. F. Triska and P. D. Finley, *Soviet Foreign Policy* (New York: Macmillan, 1968).
A. B. Ulam, *Expansion and Coexistence: Soviet Foreign Policy from 1917 to 1967* (London: Secker & Warburg, 1968).
David Vital, *The Making of British Foreign Policy* (London: Allen & Unwin, 1968).
Neville Waites (ed.), *Troubled Neighbours: Franco-British Relations in the*

Twentieth Century (London: Weidenfeld & Nicolson, 1971).

Philip Windsor, *Germany and the Management of Détente* (London: Chatto & Windus, 1971).

T. W. Wolfe, *Soviet Power and Europe, 1945–1970* (Baltimore: John Hopkins Univ, Press, 1970).

DOMESTIC POLITICS AND FOREIGN POLICY

G. A. Almond, *The American People and Foreign Policy* (New York: Praeger, 1960).

Bernard C. Cohen, *The Political Process and Foreign Policy: The Making of the Japanese Peace Settlement* (Princeton Univ. Press, 1957).

——, *The Press and Foreign Policy* (Princeton Univ. Press, 1963).

J. Frankel, *The Making of Foreign Policy* (Oxford Univ. Press, 1963).

Roger Hilsman, *To Move a Nation* (Garden City, N.Y.: Doubleday, 1967).

E. J. Meehan, *The British Left Wing and Foreign Policy: A Study of the Influence of Ideology* (New Brunswick, N.J.: Rutgers Univ. Press, 1960).

James A. Robinson, *Congress and Foreign Policy-Making* (Homewood, Ill.: Dorsey Press, 1967).

James N. Rosenau, *Domestic Sources of Foreign Policy* (New York: Free Press, 1967).

Kenneth Waltz, *Foreign Policy and Democratic Politics* (Boston: Little, Brown, 1967).

Bradford Westerfield, *Foreign Policy and Party Politics* (New Haven: Yale Univ. Press, 1955).

ALLIANCES

A. Beaufre, *NATO and Europe* (New York: Knopf, 1966).

F. A. Beer, *Alliances: Latent War Communities in the Contemporary World* (New York: Rinehart & Winston, 1970).

A. J. Cottrell and J. E. Dougherty, *The Politics of the Atlantic Alliance* (London: Pall Mall Press, 1964).

Karl W. Deutsch, Lewis J. Edinger, Roy C. Macridis and R. L. Merritt, *France, Germany and the Western Alliance* (New York: Scribner, 1967).

James A. Joyce, *End of an Illusion* (London: Allen & Unwin, 1969).

G. Liska, *Nations in Alliance: The Limits of Interdependence* (Baltimore: Johns Hopkins Univ. Press, 1962).

R. E. Neustadt, *Alliance Politics* (New York: Colunbia Univ. Press, 1970).

Robert E. Osgood, *NATO: The Entangling Alliance* (Univ. of Chicago Press, 1962).

Index